THE LEGAL FUTURE OF EMPLOYEE REPRESENTATION

EDITED BY MATTHEW W. FINKIN

ILR PRESS
ITHACA, NEW YORK

This volume is reprinted by special permission of Chicago-Kent College of Law, Illinois Institute of Technology. The papers in this volume were originally published in *Chicago-Kent Law Review* vol. 69, no. 1 (1993).

First ILR Press edition 1994

Library of Congress Cataloging-in-Publication Data

The Legal future of employee representation/edited by Matthew W. Finkin
p. cm.
"Originally published in Chicago-Kent law review vol. 69, no. 1 (1993)"—Verso t.p.
Includes bibliographical references.
ISBN 0-87546-330-4 (acid-free paper)
1. Industrial management—Employee participation—Law and legislation—United States. 2. Labor laws and legislation—United States. I. Finkin, Matthew W.
KF3369.L37 1993
344.73′01—dc20
[347.3041] 94-13490
Rev.

Copies may be ordered through bookstores or directly from

ILR Press
School of Industrial and Labor Relations
Cornell University
Ithaca, NY 14853-3901

Printed on acid-free recycled paper in the United States of America
5 4 3 2 1

Contents

Introduction / 3
Matthew W. Finkin

1. Labor Law Reform in a World of Competitive Product Markets / 13
Samuel Estreicher

2. In Despair, Starting Over: Imagining A Labor Law for Unorganized Workers / 57
Michael H. Gottesman

3. Reforming U.S. Labor Relations / 95
Joel Rogers

4. Employee Voice and Employer Choice: A Structured Exception to Section 8(A)(2) / 126
Clyde W. Summers

5. Employee Caucus: A Key Institution in the Emerging System of Employment Law / 146
Alan Hyde

6. The Road Not Taken: Some Thoughts on Nonmajority Employee Representation / 191
Matthew W. Finkin

7. Reflections on Labor Law Reform and the Crisis of American Labor / 215
Sanford M. Jacoby

8. The Overlooked Middle / 224
Thomas C. Kohler

9. Reflections on Employee Voice and Representation for the Future / 243
Peter D. Sherer

Afterword: Labor Law Reform: Waiting for Congress? / 252
Martin H. Malin

THE LEGAL FUTURE OF EMPLOYEE REPRESENTATION

INTRODUCTION

MATTHEW W. FINKIN*

What follows is a conversation—rich in analytical detail, subtle in argument, and mostly among friends—about the legal future of employee representation. All the participants agree that a need for effective representation exists; the question is how best to fill it in an economy in which a variety of factors have combined to dampen resort to collective bargaining, the only model of representation the law currently requires. What, as Michael Gottesman puts it,[1] is a labor law for the unorganized?

Why employees should be able to secure representation if they desire—as expert as possible and with as little cost or delay as necessary—was captured by the United States Supreme Court in addressing the rights of the industrially accused: "A single employee confronted by an employer investigating whether certain conduct deserves discipline may be too fearful or inarticulate to relate accurately the incident being investigated, or too ignorant to raise extenuating factors."[2] Yet the only alternative available to the unrepresented, namely individual self-representation, expects the single at will employee—intelligent but inexpert, perhaps inarticulate, and quite possibly a little diffident in the face of authority—to deal knowledgeably and confidently with her employer. With whom is the employee expected to deal and about what? With a manager of employee benefits concerning the actuarial bases for contributions to her pension? With a manager of industrial health and safety concerning the toxicology of substances to which she might be exposed? With a manager of human resources over the reliability of a psychological test she might be required to take? With an officer of industrial security concerning the factual basis for her discharge?

The authors assay a range of legal choices. One option, supported by Samuel Estreicher,[3] viewed skeptically by Clyde Summers,[4]

* Albert J. Harno Professor of Law and Professor in the Institute of Labor and Industrial Relations, University of Illinois.

1. Michael Gottesman, *In Despair Starting Over: Imagining A Labor Law for Unorganized Workers*, 69 CHI.-KENT L. REV. 59, 70 (1993).

2. NLRB v. J. Weingarten, Inc., 420 U.S. 251, 262-63 (1975).

3. *See* Samuel Estreicher, *Labor Law Reform in A World of Competitive Product Markets*, 69 CHI.-KENT L. REV. 3 (1993).

refined by Alan Hyde,[5] and favorably commented upon by Joel Rogers[6] and Michael Gottesman, concerns a relaxation of the company union prohibition of section 8(a)(2) of the National Labor Relations Act.[7] Professor Estreicher points to three changes in the workforce and the workplace as setting the stage for a lessening of the restraints on employee participative plans, so long as the plans are not sham arrangements to avoid traditional unionization:

> From the perspective of a predominantly nonunion work force, it [the law] affirmatively discourages what the law should encourage: enhanced employee voice in nonunion shops. Moreover, under current social conditions—a better educated workforce, minimum wage and other protective legislation, and a rights-conscious legal culture — it is doubtful that permitting employers to institute consultative arrangements or to use employee representatives in grievance procedures would have the effect of preventing employees from making an uncoerced decision over whether they wish to be represented by an independent union.[8]

Though Estreicher and several of the contributors deal with global economic change, which has affected the United States, some prefatory comment on these three conditions will place the larger conversation in a domestic context. Today's workforce is better educated than the workforce of the fifties, at roughly the apogee of union density, as the data supplied in Table 1 shows:

TABLE 1
EDUCATIONAL ATTAINMENT OF THE LABOR FORCE
1959-1991

Year	Labor Force Total (in thousands)	Percent Distribution					Median School Years Completed
		elementary	high school		college		
		0-8	1-3	4	1-3	4 or more	
1959	65,842	30.5	19.8	30.7	9.3	9.6	12.0
1969	76,753	18.6	17.8	38.4	12.6	12.6	12.4
1979	103,478	8.9	16.0	39.9	17.6	17.6	12.6
1991	116,886	4.6	9.8	39.0	22.1	24.5	12.9

Source: U.S. BUREAU OF THE CENSUS, U.S. DEPT. OF COMMERCE, STATISTICAL ABSTRACT OF THE UNITED STATES Table 6.1 (1992); NATIONAL CENTER FOR EDUCATIONAL STATISTICS, U.S. DEPT. OF EDUCATION, DIGEST OF EDUCATION STATISTICS Table 364 (1992).

4. *See* Clyde Summers, *Employee Voice and Employer Choice: A Structural Exception to Section 8 (a)(2)*, 69 CHI.-KENT L. REV. 129 (1993).
5. *See* Alan Hyde, *Employee Caucus: A Key Institution in the Emerging System of Employment Law*, 69 CHI.-KENT L. REV. 149 (1993).
6. *See* Joel Rogers, *Reforming U.S. Labor Relations*, 69 CHI.-KENT L. REV. 97 (1993).
7. National Labor Relations (Wagner) Act § 8(a)(2), 29 U.S.C. § 158(a)(2) (1988).
8. Estreicher, *supra* note 3, at 24, 25.

Over the past three decades the significant component of the workforce that had only an elementary education has evaporated, and the percentage of college graduates has more than doubled. Thus if one assumes that those with truly advanced educations—for example engineers and computer scientists—are better able to discern real participation and to discount its sham, it may be that the law should take account of this heightened level of formal educational attainment. But the quality of contemporary postsecondary education, no less than secondary education, has not wanted for critics;[9] and it is not at all obvious that because the median component of the workforce is now composed of persons with a year of postsecondary education, one should presume the workforce as a whole to possess greater discernment.

Clyde Summers argues that unless operational constraints are placed upon a loosening of section 8(a)(2), many employees will be deceived or be left with a shell of representation.[10] But Joel Rogers, Alan Hyde, and Michael Gottesman argue that so long as an uncoerced choice for participation in management-sponsored bodies is made, there is no reason for the law to intervene. Does it follow that because employees are better educated, assuming that to be so, they are also more autonomous, are freer to accept or reject an employer sponsored system?

However, Estreicher also points out that labor protective law has increased significantly, presumably militating toward greater employee independence. Since the fifties, Congress has enacted sweeping antidiscrimination in employment laws, welfare and pension benefits protections, occupational safety and health laws, and a cluster of discrete whistleblowing and antiretaliation laws. Federal law has regulated wage assignment, discharge for garnishment, interception of telephone communications, and the use of polygraphs. It has provided for notice of plant closings or mass layoffs, and required the granting of family and medical leave. State laws have paralleled the growth of federal labor protective law. To take the domestic jurisdiction as illustrative, by the fifties Illinois, like a great many states, had come to regulate wage payment and assignment, occupational health

9. *See, e.g.*, Denise K. Magner, *A Biting Assessment: A Report Chides Colleges for Neglecting Undergraduate Education*, CHRON. HIGHER EDUC., Dec. 8, 1993, at A26 (covering a report issued by the Wingspread Group on Higher Education decrying undergraduate education that produces too many graduates who "cannot read or write very well, too many whose intellectual depth and breadth are unimpressive, and too many whose skills are inadequate in the face of the demands of contemporary life.").

10. Summers, *supra* note 4, at 139.

and safety, child labor and homework, and to provide workers unemployment compensation. Today Illinois also regulates employee access to personnel documents maintained by the employer, whistleblowing, the use of lawful products off the premises (that is, tobacco and alcohol), and smoking in the workplace. In addition, Illinois' courts have recognized employee dignitary interests as a matter of common law. To return to the industrially accused, an employer may conduct an interrogation of an employee suspected of theft in such a manner as to render the employer liable for the wrongful infliction of emotional distress.[11]

These protections, however, often technical and legally complex, depend for their vindication upon the imponderable of the individual's ability to retain counsel. Thus Michael Gottesman explores the possibility of employees contracting with "service providers," who have "the expertise to understand the complex information and the pertinent legal constraints applicable to many of the subjects embraced by the employment relationship,"[12] to deal with their employers. But he shrinks from requiring employers to deal with them. That, he recognizes, would be a form of nonmajority representation; an idea I play out statutorily, that Joel Rogers discusses sympathetically, and that Alan Hyde develops creatively. Estreicher objects to "'watchdog' committees serving as in-house instruments of state policy,"[13] but he does not expand upon his objection. Employee-generated committees or employee subscription to a service provider would not be called into being by the State, nor would they be acting for it. Employees, by joining or subscribing, would be acting on their own felt needs and interests, the importance of which the State may have acknowledged by legislation or common law.

Estreicher also mentions the related emergence of a "rights-conscious legal culture."[14] But as the discussion of service providers evidences, the question is of how best to vindicate those rights. It remains to be seen how effective occasional litigation, or the prospect of litigation, is given the imponderable of the availability of counsel. And even assuming the individual employee is able to secure legal counsel, absent insulation for that resort an employee who insists upon legal representation—or who retains counsel in the face of po-

11. National Loss Control Serv. Corp. v. Dotti, 467 N.E.2d 937, 942 (Ill. App. Ct. 1984).
12. Gottesman, *supra* note 1, at 80-81.
13. Estreicher, *supra* note 3, at 29 n.95.
14. *Id.* at 25.

tential adverse action by the employer—is left helpless for having made that resort.[15]

A partial difficulty in the conversation on the "company union" question is the more or less interchangeable use of words—participation, representation—that may have different meanings. The idea of representation, as the image of the industrially accused conjures up, is grounded on a potential conflict of interest and a disparity between the employee and the employer in economic resources and expertness; on the need of an individual employee for protection from her employer. The idea of participation, drawing upon the theory and practice of human resource management, seeks to enlist the employee—to "tap the insights and ingenuity of the workforce"[16]—in improving the efficiency of the firm and the quality of the product. But Marc Linder has recently reminded us of Philip Selznick's admonition of two decades ago—that "to think of a man as a 'human resource' is to affront his personality."[17]

To Peter Sherer, writing from the vantage point of industrial relations—and human resource management (HRM)—the watchword of the law should be "flexibility." He discusses the variety of ways people are today engaged for the production of goods and services—one dare not say "employed," for that assumes a legal category (and conjures up the image of an on-going relationship) that has often been replaced by independent contractors, leased workers, homeworkers and contingent employees. Even the distinction between representation ("voice") and participation ("work") is collapsing.[18] The law, he argues, should accommodate a variety of models of representation; and he seems as sympathetic to internal participative plans as to external service providers—so long as there is a suitable fit.[19]

Sherer makes a powerful case, rooted in the realities of late twentieth century capitalism. But one still has to ponder whether there is a

15. An employee who appears at a disciplinary interrogation accompanied by counsel has no right under the National Labor Relations Act to insist upon the presence of counsel. TCC Ctr. Co., 275 N.L.R.B. 604, 609 (1985). Neither would such insistence be protected under state law. Winkley v. Bristol-Myers Squibb Co., 793 F. Supp. 738, 741 (E.D. Mich. 1992). In fact, an employee accused of sexual harassment may be discharged for having retained counsel to defend him against the charge. *See* Erickson v. Marsh & McLennan Co., 569 A.2d 793, 804 (N.J. 1990).

16. Paul C. Weiler, Governing the Workplace 192 (1990).

17. Marc Linder, *Governing the Workplace: The Future of Labor and Employment Law*, 9 Law & Ineq. J. 343, 353 (1991) (book review) (quoting Philip Selznick, Law, Society, and Industrial Justice 96 (1969).

18. Peter D. Sherer, *Reflections on Employee Voice and Representation for the Future*, 69 Chi.-Kent. L. Rev. 249, 250 (1993).

19. *Id.* at 257.

normative role for law in the matter of representation. Since the publication of Selznick's words, we have witnessed the rise of efforts to create comprehensive corporate cultures. Some managements have labored systematically to drench employees in a corporate ideology, not only to keep unions out, but of employees unlikely to unionize—the very engineers and computer scientists adverted to earlier—to internalize a complete identification with the company. Gideon Kunda sees these efforts as the culmination of a historical trend in managerial theory:

> [S]haping the employees' selves in the corporate image is thought to be necessary in order to facilitate the management and increase the efficiency of large-scale bureaucratic enterprises faced with what the managerial literature refers to as "turbulent environments": rapid technological change, intense competition, and a demanding and unpredictable labor force.[20]

Are the practical consequences of these efforts—"a sort of creeping annexation of the workers' selves"[21]—of societal concern? Apart from whether or not these pervasively propagandized employees are truly "free" actors, should the law carve out an area exempt from managerial control, for employees to speak and act on matters of workplace concern through means completely independent of company sponsorship or participation?

Tom Kohler takes a very different perspective, that of a general degradation of what he terms "mediating institutions"[22] in the larger society. He reminds us of the importance not of individual but of collective activity, of the imperative role of sodalities, including unions, in the Nation's social fabric. Consequently, he distinguishes meaningful participation from "dropping a check in the mail."[23]

There is no doubt that the coming together of diverse members of the community in the making of a common cause is indispensable for effective social and political action. Indeed, the establishment of in-

20. Gideon Kunda, Engineering Culture: Control and Commitment in A High-Tech Corporation 13 (1992).

21. *Id.* at 12.

22. Thomas Kohler, *The Overlooked Middle*, 69 Chi.-Kent L. Rev. 229, 235 (1993).

23. *Id.* at 238. It should be noted that sodalities can also work to maintain the social and economic status quo. Cincinnati's fraternal organizations of the 1850s, the Odd Fellows, Masons, and Red Men, though voluntary organizations, were dominated by the well-to-do and "served as social mechanisms for inculcating men with the dominant ideals of hierarchy, deference, temperance, and self-discipline." Steven J. Ross, Workers On The Edge: Work, Leisure, and Politics in Industrializing Cincinnati 1788-1860, at 165-66 (1985). So too did organized religion sometimes offer contending ideas on class loyalty. *Id.* at 166. *See also* David G. Hackett, The Rude Hand Of Innovation: Religion and Soical Order in Albany, New York 1652-1836 (1991).

dustrial labor unions is the product of just such a phenomenon.[24] From that standpoint, Kohler makes a persuasive argument that mere subscription to a service provider is a poor substitute at best for active collective engagement. But the human desire for respect and equality in the employment relationship has been a consistent theme in the emergence of wage labor.[25] Would requiring an employer to deal with the employee's chosen representative—even a lawyer paid by subscription—not conduce toward that end?

Sanford Jacoby sounds a sobering note of political reality: He doubts the prospect of any significant legislative reform, as has Willard Wirtz.[26] Wirtz argues that much could be done without legislation, with special emphasis on the leadership role of the federal government. And Martin Malin reminds us at the close of this Syposium of the ongoing even if diminished importance of the Labor Act, with a couple of helpful hints for its better administration in the matter of representation.[27] But the conclusions to be drawn from the economic diagnoses of Jacoby and the other contributors is bleak, whence Jacoby's jeremiad: "What is needed . . . is less imagination and more practicality."[28]

Does our failure adequately to take account of the political realities render this conversation, pejoratively, an "academic" exercise?

24. Such is the thrust of a superb study, *see* LIZABETH COHEN, MAKING A NEW DEAL: INDUSTRIAL WORKERS IN CHICAGO 1919-1939 (1990).

25. This has been so from the "manly" artisan of the New Republic to the deskilled industrial operative of a century later, as a random snapshot of occupational studies across this period to time will show. *See, e.g.*, SUSAN PORTER BENSON, COUNTER CULTURES: SALES WOMEN, MANAGERS, AND CUSTOMERS IN AMERICAN DEPARTMENT STORES, 1890-1940, at 138 (1986) (persistent complaints about fines imposed on employees evidence that "managers did not easily learn the lesson of more respectful conduct toward their employees."); EDWIN GABLER, THE AMERICAN TELEGRAPHER, A SOCIAL HISTORY, 1860-1900, at 165 (1988) (describing a consequence of the 1883 strike, one telegrapher told a journalist, "'We were formerly spoken to as if we were a lot of animals; but we can talk to the chief operators without falling on our knees . . . .'"); MARK A. LAUSE, SOME DEGREE OF POWER: FROM HIRED HAND TO UNION CRAFTSMAN IN THE PREINDUSTRIAL AMERICAN PRINTING TRADES, 1778-1815, at 119 (1991) (noting that journeymen printers "began with the egalitarian premise that they should be treated as their employers' equals . . . ."); MARC LENDLER, JUST THE WORKING LIFE: OPPOSITION AND ACCOMMODATION IN DAILY INDUSTRIAL LIFE 102 (1990) (study of one company's workforce in the 1970s reporting that a substantial number want "'respect'" in the employment relationship); DAVID A. ZONDERMAN, ASPIRATIONS AND ANXIETIES: NEW ENGLAND WORKERS AND THE MECHANIZED FACTORY SYSTEM 1815-1850, at 113 (1992) ("One theme that continually emerged in the operatives' critiques was that of factory 'tyranny.' These workers saw the hierarchial system of authority as a threat to the American republican ideals of justice and equity.").

26. *See* Sanford Jacoby, *Reflections on Labor Law Reform and the Crisis of American Labor Law*, 69 CHI-KENT L. REV. 219 (1993); Willard Wirtz, *Labor Unions: Not Well But Alive*, 69 CHI.-KENT L. REV. 259 (1993) (reviewing CHARLES B. CRAVER, CAN UNIONS SURVIVE? (1993)).

27. Martin Malin, *Afterword: Labor Law Reform: Waiting for Congress?*, 69 CHI.-KENT L. REV. 277 (1993).

28. Jacoby, *supra* note 26, at 227.

Jacoby confronts us with the difficult question of the role of scholars when off on reform.

In the Foreword to an earlier labor law symposium, Paul Hays warned that too much labor law scholarship was unconnected to the problems of the real world.[29] But Jacoby's criticism is different. We have attended to real problems, but we have failed in "calibrat[ing the] political feasibility" of our solutions.[30] Maybe so. But politically infeasible ideas, even thought chiliastic at one time may become commonplace by another.[31] Whether they become so or not depends upon an interaction of political and social forces—the arrival of an historical moment—over which the scholar has little influence and, perhaps, less foresight. Should the scholar, as must the politician, tailor his prescription to the prevailing political realities which, if un-

29. Paul R. Hays, *Foreword*, 59 COLUM. L. REV. 1 (1959).

30. Jacoby, *supra* note 26, at 229.

31. The "Platform of the Socialistic Labor Party" of 1883 pronounced the following "social demands":

> 1. The United States shall take possession of the railroads, canals, telegraphs, telephones, and all other means of public transportation.
> 2. The municipalities to take possession of the local railroads, of ferries, and of the supply of light to streets and public places.
> 3. Public lands to be declared inalienable. They shall be leased according to fixed principles. Revocation of all grants of lands by the United States to corporations or individuals, the conditions of which have not been complied with or which are otherwise illegal.
> 4. The United States to have the exclusive right to issue money.
> 5. Congressional legislation providing for the scientific management of forests and waterways, and prohibiting the waste of the natural resources of the country.
> 6. The United States to have the right of expropriation of running patents, new inventions to be free to all, but inventors to be remunerated by national rewards.
> 7. Legal provision that the rent of dwellings shall not exceed a certain percentage of the value of the buildings as taxed by the municipality.
> 8. Inauguration of public works in times of economical depression.
> 9. Progressive income tax and tax on inheritances; but smaller incomes to be exempt.
> 10. Compulsory school education of all children under fourteen years of age, instruction in all educational institutions to be gratuitous, and to be made accessible to all by public assistance (furnishing meals, clothes, books, etc.). All instruction to be under the direction of the United States and to be organized on a uniform plan.
> 11. Repeal of all pauper, tramp, conspiracy, and temperance laws. Unabridged right of combination.
> 12. Official statistics concerning the condition of labor. Prohibition of the employment of children in the school age, and the employment of female labor in occupations detrimental to health or morality. Prohibition of the convict labor contract system.
> 13. All wages to be paid in cash money. Equalization by law of women's wages with those of men where equal service is performed.
> 14. Laws for the protection of life and limbs of working people, and an efficient employer's liability law.
> 15. Legal incorporation of trades-unions.
> 16. Reduction of the hours of labor in proportion to the progress of production; establishment by Act of Congress of a legal work-day of not more than eight hours for all industrial workers, and corresponding provisions for all agricultural laborers.

Reprinted in RICHARD T. ELY, THE LABOR MOVEMENT IN AMERICA 366, 368-70 (1886).

promising, is to seek little for the little to be sought? Or does the University not also serve by being "an intellectual experiment station, where new ideas may germinate and where their fruit, though still distasteful to the community as a whole, may be allowed to ripen until finally, perchance, it may become a part of the accepted intellectual food of the nation or of the world."[32]

32. American Association of University Professors, General Report of the Committee on Academic Freedom and Academic Tenure (1915), *reprinted in* Freedom and Tenure In the Academy 391, 400 (W. Van Alstyne ed., 1993).

1. LABOR LAW REFORM IN A WORLD OF COMPETITIVE PRODUCT MARKETS

Samuel Estreicher*

U.S. private sector unionism is in decline. From a high watermark in 1953 of around 35.7% of the private nonagricultural workforce, union membership has fallen to 11.5% and unions represent under 13% of private sector workers.[1] Absent reform of the labor relations system,[2] the trend is clear. Unions will remain a significant force in government employment, big-city commercial construction, rail and air transportation, and certain shrinking mining and manufacturing industries. Aside from these pockets of unionism,

* Professor of Law, New York University. A.B., Columbia College, 1970; M.S. (Industrial Relations), Cornell University, 1974; J.D., Columbia Law School, 1975. A version of this article was given as the Kenneth M. Piper Lecture in Labor Law at the Chicago-Kent College of Law on March 23, 1993, and published as *Employee Voice in Competitive Markets*, 14 The American Prospect, Summer 1993, at 48-57. I have benefitted from the suggestions of David Abraham, Orley Ashenfelter, Aleta G. Estreicher, Michael C. Harper, Alan Hyde, Marcel Kahan, Bruce E. Kaufman, Michael Klausner, Thomas C. Kohler, Lewis Kornhauser, Robert Kuttner, Martin Malin, Ricky Revesz, Stuart Schwab, David M. Silberman, Peter Swenson, Leo Troy, David Westfall, and the students in my Seminar on Labor Law Theory, 1990-93; the opportunity to present earlier drafts to law school workshops at Cornell, NYU, Pennsylvania, and Seton Hall universities; and from the able research assistance of Martin Moe, NYU Class of 1994. All errors that persist are entirely my own. The financial support of the Filomen D'Agostino and Max E. Greenberg Research Fund at the New York University School of Law is also gratefully acknowledged.

1. "Union density" is the percentage of wage and salary workers who are members of unions and employee associations or are represented by such organizations. (Until the early 1980s, the Labor Department obtained membership data from the organizations themselves. Since 1985, this information is derived from the Department's monthly household employment survey (conducted by the U.S. Bureau of the Census—called the "Current Population Survey"). Prior to 1980, the Labor Department did not separate public from private unionism. The 1953 figure is from Leo Troy & Neil Sheflin, Union Sourcebook: Membership, Structure and Finance Directory app. A, at A-1 (1st ed. 1985).

In 1991, 13.1% of employees in private firms, or 10.9 million workers, were either members of unions and employee associations or represented by such organizations. In 1992, the union density rate dropped to 12.7%, or 10.6 million workers. *See Union Membership: Proportion of Union Members Declines to Low of 15.8 Percent*, Daily Lab. Rep. (BNA) No. 25, at B-5 (Feb. 9, 1993). Some employees covered by union contracts pay union dues but are not union members. The proportion of the private workforce who were members of labor organizations was 11.9%, or 9.9 million workers, in 1991, and 11.5%, or 9.7 million workers, in 1992. *Id.*

2. Although this Paper addresses labor law reform, I am not suggesting that any change in the legal framework for the conduct of labor relations can itself stem or redirect the larger economic and socio-cultural forces at work. However, to the extent the legal system inhibits the development of alternative institutional arrangements and encourages the actors in the system to perceive and advance their interests in particular ways, legal reform holds the promise of new alternatives and incentive structures, and perhaps different outcomes of the system.

however, workplace-based representation of the interests of working people will become a distinctly marginal phenomenon in our society.

The falling fortunes of the organized labor movement do not, standing alone, establish a case for reform of existing arrangements. However, whatever our views of unions, collective bargaining, strikes, and the like, the prospect of a virtual disappearance in private firms of mechanisms for employees to have a say in the terms and conditions of their employment should be a cause for public concern.

With a new labor-friendly administration in Washington, and the appointment of the Commission on the Future of Worker-Management Relations (chaired by former U.S. Secretary of Labor John T. Dunlop),[3] a window of opportunity has opened to revisit basic ground rules. Such openings are rare in our political history and should not be squandered. In shaping the reform agenda, we need to squarely confront the underlying causes of labor's decline.

I. The Causes of Union Decline in the Private Sector

A. *The Employer Opposition View*

The consensus among academic commentators sympathetic to organized labor, such as Paul Weiler of the Harvard Law School and Richard Freeman of the Harvard economics department, identifies employer resistance to unionism as the principal culprit behind the plummeting unionization rate.[4] These writers acknowledge the impact of structural shifts in the economy—the shrinkage in the manufacturing sector and the growth of service industries, traditionally infertile terrain for union drives—but downplay the impact of such

3. On March 24, 1993, Secretary of Commerce Ron Brown and Secretary of Labor Robert B. Reich jointly announced the formation of the Dunlop panel. The Commission is charged with reporting back to the Secretaries within a year on (1) what (if any) "new methods or institutions" should be encouraged to enhance productivity "through labor-management cooperation and employee participation"; (2) what (if any) changes in legal framework and bargaining procedure should be made "to enhance cooperative behavior, improve productivity and reduce conflict and delay"; and (3) what (if anything) should be done "to increase the extent to which workplace problems are directly resolved by the parties themselves" rather than by recourse to the courts or regulators. U.S. Dept. of Labor, Office of Information, News, USDL 93-105 (Mar. 24, 1993) (Mission Statement). Subsequently, the Commission announced that it would issue a fact-finding report in May 1994, and its recommendations in November of that year.

4. *See, e.g.,* Richard B. Freeman, *Contraction and Expansion: The Divergence of Private Sector and Public Sector Unionism in the United States, in* Labor Markets in Action: Essays in Empirical Economics 221 (1989); Richard B. Freeman & Morris M. Kleiner, *Employer Behavior in the Face of Union Organizing Drives*, 43 Indus. & Lab. Rel. Rev. 351 (1990); Paul Weiler, *Promises to Keep: Securing Workers' Rights to Self-Organization Under the NLRA*, 96 Harv. L. Rev. 1769 (1983).

forces.[5] Rather, they suggest, the dominant explanation for labor's plight is the persistent, if not increasingly emboldened, refusal of employers to come to terms with basic rights of employees to form unions and engage in collective bargaining.

Doubtless, employer illegality has played a role, and I favor stiffer penalties for unlawful discharge of union organizers. Professor Weiler estimates that one in twenty union supporters are unlawfully discharged.[6] Professor Bernard Meltzer and Robert LaLonde at the University of Chicago put the figure at one in sixty, which "represents a potentially significant disregard by employers of the Act's statutory protections."[7] Either figure is too high and calls for remedies with a real "bite."

Weiler's and Freeman's real point is not employer illegality but employer opposition—the fact that, entirely within the law, employers are resisting union organizing drives, demanding wage concessions, and exploiting weaknesses in the labor law that have existed from the

5. Professors Freeman and Medoff report that on one level the changing structure of the workforce, in terms of its personal, job and geographic characteristics, explains "72 percent of the observed decline" in unionization for the 1954-79 period, but argue that such "technocratic explanations" assume that worker preferences do not change over time and cannot account for union successes in the public sector and other countries (notably Canada). *See* RICHARD B. FREEMAN & JAMES L. MEDOFF, WHAT DO UNIONS DO? 225-28 (1984). Looking at a more limited period, Professor Farber and Krueger conclude that "[a]bout 35 percent of the 4.8 point decline in unionization between 1977 and 1984 can be accounted for by structural changes in the labor force." Henry S. Farber & Alan B. Krueger, *Union Membership in the United States: The Decline Continues*, *in* EMPLOYEE REPRESENTATION: ALTERNATIVES AND FUTURE DIRECTIONS 105, 115 (Bruce E. Kaufman & Morris M. Kleiner eds., 1993) [hereinafter EMPLOYEE REPRESENTATION].

Professor Freeman's and Medoff's 1984 account of the role of the structural factors, coupled with Professor Freeman's later emphasis on the contribution of union wage premium policies and competitive product market forces to union decline, *see infra* note 43 and accompanying text, suggests that structural change is likely to be a more significant causal factor than these writers are prepared to acknowledge. In my view, the increasing competitive pressures on private firms has affected significantly both the attitudes of workers about the wisdom of opting for traditional union representation and the costs on employers of operating under traditional union programs. *See infra* notes 31 to 45 and accompanying text.

6. Weiler, *supra* note 4, at 1781. Professor Weiler's estimate is based on the fact that the NLRB in 1980 secured reinstatement for more than 10,000 employees who had been illegally discharged and obtained back pay settlements for another 5000 employees, and an additional number of discriminatees did not file charges. He then suggests that of the at least 10,000 employees who were fired in 1980 for involvement in representation campaigns, the employees most at risk were among the 200,000 who voted for union representation in 1980. *Id.* at 1780-81. Hence, the 1:20 ratio.

7. *See* Robert J. LaLonde & Bernard D. Meltzer, *Hard Times for Unions: Another Look at the Significance of Employer Illegalities*, 58 U. CHI. L. REV. 953, 1006 (1991). Professors LaLonde and Meltzer argue that Professor Weiler's estimate mistakenly assumes that most illegal discharges occur during organizing drives, that an insignificant percentage of discharges occur in established bargaining units, and that each § 8(a)(3) violation in an organizational campaign is likely to result in substantially the same number of reinstatees as would result from a § 8(a)(3) violation in an established bargaining unit. *Id.* at 992.

very beginning (such as the right to hire permanent replacements for economic strikers). Although an important factor in union decline, employer opposition cannot be the full story, and it would be a mistake to ground the reform prescription entirely on this diagnosis.

B. Other Causes

The shift from a manufacturing to a service economy has eroded the base of the strong industrial unions that previously set the pattern for workers nationwide. For example, the Steelworkers Union lost a half million members from 1975 to 1985—principally because of job loss in a contracting industry—and half of its membership is now drawn from workers outside of the metals industries.[8] None of the major industrial unions ranks among the AFL-CIO's largest affiliates.[9]

The extent of union organization is a function of both the supply of unionized jobs and the demand for union services.[10] On the supply side, union organizing efforts have plainly ebbed. Although the rate of organization (eligible voters in NLRB elections as a percentage of all unorganized workers) has been falling since the early 1950s,[11] it

8. *Statement of USW Wage Policy Committee's Bargaining Goals,* Daily Lab. Rep. (BNA) No. 243, at D-8 (Dec. 17, 1992); *AFL-CIO Statistics on Paid Membership of Union Affiliates From AFL-CIO Executive Council Report to 20th Constitutional Convention*, Daily Lab. Rep. (BNA) No. 187, at D-3 (Sept. 29, 1993) [hereinafter *AFL-CIO Statistics*]. On conditions in the steel industry, see JAMES B. BURNHAM, CHANGES AND CHALLENGES: THE TRANSFORMATION OF THE U.S. STEEL INDUSTRY (Center for Study of American Business Policy Study No. 115, 1993); JOHN P. HOERR, AND THE WOLF FINALLY CAME: THE DECLINE OF THE AMERICAN STEEL INDUSTRY (1988). On the transformation of industrial unions into "general" unions, see Victor G. Devinatz, *From Industrial Unionism to General Unionism: A Historical Transformation*, 44 LAB. L. J. 252 (1993).

9. The largest AFL-CIO affiliate, the International Brotherhood of Teamsters (IBT)—an organization that early on began organizing outside of its traditional industry—reports 1.3 million members in 1993, followed by the American Federation of State, County and Municipal Employees (AFSCME), with 1.2 million members, and two unions operating in the service sector, the United Food and Commercial Workers (UFCW) with 997,000 members, and the Service Employees International Union (SEIU) with 919,000 members (a good many of whom work for public employers). *See AFL-CIO Statistics*, *supra* note 8, at D-1 to D-3.

10. *See generally* Orley Ashenfelter & John Pencavel, *American Trade Union Growth: 1900-1960*, 83 Q. J. ECON. 434 (1969).

11. *See* William T. Dickens & Jonathan S. Leonard, *Accounting for the Decline in Union Membership, 1950-1980,* 38 INDUS. & LAB. REL. REV. 323, 332-33 (1985). Professor Flanagan reports:

> Recent research casts doubt on the idea that declining union election success is the main source of falling union representation . . . . The percentage of the nonunion labor force involved in certification elections fell from about 2.6 percent in 1950 to about 1 percent in 1980. Most of the decline occurred rather precipitously in the 1950s, but the decrease continued, at a slower rate, throughout the 1970s. The decline after 1950 in the union success rate in those elections that did occur reinforced the effect of reduced organizing activity.

plummeted during the 1980s. While the union victory rate in NLRB elections stayed constant at slightly under 50%, the number of elections sought by unions fell from around 6858 in 1980 to 3561 in 1982 and has remained at the 1982 level for the remainder of the decade. From 1982 to 1987, the average annual gain of employees in new units was less than half of the average from 1975 to 1981.[12] Although it is debatable whether organizing efforts at, say, the level of the 1950s could have fully reversed the decline,[13] labor's failure to invest in organizing[14] contributed to the emergence of nonunion firms in traditionally unionized industries, and an all but faint union presence in the rapidly growing service sector.[15]

Unions are rational actors, and to the extent employer resistance (or other factors) has raised the costs of organization drives, they may well have decided that more could be gained from deploying limited resources in political or other arenas than in attempting to win new members. However, the example of the Service Employees International Union—which increased its ranks by 250,000 since 1985[16]—suggests that vigorous organizing can yield membership gains, and that other unions could have done more to improve their position.

On the demand side, there is also reason to believe that traditional union programs may not appeal to the "Baby Boomer" genera-

Robert J. Flanagan, *NLRA Litigation and Union Representations*, 38 STAN. L. REV. 957, 983 (1986).

12. *See* Gary N. Chaison & Joseph B. Rose, *The Macrodeterminants of Union Growth and Decline*, *in* THE STATE OF THE UNIONS 3, 26-27 (George Strauss et al. eds., 1991); Gary N. Chaison & Dileep G. Dhavale, *A Note on the Severity of the Decline in Union Organizing Activity*, 43 INDUS. & LAB. REL. REV. 366, 369-70 (1990).

13. *See* Dickens & Leonard, *supra* note 11, at 333 ("hypothetically fixing both the level of organizing activity relative to union membership and the success rate of organizing activity at their early (1950-54) high levels results in a drop of only two percentage points in the unionized share over the 1955-80 period"); STEPHEN G. BRONARS & DONALD R. DEERE, NATIONAL BUREAU OF ECONOMIC RESEARCH, UNION ORGANIZING ACTIVITY AND UNION COVERAGE 1973-1988, 17 (1989) (only 13% of the decline in union coverage for the 1973-1988 period can be attributed to lessened organizing activity).

14. Professor Voos notes that unions failed to increase organizing expenditures as decline began in the 1970s. Whereas during an earlier period of relative membership stability (1953-1964), organizing expenditures per member increased 32%, from 1970-1974, such expenditures fell by 2%. *See* Paula A. Voos, *Trends in Union Organizing Expenditures, 1953-1977*, 38 INDUS. & LAB. REL. REV. 52 (1984).

15. *See* Ethel B. Jones, *Private Sector Union Decline and Structural Employment Change, 1970-1988,* 13 J. LAB. RES. 257 (1992).

16. *See AFL-CIO Statistics*, *supra* note 8, at D-3. Some of the SEIU's growth was in the public sector, including the absorption in 1989 of units of the former Hospital and Health Care Employees (58,000 members); other hospital units were merged into AFSCME. *Id.* at D-2 & D-3. Although gains are not reflected in the AFL-CIO statistics, the United Food and Commercial Workers (UFCW) is reported to have increased its ranks by 100,000 during the 1980s. *See* Tim W. Ferguson, *Food Union Tastes Gains Even as Trends Eat at Base,* WALL ST. J., Feb. 16, 1993, at A15.

tion[17] and to professionals or other "symbolic analysts" (to use Robert Reich's term) in growth sectors of the economy. Partly due to the example (or threat) of unionization but also in response to the needs of modern firms, management practices in the nonunion sector are more sophisticated and employee-friendly than may have been true in earlier times. Legal developments providing employee protections may also have had a union-substitution effect. Thus, Henry Farber and Alan Krueger, Princeton economists, identify the job satisfaction level of nonunion employees as the principal factor explaining the decline in union density from 1977 to 1991.[18] (This can change if layoffs by nonunion firms increase job insecurity and unions come to be seen as effective agents for improving terms and conditions in a modern economy.)

Employer opposition can, of course, affect the demand, as well as supply, side of the story. Professors Richard Freeman and Joel Rogers discount the Farber-Krueger studies. Pointing to opinion polls suggesting that at least a third of the nonunion workforce desires union representation,[19] they argue that awareness of the "personal

17. *But cf.* LOUIS HARRIS & ASSOCIATES, AFL-CIO, A STUDY OF THE OUTLOOK FOR TRADE UNION ORGANIZING 63 tbl. 20 (AFL-CIO Study No. 843008, 1984) (on file with author) [hereinafter HARRIS STUDY] (workers 18-24 years old were most likely (42%) to vote union; workers in the 15-34 years (28%) and 35-44 years (27%) brackets were only slightly less likely to vote union than their counterparts in the 45-54 years (30%) category).

18. Professors Farber and Krueger find that:

> [V]irtually all of the decline in unionization between 1977 and 1991 seems to be due to decline in demand for union representation. There is no evidence that any significant part of the decline in unionization is due to increased employer resistance other than the sort of resistance that would be reflected in lower demand for unionization by workers.

Farber & Krueger, *supra* note 5, at 118. The authors acknowledge that further inquiry is needed to determine whether the decline in demand is due to the fact that "the services unions provide are no longer perceived as valuable by nonunion workers, or that unions have not been able to convince workers of the value of union representation, perhaps because of poor public relations." *Id.* at 130.

This Farber-Krueger study confirms Professor Farber's earlier finding that virtually all of the 1977-1984 decline in union demand for union representation could be accounted for by an increase in nonunion workers' job satisfaction, particularly with respect to pay and job security. *See* Henry S. Farber, *The Decline of Unionization in the United States: What Can be Learned from Recent Experience?*, 8 J. LAB. ECON. S75 (1990).

19. *See* Richard B. Freeman & Joel Rogers, *Who Speaks for Us? Employee Representation in a Nonunion Labor Market*, *in* EMPLOYEE REPRESENTATION, *supra* note 5, at 13, 32. Farber and Krueger concede, however, that "frustrated demand" (the probability that a worker prefers union representation but is not employed on a union job) "remained fairly constant at about 28 percent of the work force" from 1977 to 1991. *See* Farber & Krueger, *supra* note 5, at 117 tbl. 40.

There are several questions about these survey results that merit further consideration. First, can we assume that the 28-33% of nonunion workers desiring union representation are randomly distributed in all work places, such that this level of union support can be expected at any work site? Second, what do we know about the intensity of preferences involved, for after all 65% of the nonunion workers in, say, the Harris poll, indicated they would definitely or probably vote against a union? *See* HARRIS STUDY, *supra* note 17, tbl. 20. Third, to what extent

costs of seeking union organization against management wishes" is "likely to depress affirmative responses to questions about the willingness to vote for a union in an NLRB election and contaminate efforts to infer an intrinsic 'demand for unionism' from questions about voting intentions . . . ."[20]

II. Explaining the Persistence of Employer Opposition

I am not an econometrician and for present purposes leave to others the task of teasing out the precise contribution of each factor outlined above to the decline in unionization. Even if, for the sake of argument, structural factors (narrowly conceived as the changing personal, job, and geographic characteristics of U.S. workers) are discounted as too static an explanation[21] and employer opposition is viewed as the principal cause, we need a dynamic account: what has changed? What explains the resilience, if not rise, of employer opposition, and why has it succeeded in reducing the power of unions and the prevalence of collective bargaining? Blame is often laid at the door of the Reagan administration, which displayed a level of hostility to unions, as demonstrated by its 1981 firing of air traffic controllers for engaging in an illegal strike and some of its appointments to the NLRB.

Although the PATCO strike and decisions of the Reagan Labor Board influenced employer behavior at the margin, this point is largely a rhetorical one.[22] Private sector unionism was in decline throughout the 1960s and 1970s. That was why a major campaign for labor law reform was launched during the Carter years (but could not overcome a Senate filibuster). We entered the 1980s at a union-den-

are the preferences evinced through a survey instrument uninformed choices that quickly change once information about the expected costs of union organization is provided?

20. Freeman & Rogers, *supra* note 19, at 32. The 1984 Harris poll, commissioned by the AFL-CIO, found that only 2% of the nonunion employees who indicated they would definitely or probably vote against a union in their workplace gave "Fear of employer retaliation" as the "main" reason, yet 62% of these workers agreed with the statement that if a group of employees attempted to form a union at their workplace, employers would "make life difficult for those who supported a union." *See* Harris Study, *supra* note 17, tbls. 22 & 26.

21. *But see supra* note 5.

22. As Professors Blanchflower and Freeman acknowledge, "[T]he decline in U.S. union density is not an aberration—the result of Reagan's breaking the air traffic controllers union, of stodgy, incompetent union leadership, or of the decline in manufacturing in the 1980s—but is structurally rooted in what U.S. unions do on the wage front." David G. Blanchflower & Richard B. Freeman, *Unionism in the United States and Other Advanced OECD Countries*, *in* Labor Market Institutions and the Future Role of Unions 56, 76 (Mario F. Bognanno & Morris M. Kleiner eds., 1992).

sity rate of around 20%.[23] We are now at 13%. At the most, Reagan administration policy arguably accelerated the rate of decline.[24]

Something more fundamental is at work. The labor laws have allowed permanent replacement of strikers at least since 1938[25] and lawful employer opposition to union organizing drives since 1947 (if not earlier[26]), and have never provided other than mild remedies for employer infractions. The conflicts of interest between labor and management, and hence the incentive to economize on labor costs, have been with us since the very beginning. American managers have never welcomed unions, and yet unions grew from 1935 to 1954 and have declined ever since.

The change in labor-management relations, and the relative position of unions, is essentially due to an unleashing of competitive forces in the markets for American products and services. Given a large domestic market and barriers to entry in many industries, unions for many years were able to pursue traditional high-labor-cost policies across entire product markets and thus grow or at least maintain their positions despite hostile, or at best grudging, managements and a relatively toothless labor law. As we enter an era of intense product market competition, however, the underlying strains in the system are now apparent.

A. *Premises of the U.S. Labor Relations System*

The persistence and growth of employer opposition (and perhaps other causes of union decline) stem from an incompatibility between the premises of our labor relations system and the pressures of competitive product markets. Consider the following features of our system.

First, it is decentralized. Largely because unions seek elections on the basis of the smallest organizing unit, NLRB elections are held

23. *See* Chaison & Rose, *supra* note 12, at 15; Larry T. Adams, *Changing Employment Patterns of Organized Workers*, 108 MONTHLY LAB. REV., Feb. 1985, at 25. TROY & SHEFLIN, *supra* note 1, app. A. at A-2, put the figure at 20.6% for 1980.

24. This is disputed in Farber & Krueger, *supra* note 5. *See supra* note 18 and accompanying text.

25. Dictum in the 1938 decision in NLRB v. Mackay Radio & Tel. Co., 304 U.S. 333 (1938), recognizes the employer's right to attempt to maintain operations during an economic strike by hiring permanent replacements. The distinctly pro-union NLRB of the time was of the same view. *See* Reply Brief for the National Labor Relations Board at 15-17, NLRB v. Mackay Radio & Tel. Co., 304 U.S. 333 (1938) (No. 37-706).

26. *See* NLRB v. Virginia Elec. & Power Co., 314 U.S. 469 (1941) (questioning the Labor Board's authority to find as an unfair labor practice non-coercive employer expression in opposition to a union drive).

at the plant level,[27] usually among a subset of the workers—with craft workers and professionals having the right to opt for separate representation. Multiemployer bargaining units are formed only by consent[28] and in many industries have unravelled. Union organizers like small organizing units, and decentralized structures often ensure a relatively high level of responsiveness to affected employees.

Second, the system is based on an adversarial model of labor-management relations. Admittedly, the system does not "require" adversarial unions or managements. However, an essential premise of the NLRA is that there is a fundamental conflict of interest—a chasm—between labor and management, that is thought to require structural guarantees to keep separate their respective spheres of influence. Thus, employers can play no role in forming labor organizations or providing assistance to them. Similarly, the representatives of management, including supervisors and nonsupervisory personnel having a role in the making or implementation of policy, have no right to form unions and are aligned by the statute against the ranks of the organized, largely blue-collar workers. Also, the scope of mandatory bargaining is defined so as to rigidly separate the domains of labor and management.

Third, unions are multiemployer organizations representing employees of competing firms. This makes it very difficult for any firm to share proprietary information with, or to secure variable labor terms from, the multiemployer union. For example, in the still-unresolved Caterpillar-UAW dispute, at stake is not the rather modest economic differences between the two sides. Rather, the union's concern is its ability to maintain "pattern" bargaining—in this case, to impose on Caterpillar the terms agreed to by its weaker, less export-sensitive competitor, Deere, and also to preserve that strategy for bargaining with the Big Three auto manufacturers.

Finally, unions are institutionally insecure. In the old days, the competition came from rival unions. This has diminished since the 1955 merger of the AFL and CIO (although the demise of manufac-

27. For example, the Labor Board regards the single worksite unit as presumptively appropriate in retail settings. *See, e.g.*, Sav-On Drugs, Inc., 138 N.L.R.B. 1032 (1962); Frisch's Big Boy Ill-Mar, Inc., 147 N.L.R.B. 551 (1964), *enforcement denied*, 356 F.2d 895 (7th Cir. 1966).

28. The Wagner Act makes no provision for NLRB-directed elections among multi-employer units. *See* 29 U.S.C. § 159(b) (1988) ("the unit appropriate for the purposes of collective bargaining shall be the employer unit, craft unit, plant unit, or subdivision thereof"). Professor Gross suggests that craft union leaders (as well as employers) opposed multi-employer units out of fear that such units would strengthen the position of rival industrial unions. *See* JAMES A. GROSS, THE MAKING OF THE NATIONAL LABOR RELATIONS BOARD: A STUDY IN ECONOMICS, POLITICS, AND THE LAW 145-46 (1974).

turing has spawned a new form of competition among "general" unions for employees in the growing service and public sectors). Today the unions' vulnerability comes from the growing nonunion sector, and the various mechanisms for policing union responsiveness, such as decertification elections, the employers' ability to test majority support by withdrawing recognition, duty of fair representation suits, the rights of nonunion members to seek rebates of union dues used for non-collective-bargaining purposes, and union democracy safeguards. All other things being equal, union leaders would like to maintain (and increase) employment levels. Internal political pressures require them, however, to cater to the preferences of the median voter in the bargaining unit—typically long-service, older workers who are relatively free of the risk of layoff because of seniority rules.[29] Absent a palpable crisis threatening the jobs of those voters, flexibility in bargaining objectives and cooperation with management in reducing labor costs are politically unpopular, as Donald Ephlin, an advocate for greater union-management cooperation, learned during his leadership of the UAW's GM department.[30]

B. The Illusive Quest: "Taking Wages Out of Competition"

The features I have described are, on one level, desirable and certainly understandable. As a general matter, they help promote independent unions that are responsive to rank-and-file preferences, and reflect individualist values of our political culture. Also, for several decades they coexisted with union growth and strong unionism. This was largely because unions could credibly promise unionized firms that they would, in due course, organize all firms in the relevant product market, and hence ensure that any gains at the bargaining table would be imposed on all competitors. Consumers might lose in such a world,[31] but most importantly the union-represented firm suffered no competitive disadvantage.

29. *See generally* Bruce E. Kaufman & Jorge Martinez-Vasquez, *Monopoly, Efficient Contract, and Median Voter Models of Union Wage Determination: A Critical Comparison*, 11 J. LAB. RES. 401 (1990).

30. In March 1993, Michael Bennett, president of United Auto Workers Local 1853, a strong proponent of the teamwork concept at GM's innovative Saturn subsidiary, faced a tough challenge from dissidents complaining that Bennett had "lost touch with the membership." Neal Templin, *Union Boss at GM's Saturn Unit Faces Tough Runoff Bid*, WALL ST. J., Mar. 29, 1993, at B6C. Ephlin's and Bennett's difficulties may have had more with leadership style than substance, but it is telling that the rhetoric of the opposition in both cases sought to exploit disquiet with labor-management cooperation.

31. To the extent union gains are taken from a firm's monopoly profits, there should be no loss of consumer welfare. *See* Kenneth G. Dau-Schmidt, *A Bargaining Analysis of American*

This story has changed because American industry and the U.S. place in the world economy has changed.[32] The ability of unions to "take wages out of competition" has declined substantially thanks to the competitive forces unleashed by the emergence of global product markets;[33] the deregulation of previously union-dense industries, such as airlines, trucking,[34] and telecommunications; and technological change altering needs for skilled labor and reducing the advantages of local producers.[35]

Labor Law and the Search for Bargaining Equity and Industrial Peace, 91 MICH. L. REV. 419, 481 (1992).

32. Professor Freeman acknowledges in a recent essay that the book he coauthored in 1984 with Professor Medoff, WHAT DO UNIONS DO?, *supra* note 5, failed to link past successes of U.S. unions with the changing position of the United States in the world economy:

> When the U.S. had a technological and productivity lead over the rest of the world, American producers had potential "monopoly rents" that unions could extract for workers with little adverse effect on investment . . . . However, after the oil shock, the loss of the U.S. productivity edge, and the deregulation of the 1970s and 1980s, unions could no longer simply bargain for workers' share of a company's economic rent. The rent was no longer there. From this sweeping perspective, the slow adjustment of unions and unionized firms to the loss of American economic dominance contributed to the decline in union density. What worked for unions in the 1950s and 1960s did not work in the 1970s and 1980s.

Richard B. Freeman, *Is Declining Unionization of the U.S. Good, Bad, or Irrelevant?*, *in* UNIONS AND ECONOMIC COMPETITIVENESS 143, 165-66 (Lawrence Mishel & Paula B. Voos eds., 1992).

33. The impact of international product market competition has been principally felt in the manufacturing sector—in particular, the clothing, steel, automobile, rubber, and electronics industries. Union decline in mining, construction, transportation, communications, and public utilities is largely due to other factors since the products or services of these industries are generally not imported. However, the decline of manufacturing can affect demand for unionized construction work, according to Bob Wood, Remarks on Papers Dealing with Construction Union Density at the AFL-CIO/Cornell University Conference on Labor Law Reform (Oct. 25, 1993).

34. *See* Barry T. Hirsch, *Trucking Deregulation and Labor Earnings: Is the Union Premium a Compensating Differential?*, 11 J. LAB. ECON. 279, 297-98 (1993) (cost pressures due to deregulation narrowed union-nonunion wage differentials but insufficiently to prevent decline in unionization rate in the previously regulated for-hire sector of the trucking industry from about 60% during the regulatory period to about 25% by 1990).

35. At an October 1, 1993 Roundtable on Labor Law Reform, sponsored by the University of Pennsylvania's Institute of Law and Economics, David M. Silberman, head of the AFL-CIO's task force on labor law reform, criticized my failure to account for employer opposition in service industries, such as hotels and restaurants, that have been unaffected by international competition, deregulation, or technological change. But these industries have always been difficult to organize precisely because of the cost pressures due to intense product market competition. In 1991, whereas 13.1% of private nonagricultural workers were represented by unions, 7.3% of the workers in the retail trade industry and 6.8% of workers in the service industry were represented by unions. Among broad occupational categories, excluding executives and farming, sales (6.0%) and nonprotective services (10.9%) registered the lowest unionization rates. *See* U.S. Dept. of Labor, Bureau of Labor Statistics, Employment and Earnings 229 (1992). On the problems of organizing service-sector workers, see generally Howard Wial, *The Emerging Organizational Structure of Unionism in Low-Wage Services*, 45 RUTGERS L. REV. 671 (1993). These problems are similarly present in Canada despite a distinctly more favorable legal regime. *See* Noah Meltz, *Unionism in the Private-Service Sector: A Canada-United States Comparison*, *in* THE CHALLENGE OF RESTRUCTURING: NORTH AMERICAN LABOR MOVEMENTS RESPOND (Jane Jenson & Rianne Mahon eds., 1993).

U.S. unions can no longer credibly promise employers that they will succeed in imposing the costs of union contracts on their competitors. However, to retain the support of their members and attract new ones, many unions must continue to pursue "wage premium"[36] and "job control" policies that raise labor costs in excess of the productivity gains attributable to unionization.[37] (The studies of Robert Lawrence[38] now at Harvard's Kennedy School and Michael Wachter of Wharton[39] and their associates suggest that the union wage premium actually increases as union density declines in some industries.) Share prices usually fall in response to union organizing drives.[40]

Even Richard Freeman and James Medoff's celebrated 1984 defense in *What Do Unions Do?*[41] concedes that unions reduce firm profits.[42] In a subsequent essay, Richard Freeman and David Blanchflower observe that in the United States "unionism is associated with markedly lower profitability"—a "profits effect" that is the result of "the large effect of unionism on wages, which exceeds the positive

36. Professor Flanagan maintains that between 1969 and 1982, "the ratio of union to nonunion wages rose steadily, gaining 13.5 percentage points in manufacturing." Flanagan, *supra* note 11, at 983. *See also* George E. Johnson, *Changes Over Time in the Union-Nonunion Wage Differential in the United States*, *in* THE ECONOMICS OF TRADE UNIONS: NEW DIRECTIONS 3, 5-7 (Jean-Jacques Rosa ed., 1984). Professors Linneman, Wachter and Carter find that reports of a relatively stable aggregate wage premium since 1973 are deceptive:

> [U]nion wage premiums increased significantly across a broad spectrum of industries between 1973 and 1986, particularly in sectors where premiums were already high. On the other hand, premiums were stable or declining in construction, finance, and services. These changes, combined with systematic compositional shifts . . . create the statistical artifact of a relatively stable aggregate premium.

Peter D. Linneman et al., *Evaluating the Evidence on Union Employment and Wages*, 44 INDUS. & LAB. REL. REV. 34, 43 (1990).

37. There is large body of work, reported in FREEMAN & MEDOFF, *supra* note 5, to the effect that unions improve productivity, but even Professors Freeman and Medoff do not argue that the wage premiums unions seek are fully "paid for" by productivity gains. *See, e.g., id.* at 183. Moreover, such studies may overstate the productivity-enhancing role of unions because they use measures of productivity that reflect the ability of union-represented firms to pass through higher costs via higher prices, and take account only of the effect of unions on surviving firms. *See* John T. Addison & Barry T. Hirsch, *Union Effects on Productivity, Profits and Growth: Has the Long Run Arrived?*, 7 J. LAB. ECON. 72 (1989).

38. *See* Colin Lawrence & Robert Z. Lawrence, *Manufacturing Wage Dispersion: An End Game Interpretation*, BROOKINGS PAPERS ON ECON. ACTIVITY, No. 1, 1985, at 47.

39. *See, e.g.*, Linneman et al., *supra* note 36; Michael L. Wachter & William H. Carter, *Norm Shifts in Union Wages: Will 1989 Be a Replay of 1969?*, 1989 BROOKINGS PAPERS ON ECON. ACTIVITY, No. 2, 1989, at 233; Peter Linneman & Michael L. Wachter, *Rising Union Premiums and the Declining Boundaries Among Noncompeting Groups*, 76 AM. ECON. REV., 103-08 (1986).

40. *See* Richard S. Ruback & Martin B. Zimmerman, *Unionization and Profitability: Evidence from the Capital Market*, 92 J. POL. ECON. 1134 (1984).

41. FREEMAN & MEDOFF, *supra* note 5.

42. *See id.* at ch. 12.

effect of unions on productivity."[43] Because unions represent an increase in the cost of capital, the upshot is that capital increasingly withdraws from the union sector.[44]

A union movement that today represents a little under eleven million private sector workers will continue to be a factor and, it must be noted, that unions like the Steelworkers, Autoworkers, and Rubberworkers have reached creative and constructive solutions with managements in some settings to preserve jobs and enhance the firm's market position.[45] But these are the unions whose memberships are dropping the fastest, and they have reached these accommodations against a background of forces that spell a diminishing role for unions. To avoid this fate, there must be a change in union objectives, management responses, and, ultimately, the labor-management climate.

III. Comparisons to Other Systems

Labor relations specialists like Weiler and Freeman would respond to my diagnosis by pointing to the examples of Canada and Germany, where strong union movements coexist with competitive product markets because of prounion labor laws.[46]

A. Germany

In the case of Germany, however, we have a radically different framework for labor-management relations. The Germans have institutionalized their unions through a system of centralized, industry-

43. Blanchflower & Freeman, *supra* note 22, at 69. These authors attribute the decline in unionization of the late 1970s and 1980s to the jump in the union-nonunion wage differential from 15% to 20-25% during this period. *See id.* at 71.

44. Employment growth is significantly slower in union plants. *See* Jonathan S. Leonard, *Unions and Employment Growth*, 31 Indus. Rel. 80 (1992); *cf.* Richard J. Long, *The Effect of Unionization on Employment Growth of Canadian Companies*, 46 Indus. & Lab. Rel. Rev. 691 (1993). Moreover, unionized firms invest significantly less in research and development and long-lived fixed capital than their nonunion counterparts. *See* Barry T. Hirsch, Labor Unions and the Economic Performance of Firms 87-88 (1991); Brian E. Becker & Craig A. Olson, *Unions and Firm Profits*, 31 Indus. Rel. 395 (1992); Barry T. Hirsch & Robert A. Connolly, *Do Unions Capture Monopoly Profits?*, 41 Indus. & Lab. Rel. Rev. 118 (1987); Robert A. Connolly et al., *Union Rent Seeking, Intangible Capital, and the Market Value of the Firm*, 68 Rev. of Econ. & Stat. 567 (1986).

45. Consider also the interesting recent agreement between the Amalgamated Clothing Workers (ACTWU) and clothing manufacturers permitting use of nonunion, largely overseas, shops for up to 10% of production in exchange for certain investment and job guarantees and conformity to international labor standards. The pact permits union producers to offer a full range of products, not just domestically-produced, expensive lines. *See Labor Letter*, Wall St. J., Oct. 19, 1993, at A1.

46. Professor Freeman recognizes, however, that despite pro-union legislation in Canada, union density has fallen in Canadian manufacturing because of a similar union-nonunion wage differential and resulting "profits effect." *See* Blanchflower & Freeman, *supra* note 22, at 74-75.

wide collective bargaining coupled with extension by law of collective agreements to unorganized firms. Union members (defined as dues-payers) represent approximately one-third of private sector workers,[47] but union contracts cover over 90% of private sector workers.[48] Also, German social legislation—often prompted by the political power of the labor movement—regulates many of the substantive areas handled in the U.S. through collective bargaining. Given the extent of union-contract coverage, the fact that bargaining takes place at the multienterprise level, and the prominent role of social legislation, collective bargaining in Germany might better be seen as a means of negotiating the rate of inflation for broad sectors, if not the society as a whole.

Most important, the Germans have found a way to reconcile a major union role in setting standards for labor market competition while allowing flexibility in setting a firm's compensation and staffing levels. The industry-wide collective bargaining agreement sets true minima—there is no statutory minimum wage—while as much as 25% of average compensation is set at the level of the firm.[49] Notably, such

47. *See* Jelle Visser, *Trends in Trade Union Membership*, *in* OECD EMPLOYMENT OUTLOOK 97, 101 tbl. 4.1 (1991).

48. *See, e.g.*, Otto Jacobi et al., *Germany: Codetermining the Future?*, *in* INDUSTRIAL RELATIONS IN THE NEW EUROPE 218, 250 (Anthony Ferner & Richard Hyman eds., 1992); Chaison & Rose, *supra* note 12, at 11.

49. Two terms are used in the literature to describe such supplementary compensation: "wage gap" refers to the difference between the collectively bargained wage and the effective wage paid at the level of the firm; "wage drift" refers to the difference in the rate of change between collective wage rates and firm wage rates. Both "wage gap" and "wage drift" appear to have been quite substantial in the 1950s and 1960s. *See* KATHLEEN A. THELEN, UNION OF PARTS: LABOR POLITICS IN POSTWAR GERMANY 82 (1991) ("Between 1960 and 1970, collectively bargained wages increased at an average annual rate of 7.3 percent. Workers' effective wages in that period, however, rose at an average annual rate of 9.4 percent."). It has been suggested that "wage drift" has become less important in the 1980s, see Jacobi et al., *supra* note 48, at 250; Wolfgang Streeck, Pay Restraint Without Incomes Policy: Institutionalized Monetarism and Industrial Unionism in Germany 9 n.10 (Aug. 1993) (unpublished manuscript, on file with author). However, "wage gap"—despite cutbacks in a changing economy, see PETER SWENSON, FAIR SHARES: UNIONS, PAY, AND POLITICS IN SWEDEN AND WEST GERMANY 81-82 (1989) (unofficial strikes in 1973 protesting employer reductions in supplementary pay as high as 30% of contract wages)—continues to be an important phenomenon. In a 1989 essay, Professor Streeck observed that "wages at the big car assemblers are about 20 to 25 percent higher than stipulated by the metal industry agreement." Wolfgang Streeck, *Successful Adjustment to Turbulent Markets: The Automobile Industry*, *in* INDUSTRY AND POLITICS IN WEST GERMANY: TOWARD THE THIRD REPUBLIC 113, 125 (Peter J. Katzenstein ed., 1989). A recent Labor Department publication reports that Daimler Benz, Germany's largest company, pays, on average, 17% more than the contractual rate set in the metal industry's central agreement. *See* U.S. DEP'T OF LABOR, FOREIGN LABOR TRENDS REPORT, FEDERAL REPUBLIC OF GERMANY 31 (1991-1992).

Quantitative data are difficult to come by. U.S. Department of Labor statistics suggest that in 1992 "other direct pay"—which "consists primarily of vacation and holiday pay and seasonal bonuses"—accounted for only 6.6% of hourly compensation costs for production workers in

supplementary compensation is negotiated not with multienterprise organizations but determined at the enterprise level, where a statutory works council represents all of the nonexecutive employees and is prohibited by law from striking.[50]

Despite these structural advantages,[51] German unions have trouble retaining membership because of the serious "free rider" aspects of their system. The German system is also facing pressures for change: rising unemployment (from one-seventh of U.S. levels in 1973 to parity with the U.S. by the mid-1980s and a rate in excess of U.S. levels in 1993);[52] joblessness of exceptionally long duration;[53] a grow-

manufacturing in the United States, but for 21.4% of hourly compensation costs in Germany. *See* Bureau of Labor Statistics, U.S. Dep't of Labor, International Comparisons of Hourly Compensation Costs for Production Workers in Manufacturing, 1992, at 14 tbl. 10 (1993). Admittedly, this statistic reflects generous vacation pay practices as well as bonuses. The background documents used by the Labor Department indicate, however, that in 1988 bonuses and other "special payments" represented 10.05% of the hourly compensation costs for German manufacturers with 1000 or more employees. *See* Loehne und Gehalter, Arbeitskostenerhebung, Fachserie 16, Heft 1: Arbeitskosten im Produzierenden Gewerbe, 1988, at 77 (Statistisches Bundesamt, Wiebasden, Germany 1990) (on file with author); telephone interview with Alexander Strand, Bureau of Labor Statistics, Office of Productivity and Technology (Oct. 14, 1993); letter from Alexander Strand (Nov. 15, 1993) (on file with author).

50. Interest arbitration is also not available. Under § 87 of the Works Constitution Act, the works council has "a right of co-determination" with respect to certain matters to the extent not prescribed by legislation or collective bargaining. Works Constitution Act 1972, § 87 (F.R.G.). As to these subjects, the employer must obtain the consent of the works council or, barring agreement, resolution by a tripartite "conciliation committee." *Id.* § 76. However, it is doubtful whether supplementary compensation comes within the category of subjects triggering a "right of co-determination." *Cf. id.* § 87 pts. 4 & 10-11. Indeed, it appears that employers can unilaterally reduce supplementary compensation:

> As by law employers are obligated to pay only contract minima, extra-contractual pay (*ubertarifliche Lohnbestandteile*) is a matter about which employers alone have final say. In practice, works councils frequently haggle with employers about extra-contractual changes, patterning their increases and structure generally after contractual changes (thus maintaining the wage gap). On the other hand, employers frequently exercise their right unilaterally to reduce and restructure extra-contractual pay.

Swenson, *supra* note 49, at 81. During the current economic downturn, such cut-backs have been quite common. Interview with Wolfgang Trittin, Industriegewerkschaft Metall Vorstand (IG Metall), in Frankfurt am Maim (July 26, 1993).

51. However, the few empirical studies to date do not indicate that German works councils contribute to firm productivity or profits. *See* John T. Addison et al., *German Works Councils and Firm Performance*, *in* Employee Representation, *supra* note 5, at 305-38.

52. In 1982, the unemployment rate for the *lander* or states comprising the former West Germany was 5.8%; it rose to 7.5% in July 1993. *German Unemployment Up to 7.5% in July, Data Show*, Daily Lab. Rep. (BNA) No. 151, at A-10 (Aug. 9, 1993). OECD projects an unemployment rate of 8.3% for 1993, and 9.9% for 1994. The situation is far worse in the former East Germany. *See* 53 OECD Economic Outlook, 71 (1993); *see also* Ronald E. Kutscher & Constance E. Sorrentino, *Employment and Unemployment Patterns in the U.S. and Europe, 1973-1987*, 10 J. Lab. Res. 5, 12 & tbl. 4 (1989).

53. *See* Kutscher & Sorrentino, *supra* note 52, at 15 tbl. 5 (noting that in 1986, 52.2% of total unemployed in Germany were out of work six months or more and 32.2% were out of work for twelve months or more, with the comparable U.S. figures 14.4% and 8.7%, respectively).

ing contingent, part-time workforce;[54] and the opening of German production facilities in other countries, such as the BMW plant in Spartansburg, South Carolina and the planned Mercedes-Benz facility in Alabama.[55]

B. Canada

The Canadian experience is more relevant. In many respects, we share a common culture and, increasingly, a common market with the Canadians. The labor laws in the Canadian provinces and at the federal sector are markedly more prounion than our own. Several of the provinces allow unions to obtain bargaining rights on the basis of authorization cards in lieu of contested elections, impose interest arbitration in first-contract situations (where the parties cannot reach agreement on their own), and prohibit the hiring of permanent replacements during strikes. (Indeed, Quebec and Ontario bar resort even to temporary replacements.)[56]

The union density figures (combining public- and private-sector unionism) in Canada are twice as high as our own, and despite a decline in the 1970s, appear in recent years to have levelled off or slightly increased. The extent to which unions have maintained their positions in *private* firms during the turbulent late 1970s and 1980s is a matter of considerable dispute. However, it is not contested that—despite favorable prounion laws—unionization in the private sector is well under 50% of the level in the public sector, and that private sec-

54. "In 1986 . . . , about 25 percent of West Germany's workers were under nonpermanent, nonfulltime contracts, and 1 out of 12 unemployed workers could find work only on a fixed-term basis." *The European Labor Market: Some Background*, *in* European and American Labor Markets: Different Models and Different Results 117 app. at 119 (Richard S. Belous et al. eds., 1992). The Employment Protection Act of 1985, as amended in 1989, accelerated this trend by permitting initial hires on fixed-term contracts for up to eighteen months. Presumably, such contracts may be terminated free of the scriptures of German wrongful dismissal law. *See* Jacobi et al., *supra* note 48, at 240.

55. The German labor relations system is in a state of ferment. In September 1993, Gesamtmetall, the employers federation, for the first time in history took the initiative and cancelled its wage agreements with IG Metall, announcing it would be seeking cut-backs in holiday time and vacation pay and greater freedom for individual firms to set wages with local works councils. Some companies, like IBM's German subsidiary, are seeking to exclude much of their operations from the multi-employer framework. *See Time to Leave the Cocoon?*, Bus. Wk., Oct. 18, 1993, at 46-47; Terence Roth, *German Industry Group Cancels Wage Pact, Pre-Empting Union*, Wall St. J., Sept. 29, 1993, at A15.

56. In June 1992, the New Democratic Party government in Ontario repealed a law that allowed employers to hire permanent replacements after the sixth month of an economic strike, and substituted rules that significantly limit the ability of employers to maintain operations during an economic strike (including the use of temporary help). *See* Ontario Labour Relations Act § 73, 3 Can. Lab. L. Rep. (CCH) ¶ 60,373 (1992).

tor unionism, particularly in manufacturing, has declined.[57] The disagreement is over the extent of the union slide, and whether the decline has been halted in Canada by public policy.[58]

Without venturing into the methodological thicket of the debate over the U.S.-Canada "density gap,"[59] I am willing to assume, for present purposes, that Canadian prounion legislation has retarded the decline in private sector unionism in that country. But these laws have not prevented the erosion of traditional union sectors, where the available evidence suggests a significant shift of capital to nonunion

57. *See, e.g.*, Blanchflower & Freeman, *supra* note 22, at 74 ("In manufacturing, density was stable throughout the 1970s but fell from 49 percent organized in 1977 to 42 percent organized in 1986 . . . ." (citation omitted)); Noah Meltz & Anil Verma, *Developments in Industrial Relations and Human Resource Practices in Canada: An Update from the 1980s*, *in* EMPLOYMENT RELATIONS IN A CHANGING WORLD ECONOMY tbl. 1 (Thomas A. Kochan et al. eds., forthcoming 1994) (union density in manufacturing declined from 43.2% in 1980 to 36.7% in 1990; however, overall private sector density remained stable at a little under 21%); Leo Troy, *Is the U.S. Unique in the Decline of Private Sector Unionism?*, 11 J. LAB. RES. 111, 127 tbl. 4 (1990) (overall decline in private union density from 25.7% in 1975 to 20.7% in 1985); MARY LOU COATES, IS THERE A FUTURE FOR THE CANADIAN LABOUR MOVEMENT?, 3 cht. 2 (Industrial Relations Centre, Queen's University Current Issues Series, 1992) (unionization rate declined from 1977-1988 in mining and manufacturing, but grew in transportation and services while remaining stable in construction, communications and utilities).

58. Professors Meltz and Verma find that private sector union density stabilized during the 1980s at 20.7%, with unions strengthening their position in growing trade and finance services to compensate for losses in goods-producing industries. *See* Meltz & Verma, *supra* note 57, at 17-18. By contrast, Professor Troy projects a continuing decline in union membership, explaining that the present higher Canadian unionization rate is a function of differences in the timing of structural changes such as the shift from manufacturing and primary industries to services. *See* Troy, *supra* note 57; Leo Troy, *Convergence in International Unionism, etc.: The Case of Canada and the U.S.A.*, 30 BRIT. J. OF INDUS. REL. 1 (1992).

59. Using data from a 1984 household Survey of Union Membership by Statistics Canada, Professor Riddell pegs the private sector unionization rate at 29% (workers who are union members) and 34% (workers covered by collective agreement)—figures considerably higher than the Meltz-Verma or Troy estimates of around 21% for the same period. *See* W. Craig Riddell, *Unionization in Canada and the United States: A Tale of Two Countries*, *in* SMALL DIFFERENCES THAT MATTER: LABOR MARKET AND INCOME MAINTENANCE IN CANADA AND THE UNITED STATES 109, 136 tbl. 4.9 (David Card & Richard B. Freeman eds., 1993).

Some of the disparity in the published results may be due to the fact that the survey Riddell relies upon lumps together membership in unions with membership in professional associations (whether or not they engage in collective bargaining). *See* Farber & Krueger, *supra* note 5, at 124-25. There is also a definitional disagreement over whether to include all employees in health, welfare services and education in the public sector; public monies fund these services, but some of the employees work for private employers. *See* Riddell, *supra*, at 134 & n.23. Moreover, as Professor Riddell acknowledges, Canadian "Crown Companies" operate in traditional private-sector fields. *Id.* at 139. In 1984, 500,000 employees (or 5% of the nonagricultural work force) worked in such government enterprises. *See* Allen Ponak, *Public Sector Collective Bargaining*, *in* UNION-MANAGEMENT RELATIONS IN CANADA 343-44 tbl. 1 (J.C. Anderson et al. eds., 1989) [hereinafter UNION-MANAGEMENT RELATIONS]; Mark Thompson, *Collective Bargaining by Professionals*, *in* UNION-MANAGEMENT RELATIONS, *supra*. Finally, differences may also stem from the use of different data bases, with Riddell relying on the 1984 household survey and Troy relying on union surveys conducted by Statistics Canada and Labour Canada. *See generally* Pradeep Kumar, *Estimates of Unionism and Collective Bargaining Coverage in Canada*, 43 REL. INDUSTRIELLES 757 (1988).

firms.[60] The situation is likely to get worse as the free trade agreement with Canada continues to narrow labor-cost differentials between the two countries.[61] As in the United States, Professors Blanchflower and Freeman observe, high union-nonunion wage differentials in Canada "have begun to cut into membership where unionized employers competed with overseas firms, including increasingly deunionized U.S. manufacturers."[62]

The question for U.S. public policy is whether the dominant thrust of labor law reform should be essentially to mimic the Canadian approach—through protective laws that help U.S. unions maintain their position while they pursue their traditional program—or whether other avenues should be explored to enhance employee voice, union and nonunion, in competitive markets.

IV. What Should Be Done?

A. *The Case for Change*

The decline of union density on its own does not state a case for change in U.S. labor law. One option is to do nothing and let the chips fall where they will. Much depends on the view one takes of the value of workplace representation of employee interests. I believe that we are worse off as a society if workers are bereft of a meaningful opportunity for collective voice in factories and offices.[63]

60. *See* Richard J. Long, *The Effect of Unionization on Employment Growth of Canadian Companies*, 46 Indus. & Lab. Rel. 691, 698 (1993) ("With controls for industry, firm size, and firm age, union manufacturing firms grew about 3.7% per year more slowly than their nonunion counterparts, and union nonmanufacturing firms grew about 3.9% more slowly than their nonunion counterparts.").

61. *See* Brian A. Langille, *Canadian Labour Law Reform and Free Trade*, 23 Ottawa L. Rev. 581 (1991). Canada is presently suffering from double-digit unemployment rates in all of its provinces, save Saskatchewan (8.1%) and Manitoba (9.4%). *See Canadian National Unemployment Rate Decreased to 11.2 Percent in September*, Daily Lab. Rep. (BNA) No. 195, at A-8 (Oct. 12, 1993).

62. Blanchflower & Freeman, *supra* note 22, at 74.

63. Professor Richard Epstein of Chicago urges wholesale deregulation, *see* Richard A. Epstein, *A Common Law for Labor Relations: A Critique of the New Deal Labor Legislation*, 92 Yale L.J. 1357 (1983), but a deregulatory agenda is difficult to assess without knowing what the background rules will be after the Wagner Act and Railway Labor Act are repealed. Presumably, Epstein would keep in place common-law and statutory antitrust restrictions on union picketing and secondary boycotts. In any event, it is far from clear that labor markets operate like commodity markets in the manner described by standard microeconomic price theory—both because workers make undiversified investments of their labor in firms, and firms in many situations act more like wage-setters than wage-takers. Moreover, if workers wish to be represented by a collective agency, norms of self-determination and freedom of association argue for requiring employers to negotiate with the chosen representative of the workers. *See, e.g.*, Charles Fried, *Individual and Collective Rights in Work Relations: Reflections on the Current State of Labor Law and its Prospects,* 51 U. Chi. L. Rev. 1012, 1023-25 (1984).

However, the case for reform cannot be persuasively based on the "monopoly" role of unions as agents for effecting a redistribution of wealth from capital to labor. Tax and spending measures are better suited for this purpose than is collective bargaining. Freeman and Medoff acknowledge that union wage gains at the expense of profits are largely confined to industries sheltered from vigorous competition.[64] Whatever force collective bargaining once may have had as a redistributive strategy, unions will have difficulty pursuing traditional wage premium and job control policies in a world of competitive product markets.[65]

It is, rather, the "voice" benefits of workplace representation—whether supplied by unions or other mechanisms—that argue for reform. To use Albert Hirschman's influential terminology, workers have a need for "voice" because of a limited ability to "exit," as they are rooted in their communities and tied to the firm by training and benefits policies that discourage mobility. Voice is important not only because of the contribution it makes to the dignity and autonomy of the individual worker. Voice mechanisms in the workplace also promote efficient contracts between workers and firms. Some contractual terms like a meaningful grievance procedure are "collective goods" that are likely to be underproduced in individual bargains, and

64. Freeman and Medoff write in WHAT DO UNIONS DO?, *supra* note 5, at 186:

> These data suggest that unionism has no impact on the profitability of competitive firms. Among highly concentrated industries, by contrast, the table shows enormous differences in profitability by union density; the highly unionized industries have considerably lower profitability in all calculations . . . . What unions do is reduce the exceedingly high levels of profitability in highly concentrated industries toward normal competitive levels. In these calculations, the union profit effect appears to take the form of a reduction of monopoly profits.

Professors Addison and Hirsch question whether concentration is a major source of union gains, and argue that the union effect on profits influences adversely firm investments by keeping in place inefficient capital as a means of moderating union demands. *See* Addison & Hirsch, *supra* note 37, at 94. Under either account, traditional union wage premium policy will be difficult to maintain in competitive product markets.

65. Professor Dau-Schmidt's recent article, *supra* note 31, attempts to ground a public policy of fostering unions and collective bargaining in redistributive terms. Dau-Schmidt's essay assumes that persisting union gains are drawn exclusively from a "cooperative surplus" derived from a combination of the firm's supracompetitive profits and productivity gains attributable to unions. In his model:

> [E]mployers and unions who seek to maximize the monetary value of the employer rents they divide will employ the same amount of labor and set the same product price as they would in the absence of a union. Inefficiency in production and consumption will occur only to the extent that the union is willing to trade employment for wages at the expense of maximizing the monetary value of the cooperative surplus and to the extent that the union derives its wage increase from an effective labor cartel.

Id. at 491. This is not the place for an extensive discussion of this interesting article, other than to note that Dau-Schmidt offers no evidence of the extent to which unionized firms in today's economy enjoy such supracompetitive "rents."

unilateral employer promulgation may not adequately capture employee preferences. In addition, many productivity-enhancing improvements in the workplace such as employee involvement programs and flexible pay schemes are difficult to put in place without a mechanism for representing employees and eliciting their cooperation and trust.

There may also be a direct relationship between the decline of workplace representation and the rise in demand for social legislation. In some cases, as suggested by today's debate over workplace-based health insurance, appropriate legislation may be preferable to reliance on the outcomes of decentralized collective bargaining or unilateral employer policies. However, the demand for legislation can also take the form of an ever-growing list of "mandates" that may poorly reflect employee preferences, deter needed job growth, and divert resources to the litigation system. Unions or other institutions for employee voice, when they effectively communicate employee preferences, provide an important alternative to such "minimum terms" legislation.

The Wagner Act framework was intended to recognize these benefits of collective representation, but it no longer serves most workers. If we do nothing, the opportunity for collective voice may well disappear from the American workplace. In the absence of reform, we will be poorer as a society.

B. Models of Labor Law Reform

Several models of labor law reform have been proposed in the literature. In the main, these proposals are deficient because of incompleteness, lack of fit with U.S. institutional arrangements, or a failure to confront the challenge of competitive markets for traditional union programs. I offer an alternative approach later in these pages.

1. Collaborative Representation

Some, though not all, voices in U.S. management would like to see a significant relaxation of the existing prohibition in section 8(a)(2) of the NLRA of company-dominated or supported "labor organizations."[66] Although the original impetus for this provision was to prevent employers from installing sham unions, the term "labor or-

66. In response to the NLRB's ruling in Electromation, Inc., 309 N.L.R.B. 990 (1992), bills (H.R. 1529, S. 669) were introduced in March 1993 to amend § 8(a)(2) to allow for the establishment of employee participation programs dealing with productivity and efficiency. The House version, offered by Representitive Steven Gunderson (R-Wis.), currently has twenty-four sponsors. Some management advocates do not believe any change in the law is needed. *See Former*

ganization" was broadly defined to include "any organization of any kind, or any agency or employee representation committee or plan," in which employees participate for the purpose of "dealing with" their employer, even if such dealings fall short of actual bargaining over contracts.[67]

In December 1992, the Labor Board issued its long-awaited ruling in *Electromation, Inc.*,[68] in which the agency found a company guilty of no other impropriety than forming employee "action committees" for joint dealings with management over absenteeism, pay progression, and no-smoking policies. A portion of the U.S. management community fears that *Electromation* (and a related ruling in the union setting[69]) will place in jeopardy current strategies of workplace organization that emphasize reduced layers of supervision and increased employee involvement in work redesign and product and service delivery improvements.[70]

Although it is too early to tell how far-reaching *Electromation*'s impact will be, there is some cause for concern. It appears that practices that involve complete delegations of managerial authority to work teams or grievance boards,[71] or avoid any element of what the Labor Board terms, "a bilateral process involving employees and management in order to reach bilateral solutions on the basis of employee-initiated proposals,"[72] will survive scrutiny. However, practices involving any representational element at all,[73] or any "bilateral process" that can be viewed as distinct from of a natural work group-

NLRB Chairman Miller Calls Electromation *Problem 'Myth,'* Daily Lab. Rep. (BNA) No. 201, at D-7 (Oct. 20, 1993).

67. *See* NLRB v. Cabot Carbon Co., 360 U.S. 203 (1959).

68. 309 N.L.R.B. 990 (1992).

69. *See* E.I. du Pont de Nemours & Co., 311 N.L.R.B. No. 88, 1992-1993 NLRB Dec. (CCH) ¶ 17,862 (May 28, 1993).

70. *See generally* Edward E. Potter, Quality at Risk: Are Employee Participation Programs in Jeopardy? (1991); Paul Osterman, *How Common is Workplace Transformation and Who Adopts It?*, 47 Indus. & Lab. Rel. Rev. 173 (1994).

71. *Electromation*, 309 N.L.R.B. at 995, *citing* General Foods Corp., 231 N.L.R.B. 1232 (1977); Mercy-Memorial Hospital, 231 N.L.R.B. 1108 (1977); John Ascuaga's Nugget, 230 N.L.R.B. 275 (1977).

72. *Electromation*, 309 N.L.R.B. at 997.

73. The Labor Board left open the question whether the putative "labor organization" must be acting in a representational capacity. However, the agency found a representational element in *Electromation*'s "Action Committees" on rather meager facts:

> It is also clear that Respondent contemplated that employee-members of the Action Committees would act on behalf of other employees. Thus, after talking 'back and forth' with their fellow employees, members were to get ideas from other employees regarding the subjects of their committees for the purpose of reaching solutions that would satisfy the employees as a whole. This would occur only if the proposals presented by the employee-members were in line with the desires of other employees. In these circumstances, we find that employee-members of the Action Committees ac-

ing or the workforce as a whole,[74] are likely to elicit regulatory action.[75]

Electromation brings to the fore the basic theory of the Wagner Act: employees should be put the choice of collective representation by a union or unilateral decisionmaking by their employer. Senator Wagner and his colleagues were of the view that any form of representation by mechanisms other than an independent organization would be likely to manipulate workers and forestall the conditions for independent unionism.[76]

This is not the place for an extended analysis of section 8(a)(2) and its legislative history.[77] Whatever its original justification, this provision has not spurred union growth and has had largely negative effects. From the perspective of a predominantly nonunion work

> ted in a representational capacity and that the Action Committees were an "employee representation committee or plan" as set forth in Section 2(5).

Id. As then NLRB General Counsel Jerry M. Hunter observed, in a memorandum to regional directors, "should the Board ultimately conclude the statute requires employee committees to act in a representational capacity, such a factual test may not be difficult to meet," and hence representational capacity "may not be an issue in many cases . . . ." Memorandum from NLRB General Counsel GC 93-4, Guideline Memorandum Concerning *Electromation, Inc.*, 309 N.L.R.B. No. 163 (Apr. 15, 1993), *reprinted in* Daily Lab. Rep. (BNA) No. 78, at G-1, G-6 (Apr. 26, 1993).

74. There is a suggestion in Member Oviatt's concurrence that programs confined to narrowly-conceived "productivity" and "quality" issues do not come within the subjects of "dealing" reached by § 2(5) ("grievances, labor disputes, wages, rates of pay, hours of employment or conditions of work"). This suggestion is of doubtful practical utility because "[t]he very foundation of employee participation programs is the notion that employees should be consulted because they have knowledge and experience concerning the workplace." Harold J. Datz, *Employee Participation Programs and the National Labor Relations Act—A Guide for the Perplexed*, Daily Lab. Rep. (BNA) No. 30, at E-1, E-2 (Feb. 17, 1993).

75. Thus, for example, a complaint to the Labor Department caused Polaroid to disband a system of committees that had been in place since 1946—and was lauded in DAVID EWING, JUSTICE ON THE JOB: RESOLVING GRIEVANCES IN THE NONUNION WORKPLACE 299-308 (1989)—for airing shop-floor grievances and adjusting layoffs and other personnel practices, with third-party arbitration as the final step. *See Polaroid Dissolves Employee Committee in Response to Labor Department Ruling*, Daily Lab. Rep. (BNA) No. 121, at A-3 (June 23, 1992). A new employee advisory structure set up by Polaroid has resulted in the issuance of an NLRB complaint, Polaroid Corp, 1-CA-29966 & 1-CA-30063 (May 28, 1993). *See NLRB Charges Polaroid with Forming New Employer-Dominated Labor Committee*, Daily Lab. Rep. (BNA) No. 105, at A-1 (June 3, 1993).

76. *See generally* Mark Barenberg, *The Political Economy of the Wagner Act: Power, Symbol and Workplace Cooperation,* 106 HARV. L. REV. 1379 (1993).

77. Section 8(a)(2) may have been a broader restriction than was necessary to address the specific evils before the 1935 Congress. Much of the experience with company unions during the National Industrial Recovery Act (NIRA) period involved firms that used their in-house employee representation plans to refuse to bargain with outside unions even in the face of strikes reflecting clear majority support. *See, e.g.*, the Edward G. Budd Mfg. Co. case, described in IRVING BERNSTEIN, TURBULENT YEARS: A HISTORY OF THE AMERICAN WORKER, 1933-1941 at 179 (1970); *Hearings on S. 2926 Before the Comm. on Education and Labor*, 73d Cong., 2d Sess. 104-06 (1934) (testimony of William Green), *reprinted in* 1 NLRB LEGISLATIVE HISTORY OF THE NATIONAL LABOR RELATIONS ACT, 1935 at 134-36 (1985).

force, it affirmatively discourages what the law should encourage: enhanced employee voice in nonunion shops. Moreover, under current social conditions—a better educated workforce, minimum wage and other protective legislation, and a rights-conscious legal culture—it is doubtful that permitting employers to institute consultative arrangements or to use employee representatives in grievance procedures would have the effect of preventing employees from making an uncoerced decision over whether they wish to be represented by an independent union.

A substantial modification of section 8(a)(2) is called for as part of a broader package of reforms of the labor laws. I propose limiting section 2(5)'s definition of "labor organization" to entities that "bargain with" their employer over terms and conditions of employment. Employers should not be able to establish and dominate representational structures that purport to function as bargaining agents for the employees, so as to deceive employees into believing they are represented by independent unions when, in fact, they are not. Formal agreements would not be required to trigger the statutory prohibition; it would reach any employer-dominated or supported structure that purported, or was reasonably perceived by the employees, to function as a collective bargaining agency.[78] Employees would retain their section 7 rights to engage in concerted activity for self-representation and "other mutual aid and protection," and, most importantly, their section 9 right to petition for independent unions. No agreement with an employer-dominated committee could bar an election. In addition, employers should not be permitted to install employee committees as a purely strategic device to win over workers in the midst of an NLRB representation election.[79]

78. Section 8(a)(2), as amended, would still prohibit an employer's recognition of a minority union as an exclusive bargaining agent and negotiation of an agreement providing for the checkoff of union dues. *See* ILGWU v. NLRB, 366 U.S. 731 (1961). (I would, however, relax the prohibition of prehire contracts under certain conditions described below.) In the *Electromation* case, the "Action Committees" were found to have violated § 8(a)(2) without any basis in the record that the employees in that plant believed, reasonably or otherwise, that the committees were acting as their bargaining agent. Whether or not such committees promote greater job satisfaction, they should pose no threat to the employees' ability to make an uncoerced decision as to representation by independent unions, if the NLRA is also amended to strengthen the legal protection of employees opting for independent unions. Under my proposal, such committees would not be treated as a "labor organization" triggering § 8(a)(2).

79. Under current law, employers are prohibited from changing terms and conditions of employment for the purpose of affecting the outcome of a pending NLRB election. *See* NLRB v. Exchange Parts Co., 375 U.S. 405 (1964). There is also merit in extending the prohibition to an earlier point, say, when the employer receives a demand for recognition from a union organizing its work force, or perhaps first learns of the organizing drive. Professor Gottesman would extend the constraint to situations where there had been an organizing drive in the past

But a relaxation of the section 8(a)(2) prohibition, standing alone, is likely to distort the cost-benefit calculus of workers if they are confronted simply with the choice between a "free" form of representation under the employer's plan and risk of job loss in opting for independent unionism.[80] Workers dissatisfied with collaborative representation must be able, with minimum cost, to choose independent unions. Reform, if it is to take place, should be part of an integrated package that includes a substantial bolstering of the legal protections for workers opting for independent organizations to advance their interests.

We should resist, however, suggestions that any employer plan or committee system seeking freedom from section 8(a)(2)'s strictures must provide for an elaborate set of safeguards—including a secret-ballot election, independent resources for employee representatives, separate representation of supervisory and nonsupervisory personnel, protection from discharge of employee representatives, and the like—that would approximate the state of affairs that would obtain if an independent union had been voted in.[81] Such requirements would be

two years. *See* Michael H. Gottesman, *In Despair, Starting Over: Imagining a Labor Law for Unorganized Workers*, 69 CHI.-KENT L. REV. 59, 87 (1993).

80. In a thoughtful essay, Laurence Gold, the AFL-CIO's able general counsel, has suggested that any opening up of § 8(a)(2) will distort the employee's cost-benefit analysis in deciding whether to be represented by an independent union. *See* Laurence Gold, *The Legal Status of "Employee Participation" Programs After the Labor Board's* Electromation *and* du Pont *Decisions*, *in* PROCEEDINGS OF NEW YORK UNIVERSITY 46TH ANNUAL NATIONAL CONFERENCE ON LABOR 21-24 (Bruno Stein ed., forthcoming 1994).

Admittedly, liberalization of § 8(a)(2) may enhance job satisfaction, and otherwise raise union organizing costs by offering employees an alternative form of representation presently denied to them. However, I believe Mr. Gold overstates the magnitude of the distortion of the cost-benefit calculus (the implications of his view would also require prohibition of voluntary recognition of unions without elections)—provided (1) the employer-dominated structure is not permitted to function as a bargaining agency; and (2) meaningful protection against retaliatory discharge and union rights of access to the employee electorate are put in place. *See infra* note 81 and accompanying text.

81. This appears to be the thrust of Professor Summers' proposal in this Symposium. *See* Clyde W. Summers, *Employee Voice and Employer Choice: A Structured Exception to Section 8(A)(2)*, 69 CHI.-KENT L. REV. 129, 141-48 (1993); *see also* Janice Bellace, Electromation: *The Dilemma of Employee Participation under the NLRA*, *in* PROCEEDINGS OF NEW YORK UNIVERSITY 45TH ANNUAL NATIONAL CONFERENCE ON LABOR 225, 236-43 (Bruno Stein ed., 1993) [hereinafter NYU PROCEEDINGS]. If required to choose, I much prefer Professor Hyde's approach (also in this Symposium), requiring only a secret-ballot election, notice that the employees are free to oppose the employee representation plan, and periodic reauthorization elections. *See* Alan Hyde, *Employee Caucus: A Key Institution in the Emerging System of Employment Law*, 69 CHI.-KENT L. REV. 149, 188 (1993). But election requirements make little sense if the employees are part of a natural work grouping or are chosen to participate in, say, a safety committee because of their expertise. Even in the case of *Electromation*-type committees, for those employers who seek employee participation programs as a means of reinvigorating a low-productivity, low-morale work force, Professor Hyde's proposal gives employees an effective veto over what may be needed changes in the workplace culture. Moreover, any election re-

entirely inappropriate for employee involvement programs based on natural work groupings. Moreover, even for "off-line" commitees such as those at issue in *Electromation*, these strictures would essentially be self-defeating, for employers are not seeking to put in place independent—or depending on your point of view, adversarial—structures of their own making.[82] Moreover, it is important to maintain conceptual and practical distance between collaborative structures and independent employee organizations in order to preserve the conditions for employee free choice; employees should clearly understand that the employer's committee system is a vehicle for participation in workplace decisions, in aid of management's objectives, not an alternative form of union representation.

2. German-Style Labor Law Reform

Another approach to labor law reform would be to attempt to replicate the system of another country that we think does a pretty good job of promoting worker representation values and firm competitiveness. If we were to adopt the German model, for example, the labor laws might require industry-wide collective bargaining (though not mandated by German law), an extension procedure enabling unions and employers to petition the state to extend collective agreements to the unorganized sector, union representation in the corporate board room, and the establishment of works councils at the enterprise level.[83]

Although proposals for mandating union or employee representation on corporate boards have been floated in the past, this aspect of the German "codetermination" system is not a prominent feature of the current debate.[84] However, there appears to be considerable support for mandatory works councils (at least in academic circles).[85]

quirement is likely substantially to raise the costs for union organizers (in Mr. Gold's terms, see *supra* note 80) by endowing the collaborative representation structure with the trappings of independent representation.

82. Apparently, Professor Gottesman is in accord. *See* Gottesman, *supra* note 79, at 86.

83. Proposals to import a particular feature of the German system must consider how that feature relates to other aspects of that country's labor relations framework, and whether that feature would present the same mix of costs and benefits within the U.S. framework. *See generally* Otto Kahn-Freund, *On Uses and Misuses of Comparative Law*, 37 MOD. L. REV. 1 (1974).

84. For a proposal envisioning a limited "voice" role for employee directors, see Robert J. Borzone, Jr., Codetermination in the United States (paper prepared for NYU Law School Seminar on Labor Law Theory, Spring 1993) (unpublished manuscript, on file with author). Apparently, Professor Gottesman is working on a similar project. *See* Gottesman, *supra* note 79, at 93-96.

85. *See, e.g.*, PAUL C. WEILER, GOVERNING THE WORKPLACE: THE FUTURE OF LABOR AND EMPLOYMENT LAW 283-95 (1990); Summers, *supra* note 81, at 131 ("The obstacle is not struc-

Professor Weiler has offered a particularly nuanced proposal. He would urge legislation requiring every firm above a certain size to establish an Employee Participation Committee (EPC), elected through a proportional scheme to reflect the different constituencies in the firm. The EPC's function would be to address "the broad spectrum of resource policies of the firm," with some initial responsibility for the administration of public laws; the range of subject matter would be "even broader than what is now required by the NLRA for employers engaged in full-fledged bargaining with a national union."[86] The law would require extensive information-sharing concerning not only the firm's personnel policies but also its "broader financial, investment, and profit situation"; and would oblige management to meet and confer with the EPC over its plans for the firm.[87] Although the EPC's consent would not be required as a prerequisite to management action, the EPC could exercise its section 7 rights under the NLRA to strike or form independent unions.[88]

If we put aside nagging questions about whether works councils in Germany actually contribute to, rather than detract from, firm productivity and profits,[89] and whether there is a political constituency for such a sweeping change,[90] mandatory works councils of the German variety, in the abstract, offer an attractive framework for ensuring collective employee voice without some of the costs associated with the U.S. system of multienterprise unionism and decentralized collective bargaining. But Professor Weiler's approach differs significantly from the German version. Notably, it preserves a right to strike and the option of converting the EPC into an independent union. By contrast,

tural, but political"); Clyde W. Summers, *Codetermination in the United States: A Projection of Problems and Potentials*, 4 J. COMP. CORP. L. & SEC. REG. 155 (1982); *see also* Clyde W. Summers, *An American Perspective of the German Model of Worker Participation*, 8 COMP. LAB. L.J. 333 (1987); Janice R. Bellace, *Mandating Employee Information and Consultation Rights*, 43 INDUS. REL. RES. ASS'N 137-44 (1990). I intimated a similar view in Samuel Estreicher, *Some Reflections on the Future Development of Collective Representation and Individual Rights in the Workplace*, *in* NYU PROCEEDINGS, *supra* note 81, at 170-73.

Legislation has been introduced, dubbed the Comprehensive Occupational Safety and Health Reform Act, S. 575, H.R. 1280, 103d Cong., 1st Sess. (1993), that would, inter alia, mandate worker-management safety committees for all firms with eleven or more employees. On the Canadian experience with statutory works councils, see Amy Timlin, Statutory Works Councils in Canada: The Benefit of Worker Participation (Aug. 1991) (unpublished M. Indus. Lab. Rel. thesis, Queen's University); Roy J. Adams, *Should Works Councils be Used as Industrial Relations Policy?*, MONTHLY LAB. REV., July 1985, at 25-29.

86. WEILER, *supra* note 85, at 285.

87. *Id.* at 285-86.

88. *Id.* at 288.

89. *See* Addison et al., *supra* note 51.

90. *See* Michael H. Gottesman, *Wither Goest Labor Law: Law and Economics in the Workplace*, 100 YALE L.J. 2767, 2807 (1991).

German works councils are prohibited by law from striking and operate as a body independent of unions with a set of functions and responsibilities separate from the realm of centralized collective bargaining.[91]

It seems doubtful that EPCs of the Weiler strain will function on American soil as integrative organizations. Predictions as to the likely impact of EPCs vary. The French experience suggests that works councils do not function well where unions are weak, and multienterprise collective bargaining has been unsuccessful.[92] In the United States, I suspect, they are likely to be seedbeds of traditional unionism, if they take hold at all.[93]

The problem proponents of mandatory works councils have is that our existing system is committed to legal protection of the right to form independent unions that organize and bargain at the level of the firm. Works councils and trade unions are both firm-based organizations. Unless the range of subjects lodged with works councils is severely curtailed, they will either threaten extinction for conventional unions (at least where such unions do not perform a hiring hall function, as in construction), or they will become unions in all but name.

Seeking a way out of this conundrum, Professors Freeman and Rogers advocate withholding "tax breaks" from employers who fail to establish EPCs that would have rights to information and consultation over labor policies and would help enforce government policies in such as areas as occupational safety and health, job training, and job closings, while steering clear of "wage bargaining" and presumably other matters commonly addressed in collective bargaining.[94] They

91. Admittedly, the Works Constitution Act of 1972 broadened the union role by granting union officials access to plants and permitting works councillors to engage in union activities within plants. *See* ANDREI M. KARKOVITS, THE POLITICS OF THE WEST GERMAN TRADE UNIONS: STRATEGIES OF CLASS AND INTEREST REPRESENTATION IN GROWTH AND CRISIS 49 (1986). German unions have made substantial inroads, with 76.3% of works councillors members of DGB-affiliated unions. *See* Jacobi et al., *supra* note 48, at 243-44 & tbl. 7.9. On the successful adaptation of unions to works councils, see THELEN, *supra* note 49; LOWELL TURNER, DEMOCRACY AT WORK: CHANGING WORLD MARKETS AND THE FUTURE OF LABOR UNIONS 95-103 (1991).

92. On the French experience, see François Eyraud & Robert Tchobanian, *The Auroux Reforms and Company Level Industrial Relations in France*, 23 BRIT. J. INDUS. REL. 241 (1985); Mary Ann Glendon, *French Labor Law Reform 1982-1983: The Struggle for Collective Bargaining*, 32 AM. J. COMP. L. 449 (1984).

93. *Compare* Alan Hyde, *Endangered Species*, 91 COLUM. L. REV. 456, 466 (1991) (reviewing PAUL C. WEILER, GOVERNING THE WORKPLACE: THE FUTURE OF LABOR AND EMPLOYMENT LAW (1990)) (such organizations will be potent rivals for union power) *with* Gottesman, *supra* note 90, at 2807 (absent provision of interest arbitration, they are likely to be ineffectual, producing "mere frustration").

94. *See* Freeman & Rogers, *supra* note 19, at 63-64; *A New Deal for Labor*, N.Y. TIMES, Mar. 10, 1993, at A14. *See also* Gottesman, *supra* note 90, at 44-45.

also advocate allowing 40% of the workers in a unit to insist upon EPCs in their shops.

If such proposals envision narrow-purpose works councils set up largely to police conformity with external law, they are, I submit, misguided.[95] If we think it appropriate to mandate, or use tax policy virtually to compel, collaborative representation, such works councils should be allowed to address constructively the entire range of issues—productivity improvements, wages, hours and benefits, as well as occupational safety and plant closings—affecting the welfare of the employees and the competitive position of the firm.[96]

3. Canadian-Style Labor Law Reform

Should we enact Canadian-style labor laws to strengthen the hand of existing unions? New rules could be put in place to facilitate union organization by permitting certification on the basis of card showings in lieu of elections and using arbitrators to impose labor contracts on newly organized units where the parties cannot reach agreement. We could also boost union bargaining power by allowing secondary boycotts in aid of organizing drives and strikes, and we could ban the hiring of permanent replacements (and perhaps temporaries as well, as in Ontario and Quebec).

The laws in Canada on "automatic" certifications without elections are designed to ease the union's organizing task, and exclude the employer from any role in the representational process. In Ontario, if more than 55% of the employees in a unit are members of, or have applied for membership (by making a token payment) in, a union, the labor board may (and typically will) certify the union outright.[97] The agency will not consider evidence of membership or disavowal of membership filed or presented after the date of the union's application for certification.[98] Evidence filed prior to the application date

95. My objection here is to "watchdog" committees serving as in-house instruments of state policy, as opposed to committees established with a constructive problem-solving mission—e.g., to administer government grants or to develop jointly agreed-upon standards for training programs.

96. Mandatory works councils, I would urge, should be relegated to a future reform agenda *after* we have strengthened the independent union option, developed experience with collaborative representation in the non-union sector, and have a better understanding of the role independent unions might play in U.S.-style works councils.

97. Ontario Labour Relations Act § 8(2), 3 Can. Lab. L. Rep. (CCH) ¶ 60,308 (1992).

98. *Id.* §§ 8(4)-(6). This freezing of the status quo at the time of application is also the law in Quebec, Alberta, British Columbia, Newfoundland, and the federal sector. *See* James D. Merriman, Certification in Canadian Labor Law: Towards the "Ideal" Mix (June 9, 1993) (unpublished manuscript, on file with author). Ontario had previously provided for a "return date" of ten days during which workers could revoke their membership. Professor Weiler recommends a

will be considered only if in writing and signed by each employee, but the board will not examine whether the employee made an informed choice.[99] However, such informality does not attend the process of decertification. Petitions will not be entertained during the first year after certification, and if a collective agreement is in place, they will be entertained only during the last two months of the third year of the term (or of each succeeding year). They must be signed by 45% of the unit, and the signatures must not be tainted by management influence or solicitation going beyond the "acceptable bounds of salesmanship."[100] If the petition satisfies the formalities, the board holds a decertification vote.[101]

The question for U.S. public policy is whether the deficiencies in our representational process are so beyond repair that NLRB-supervised elections should be dispensed with altogether as the principal avenue (absent voluntary recognition) for the union's acquisition of bargaining authority. As developed below, I prefer to retain the electoral model bolstered by enhanced penalties for retaliatory discharge and union access rights to the electorate. Except where the employer's illegality has precluded fair election conditions, a secret ballot is still the best way to determine employee preferences.[102] NLRB policy over the decades has recognized that employees often sign cards (even when properly worded) under the mistaken impression that they are merely authorizing an election or simply to avoid a personal encounter with the union organizer. Moreover, the conversation between the employee and the union organizer is understandably one-

ten or fifteen day period to enable workers to change their minds. PAUL WEILER, RECONCILABLE DIFFERENCES: NEW DIRECTIONS IN CANADIAN LABOUR LAW 43 (1980).

99. Ontario Labour Relations Act § 8(6); *e.g.*, Johnson Controls Ltd. and C.A.W.-Canada, 8 C.L.R.B.R.2d 198, 203 (1991) (Ont.). In *Johnson Controls*, an individual had signed an authorization card and paid a $1 membership after campaigning against the union:

> There is no dispute that S. McKibbon had been drinking. However, the Board finds that he knew full well the nature of the transaction. His motive in signing the card (whether he sought to impress his friends, for example) is of no concern to the Board as the Board is satisfied his act in joining the union was voluntary.

Id. at 207.

100. *See* Sandra Taylor and United Food and Comm'l Workers Int'l, Locals 175 and 633, 4 C.L.R.B.R.2d 246, 252 (1990) (Ont.) (upholding decertification application).

101. Ontario Labour Relations Act § 57(3), 3 Can. Lab. L. Rep. (CCH) ¶ 60,357 (1992).

102. Consider Professor Cooper's findings:

> Only when a union had cards from more than 60% of employees did it achieve at least an even chance of winning the election. Another interesting finding . . . is that an increase in the proportion of authorization cards collected over 70% did not substantially increase the union's chance of success. Unions with authorization cards from 90-100% of employees still won only 65.7% of the time.

Laura Cooper, *Authorization Cards and Union Representation Election Outcome: An Empirical Assessment of the Assumption Underlying the Supreme Court's* Gissel *Decision*, 79 NW. U. L. REV. 87, 119 (1984).

sided; the arguments against union representation and collective bargaining are not presented. Union representation is not always the right choice for workers; if it were, the law would simply mandate a union for every plant. Where an employer is unwilling voluntarily to extend recognition, and has no independent basis to believe the union is a majority representative,[103] employees should be able to choose whether to be represented by a union or not after hearing opposing views and in a secret ballot.

As for some other aspects of the Canadian-style package of proposals, I am skeptical that lasting improvements are possible simply by enacting aggressively pro-union laws that do not take account of fundamental causes of the current state of affairs. Consider, for example, the AFL-CIO's campaign to secure an absolute ban on the hiring of permanent replacements for economic strikers.[104] Change is needed; an employer should have to show that operations could not be maintained with temporary replacements, and even then should be required to engage in collective bargaining for a significant period of time before resorting to permanent replacements.[105] However, an absolute ban is a mistake. It will help unions prevail in particular disputes, but ignores the larger forces at work. What is needed is not greater insulation of unions from competitive pressures but a redirec-

103. The NLRB is free to abandon the agency policy sustained in Linden Lumber Div. v. NLRB, 419 U.S. 301 (1974), and require an employer to bargain with a union where it has independent knowledge, say, because of employee participation in a peaceful, clearly placarded recognitional strike, that the union enjoys majority support.

104. The House of Representatives passed H.R. 5, 103d Cong., 1st Sess. (1993) (Cesar Chavez Workplace Fairness Act), on June 15, 1993; the bill would amend the NLRA and the Railway Labor Act to bar the hiring of permanent replacements for strikers. The identical Senate version, S. 55, cleared the Senate Labor and Human Resources Committee on May 5, 1993, but its prospects for surmounting a threatened filibuster are unclear. Similar legislation failed to survive a Senate filibuster during the 102d Congress.

105. In a work in progress, *Collective Bargaining or "Collective Begging"?: Economic Conflict Under the NLRA*, I argue against an absolute ban on the hiring of permanent replacements in favor of a six-month period during which strikes are insulated from such labor-market pressures. I would also authorize the NLRB to decline to consider representational issues during an active strike, and would require a showing on the employer's part—keyed to objective indicators such as unemployment rates in the particular industry or locality—that temporary replacements could not be hired for the wages and benefits offered to the striking workers; the use of permanent replacements where temporary workers are available inflicts a penalty on strikers for no legitimate purpose. For this latter proposal, it would be essential that the NLRB (or some other entity) be authorized to issue a prompt determination as to the availability of temporary workers, with provision for expedited review in the court of appeals. Workers should not be betting their jobs on the hope that the Labor Board will at some point in the distant future treat them as "unfair labor practice strikers" entitled to displace their replacements. Employers, too, should be able to respond to union demands with a minimum of legal uncertainty. *See generally* Samuel Estreicher, *Strikers and Replacements*, 3 LAB. LAW. 897 (1987).

tion of existing rules to enable independent unions better to take account of the competitive position of union-represented firms.

4. Nonmajority Unionism

A number of writers have urged modification of the exclusivity principle of American labor law as a means of broadening the opportunities for collective representation.[106] These proposals would retain the rule that the majority representative is the exclusive representative of the workers in an appropriate unit. But absent majority support for a particular labor organization, employers would be obligated to bargain with any organization commanding the support of any, or some minimum percentage, of the work force.[107]

There are a number of difficulties of considerable practical importance with this proposal. One is the costs to the firm of dealing with a proliferation of bargaining obligations in a particular plant. Professor Finkin's thoughtful piece in this Symposium offers a solution: allow the employer to demand joint bargaining "with respect to matters which have customarily been provided on a uniform basis," and in the absence of consent to such joint bargaining, to conclude an agreement with the organization which represents the largest number of employees and impose that agreement on the other organizations. Unions could demand joint bargaining, but employers would not be required to deal with a coalition.[108] Other problems include the spectre of discriminatory exclusion of disfavored groups.[109] Professor Gottesman also voices concern over how to deal with "ever-shifting populations," strategic combinations to escape contracts by petitioning for NLRB certification, and conflicting demands from rival minorities in the work force.[110]

The core difficulty is one of institutional fit. Plural unionism means something very different in a system like France's—hardly a success story—where collective bargaining occurs at the supraenter-

106. *See, e.g.*, Matthew W. Finkin, *The Road Not Taken: Some Thoughts on Nonmajority Employee Representation*, 69 CHI.-KENT L. REV. 195 (1993); *see also* Richard R. Carlson, *The Origin and Future of Exclusive Representation in American Labor Law*, 30 DUQ. L. REV. 779 (1992).

107. "Members only" collective bargaining is currently permitted. *See* Alan Hyde et al., *After Smyrna: Rights and Powers of Unions That Represent Less Than a Majority*, 45 RUTGERS L. REV. 637, 638 (1993); Clyde Summers, *Unions Without Majority—A Black Hole?*, 66 CHI.-KENT L. REV. 531 (1992). But the employer is under no duty to bargain with nonmajority unions.

108. *See* Finkin, *supra* note 106, at 205-06.

109. *See* George Schatzki, *Majority Rule, Exclusive Representation, and the Interests of Individual Workers: Should Exclusivity be Abolished?*, 123 U. PA. L. REV. 897, 935 (1975).

110. *See* Gottesman, *supra* note 79, at 88-90.

prise, industry-wide level among unions representing political coalitions with little interest in plant-level issues[111] than it would in the U.S. system based on decentralized collective bargaining which contemplates a comprehensive local agreement on terms and conditions of employment. In practice, the proposal to mandate nonmajority collective bargaining is likely to pull us further away from the goal of an integrative positive-sum labor relations system capable of providing employee voice in competitive markets.

5. Labor Law Reform for Competitive Product Markets

If labor law reform is to stand a reasonable chance not only of being enacted but also of promoting employee voice and changing the labor-management climate, it must take account of existing institutional arrangements. Whatever we may think of, say, the German system, we cannot simply waive the legislators' wand and mandate centralized collective bargaining over minimum terms,[112] works councils in every enterprise, and tripartite labor courts.

Of the several premises of the U.S. system previously discussed, the commitment to decentralized collective bargaining and multiemployer labor organizations seems particularly entrenched. Legal reform can, however, substantially reshape the arrangements that exacerbate adversarial labor-management relations and mitigate the institutional insecurity of independent employee organizations.

The reforms I have in mind would (i) remove legal restraints on the evolution of alternative workplace arrangements, (ii) strengthen the independent union option by bolstering remedies for employer illegality and enhancing union's access to workers during organizing drives, and (iii) for unionized firms alter the system of incentives that contributes to adversarial labor-management relations.

111. The best writing on this subject remains Derek C. Bok, *Reflections on the Distinctive Character of American Labor Laws*, 84 HARV. L. REV. 1394 (1971).

112. Professor Rogers' piece in this Symposium, Joel Rogers, *Reforming U.S. Labor Relations*, 69 CHI.-KENT L. REV. 97, 115-16 (1993), suggests, without offering details, a presumptive "requirement" of multi-employer and "sectoral" bargaining. With union density under 13% of the work force and the breakdown of multiemployer bargaining in many industries, it is difficult to see how this "requirement" could be implemented, even if the political will were found to enact such legislation. In any event, any proposal to extend union wages to unorganized firms runs up against the practical difficulty for unions of "free riding" and, more importantly, fails to take account of the need for a fundamentally different union program in a world of competitive product markets.

C. *Outline of an Agenda for Reform*[113]

1. Amend the "Company Union" Prohibition

Under our labor laws, workers must choose between an independent union or no workplace representation at all. Companies that establish representative bodies, whether to hear employee grievances or to elicit employee input into managerial decisions, run afoul of the law. An employer who establishes a German-style works council for her employees faces considerable legal obstacles, even if there is a union in the shop.[114] Moreover, unions are skeptical of "employee governance" proposals, in part because—as faculty unions have learned—individual workers who participate in the making or implementation of managerial policy are deemed part of management and excluded from union representation rights.

Alternatives to traditional unionism—or, to put the point somewhat differently, competitive pressures that might force a change in the labor relations climate—can never emerge if the law insists on one form of workplace representation or none at all. Through a narrowing of the definition of "labor organization" to reach only representational structures that purport to engage in a form of collective bargaining, the reach of the section 8(a)(2) prohibition would be confined to truly coercive or deceptive practices. Workers would still have the right to seek representation by independent unions, and would retain existing protection for concerted activities.

2. Ensure a Realistic Option to Choose Independent Representation

To prevent employer-based schemes from becoming mere tools to manipulate workers, the option to choose an independent union must be a realistic one. The law should be amended to substantially reduce the costs to employees—principally fear of job loss—who exercise their right to choose independent representation. Without the prospect of significant liability, it is too easy—even if Professors Meltzer and LaLonde are right that the risk of unlawful discharge is only 1

113. The proposals that follow are sketched here. They will be developed in more detail in a book under preparation with Harvard University Press.

114. Where a union is present, the employer must respect the employees' choice to be represented by an independent union. Any different or supplementary *representational* structure requires the consent of the union. I thus would have found it unnecessary to consider the § 8(a)(2) issue in E.I. du Pont de Nemours & Co., 311 N.L.R.B. No. 88, 1992-1993 NLRB Dec. (CCH) ¶ 17,862 (May 28, 1993), because the exclusive bargaining representative in that case had refused to accept the employer's committee system.

in 60[115]—for unscrupulous employers to frustrate employee free choice by the simple expedient of firing supporters of the union drive.

When prounion workers are improperly fired, delay in achieving redress can undermine the most determined organizing drive. By the time the case works its way through the administrative process and on appeal, the original workers are often long gone and management has succeeded in eviscerating the momentum of the organizing campaign. These are avoidable costs of union organization. The NLRB should be authorized to impose strict penalties (not tied to the workers' economic losses) to deter flagrant unfair labor practices.[116] Areas where courts have resisted broader remedies require explicit authorization. Section 10(j) should be rewritten to make clear that preliminary injunctive relief is available to reinstate improperly discharged union supporters pending the outcome of administrative hearings. Interim reinstatement orders, when coupled with the prospect of substantial penalties, should bring home to employees that they indeed have a legal entitlement to be represented by unions, and to employers that retaliatory discharge may not be a very sound course after all.[117] Also, where employer illegality undermines fair election conditions, the law should explicitly provide[118] that bargaining orders without elections are an appropriate remedy, whether or not there has been employee turnover.[119]

115. *See supra* note 7 and accompanying text.

116. The initial version of labor law reform legislation introduced during the Carter administration would have provided for a doubling of backpay without mitigation. *See* H.R. 8410, 95th Cong., 1st Sess. (1977); S. 2467, 95th Cong., 2d Sess. (1978).

117. Writing in 1983, Professor Weiler stated that "[i]t is simply unrealistic to expect that the Board could give 'priority' to the investigation of 17,000 discriminatory discharge cases a year, and that the federal courts could dispose of 3500 injunction applications annually within the two- to three-month period that is crucial to the effective use of reinstatement to ensure the fairness of the representation process." Weiler, *supra* note 4, at 1803. This observation assumes, however, that interim reinstatement orders must be sought in every case to achieve the right level of deterrence. If the Board makes clear it is prepared to pursue this remedy aggressively, and the courts are directed to be receptive to such applications, employers—especially the small companies that are likely targets of § 10(j) relief—will soon internalize the message. I may be wrong, but only actual experience under new rules will tell.

118. Express statutory authority might avoid some of the persisting court-agency conflicts over bargaining orders under NLRB v. Gissel Packing Co., 395 U.S. 575 (1969). I surveyed the status of *Gissel* bargaining orders in the Second Circuit, in Samuel Estreicher, *The Second Circuit and the NLRB 1980-1981: A Case Study in Judicial Review of Agency Action*, 48 Brook. L. Rev. 1063, 1084-94 (1982).

119. There is much the Labor Board can do administratively to streamline pre-election procedures to ensure that elections are held promptly after a petition has been filed. The Supreme Court has given the NLRB a "green light" to promulgate rules through notice-and-comment procedures, pursuant to § 553 of the Administrative Procedure Act, in lieu of case-by-case adjudications. *See* American Hosp. Ass'n v. NLRB, 499 U.S. 606 (1991). This authority should be used to simplify unit determinations and to clarify disputed policies, such as those governing issuance of *Gissel* bargaining orders, that have met with resistance in the courts of appeals. *See*

In addition, we need to improve the access rights of unions in order to ensure that the NLRB-supervised election truly provides an accurate poll of employee wishes. That is, after all, the rationale for preferring the electoral model over "automatic" certification procedures. The Supreme Court's recent *Lechmere* decision[120] should be overruled; parking lots in shopping malls are generally open to the public and should be available to union organizers for nondisruptive informational picketing and handbilling.[121] The union's access can never be fully equal to the employer's, but more can be done to enable employees to hear both sides. The Board should be authorized to allow unions who secure card signatures from 30% of the employees access to names and addresses well before an election is scheduled,[122] absent a showing of union misconduct (in that case or other cases involving the same labor organization). Also, since employers presently have the right to hold "captive audience" addresses on their property,[123] unions should have the right to come on the premises to address the workers at a scheduled time shortly before an NLRB election.

Legislative change is also needed to reduce current incentives to use the appeal process as a means of delaying effective bargaining with certified majority representatives. NLRB orders could be made self-enforcing without need to petition the courts of appeals in every case. Judicial review of representation case determinations and first-time bargaining orders also should not be a cost-free opportunity to stymie employees' desire for collective representation; costs, including attorney's fees, should be awarded to the prevailing party on appeal (at least absent a "substantial justification" for bringing the appeal).[124]

generally Samuel Estreicher, *Policy Oscillation at the Labor Board: A Plea for Rulemaking*, 37 Admin. L. Rev. 163 (1985).

120. *See* Lechmere, Inc. v. NLRB, 112 S. Ct. 841 (1992).

121. The same principle would extend to non-disruptive solicitation in hospital cafeterias open to the public. *Cf.* Oakwood Hosp. v. NLRB, 983 F.2d 698 (6th Cir. 1993).

122. The current rule requires the employer to furnish the union with an *Excelsior* list within seven days after an order directing an election. *See* Excelsior Underwear, Inc., 156 N.L.R.B. 1236 (1966).

123. *See* NLRB v. United Steelworkers (NuTone and Avondale), 357 U.S. 357 (1958).

124. The Labor Board presently faces such costs, in the absence of "substantial justification" for its position, under the Equal Access to Justice Act, 28 U.S.C. §§ 2412(d)(1)(A), (d)(2)(D) (1988); *see* discussion in Samuel Estreicher & Richard L. Revesz, *Nonacquiescence by Federal Administrative Agencies*, 98 Yale L.J. 679, 758 nn. 347-48 and accompanying text (1989). There is authority that an employer may be assessed a union's attorney's fees and litigation costs occasioned by "patently frivolous" litigation before the agency. *See* International Union of Elec., Radio and Mach. Workers v. NLRB, 502 F.2d 349, 358-59 (D.C. Cir. 1974), *cert. denied*, Tiidee Products, Inc. v. NLRB, 421 U.S. 991 (1975).

3. Encourage Alternatives to Strikes

Strikes are sometimes necessary to resolve disputes but they are often the product of bargaining failures. They promote an adversarial climate, and too often result in pitched battles destructive of entire communities and yielding little social benefit. Reform is needed to improve the flow of information and to encourage the parties to consider alternatives to strikes.

Both workers engaged in a strike and employers responding to a strike should make an informed decision: as a precondition to a lawful strike, all of the employees in the bargaining unit (including mere dues-payers who have not joined the union as such) should have a statutory right to vote by secret ballot on the employer's final offer and on whether or not they authorize a strike.[125]

Interest arbitration—the use of neutral arbiters to resolve disputes over the content of labor contracts—is common in the public sector, but rarely used in the private sector. Under current law, interest arbitration is not within the scope of mandatory bargaining: a party desiring such a term cannot require the other side to bargain or use its economic leverage to insist upon it as a condition of an overall agreement.[126] Such barriers should be removed, and tax and other incentives to experiment with strike alternatives should be ex-

We should await experience with enhanced § 8(a)(3) remedies and two-way fee shifting in deterring egregious refusals to bargain with newly-certified unions before embarking down the Canadian path of first contract arbitration. *See* Sabrina Sills, First Contract Arbitration in Ontario: Success or Failure? 1986-1990, at 30 (Aug. 1991) (M. Indus. Lab. Rel. thesis, Queen's University) (limited data suggests that first contract arbitration in Ontario "is not very successful in establishing enduring relationships").

125. Under current law, such votes are strictly a matter of internal union governance for the union to structure as it chooses. This practice creates unnecessary agency costs of unionism. In a number of highly-publicized strikes, unions have allowed constituencies other than the immediately affected workers to determine the outcome of strike and contract ratification votes. *See, e.g.*, Henry J. Holcomb, *Port Workers Reject Pact, Face Job Loss Wage Cuts and Rule Changes*, PHILA. INQUIRER, Sept. 29, 1993, at A1 (Wilmington port workers voted against concession pact for Philadelphia port workers, even though Chilean fruit shipper threatened to divert traffic to lower-cost Wilmington port); Alex S. Jones, *Paper Brinkmanship: Times and Drivers Are Joined in Fear Both Would Lose All-Out Labor War*, N.Y. TIMES, May 15, 1992, at B2 (deal between New York Times and its drivers subject to majority vote of entire union including drivers for competitors, The Daily News and The New York Post).

The Taft-Hartley experience with employee votes on management's final offer suggests, however, that employees will typically vote to reject. *See* DONALD E. CULLEN, NATIONAL EMERGENCY STRIKES 56-57 tbl. 6, 61 (1968). It is unclear whether this would occur generally outside of Taft-Hartley's "emergency disputes" context. In any event, whether or not the procedure reduces the incidence of strikes, employers (and the public) should know that a strike enjoys the informed support of the affected employees rather than adherence to a top-down direction from the union leadership.

126. *See, e.g.*, Sheet Metal Workers, Local 59, 227 N.L.R.B. 520, 520-21 (1976) (future contract dispute resolution by third party is a permissive subject of bargaining).

plored.[127] Also, as discussed below,[128] the "quick fix" of hiring permanent replacements in response to an economic strike should be substantially curtailed, and, possibly, some form of advisory interest arbitration might be required prior to resort to economic conflict.[129]

4. Allow Free Collective Bargaining

Existing law draws a sharp distinction between "mandatory" and "permissive" subjects. Under the *Borg-Warner* rule,[130] the parties have a duty to bargain and a right to press disagreements over "mandatory" subjects defined narrowly to encompass only issues of immediate concern to employees. But management is not required to bargain over issues affecting the scope and direction of the enterprise, such as plant closings or capital investment;[131] nor is the union allowed to strike over such issues.[132] If collective bargaining is to succeed, the parties should be able to shape a deal that meets their needs without the government deciding which subjects can be deal-breakers.[133] Such reform might unleash the creative potential of collective

127. For a useful survey, see Merton C. Bernstein, *Alternatives to the Strike*, 58 AAUP Bull. 404-12 (1972). The so-called "statutory strike" procedure imposes financial penalties on the parties for prolonged disagreement without entailing the disruption of a strike. *See, e.g.*, Thomas J. Raleigh, *Ease the Pain of Labor Negotiations*, Wall St. J., June 29, 1992, at A14.

128. *See supra* note 105; *infra* text accompanying note 160.

129. In a last-minute, unsuccessful attempt in June 1992 to overcome a filibuster on AFL-CIO backed legislation to bar the hiring of permanent replacements for strikers, Senators Packwood (R-Ore.) and Metzenbaum (D-Ohio), with labor backing, offered a compromise that would have made a proffer of binding interest arbitration a mandatory condition to resort to economic conflict. Under this proposal, an employer who refused to participate in arbitration or to accept an arbitration award could not hire permanent replacements; and if the union chose to strike without proffering interest arbitration or accepting the award, the employer would be free to use such replacements. *See* S. Res. 55, 102d Cong., 2d Sess. (1992). Another proposal would require submission of unresolved issues to advisory arbitration and impose mild sanctions as an additional settlement impetus. *See* George S. Roukis & Mamdouh I. Farid, *An Alternative Approach to the Permanent Striker Replacement Strategy*, 44 Lab. L.J. 80, 89-90 (1993). These and other approaches will be evaluated in a forthcoming article, *see supra* note 105.

130. *See* NLRB v. Wooster Div. of Borg-Warner Corp., 356 U.S. 342 (1958).

131. *See* First Nat'l Maintenance Corp. v. NLRB, 452 U.S. 666 (1981).

132. *See* Michael C. Harper, *Leveling the Road from* Borg-Warner *to* First National Maintenance: The Scope of Mandatory Bargaining, 68 Va. L. Rev. 1447 (1982) (purpose of permissive-mandatory distinction is to mark out the sphere of decisions unions should be able to influence through collective pressure).

133. I am urging here legislation adopting Justice Harlan's view of the bargaining process in the *Borg-Warner* case. In essence, the "right to insist" should be broader than the "duty to bargain"; either party can insist on subjects outside of the scope of mandatory bargaining, subject to an overall duty to bargain in good faith. *See* 356 U.S. at 351 (Harlan, J., with whom Clark and Whittaker, JJ., join, concurring in part and dissenting in part). At the October 1, 1993 Roundtable on Labor Law Reform, *supra* note 35, former NLRB member Marshall Babson suggested that Harlan's position, if enacted into law, would enable parties to act strategically, to insist on matters of little underlying substantive interest in order to gain leverage or delay signing contracts. By way of response, I offer Justice Harlan's caveat:

bargaining—for example, agreements over wages and job-bidding rights for a seat on the corporate board and enforceable guarantees of job security.[134]

5. Lengthen and Broaden Union Horizons

Labor laws should narrow, rather than widen, the divergence of perspective between the union and firm. For starters, long-term contracts should be encouraged. The typical term of labor agreements is three years, largely because the NLRB will not recognize a "contract bar" to challenges to the union's bargaining authority beyond three years. Successful relationships can bypass such hurdles.[135] Thus, the Steelworkers Union-Magna Copper contract runs for 15 years (with provision for interest arbitration at 5-year intervals)[136] and the union has reached similar long-term agreements with other steelmakers.[137] Employers should be allowed to waive by contract their (*not* the employees') right to challenge the union's authority for any agreed-upon period.[138]

> I do not deny that there may be instances where unyielding insistence on a particular item may be a relevant consideration in the over-all picture in determining "good faith," for the demands of a party might in the context of a particular industry be so extreme as to constitute some evidence of an unwillingness to bargain.

Id. at 359. There may also be a narrow category of subjects that should be placed beyond the reach of either party's insistence, such as proposals to alter or dilute the representative status of a union. *See, e.g.*, Boise Cascade Corp., 283 N.L.R.B. 462, 469 (1987) (proposal to consolidate two maintenance employee units involves a permissive subject), *enforced*, 860 F.2d 471 (D.C. Cir. 1988). Employer-initiated employee representation committees would also come within this category. *See supra* note 114.

134. On the problems sophisticated union negotiators face under current law in crafting enforceable job-security guarantees, see Kathryn A. English, Adapting The Mandatory-Permissive Distinction to an Era of Corporate Instability (Spring 1993) (unpublished manuscript, on file with author); James D. English & Samuel A. Flax, Bargaining in Anticipation of Corporate Reorganizations (n.d.) (unpublished manuscript, on file with author).

135. Professor Jacoby's Essay in this Symposium, Sanford M. Jacoby, *Reflections on Labor Law Reform and the Crisis of American Labor*, 69 Chi.-Kent L. Rev. 219, 225 n.24, misconstrues my position on the effect of the Board's "contract bar" rule. Plainly, the rule does not create an absolute "obstacle" to long-term contracts, but to the extent the union cannot contract for a waiver of the employer's ability to test its majority support for a coterminous term, the rule discourages the writing of such contracts.

136. *See* Magma Copper, *Unions Propose Historic Contract Agreement*, Daily Lab. Rep. (BNA) No. 199, at A-9 (Oct. 15, 1991).

137. *See, e.g.*, Dana Milbank, *Inland Steel Sets Accord with Steelmakers*, Wall St. J., May 28, 1993, at A2. *See also* the very interesting *Statement of USW Wage Policy Committee's Bargaining Goals*, Daily Lab. Rep. (BNA) No. 243, at D-1 (Dec. 17, 1992).

138. There is, of course, a tradeoff between rules promoting long-term perspectives and rules ensuring union responsiveness to rank-and-file pressures. To the extent, as I argue, the law should allow long-term contracts barring employer petitions and also prevent employers from withdrawing recognition from unions without elections, *see infra* text and accompanying notes 150-51, the employer's role as an agent for ensuring union responsiveness will be considerably diminished. Employers were, however, never terribly faithful agents of employees in this process. It is far better, in my view, to rely on the employees themselves to monitor their represent-

Current law also encourages information-hoarding rather than information-sharing by overregulating the bargaining process. If an employer acknowledges an "inability"—rather than mere unwillingness—to pay for the union's proposals,[139] this triggers a duty of disclosure and protracted agency oversight which the union can exploit as a source of leverage. Constructive bargaining over major corporate decisions, such as plant closings, is hampered by doctrines penalizing candor and excluding subjects affecting job security from all information-sharing and bargaining duties. If the parties have learned to work together, here too they can negotiate around the law. For example, the agreement between General Electric and the electrical workers union (IUE) provides for advance notice and consultation rights over plant closings and use of subcontractors.[140]

But the law can help reverse, rather than perpetuate, the distrust that mars other relationships. The rigidity of current law which links disclosure duties to the apparatus surrounding "mandatory" bargaining subjects needs change. The building of trust requires candid exchange of information, which should occur without fear that such action creates an entitlement to additional rounds of disclosure or means of delaying impasse. An employer should be required to give advance notice of, and consult with the union over, significant investment decisions, plant shutdowns, and the like. However, meaningful reform must also address legitimate employer concerns, by preventing disputes over financial information from being used to protract bargaining[141] and requiring safeguards to prevent unions from sharing

atives. Employees need information to perform this role. This includes clear notice of their right to petition for decertification elections and a § 7 right to cast a secret-ballot vote on the employer's final contract offer, any proposed contract, and any strike authorization. They also need procedures that reduce the transaction costs of collective monitoring. This might take the form of a relaxation of contract bar rules for employee-initiated decertification petitions filed after the third year of a long-term contract, or provision of a regularly scheduled secret-ballot reauthorization election (untainted by employer illegality). Also, employees who are union members have rights to participate in the internal governance of their unions, as safeguarded by the Landrum-Griffin Act of 1959—a subject that is beyond the scope of this article. I will be exploring these and related questions in a forthcoming article, tentatively entitled *Rethinking Employee Choice in U.S. Labor Law*.

139. *See, e.g.*, United Steelworkers of Am., AFL-CIO-CLC, Local Union 14534 v. NLRB, 983 F.2d 240 (D.C. Cir. 1993); United Paperworkers Int'l Union v. NLRB, 981 F.2d 861 (6th Cir. 1992) (both holding that insistence on concessions in order to remain competitive is not tantamount to a plea of poverty requiring access to financial substantiation under NLRB v. Truitt Mfg. Co., 351 U.S. 149 (1956)).

140. *See* 1991-1994 GE-IUE National Agreement § 5 (on file with author).

141. Information-sharing and consultation rights over major corporate decisions should be clearly defined in the form of "safe harbor" rules to prevent the unions or the NLRB from forestalling a declaration of "impasse" when the parties are plainly in deadlock.

proprietary information with competitor firms or the general public.[142]

As a general matter, the labor laws should be encouraging representational structures that are broadly inclusive of all of the nonexecutive workers of a firm. The Supreme Court's *Bell Aerospace* decision[143] is badly in need of overhaul; workers should not be deprived of the right to seek independent representation because of their involvement in the making or implementation of company policies.[144] Unions should also be freed of existing constraints in seeking units commingling professional and nonprofessional workers[145] or craft with unskilled workers.

With due acknowledgment of the preferences of union organizers and the value of limiting initial recognitional authority to fairly small, cohesive units, current unit determination policies that allow fragmentation of bargaining structures within the firm should be reexamined. An employer and a union representing a threshold percentage of the workforce should be permitted, without need for a NLRB election, to extend labor agreements throughout the plant and, perhaps, other plants within the same commuting area, with an opportunity for a later NLRB-supervised secret-ballot poll of the affected employees.[146]

142. *Cf.* NLRB v. New England Newspapers, Inc., 856 F.2d 409, 414 (1st Cir. 1988) (noting favorably the Board's "sensitivity" in allowing the company to strike irrelevant price information from sales contract and ordering the union to keep the contents of the contract confidential). The Labor Board should use its rulemaking authority to develop "Chinese wall" rules to ensure that unions maintain internal procedures to preclude disclosure of a firm's confidential financial data from union officials who represent employees of competing firms.

143. *See* NLRB v. Bell Aerospace Co., 416 U.S. 267 (1974).

144. *See* David M. Rabban, *Distinguishing Excluded Managers from Covered Professionals Under the NLRA*, 89 Colum. L. Rev. 1775 (1989). One question is whether such liberalization should extend to at least low-level supervisory personnel, in light of the largely unfavorable public-sector experience with foreman unionism. Any extension of NLRA protections to supervisors should provide that they are represented in separate units in order to permit agreements enabling management to call on supervisors to maintain operations during a strike by nonsupervisory personnel.

145. *See* Leedom v. Kyne, 358 U.S. 184 (1958).

146. Such agreements do occur, *see SEIU Master Pact for Washington Janitors Includes Area-wide Recognition Provision*, Daily Lab. Rep. (BNA) No. 193, at A-5 (Oct. 7, 1993), but it is unclear whether current law permits, in the absence of a functional accretion of units, the extension of contracts to new locations, even when conditioned by a later card showing of majority support. *See* Houston Div. of the Kroger Co., 219 N.L.R.B. 388 (1975); Majestic Weaving Co., 147 N.L.R.B. 859 (1964), *enforcement denied on other grounds*, 355 F.2d 854 (2d Cir. 1966). Moreover, current rules make it difficult to attack facially valid agreements after six months, *see* Machinists v. NLRB, 362 U.S. 411 (1960), and require any decertification elections to be held on the basis of the expanded unit (rather than the portion accreted), *see* George Brooks & Mark Thompson, *Multi-Plant Units and Employee Choice*, 20 Indus. & Lab. Rel. Rev. 363 (1967). Would it not be better to permit accretion agreements that provide for (1) a later secret-ballot authorization poll of the accreted work force, and (2) opportunity to petition for a decertification election on the basis of the accreted unit?

6. Promote Union Institutional Security

Responsible unionism requires institutionally secure unionism. UAW's innovative agreement with GM's Saturn division was negotiated before any of the employees were hired for the new Tennessee facility. By stipulating to the UAW's bargaining authority in advance, the Saturn management was able to encourage the union to experiment with broadened job classifications and a participative "team structure" at variance with the national UAW-GM agreement.[147] Saturn's success, however, should not obscure the fact that the agreement with the union was of questionable legality under the NLRA.

Prehire agreements outside of the construction industry are unlawful. The Saturn agreement was saved by an ingenious argument that General Motors and the UAW were really engaged in a form of "effects" bargaining for UAW-represented workers laid off in other plants.[148] Even this tack could not be used for foreign firms establishing plants here. The upshot is that companies like Mercedes and BMW have no vehicle for testing the union's receptivity to doing things differently; neither do American firms deciding whether to invest in new plants here or abroad. The law should encourage, rather than hinder, labor-management cooperation experiments in new "greenfield" plants by relaxing the prohibition of prehire agreements. The wishes of the employees ultimately hired can be ascertained in a less self-defeating, and more reliable, manner than by barring such agreements.[149]

Employers also should not be able unilaterally to withdraw recognition from unions; any test of the union's authority should occur only in a secret-ballot NLRB election (and only where employers have not waived their right to do so by contract). Current law allows the employer to claim that the union no longer represents its employees and

147. *See* BARRY BLUESTONE & IRVING BLUESTONE, NEGOTIATING THE FUTURE: A LABOR PERSPECTIVE ON AMERICAN BUSINESS 189-201 (1992); Saul Rubinstein et al., *The Social Partnership: Co-Management and the Reinvention of the Local Union*, *in* EMPLOYEE REPRESENTATION, *supra* note 5, at 339-70.

148. *See Advice Memorandum Issued by NLRB Associate General Counsel on UAW-GM Saturn Agreement*, Daily Lab. Rep. (BNA) No. 110, at E-1 (June 9, 1986).

149. For an initial period, such pre-hire agreements should not erect a "contract bar" to an employee decertification—as opposed to employer—petition, and it would be desirable to provide for a secret-ballot "authorization election" by the second year of operations. Compare the rules governing pre-hire contracts in the construction industry. *See* John Deklewa & Sons, 282 N.L.R.B. 1375 (1987), *enforced sub nom.* Iron Workers Local 3 v. NLRB, 843 F.2d 770 (3d Cir. 1987), *cert. denied*, 488 U.S. 889 (1988).

to stop bargaining as soon as the prior contract expires.[150] Such a move risks unfair labor practice charges, but in the two to three years it takes to resolve the issue the union may be gone. The employer's ability to withdraw recognition is not a very good, and hardly the best, mechanism one could devise to ensure that the union continues to enjoy majority support.[151]

Under current "successorship" doctrine, union workers have no right to be hired by purchasers who take only the firm's assets and not its stock.[152] Indeed, current law creates perverse incentives on the purchaser's part to select an entirely new work force and thereby escape the union contract altogether.[153] This rule should be changed[154] to require that firms buying a company's assets maintain the same work force and bargain with the union over the terms and conditions of employment,[155] even if they do not purchase stock as well.

Some rules designed to protect dissenting voices exacerbate the union's institutional insecurity without adequate justification. For instance, section 14(b) of the NLRA, which allows states to enact "right to work" laws, enables those who benefit from the unions a "free ride," thus hampering unions' effectiveness as bargaining agents. It should be repealed; all employees benefited by collective representation should have to pay their share of the costs of that representation (whether or not they formally join the union). Also, union coopera-

150. Conceivably, the Supreme Court left open the validity of this long-standing practice in NLRB v. Curtin Matheson Scientific, Inc., 494 U.S. 775, 787 n.8 (1990); *see* Brief for the AFL-CIO as Amicus Curiae Supporting Petitioner, NLRB v. Curtin Matheson Scientific, Inc., 494 U.S. 775 (1990) (No. 88-1685); Joan Flynn, *The Economic Strike Bar: Looking Beyond the "Union Sentiments" of Permanent Replacements*, 61 TEMPLE L. REV. 691 (1988).

151. For a preferable approach, see *supra* note 138.

152. In NLRB v. Burns Int'l Sec. Serv., Inc., 406 U.S. 272, 294-95 (1972), the putative successor, a company that won a competitive bid to provide security services, was not required to hire the predecessor's employees and was under no duty to bargain with the predecessor union until it hired a majority from the predecessor work force. The rules announced in *Burns* make sense in the context of that case, but they have been extended to consensual transactions as well. *See* Howard Johnson Co. v. Detroit Local Joint Executive Bd., 417 U.S. 249 (1974). *See generally* Samuel Estreicher, *Successorship Obligations*, *in* LABOR LAW AND BUSINESS CHANGE 63-78 (Samuel Estreicher & Daniel G. Collins eds., 1988).

153. Admittedly, the new employer cannot discriminate against union-represented employees, but under the *Burns* decision, a preference for new workers would not be sufficient proof of anti-union animus. *See, e.g.*, Southward v. South Cent. Ready Mix Supply, 7 F.3d 487 (6th Cir. 1993).

154. Unions can bargain around the rule by negotiating "successorship" clauses, but these can be of doubtful practical utility if the union is unable to obtain an injunction to block the transaction. *See* Estreicher, *supra* note 152, at 68-69; Katherine Van Wezel Stone, *Employees as Stakeholders Under State Nonshareholder Constituency Statutes*, 21 STETSON L. REV. 45, 62-63 (1991).

155. Absent an express assumption, the predecessor's contract should not be binding on the purchaser, but it may serve to define the operational status quo for bargaining new terms.

tion with workplace discipline and job shifts is undermined by the spectre of jury trials for unfair representation brought by disgruntled employees; adjudicated violations of the fair-representation duties should trigger only a rearbitration remedy.[156]

7. Lengthen and Broaden Employee Horizons

Unions at their best are only bargaining agents reflecting the preferences of their principals; the horizons of the workers themselves need to be lengthened and broadened. Communicating reliable information about the firm's economic position would help.[157] Tax laws should affirmatively promote "gain sharing" and profit sharing in compensation packages as a way to enhance worker productivity and to facilitate employment stability during difficult economic times.[158] Employees and unions understandably resist productivity improvements that may cause job loss. To promote greater receptivity to changes that will improve the health of the firm and, in the long run, the competitiveness of U.S. industry, public policy must address the problem of job security. The government should make transition easier by making benefits portable, offering relocation assistance, and retraining workers in growing sectors of the economy.[159]

8. Lengthen and Broaden Management Horizons

Management attitudes and practices also need overhauling. We must prevent companies from using the "quick fix" of hiring permanent replacements during a strike. The employer's unconstrained ability under current law to replace striking workers with permanent employees undermines the bargaining process. Management has a legitimate need to keep operating during a strike, but it can usually meet this need with temporaries. Even where this cannot be done, companies should have to wait six months before permanently replacing strikers, as was the law until recently in Ontario.[160]

156. *See generally* David E. Feller, *A General Theory of the Collective Bargaining Agreement*, 61 CAL. L. REV. 663 (1973).

157. Even in the union-represented sector, management should be permitted to communicate directly with employees (with union representatives present) on matters such as final bargaining offers and the reasons for particular business decisions.

158. *See generally* PAYING FOR PRODUCTIVITY: A LOOK AT THE EVIDENCE (Alan S. Blinder ed., 1990).

159. *See generally* Samuel Estreicher, *Laws Promoting Worker Training, Productivity, and Quality*, 9 LAB. LAW. 19 (1993) (also published in 44 LAB. L.J. 110 (1993)).

160. Details will be developed in a forthcoming article. *See supra* note 138.

Union representation on corporate boards is rare, and when it occurs it is usually in a concessionary or distress bargaining context in which the union agrees to wage and benefit reductions in exchange for stock. To the extent the labor laws or state corporate law prevent parties in healthy firms from addressing proposals in which union or employee directors representing employee interests have a role in corporate governance, those restrictions should be reexamined.

Government should widely disseminate information about labor-management success stories where unions have been made an integral part of the "employee involvement" program, such as prevail between Xerox and the Clothing Workers, AT&T and the Communications Workers, Inland Steel and the Steel Workers, and Goodyear and the Rubber Workers, among others. The Secretary of Labor's and the President's "bully pulpit" could profitably be employed to promote changes in labor-management culture.

Ultimately, however, stock-market-driven incentives need to be addressed. Management's obsession with short-term share price spurs workforce reductions that undermine the atmosphere of trust that is essential to cooperative unionism, wage flexibility, and long-term productivity. The debt-load legacy of the 1980s suggests that the benefits of the market for corporate control are vastly overrated, and costs of leveraging and short-termism understated.[161] Tax and corporate law rules need redirection to promote longer-term perspectives.

* * *

There are bright spots in the current scene—employee involvement programs in the nonunion sector and labor-management cooperation experiments in the one-time "mass production" industries are eliciting the guarded approval of unions like the UAW, Steel Workers, and Rubber Workers. We need a revitalization of our labor laws—one responsive to the forces at play in a world of competitive product markets—so that collective voice for employees in high-quality competitive firms becomes the norm and not the exception.

161. *See* Aleta G. Estreicher, *Beyond Agency Costs: Managing the Corporation for the Long Term*, 45 RUTGERS L. REV. 513 (1993).

2. IN DESPAIR, STARTING OVER: IMAGINING A LABOR LAW FOR UNORGANIZED WORKERS

MICHAEL H. GOTTESMAN*

I began representing unions—principally the Steelworkers Union—in 1961. Those were the halcyon days. Union density was near its all-time high, close to forty percent.[1] The *Steelworkers Trilogy* had just been decided, in which the Supreme Court waxed romantic about collective bargaining and labor arbitration.[2] In just a few years, the Steelworkers would negotiate the Experimental Negotiating Agreement (the "ENA") with the steel industry, substituting interest arbitration for strikes as the terminal point in negotiations,[3] as well as the Steel Industry Civil Rights Decree, hailed by the Fifth Circuit as implementing Title VII's policies "to an exceptionally thorough degree."[4] Throughout the 1970s, the Steelworkers (and other industrial

* Professor of Law, Georgetown University Law Center. I wish to thank Amy Patricia Walters for superb research assistance. I have benefitted from conversations with a number of labor law academics, including all of the principal contributors to this Symposium, about the proposals contained in this article.

1. Union density as a percentage of *private* nonagricultural wage and salary workers has declined from a high of 38% in 1954 to 11.5% in 1992. The 1954 figure is available in Paul C. Weiler, *Promises to Keep: Securing Workers' Rights to Self-Organization Under the NLRA*, 96 HARV. L. REV. 1769, 1772 n.4 (1983). For the 1992 figure, see *New Administration is Seen as Giving Labor Chance to Check Declining Unionization*, 142 Lab. Rel. Rep. (BNA) 300 (Mar. 15, 1993) [hereinafter *New Administration*]. Organized labor as a percentage of the overall work force (public and private combined) declined from 34.7% in 1954 to 15.8% in 1992. For the 1954 figure, see U.S. BUREAU OF THE CENSUS, THE STATISTICAL HISTORY OF THE UNITED STATES I, at 178 (1976). For the 1992 statistic, see *New Administration*, *supra*, at 297.

2. In the *Steelworkers Trilogy*, the Supreme Court limited judicial intervention in private sector contract disputes between labor and management, and promoted arbitration as the proper vehicle to maintaining the vitality of the collective bargaining process. United Steelworkers v. American Mfg. Co., 363 U.S. 564 (1960); United Steelworkers v. Warrior & Gulf Navigation Co., 363 U.S. 574 (1960); United Steelworkers v. Enterprise Wheel & Car Corp., 363 U.S. 593 (1960).

3. For a description of the ENA, see Charles J. Morris, *The Role of Interest Arbitration in a Collective Bargaining System*, 1 INDUS. REL. L.J. 427, 498-503 (1976). See also, descriptions by principal negotiators for the steel industry and the Steelworkers Union, R. Heath Larry, *Inflation, Labor and the Law*, 13 DUQ. L. REV. 203, 218-21 (1974); Bernard Kleiman, *Collective Bargaining in Perspective*, 13 DUQ. L. REV. 481, 490-92, 497 (1975).

4. United States v. Allegheny-Ludlum Indus., Inc., 517 F.2d 826, 881 (5th Cir. 1975), *cert. denied sub nom.* Harris v. Allegheny-Ludlum Indus., Inc., 425 U.S. 944 (1976). The decree radically altered seniority systems throughout the steel industry, so that workers of all races could transfer to seniority units other than the one to which they were initially assigned. As blacks had been disproportionately assigned by employers to the lower-paid and uncomfortable hot-end departments (coke ovens and blast furnaces), they benefitted disproportionately from this new opportunity. The decree also established quotas based on race and sex for the filling of trade, craft and apprenticeship vacancies. Comparable provisions were negotiated in 1974 by the Steel-

unions, such as the Auto Workers) would win enormous wage and benefit increases that produced a standard of living for industrial workers unprecedented in American history.[5]

Like most of my colleagues who represented unions, I thought the National Labor Relations Act (the "NLRA"),[6] and the system of collective bargaining it established and fostered, an unqualified triumph. This rosy view was shared by labor law academics, virtually all of whom devoted their energies in that era to lauding the NLRA and advocating methods for incrementally improving its virtually (but not quite totally, for what need would there be for scholars if perfection were already at hand?) perfect design.[7]

Looking back, I can see that the decline of the NLRA was underway even as I began my optimistic journey. The ENA was not merely, as we thought it then, a solution to a short-term problem,[8] but an early

workers Union and the aluminum industry, without the umbrella of a court-approved consent decree, and gave rise to the litigation that ended with the Supreme Court's decision in United Steelworkers v. Weber, 443 U.S. 193 (1979) (holding that a racial quota negotiated voluntarily by private employer and union to address underrepresentation of minorities in craft jobs does not violate Title VII, even though there is no history of prior discrimination by the employer or union).

5. Average weekly earnings of production workers in "blast furnaces and basic steel products" rose from $166.40 in 1970 to $509.04 in 1981. Bureau of Labor Statistics, U.S. Dep't of Labor, Bull. No. 2340, Handbook of Labor Statistics 318-19 (1989). The comparable figures for production workers in "motor vehicles and equipment" were $170.07 and $450.72, and in "petroleum and coal products" $183.18 and $491.62. *Id.*

6. National Labor Relations Act of 1935, Pub. L. No. 74-198, 49 Stat. 449 (1935) (codified as amended at 29 U.S.C. §§ 151-169 (1982 & Supp. 1993)).

7. *See, e.g.*, Julius G. Getman et al., Union Representation Elections: Law and Reality (1976); Derek C. Bok, *The Regulation of Campaign Tactics in Representation Elections Under the National Labor Relations Act*, 78 Harv. L. Rev. 38 (1964); David E. Feller, *A General Theory of the Collective Bargaining Agreement*, 61 Cal. L. Rev. 663 (1973); William B. Gould, *The Question of Union Activity on Company Property*, 18 Vand. L. Rev. 73 (1964); Howard Lesnick, *The Gravamen of the Secondary Boycott*, 62 Colum. L. Rev. 1363 (1962); Clyde W. Summers, *Collective Agreements and the Law of Contracts,* 78 Yale L.J. 525 (1969). Some scholars today remain optimistic that with appropriate amendments to the NLRA there can be a resurgence of collective bargaining through exclusive representatives. *See, e.g.,* Charles B. Craver, Can Unions Survive?: The Rejuvenation of the American Labor Union (1993); Charles B. Craver, *The National Labor Relations Act Must Be Revised to Preserve Industrial Democracy,* 34 Ariz. L. Rev. 397 (1992) [hereinafter Craver, *National Labor Relations Act*]; William B. Gould IV, *Some Reflections on Fifty Years of the National Labor Relations Act: The Need for Labor Board and Labor Law Reform,* 38 Stan. L. Rev. 937 (1986); Donna Sockell, *The Future of Labor Law: A Mismatch Between Statutory Interpretation and Industrial Reality*, 30 B.C. L. Rev. 987 (1989).

8. The steel industry had endured a lengthy strike in 1959, which ended only when the Supreme Court upheld a Taft-Hartley injunction after 116 days of strike. United Steelworkers v. United States, 361 U.S. 39 (1959). As the parties began negotiations in each triennial period thereafter, steel industry customers, concerned that they might be without steel should another strike occur, began stockpiling. Unable to secure sufficient steel from the American producers to build an adequate stockpile, the steel customers began buying from foreign steel producers. Although no steel strikes occurred after 1959, customers could not know that in advance; thus, there were periodic intervals when steel customers turned to foreign producers to help build

signal that the economic conditions that had enabled the NLRA to succeed were coming to an end.

Today, of course, the global economy is an ever-present reality, the Steelworkers Union, despite exceptional leadership, is half its former size,[9] and the system of collective bargaining that the NLRA promotes is invoked by an ever-shrinking percentage of American workers. At latest count, less than twelve percent of the workers covered by the NLRA are union-represented.[10] "Our national labor policy"[11] is not serving eighty-eight percent of America's workers.[12]

In Part I, I proffer my views as to why the NLRA has fallen so far. I suggest that the ills that afflict the NLRA are only partially curable by amendment of its now-evident weaknesses. The reality is that the vast majority of American workers likely would not embrace collective bargaining as we know it (i.e., exclusive representation by national unions that attempt to organize employees of all employers in an industry) even if such bargaining were available free of all the present legal infirmities. And while collective bargaining through employer-specific or workplace-specific institutions ("enterprise unions")[13] is imaginable, it is not likely to develop spontaneously out of

their stockpiles. The foreign producers, in turn, ultimately realized that they could exploit the *periodic* need for their product by conditioning their willingness to satisfy it upon the customers' entering into *long*-term purchasing commitments. The ENA was designed to prevent this "tying" tactic of foreign producers by providing assurance to American customers that there would be no steel strikes and thus no need to turn to foreign producers to build stockpiles. It was believed at the time that this would effectively eliminate the threat of foreign competition. *See* Morris, *supra* note 3, at 498-99; Larry, *supra* note 3, at 218 n.63.

9. Membership in the Steelworkers Union fell during the seventies from a high of over 1,000,000 in 1975 to 481,000 by 1989. *See* U.S. Bureau of the Census, U.S. Dep't of Commerce, Statistical Abstract of the United States 401 (1988) (average per capita membership of actively employed members for a two-year period ending the year cited); U.S. Bureau of the Census, U.S. Dep't of Commerce, Statistical Abstract of the United States 424 (1991).

10. *New Administration, supra* note 1, at 300.

11. *See, e.g.,* Trans World Airlines, Inc. v. Hardison, 432 U.S. 63, 79 (1977); Lodge 76, Int'l Ass'n of Machinists v. Wisconsin Employment Relations Comm'n, 427 U.S. 132, 136 (1976); Teamsters Union v. Morton, 377 U.S. 252, 260 (1964).

12. Worse still, the NLRA to some extent obstructs the opportunity for workers to negotiate with their employers through other mechanisms. Section 8(a)(2) of the NLRA forbids the creation of some mechanisms for employer-employee dialogue, *see infra* text accompanying notes 93-98, and the Act as a whole preempts the authority of state legislatures to promote other forms of collective activity (e.g., legal enforcement of a duty to bargain with minority unions, such as Matthew Finkin advocates). Matthew W. Finkin, *The Road Not Taken: Some Thoughts on Nonmajority Employee Representation,* 69 Chi.-Kent L. Rev. 195 (1993). For a description of the NLRA's preemptive sweep, see generally, Michael H. Gottesman, *Rethinking Labor Law Preemption: State Laws Facilitating Unionization,* 7 Yale J. on Reg. 355, 374-83 (1990).

13. *See, e.g.,* Paul C. Weiler, Governing the Workplace: The Future of Labor and Employment Law 218-24 (1990).

a legal regime focused solely on promoting the right to collective bargaining.

If my predictions are accurate, there is need to examine what role (if any) the law should play with respect to workplaces where no union has been chosen. That is the subject of Part II.

I. Why the NLRA Has Failed: Employee Fear of Job Loss

The diagnosis that follows is not predicated on an empirical study, nor on other traditional academic foundations. It represents merely the conclusions of one who participated actively for nearly three decades as a lawyer for a broad cross-section of American labor unions. The proposals for legal change put forth in Part II are not necessarily dependent on the accuracy of this diagnosis—I believe the proposals would have merit *whatever* the explanation for the precipitous decline in resort to collective bargaining—but the reader is surely entitled, as a predicate for evaluating those proposals, to know where their proponent is coming from.

A. *The Obsolescence of Industry-Wide Unions*

In a nutshell, I believe that the principal reason employees do not opt in greater numbers for unionization today is a fear that, one way or another, going that route will jeopardize their job security.[14] There are many reasons for that fear, only some of which are attributable to defects in the NLRA, and only some of which, therefore, are curable by amending the NLRA.

The NLRA's contributions to this employee fear are well known. The NLRA does not protect workers meaningfully against employer reprisal for attempts to unionize, and it authorizes employers to replace permanently workers who opt to strike.

Workers fear that if they attempt to unionize the employer will retaliate against them. The fear is amply justified. While the NLRA purports to outlaw employer discharges against employees for union-

14. No doubt some part of the explanation of the low rate of unionization is attributable to causes other than those discussed in text. *See, e.g.*, Weiler, *supra* note 13, at 10-15, 105-18 (listing other causes for the decline in union density). But these other causes would not produce the widespread declination of unionization that now exists in the United States, and indeed would have little independent weight were the principal impediments (discussed in text) not also present. For example, it is undoubtedly true that a handful of unions were corrupt, and no doubt some employees declined to select corrupt unions as their representatives. But that would not explain why those employees declined to select *other* unions that were *not* corrupt.

izing,[15] the Act catches but a fraction of the culprits, even then only too late, and ultimately visits sanctions on those caught that are so small as to make union-busting the economically rational choice.[16] Not surprisingly, union-busting is going full tilt.[17] Workers otherwise disposed to unionize will decline the opportunity if they think they will be fired for trying.

Workers likewise fear that if they unionize, and then strike, they will be permanently replaced and lose their jobs in that manner.[18] That fear, too, is justified, given the historic but indefensible interpretation of the NLRA's ban on discharge for striking as allowing employers to permanently replace strikers (indeed, to replace permanently even when an adequate supply of temporary replacements is available).[19]

The employee fears thus far identified are attributable to curable defects in the NLRA. There have been proposals for decades to strengthen the prohibition against discharge for organizing.[20] And a bill is pending in Congress to ban permanent replacement of strikers.[21] These proposals are so patently justified that no creditable argument can be advanced against them—except, of course, an argument that the scheme of labor relations they are meant to lubricate (collective bargaining) is itself undesirable. That these proposals have *not* been adopted by Congress suggests that our society has

15. The NLRA protects the workers' right to "engage in concerted activities for the purpose of collective bargaining," 29 U.S.C. § 157 (1982), and forbids discrimination against employees for exercising that right. 29 U.S.C. § 158(a)(3) (1982).

16. *See* Weiler, *supra* note 13, at 236-41; Weiler, *supra* note 1, at 1769, 1776-87; Paul C. Weiler, *Striking A New Balance: Freedom of Contract and the Prospects for Union Representation*, 98 Harv. L. Rev. 351, 353-63 (1984) [hereinafter Weiler, *New Balance*].

17. *See* Weiler, *supra* note 13, at 111-18; Weiler, *supra* note 1, at 1776-81; Robert J. LaLonde & Bernard D. Meltzer, *Hard Times for Unions: Another Look at the Significance of Employer Illegalities*, 58 U. Chi. L. Rev. 953, 954-69 (1991).

18. Though the NLRA forbids the retaliatory discharge of workers engaged in concerted action, the Act has been interpreted to permit employers to hire permanent replacements for strikers. *See* NLRB v. Mackay Radio & Tel. Co., 304 U.S. 333, 345-46 (1938).

19. *See id.*; *see also* Trans World Airlines, Inc. v. Independent Fed'n of Flight Attendants, 489 U.S. 426 (1989).

20. *See* Weiler, *supra* note 13, at 96-99, 294; Weiler, *supra* note 1, at 1804-22; Gerald E. Rosen, *Labor Law Reform: Dead or Alive?* 57 U. Det. J. Urb. L. 1 (1979).

21. The House of Representatives passed the Cesar Chavez Workplace Fairness Act H.R. 5, 103d Cong., 1st Sess. (1993) on June 15, 1993 with a vote of 239 to 190. The bill amends the NLRA and the Railway Labor Act and makes it an unfair labor practice for employers to hire or threaten to hire permanent replacements for economic strikers. *See* 139 Cong. Rec. H3518-68 (daily ed. June 15, 1993). The identical Senate version of the bill, S. 55, 103d Cong., 1st Sess. (1993), cleared the Senate Labor and Human Resources Committee on May 5, 1993 by a vote of 10 to 7. *Striker Replacement Bill Clears Labor Committees*, 143 Lab. Rel. Rep. (BNA) 78 (May 17, 1993). Similar legislation was debated during the 102d Congress, but the Senate version failed to survive a senate filibuster.

turned against collective bargaining as the ordering scheme for employer-employee relations; or, more precisely, has abandoned it as the ordering scheme for any but the small fraction of workplaces where collective bargaining has thrived despite the obstacles.

But even if the proposed changes in the NLRA could somehow be enacted, I doubt that we would see a resurgence of collective bargaining to the eminence it enjoyed in the 1950s and 1960s. There might well be a few million workers who would unionize if relieved of the fears of employer reprisal and permanent replacement (and that would be a significant contribution in its own right—how many statutes provide material benefit to that many citizens?), but I know of no serious observer who believes that just curing the NLRA's ills would lift unionization in the private sector beyond the twenty percent mark.

What is it, then, that is deterring the rest of America's workers from unionizing? It is fear of job loss here, too, but fear of a different kind.

If one charts the industries where unions were successful, they are characterized by one common ingredient: the union was able to eliminate competition among employers based on labor costs. In large part, the industries that were unionized were themselves cartelized, and were able to pass much of the increase in labor costs on to consumers.[22] In others, the employers all joined together in multiemployer bargaining (e.g., trucking), or at least coordinated their bargaining with the union (e.g., steel), to assure that labor costs would be equalized.[23] Still other industries were covered by prevailing wage laws that assured that labor costs were not a basis for competition (e.g., public works construction), or by regulatory regimes that fixed prices among competitors and thereby removed any incentive to compete over labor costs (e.g., airlines).

The falloff in union density has coincided with the shrinkage or disappearance of industries in which it is possible for unions to remove labor costs as a ground for employer competition. Foreign com-

22. The automobile and electrical equipment industries are textbook examples of cartelized industries that are also highly unionized. Such oligopolistic industries are characterized by a high degree of interdependence among its members. Even without outright price collusion, there is a game theoretic at work that enables firms within the industry to pass costs along to consumers. *See, e.g.*, EDWIN MANSFIELD, MICROECONOMICS THEORY AND APPLICATIONS ch. 12 (4th ed. 1982).

23. Steel industry negotiations were in form like multi-employer bargaining—the companies joined together and negotiated as a group—but the negotiations eventually resulted in separate collective bargaining agreements for each company with variations in noneconomic provisions.

petition by producers with much lower labor costs has of course been the most dramatic change, but deregulation and easier access of new entrants have also furnished increased incentives for cost competition, and have led employers increasingly to attempt to gain a competitive edge through lower labor costs.[24]

At the same time, this country has experienced (perhaps not coincidentally) a chronic shortage of jobs. That shortage would in any climate make employees risk averse about losing the jobs they currently hold. But the fear is magnified, for there is a widespread perception that the shortage may be a permanent condition, as the rest of the world increases its share of the global market's business.[25]

The fear that grips most workers today is not that they will be fired or permanently replaced, but that their jobs will disappear. They worry that their employer will lose out in the competitive world and go under, or that the investors will move their capital (and thus the jobs) to another locale (perhaps another country) whose lower wage scales enable more effective competition. Having absorbed this message, workers today have become persuaded that the key to the survival of their jobs is that their employer be an effective competitor—including, if necessary, a competitor based on lower labor costs.[26]

This altered economic climate has profound implications for traditional unionism. In the past, unions held out the promise that, by organizing an entire industry and equalizing wages, they could secure a larger share of the pie for workers. Within an industry, employees

24. The suffering of the automobile and steel industries in the face of increased foreign competition, and the labor struggles of the airline industry in the wake of deregulation, are too well known to require documentation.

25. Of course, long-service employees would be risk-averse about losing their present jobs even in a healthy job market, for the workplace-specific capital they accumulate cannot be replicated if they transfer to a job with another employer. *See* WEILER, *supra* note 13, at 76, 141.

26. When sharing informally with union lawyers the thoughts expressed in this article, the point most often challenged is my perception that workers today have internalized their employers' desire to compete based on lower labor costs. I said at the outset that my diagnoses are not predicated on empirical research. But I have noticed that non-unionized employers, when confronted with an organizing campaign, frequently invoke the following theme:

> Remember company X down the block. It was a thriving firm until the employees selected a union. The union forced labor costs up despite the company's warning that it couldn't afford them, and the company closed the plant [moved, went out of business, etc.]. Do you want this to happen here?

This theme appears to be part of the standard bag-of-tricks used by management consultants who are retained to resist organizing campaigns. I surmise that these consultants, who are presumed to have expertise in what will scare workers (otherwise why would employers retain them?), have detected employee labor-cost conservatism. And the results of organizing drives resisted by these consultants hardly serve to refute that hypothesis.

of one company furnished "mutual aid and protection"[27] to employees of competing companies, as they waged a common war against the corporate barons. Today, employees do not expect that all employers in an industry will survive. The fittest will survive, and they want their employer to be in that number. Far from joining a movement for equality among all workers in an industry, the endangered worker today is anxious to assure that his or her employer has a competitive edge over others in the industry. And, if labor cost competition is necessary to facilitate gaining that edge, well, it's better than losing one's job altogether.[28]

In sum, as employers within an industry compete with each other to survive, so do their employees. Today's employee wants to win the battle for survival, if necessary at the expense of other employees in the industry working for other employers.[29]

Thus, the traditional union appeal is not congruent with the fears of modern workers. Indeed, the union that appears at the door of an unorganized workplace may be seen by the employees as having dual interests. To be sure, the union hopes to improve the lot of those it seeks to enroll. But at the same time, an important reason for the union's desire to improve their lot (i.e., to bring their labor standards up to those of the already-organized employers) is *to eliminate the competitive advantage the unorganized employer (and derivatively its employees) presently enjoys.*

What is more, the traditional weapon that the NLRA offers to extract better terms from the employer—the strike—is, even apart from the fear of permanent replacement, an anachronism in this competitive world.[30] The last thing the worker frightened for the survival

27. The NLRA seeks to overcome unequal bargaining power between employers and employees, "by encouraging the practice and procedure . . . of association, self-organization, and designation of representatives of their own choosing, for the purpose of negotiating the terms and conditions of their employment or other mutual aid and protection." 29 U.S.C. § 151 (1982).

28. *See supra* note 26.

29. This is, to be sure, a sorry picture. Indeed, it accounts for another recent phenomenon: the willingness of employees to cross picket lines and take permanently the jobs of strikers. There was a day when it was thought unethical to "steal" the job of a long-term employee who was simply attempting to better his working conditions. Nowadays, the prevailing ethic is different: one who strikes has stupidly left his property (his job) lying unattended so that anyone who happens along can take it (finders keepers!). One hopes that the economy can be transformed so that these incentives disappear. I report them as I see them; I should not be understood to be embracing as desirable the libertarian world that creates these incentives.

30. Collective bargaining under the NLRA has been described as a "mutual deterrence system," where both sides wield economic weapons to exert the necessary pressure for compromise. Weiler, *New Balance, supra* note 16, at 367.

of the firm wants is to engage in "economic warfare"[31] that will cripple the employer's ability to compete. In the golden days of steel and auto unionism, a strike was not a job-threatening undertaking. Wounding one employer was wounding all, for the gains extracted from one would be enjoyed ultimately by the workers of all. Today, wounding one's own employer is wounding one's self.

Of course, the grim scenario I have just recounted does not characterize every industry in America. The principal growth areas in our economy are in services, such as hospital care, in which employers do not face global or even national competition. In these areas, unionization may well flourish under a properly-amended NLRA. Indeed, if there were a significant turnaround in job prospects in this country, it might well be that unionization could expand in quantum leaps that would exceed my prognoses. But so long as vast parts of the employment map are marked by endangered workplaces facing competition based in part on labor costs, it seems unrealistic to expect that employees will opt for a regime that is centered on the strike threat and depends upon industry-wide wage equalization to prosper.

B. The Barriers to Enterprise Unionism

The account to this point, if accurate, explains the reluctance of employees to join industry-wide unions, but it does not foreclose the possibility that they would join unions confined to a single company or, perhaps, to a single workplace. (Even within a single company, employees at different plants may be competing. The recent episode in which General Motors engaged in a lengthy review of which plants to close and which to retain exemplifies the incentive for employees to make theirs the most cost-effective plant).[32]

Paul Weiler has identified enterprise unionism as the road to collective bargaining in the future,[33] and Samuel Estreicher's piece in this Symposium points in the same direction.[34] It is, indeed, imaginable that employees will evolve into enterprise unions, but I doubt that would eventuate merely from strengthening the NLRA. Employees

31. "[W]e have built into our labor relations system a species of industrial warfare by which the parties attempt to settle disputes through the deliberate infliction of severe economic losses on each other." *Id. See also id.* at 364-67.

32. *See, e.g.,* Donald W. Nauss, *GM Hoping to Cut More Jobs*, L.A. TIMES, Sept. 25, 1993, at D1; Warren Brown & Frank Swoboda, *For GM, a Makeover is Measured in Years,* WASH. POST, Apr. 4, 1993, at H1.

33. *See* WEILER, *supra* note 13, at 218-24.

34. Samuel Estreicher, *Labor Law Reform in a World of Competitive Product Markets,* 69 CHI.-KENT L. REV 3, 15-18, 20-21 (1993).

will be reluctant to commit their fate to an "exclusive" representative—one with authority to bind them—without having some basis for trusting that the representative will be competent and will operate in their interests. Employees cannot simply "create," spontaneously, an institution with the expertise needed to bargain on such complex issues as pensions, insurance and occupational health.

Enterprise unions more likely will evolve out of institutions that begin in the workplace on a less formal, nonexclusive basis and prove their worth in that capacity. A classic example is the National Education Association (the "NEA"), whose affiliates began as nonbinding entities dedicated to working with school management (indeed, whose membership included school principals) on problems of mutual professional interest, acquired and demonstrated expertise, and then evolved in the late 1960s and early 1970s into exclusive bargaining representatives for teachers. Today the NEA is America's largest union, representing teachers in virtually all the public schools in America in locales that are otherwise devoid of significant union activity. By contrast, the American Federation of Teachers, which from the start was organized as a traditional collective bargaining institution, never succeeded at organizing teachers outside the cities with strong union roots.[35] The lesson is that collective bargaining evolves out of institutions that garner employees' trust. They will not spring into existence out of a revitalized NLRA. There must be a law that enables nascent institutions to grow. I suggest in Part II that a regime that encourages "service providers" would provide the soil out of which enterprise unionism might grow.

Yes, amend the NLRA to cure its defects, and permit all who desire representation through exclusive bargaining representatives a meaningful opportunity to have it. But at the same time, let's focus on the role government should be playing vis-à-vis the majority of workplaces that will not, at least in the near future, be organized under the NLRA.

II. A Labor Law for Unorganized Workers

There exists today a haphazard labor law for workers who do not have an exclusive bargaining representative. The states have declared that the unorganized worker's relationship with the employer is contractual, and state and federal governments have enacted a variety of

35. *See* Michael Finch & Trevor W. Nagel, *Collective Bargaining in the Public Schools: Reassessing Labor Policy in an Era of Reform*, 1984 Wis. L. Rev. 1573.

substantive statutes designed to assure the provision of minimal terms to all workers.[36] In most cases, of course, the "contract" is invisible:[37] the terms and conditions are those fixed unilaterally by the employer, subject to the minima prescribed by statute. Employees "negotiate" only by accepting or rejecting the employer's proffered terms. The employer's unilateral assessment of the potential of employee exit to more beneficent employers is the only employment-related constraint influencing the terms the employer proffers.

Richard Epstein suggests that this should be the full measure of the law's concern for the unorganized worker.[38] Other contractual relationships prosper with no greater governmental intervention, so why

36. Federal minimal terms protection for employees is evident in now familiar acronyms. *E.g.*, Equal Pay Act of 1963, 29 U.S.C. § 206 (1982); Age Discrimination in Employment Act of 1967 (ADEA), 29 U.S.C. §§ 621-634 (1982); Occupational Safety and Health Act (OSHA), 29 U.S.C. §§ 651-678 (1982); Employment Retirement Income Security Act (ERISA), 29 U.S.C. §§ 1001-1461 (1982); Title VII of the Civil Rights Act of 1964 (Title VII), 42 U.S.C. §§ 2000e to 2000e-17 (1982). Every state has statutes conferring still additional minimum terms. *E.g.*, ME. REV. STAT. ANN. tit. 26, § 625-B (West 1987) (requiring employers to notify employees 60 days in advance of a plant closing and to provide severance pay to employees who lose their jobs as a result); MONT. CODE ANN. § 39-2-904 (1987) (requiring a showing of good cause for employees dismissed in retaliation for refusal to violate public policy or express personnel policies).

37. Some contracts are more visible than others. Courts in several states have found the employer's written personnel policies to constitute enforceable contractual promises. *See, e.g.*, Small v. Springs Indus., Inc. 357 S.E.2d 452, 455 (S.C. 1987) (holding that an employer may be bound by provisions of an employee handbook absent a conspicuous disclaimer); Leithead v. American Colloid Co., 721 P.2d 1059, 1062 (Wyo. 1986) (holding that an employee handbook "may change the employer's unfettered right to discharge an employee"); Toussaint v. Blue Cross & Blue Shield, 292 N.W.2d 880, 892 (1980) (holding that employer's written policy statements may create protection against discharge without cause).

38. Richard Epstein is the most prominent exponent of this view. Epstein and other neoclassical economic theorists contend that the law should not interfere with free contractual relationships unless fraud is involved. Under this theory, there is nothing unique in the employment contract that warrants legal intervention; employees have merely contracted to supply labor, the same as product suppliers agree to provide other factors of production. The NLRA abrogates freedom of contract by regulating labor-management contracts and expropriating the employer's property interests. *See, e.g.*, RICHARD A. EPSTEIN, FORBIDDEN GROUNDS: THE CASE AGAINST EMPLOYMENT DISCRIMINATION LAWS chs. 2-5 (1992); Richard A. Epstein, *A Common Law for Labor Relations: A Critique of the New Deal Labor Legislation*, 92 YALE L.J. 1357 (1983); Richard A. Epstein, *In Defense of the Contract at Will*, 51 U. CHI. L. REV. 947 (1984); Richard A. Epstein, *Agency Costs, Employment Contracts, and Labor Unions, in* PRINCIPALS AND AGENTS: THE STRUCTURE OF BUSINESS 127 (John W. Pratt & Richard J. Zeckhauser eds., 1985).

Charles Fried also claims that the NLRA system of restructuring labor markets in favor of employees should be abandoned:

> One question in particular I would like to raise is whether it is any longer necessary or even wise to retain the premise that the best protection of workers' interests is to be found in a restructured market, that is, one in which workers are assured of their rights by guaranteed access to a process of bargaining and in which their strength is assured through the monopolistic principle of exclusive representation.

Charles Fried, *Individual and Collective Rights in Work Relations: Reflections on the Current State of Labor Law and Its Prospects*, 51 U. CHI. L. REV. 1012, 1019 (1984). Instead, Fried proposes that labor relations be guided by the free market and supplemented when necessary by minimal terms. Fried's market solution, however, backs away from Epstein's position that the NLRA represents an unjustifiable redistribution of employer property towards the employees:

not the labor contract? If one truly believes this, the NLRA should be repealed (and Epstein so contends).[39]

The underlying premise of the NLRA is that market failures render the contracting process imperfect.[40] If one accepts that premise, as I do,[41] it not only justifies the NLRA's existence, but leads to the additional question that underlies this paper: If those imperfections are to be addressed by law for the organized worker, why not for the unorganized?

In an earlier day, I would have said that this is a false paradox: the NLRA provides a solution for *all* workers, and those who opt to reject it have no claim upon the government to proffer an alternative. But the conditions I have described in Part I persuade me that NLRA-style representation is not as viable an option in some industries as in others, and thus that workers whose conditions are not suited to the NLRA have a legitimate claim that government seek alternative ways to cure the market imperfections that afflict their efforts to bargain with their employers.

Legislative dictation of minimum terms is of course one way to protect unorganized employees, and certainly there is room for such legislation. But a legal regime that did no more would be arid indeed. There are vast areas of employee interest that can never be captured by such legislation (when can I take my vacation? will I get a raise this year? will I get the next promotion? can we get better food in the

> Epstein's analysis is vulnerable at its central premise: the definition of the property rights involved. Only by assuming that the preexisting common law system of property rights had some natural, preconventional status can the expropriationary thrust of the [NLRA] . . . be criticized. If, however, property rights are essentially conventional, then Epstein runs up against the problem of showing why the [NLRA] system does not represent simply a redefinition by society of what have always been social conventions in any event.

Id. at 1016.

39. *See supra* text accompanying note 38.

40. *See infra* note 86. Cass Sunstein indicates the weak link in the market theory is its assumption that the original distribution of wealth is free of market flaws:

> A common attack on [the NLRA] insists that if employees in fact value self-government, the marketplace will produce it. But this attack is vulnerable to a critique that should by now be familiar. It takes for granted the current distribution of wealth and entitlements and the current set of preferences. It fails to take account of the possibility that an unconstrained market in labor may produce relationships, attitudes, and allocations of power that are on balance highly undesirable for society in general.

Cass R. Sunstein, *Rights, Minimal Terms, and Solidarity: A Comment*, 51 U. Chi. L. Rev. 1041, 1059 (1984). For Paul Weiler, the essential labor market imperfection is the unequal bargaining power between employer and employee. Weiler, *supra* note 13, at 77-78, 183-84. Moreover, Weiler posits that the relationship of career employees to their workplace creates a special vulnerability to market imperfections. *Id.* at 136-52.

41. Michael H. Gottesman, *Wither Goest Labor Law: Law and Economics in the Workplace*, 100 Yale L.J. 2767, 2785-93 (1991).

cafeteria?). Unless one is content to rely on traditional contract law for all above the minimum (and one should not be, because of market imperfections to be discussed next), the law has an interest, beyond mere dictation of minimum terms, in facilitating a dialogue between employer and employee.[42]

Borrowing from traditional notions of market failure, and from some of the choices made in the NLRA designed to overcome market failure, I have constructed the following set of proposals that I believe are necessary to create a meaningful climate for bargaining by employees who do not opt for exclusive recognition under the NLRA.

A. *Protection Against Reprisal*

It is a curious feature of our current labor relations regime that the law protects against employer reprisal (however inadequately) those employees who seek to bargain concertedly with their employer,[43] but affords no protection against reprisal to the individual employee who attempts to bargain with the employer.

The relationship between employer and individual employee is, in every state, deemed contractual.[44] But employees must be bold indeed to insist upon actual negotiation of that contract, as opposed to simply accepting the employer's terms.

The employer-employee relationship is, on a day-to-day basis, one of domination and subordination.[45] The employer commands,

42. Moreover, governmentally dictated solutions are an imperfect mechanism for regulating the workplace. Of necessity, such solutions must be declared at a high level of generality. But often, the parties directly interested could craft workplace-specific solutions that were more desirable. *See* WEILER, *supra* note 13, at 153-56, 181-85; Gottesman, *supra* note 41, at 2794-98; Richard B. Stewart, *Reconstitutive Law*, 46 MD. L. REV. 86, 108-09 (1986).

43. *See supra* note 15.

44. *But see supra* text accompanying note 37.

45. Recently, "critical" legal scholars have sought to address the dependency and subordination of the employees by promoting workplace democracy. These scholars view the relationship between employers and employees as essentially artificial (i.e., Karl Marx' critique of capitalist enterprise as the nexus of a social relationship between the owners of the means of production and labor), and criticize the current system of labor relations as inadequate to address the skewed properties of the current system of economic production.

For example, James Raskin criticizes the current system of collective bargaining as faulty because it treats union participation as a "foreign entity" grafted onto the workplace, rather than an "organic 'activity'" that is essential to employees. James B. Raskin, *Reviving The Democratic Vision of Labor Law*, 42 HASTINGS L.J. 1067, 1071 (1991). Similarly, Karl Klare proposes that, "[l]abor law should be framed and administered with a commitment to democratizing decision making in the workplace and to redistributing power in labor markets in favor of employees . . . ." Karl E. Klare, *Workplace Democracy and Market Reconstruction: An Agenda for Legal Reform*, 38 CATH. U. L. REV. 1, 5 (1988). *See also* Karl E. Klare, *Judicial Deradicalization of the Wagner Act and the Origins of Modern Legal Consciousness, 1937-1941*, 62 MINN. L. REV. 265 (1977).

and the employee is expected to obey. A willful refusal to accommodate the employer's wishes is insubordination. Against that backdrop, the employee who manifests dissatisfaction with the employer's proffered employment terms—and, worse still, has the audacity to "demand" better—courts the employer's displeasure. Not every employer will understand or appreciate that the terms of the contract are a pre-condition to the onset of the domination-subordination relationship, and necessarily must be arrived at independent of that relationship. And even those employers who do understand this may doubt that the employee who is strident on this issue will be docile where docility is required.

Not surprisingly, then, most employees steer clear of demanding explicit negotiations of employment terms. They accept what the employer offers; if the offer ceases to be the best available, they voice their displeasure by exiting.

The threshold question is whether there is any justification for legal intervention to protect the employee who asserts a right to bargain. Typically in contract law, the parties are free to deal with whom they please. If I am put off by a contractual partner who seeks to renegotiate on terms I find annoying, or in a manner I find offensive, I am free to send him away, to terminate our relationship. I can pick my contractual partners to suit my tastes.

The NLRA manifests a consensus, that I believe still holds,[46] that the employment contract is different. The employee's inability to replace easily the existing employment (because of relative immobility, the unavailability of comparable employment elsewhere, and the accumulated firm-specific benefits that the employee would lose by transferring elsewhere)[47] means that, unless the employer is constrained from reprisal against employee efforts to negotiate, employees will be unwilling to assume their role in a traditional contractual dialogue. While there is much debate about the meaningfulness of the phrase "lack of bargaining power" I suggest that it *is* meaningful at least in this threshold sense: the typical worker in America today lacks the "power" literally "to bargain" with the employer. This is an instance of market failure attributable to the peculiar dependency of the employee on the current job, and perhaps also to the psychology of

46. *See* WEILER, *supra* note 13, at 136-52; Estreicher, *supra* note 34, at 13-15; Finkin, *supra* note 12, at 195; Clyde W. Summers, *A Structured Exception to Section 8(a)(2)*, 69 CHI.-KENT L. REV. 129 (1993).

47. *See* WEILER, *supra* note 13, at 63-71, 140-42.

subordination[48] that attends the day-to-day relationship and that must be ruptured in this instance if explicit bargaining is to occur.

I take it as a given, then, that the law may appropriately act to protect the employee's interest in negotiating without reprisal. That protection is needed all the more by the employee who attempts to negotiate individually, rather than in a group; a group may have combined leverage that will act as a deterrent against employer retaliation, but an individual (except for the rare irreplaceable employee) will not.

Yet the NLRA protects only "concerted activities" against reprisal, and despite the impassioned pleas of some scholars,[49] it has been interpreted consistent with its literal words. The upshot is that if two or more employees approach their employer with bargaining demands they enjoy NLRA protection, but if a single employee does so there is no protection. In a world in which most employees deal individually with the employer, this is a rather astonishing gap.

States might fill the gap by including reprisal for attempting to negotiate as one of the grounds of discharge that will be regarded as "wrongful" and thus a common-law tort. Presumably, state protection of this type would not be preempted by the NLRA so long as the employee is acting alone.[50] And, at least until the NLRA is reformed to provide truly meaningful protection against reprisals, coverage under state tort law might be far more beneficial for employees than amendment of the NLRA to protect individual activity.

The downside, of course, is that it would take forever for fifty states to decide to protect individual employee bargaining activity,

48. *See supra* text accompanying note 45.

49. *See, e.g.*, Robert A. Gorman & Matthew W. Finkin, *The Individual and the Requirement of "Concert" Under the National Labor Relations Act*, 130 U. Pa. L. Rev. 286 (1981) (arguing that the NLRA was intended to protect workers from retaliation whether acting individually or in concert); B. Glenn George, *Divided We Stand: Concerted Activity and the Maturing of the NLRA*, 56 Geo. Wash. L. Rev. 509 (1988) (arguing that the conservative construction of "concerted" defeats the NLRA's goal of establishing a procedural system to facilitate communication between employer and employee).

50. The Supreme Court has consistently ruled that the NLRA preempts state law that attempts to regulate conduct that is either protected or prohibited by the NLRA, or that is even arguably prohibited. Gottesman, *supra* note 12, at 355. As the NLRA does not purport to prohibit the firing of employees for activity that is not "concerted," the states presumably are free to regulate such conduct. However, if two or more employees attempt to negotiate in concert, traditional NLRA preemption doctrine suggests that the states would be preempted from providing protection, notwithstanding that NLRA remedies are woefully inadequate. *Id.* at 372-73. *But see id.* at 391-94 (arguing that the common wisdom is wrong, and that the proper construction of the NLRA would not preempt stronger state remedies for conduct prohibited by the NLRA). One can imagine cases in which an employee acts alone, but the employer alleges that it thought the employee was acting in concert with other employees; in that scenario, the employer could argue that its conduct was at least arguably prohibited by the NLRA, thus preempting state regulation.

whereas federal law could decree it in a stroke. The optimal protection would be a federal law with appropriate teeth, as outlined below. In its absence, the second-best would be expansion of the NLRA to protect individuals against reprisal, however inadequate the protection, *but without preemption of state law that provides parallel prohibitions against such reprisals (which might be stronger in substance and remedy than the federal).*

Whether federal or state, *meaningful* protection of the employee's right to bargain free of reprisal requires measures that would be regarded as radical, and beyond the realm of political acceptability, in today's climate. Employees will not be encouraged out of their shells unless the law provides a truly effective protection against the risk of job loss. Most employees will be extremely risk averse about putting their jobs on the line, and the determinative calculation in their eyes will be whether it is *possible* that by demanding negotiations they will lose their jobs. A regime such as the NLRA provides, even if extended to individual employees, would likely prove meaningless, for several reasons.

First, employees will not be assured that improperly motivated discharges will be caught and corrected.[51] The NLRA places the decision whether to prosecute upon a public official vested with unreviewable discretion. Moreover, even if the employee could be confident that an unfair labor practice complaint would be filed, so long as legal victory depends upon proving the employer's bad motive, a significant percentage of badly motivated discharges will escape condemnation for want of proof. Risk-averse employees will fear that will be their fate.

Prospects of success would be improved, of course, if the burden of proof were inverted (the employer who fires within x months of an employee bargaining demand must prove the absence of bad motive), or if a general regime of protection against discharge without just cause were instituted (so that a finding of motive would in many cases be rendered unnecessary).[52]

Still, even if employees were assured that they could prevail in such lawsuits, the deterrent effect would not be wholly removed. If the remedy is back pay and reinstatement (even if supplemented with

51. *See supra* text accompanying notes 16-17.

52. Of course, there will still be cases where the employer indeed had good cause for discharge, but would not have acted upon that cause but for the employee's protected negotiating demands. In such cases, proof of motive would remain essential. *See, e.g.*, Edward G. Budd Mfg. Co. v. NLRB, 138 F.2d 86 (3d Cir. 1943).

attorneys fees), the employee will not truly be made whole. Reinstatement to a nonunion workplace rarely works: employees are reluctant to accept it, fearing ongoing employer harassment motivated not only by the initial "insubordination" that prompted the discharge but also by the animosity engendered by the subsequent litigation; and even when employees do accept reinstatement, they usually leave shortly because such harassment does occur.[53]

To be truly effective, a remedy for reprisal discharges must fulfill one or the other of two very ambitious goals. It must either provide a remedy so attractive that employees will be willing to trade (i.e., risk) their jobs for it, or so powerful that employees can be confident their employers will be deterred from discharging. Both goals might be met if employees were entitled to opt against reinstatement, and instead to receive compensatory damages that fully reflect the degree of loss (including future loss) they have suffered by reason of the discharge. Even this would not be enough, however, if employers succeeded in escaping detection in any significant percentage of cases. In that event, as the law and economics literature teaches, the solution is punitive damages geared to the percentage likelihood of detection—the likelier the employer's escape, the higher the damages should be when the employer is caught.[54] The current NLRA's limitation to back pay is an invitation to violations: unless employers are caught virtually one hundred percent of the time, there is economic incentive to violate.

Notice that, in the case of individual bargaining, there is no "public interest" in preferring reinstatement as a remedy. In the union organizing context, the concern is that if the discharged employee does not return to the workplace a pall will have been cast over the organizing effort (and, perforce, at least one pro-union vote will have been removed from the electorate).[55] But in the context of individual bargaining, if every employee knows that he or she will receive adequate monetary compensation if discharged for proffering bargaining demands, the public has no interest in insisting upon reinstatement in disregard of the victimized employee's preference for a forward-looking compensatory remedy.[56]

53. Weiler, *supra* note 13, at 85-87; Weiler, *supra* note 1, at 1791-93.

54. A. Mitchell Polinsky, An Introduction to Law and Economics 75-84 (2d ed. 1989).

55. Phelps Dodge Corp. v. NLRB, 313 U.S. 177, 195 (1941).

56. A minor qualification is that the failure to reinstate in the individual bargaining context might act as a deterrent to future employees who might wish to organize collectively. This seems remote, however.

The remedies available under state tort law for "wrongful discharge" come closer to approximating the package I have suggested than does anything that is likely to emerge in any federal statute. When an employer has discharged an employee for a reason that a state court holds offensive to public policy, and thus tortious, that court holds that the employee is entitled to sue for past and future lost earnings, as well as punitive damages.

I would be nervous about any effort to expand the NLRA to extend protection against individual bargaining unless it were a certainty that the final product—with remedies that surely would be inadequate—was not going to preempt state law. The scenario to be feared is one in which well-intentioned legislators introduce a bill in Congress that would protect individuals against reprisal, provide adequate remedies, and explicitly preserve parallel state law, only to have the bill whittled down during consideration so that the remedies are inadequate and state law is preempted; at that point, it would be employers who would be championing its passage.[57]

B. Provision of Information

Another anomaly of existing law is that the NLRA requires the employer to provide information to a union when chosen as exclusive bargaining representative, but contains no requirement that information be provided to employees who have not chosen an exclusive representative.[58] Nor does any state mandate the provision of such information on a generic basis.

It is generally understood that there is an information imbalance between employers and employees, and that the imbalance is a form of market failure that justifies legal intervention.[59] The employer knows much more about its operations, policies, etc., than the employees. Furthermore, and perhaps more important, the employer knows what its plans for the future are, and the employees do not. The mat-

57. It should not be forgotten that Montana's just cause statute, with its minimal remedies, was championed by employers seeking to escape the powerful remedies authorized by the Montana Supreme Court for wrongful discharge. *See* Gottesman, *supra* note 12, at 368-69 n.57; MONT. CODE ANN. § 39-2-901 (1987).

58. 29 U.S.C. § 158(d) (1988); Detroit Edison Co. v. NLRB, 440 U.S. 301 (1979); NLRB v. Acme Indus. Co., 385 U.S. 432 (1967); NLRB v. Truitt Mfg. Co., 351 U.S. 149 (1956).

59. *See* Leslie K. Shedlin, *Regulation of Disclosure of Economic and Financial Data and the Impact on the American System of Labor-Management Relations*, 41 OHIO ST. L.J. 441, 458-59 (1980) (stating that the legal entitlement of union workers to information about their employer's financial condition and plans is limited in comparison with Germany); *cf.* WEILER, *supra* note 13, at 288 (indicating that employee participation committees will serve to provide workers with informational resources not otherwise available).

ters employees would most wish to discuss with their employers are those "entrepreneurial" decisions under consideration by corporate officials that might lead to elimination of jobs or radical alteration of employment conditions.[60]

Meaningful bargaining requires access to all the information possessed by the employer that is pertinent to the terms to be negotiated. The NLRA does not provide this even to unions. While information disclosure is required respecting mandatory bargaining subjects,[61] the Supreme Court has excluded from the "mandatory bargaining" category many employer entrepreneurial decisions that affect employees,[62] in part out of concern that the union (which ordinarily represents competitors of the employer) cannot be trusted to maintain the confidentiality of the information,[63] and in part out of concern that the union would exploit strategic opportunities, which the NLRA creates in the case of mandatory bargaining subjects, to delay implementation of the employer's plans and/or to strike to prevent their implementation.[64]

60. *See* Cynthia L. Estlund, *Economic Rationality and Union Avoidance: Misunderstanding the National Labor Relations Act*, 71 TEX. L. REV. 921 (1993) (arguing that mandatory bargaining should be expanded to include capital allocation decisions (e.g., locating a new plant or relocating current production) because such "economically rational" employer business choices can shield anti-union animus). *See also* Marleen A. O'Connor, *Restructuring the Corporation's Nexus of Contracts: Recognizing a Fiduciary Duty to Protect Displaced Workers*, 69 N.C. L. REV. 1189 (1991) [hereinafter O'Connor, *Nexus of Contracts*] (employers can opportunistically breach the implicit employment contract because "informational asymmetries" prevent employees from having access to operational and financial information); Marleen A. O'Connor, *The Human Capital Era: Reconceptualizing Corporate Law to Facilitate Labor-Management Cooperation*, 78 CORNELL L. REV. 899 (1993) (restructuring corporate law is necessary to prevent opportunistic breach by employers).

61. 29 U.S.C. § 158(d) (1988); Detroit Edison Co. v. NLRB, 440 U.S. 301 (1979); NLRB v. Acme Indus. Co., 385 U.S. 432 (1967); NLRB v. Truitt Mfg. Co., 351 U.S. 149 (1956).

62. The Supreme Court, declaring that "[m]anagement must be free from the constraints of the bargaining process to the extent essential for the running of a profitable business," has interpreted the NLRA's bargaining provision *not* to require bargaining "over management decisions that have a substantial impact on the continued availability of employment [unless] . . . the benefit, for labor-management relations and the collective bargaining process, outweighs the burden placed on the conduct of the business." First Nat'l Maintenance Corp. v. NLRB, 452 U.S. 666, 678-79 (1981).

63. *Id.* at 682-83 ("[M]anagement may have great need for . . . secrecy in meeting business opportunities and exigencies. It may face significant tax or securities consequences that hinge on confidentiality . . . .").

64. In the case of mandatory bargaining subjects, the employer cannot unilaterally change the status quo without first bargaining to an impasse with the union. *Id.* at 674-75; NLRB v. Katz, 369 U.S. 736, 743 (1962). The Court likewise implicitly assumed that a union's right to strike applies only to mandatory bargaining subjects, *First Nat'l Maintenance,* 452 U.S. at 679 n.17, 686 n.23, but this seems erroneous. It is a refusal to bargain within the meaning of § 8(b)(3), (d) for a union to refuse to sign an agreement on mandatory terms because striking over nonmandatory terms. But if a union announces its readiness to sign a collective bargaining agreement—an agreement that does not contain a clause forbidding strikes over nonmandatory entrepreneurial decisions—there is nothing in the NLRA that would prohibit that strike. Quite

But the objection to furnishing information to an institution that deals with the employer's rivals is inapplicable when an individual employee seeks the information, at least so long as appropriate (and enforceable) pledges of confidentiality are provided by the employee.[65] And, as the employer is under no obligation to withhold implementation pending impasse absent a certified bargaining agent (and need hardly fear a strike by a single employee) the other factors that have influenced the Court to decline ordering bargaining (and hence the employer's furnishing of information) also are inapplicable.[66]

No doubt, employers would be tempted to defy a statutory command that they turn over to employees information they would prefer not to disclose. But it need not require a vast administrative regime to enforce such a command. If there is adequate legislative will, a way can be found. The statute could specify with some precision the categories of information that employers were required to furnish upon request to employees. If the penalty for noncompliance were demonstrably greater than the potential gains from noncompliance, the employers' efficient choice would then be compliance.[67]

There are already a number of federal statutes requiring employers to disclose particular categories of information to employees (ERISA,[68] OSHA[69]), accompanied by substantial penalties for noncompliance. My proposal would merely generalize that obligation to all matters pertinent to the terms and conditions of employment.

simply, the Act contains no provision forbidding strikes over nonmandatory subjects, and unions engage in such strikes all the time (e.g., sympathy strikes). Indeed, § 13 of the Act declares that "[n]othing in this subchapter, except as specifically provided for herein, shall be construed so as either to interfere with or impede or diminish in any way the right to strike, or to affect the limitations or qualifications on such right." 29 U.S.C. § 163 (1982). Unless a strike violates some other provision—as would a strike over nonmandatory subjects that prevented agreement on mandatory subjects—it is protected by § 13.

65. The common law has always protected the employer's interest in preventing disclosure of trade secrets by current or former employees, and would surely enforce reasonable agreements restricting disclosure of other confidential information. *See, e.g.,* Schulenburg v. Signatrol, Inc., 212 N.E.2d 865 (Ill. 1965); Edmund W. Kitch, *The Law and Economics of Rights in Valuable Information*, 9 J. Legal Stud. 683 (1980).

66. The decision to relieve employers of the burden of dealing with unions about entrepreneurial decisions was driven not only by the confidentiality concern, but by others that likewise are inapplicable in the individual employee setting. The Court was concerned in *First National Maintenance* that making bargaining mandatory about these subjects would trigger the NLRA's prohibition against unilateral change until impasse is reached, and thus inject delay that might be injurious to the employer; and the Court thought (perhaps erroneously, *see supra* note 64) that by declaring such decisions nonmandatory bargaining subjects, unions could not call strikes over them. 452 U.S. at 679 n.17, 686 n.23.

67. Polinsky, *supra* note 54.

68. Employment Retirement Income Security Act of 1974, 29 U.S.C. §§ 1001-1461 (1982).

69. Occupational Safety and Health Act, 29 U.S.C. §§ 651-678 (1982).

C. Collective Goods

A third type of market failure that infects the contractual relationship between employer and individual employee is what is commonly called the "collective goods" or "public goods" problem.[70] Some conditions of employment cannot be fixed for a single employee; a change to help one necessarily affects many or all. Thus, the employee who wants cleaner air in the plant cannot obtain satisfaction of that demand without its conferral on many other employees as well. There are two implications of this truism:

(1) There are many benefits that employees would collectively "purchase" in bargaining with the employer (e.g., trading a few cents in wages per hour for a reduction in chemical toxins) that no one employee could afford to purchase alone (indeed, that would not be worth the cost for the one employee even if she could afford it).

(2) Absent a mechanism for making all employees pay for such a "collective good," there will be a tendency for many employees to free-ride, and thus for the common interest not to be obtained.[71]

There are many collective goods among the employee's possible terms and conditions of employment, i.e., benefits that cannot be provided to one employee without automatically furnishing it to others: many types of pensions, group health insurance, seniority, etc. Collective bargaining through an exclusive bargaining representative is generally thought to be uniquely suited to solving these collective goods problems. The union bargains on behalf of all the employees, and binds all, so that it can "trade" (in reduced wages) whatever is necessary to purchase the collective good.[72]

What happens to collective goods in the absence of an exclusive representative? The problem is not quite as difficult as it would be, for example, if the *neighbors* of a factory wanted clean air.[73] The factory does not have the option unilaterally to provide the clean air and "charge" the neighbors for the cost of providing it. In the nonunion workplace, however, the employer *does* have the power to provide the clean air and adjust wages appropriately to pay for it. Thus, one possible answer is that the law need not concern itself with collective goods

70. The primary resource on the public goods problem is MANCUR OLSON, THE LOGIC OF COLLECTIVE ACTION: PUBLIC GOODS AND THE THEORY OF GROUPS (1965).

71. *See* Gottesman, *supra* note 41, at 2789-90; Richard B. Stewart et al., *Market Failure: The Collective Goods and Externality Problems, in* ENVIRONMENTAL LAW AND POLICY (forthcoming 1994).

72. Gottesman, *supra* note 41, at 2788-90.

73. The factory-neighbor hypothetical is explored in Stewart et al., *supra* note 71.

problems in the workplace. The astute employer has an interest in learning what collective goods its employees would pay their "fair share" to get, and to implement them unilaterally through wage adjustments. All the employer need do is provide sufficient forum for individual employees to "signal" their preferences (a written questionnaire, for example, might do the trick).

This answer, however, seems too facile. Collective goods are expensive, and their design is usually complex. Pensions, insurance, and clean air are not simple "yes-no" items for a questionnaire. Employees are unlikely (absent retention of expert advisors) to understand all the complexities involved, let alone transmit signals clear enough for an employer to develop a package that optimizes employee interests. Intensive negotiations, with both sides assisted by experts, plainly are the best way to achieve the optimal provision of collective goods.

But is this rejoinder likewise too facile? After all, if employees would be best served by collective bargaining, would they not opt for it (or at least do so if the NLRA's imperfections were removed)? My supposition is that many employees would welcome a regime in which they could negotiate collectively with their employer over some or all collective goods problems, while retaining their right individually to deal with respect to all other issues.[74] One legal solution thus might be to expand the NLRA to afford employees the option of exclusive recognition on particular subjects, to be picked from a menu of collective goods. For example, employees who resist unionization out of fear that seniority will displace merit as the criterion for wages and promotion might opt for unionization if it applied only to pensions and insurance.

Another option would be simply to await the emergence of service providers who would aggregate a number of clients from within a particular work force and thus be able to bargain for collective goods on their clients' behalf. This cryptic observation will hopefully become clear from the discussion that follows next.

74. It is possible to achieve this under the current NLRA. The sports and entertainment unions are exclusive bargaining representatives under the NLRA, but they have opted to leave the determination of some issues (e.g., salaries above prescribed minima) to individual negotiation. But an employee voting today for an exclusive representative has no assurance that the entity, once elected, will "opt" to delegate some issues for individual bargaining. My proposal in text would provide assurances to employees *up front* that election of a union would not result in sacrificing control over issues the employee wants to retain for individual bargaining. It might, therefore, attract employees unwilling to take the risk of loss-of-control that the current NLRA poses.

D. *Service Providers*

Removing the threat of reprisals, and requiring the furnishing of information, are necessary preconditions to real bargaining by individual employees, but it is unrealistic to expect that most employees would have the expertise to use the opportunity meaningfully. Employees lack the expertise to understand the complex information and the pertinent legal constraints applicable to many of the subjects embraced in the employment relationship, such as benefit plans and occupational safety and health. Employees also lack the information about what comparable employers provide that would enable them to assess what demands might be realistic and what employer offers should be accepted. In simplest terms, employees need "experts" to assist them in the bargaining process.

In unionized workplaces, that expertise is provided by the international union. The Steelworkers Union, for example, has staffs of skilled experts in both OSHA and benefit areas, as well as a superb legal office. This centralized core of expertise reaches out to assist the bargainers at each of the discrete locations the union serves as bargaining agent. This expertise is financed out of the dues paid by the union's members.

There is no reason why comparable services could not be available to employees who are not unionized. What is needed are experts to provide similar functions for individual employees, and a funding mechanism that would make the employment of such experts feasible. Plainly, the cost of employing this expertise on an individual-by-individual basis would be prohibitive. But it is not inconceivable that an industry of service providers might spring up, offering a package of pertinent representational services, mirroring the group legal service programs that have begun to emerge.

Indeed, the institutions likeliest to offer such services are traditional unions, who would be willing to bear the costs in the hope that providing these services might lead ultimately to selection as exclusive representative.[75] But other institutions, whether socially oriented nonprofit or profit-making consultants, might devise group programs that would be economically viable.

75. The only potential problem with unions providing this service is the confidentiality problem discussed above. *See supra* text accompanying notes 61-66. The problem would not arise, of course, unless Congress truly mandated employers to provide such "entrepreneurial" information to employees, not the likeliest of my proposals to secure enactment. Even then, it might be possible for unions to build internal "Chinese walls" sufficient to remove the risk of breaching confidentiality.

To facilitate employee awareness of the availability of these services, the law could require employers to provide bulletin boards on which their wares could be advertised, and a forum at the workplace where they could meet with employees to discuss the services they offer to provide.[76] Access could also be mandated for the period after employees have chosen service-providers to facilitate communication between the provider and its employee-clients.

How would the provision of these services be funded? The simplest method, conceptually, would be small premiums paid by subscribers—an equivalent of union dues. The law could require the employer to check off such premiums from wages at employee request.[77] Is it feasible to deliver meaningful services to individual employees without prohibitive cost? I think it might be, if numbers of employees of a single employer joined in purchasing such services.[78] And, as noted, unions would have incentive to provide these services even at a loss, to gain a foothold in the enterprise.

It is foreseeable that eventually a majority of employees within a workforce might subscribe to a single service provider, at which point the subscriber would technically qualify for exclusive representation status under the NLRA.[79] If there is ultimately to be an expansion of

76. *A fortiori*, a Congress prepared to provide this access should be providing it as well to unions seeking to persuade employees to select them as exclusive bargaining representatives. I share Samuel Estreicher's view that the NLRA's failure to provide such access (more precisely, the Supreme Court's persistent refusal to permit the Labor Board to construe the NLRA to require such access) is scandalous. *See* Estreicher, *supra* note 34, at 36-37.

77. Here again, it should follow *a fortiori* that the law should require employers to check off dues to *exclusive bargaining representatives* upon employee request, upon the union's simple proffer to pay the employer's out-of-pocket costs to effectuate the transfer. The present interpretation of the NLRA, which leaves the availability of a checkoff to collective bargaining, discussed in H.K. Porter Co. v. NLRB, 397 U.S. 99 (1970), is indefensible for a statute that purports to facilitate union representation when sought by employees.

78. There are other possibilities for financing at least some of the costs of service providers. To the extent that those providers enforced employees' legal rights, their fees could be paid by the government (whose enforcement burden would be correspondingly lightened, see Gottesman, *supra* note 41, at 2808-09) or by fee awards against wrongdoing employers, as many federal statutes already provide. *See, e.g.*, Title VII, ADA, ADEA, FLSA, ERISA.

79. Section 2(5) of the NLRA defines "labor organization" as "any organization of any kind, or an agency or employee representation committee or plan, in which employees participate and which exists for the purpose, in whole or in part, of dealing with employers concerning grievances, labor disputes, wages, rates of pay, hours of employment, or conditions of work." 29 U.S.C. § 152(5) (1982). While this definition is likely broad enough to embrace the service providers I have envisioned, those providers might qualify even if they fell without the definition. For § 9 does not, in terms at least, limit employees to selecting only "labor organizations" as their bargaining agents:

> *Representatives* designated or selected for the purposes of collective bargaining by the majority of the employees in a unit appropriate for such purposes, shall be the exclusive representatives of all the employees in such unit for the purposes of collective bargaining in respect to rates of pay, wages, hours of employment, or other conditions of employment.

NLRA coverage to industries where labor costs cannot be equalized, it will likely be in the form of "enterprise" entities (whether company wide or plant wide).[80] Such entities are likelier to grow out of service providers who have furnished satisfactory representation than to spring up suddenly out of whole cloth. For it is unrealistic to expect that employees, lacking expertise or a focus for rallying together, would commit their fates exclusively, and spontaneously, to a newly formed entity that had no track record engendering trust.[81]

Some might argue that, if the marketplace would support such services, the providers already would have appeared on the scene hawking their wares; ergo, past experience demonstrates that the concept is not economically feasible. But the present legal climate is altogether inhospitable, and thus provides no indication of what might emerge under the preconditions I have outlined. Employees will fear to invoke such services unless protected by law against employer reprisal; potential providers have no capacity to render meaningful service in the absence of information that only the employer possesses.

E. Legal Compulsion on the Employer to Negotiate?

The discussion to this point has suggested creating rights in individual employees to protection against reprisal for negotiating, information necessary to bargain meaningfully, access to the workplace for employee representatives, and checkoff of fees to the representative. It has been suggested that these provisions might lead to an industry of service providers prepared to assist employees in both the negotiating and contract-law enforcement contexts. Finally, it has suggested the possibility that the NLRA be expanded to permit exclusive representation limited to collective-good subjects if the employees so elect. Harder choices remain to be discussed.

The NLRA does not merely empower employees to select unions, and require that the unions be afforded information. It goes on to oblige the employer to bargain in good faith with the union,[82] and it sanctions economic duress (a strike) as a means by which employees can induce employers to make concessions and reach agreement.[83] In both respects, the NLRA departs from traditional contract law. As

29 U.S.C. § 159(a) (1982). *See also* § 8(a)(5), (d) (declaring the employer's obligation to bargain with "representatives" chosen pursuant to § 9), 29 U.S.C. § 158(a)(5), (d) (1992).

80. *See supra* text accompanying notes 13, 34.

81. *See supra* text accompanying note 35.

82. 29 U.S.C. § 158(a)(5), (d) (1982).

83. *See supra* text accompanying notes 30-31.

noted before, contract law does not compel anyone to bargain with another.[84] And the use of concerted economic duress as a mechanism for extracting concessions in negotiations would render the ensuing contract voidable at the behest of the other party.[85]

Applying the logic employed in prior sections of this article, it would follow that the special treatment accorded by the NLRA to unionized employees (compulsion on employers to bargain, and enhancement of employee bargaining power to make agreement likelier) should be extended to unorganized employees. Is that logical step sensible? To answer that, we must first determine why the NLRA decreed these exceptions for unionized employees, so that we can determine the appropriate analogue for unorganized employees.

One plausible explanation is that Congress intended the NLRA to have a redistributional effect. The statute's quest to "equalize bargaining power" suggests that broader goal.[86] In 1935, there were virtually no statutorily prescribed minimum terms of employment, and the Nation was in the midst of the Great Depression. The enhanced leverage of compelled bargaining and sanctioned economic duress afforded employees a means to improve what were perceived to be unacceptably poor terms and conditions of employment. Today, with statutory minima everywhere, it is plain that Congress is prepared to legislate what are thought to be minimally acceptable employment terms, and thus it is less evident that compelled bargaining and enhanced leverage are needed for that purpose. (Indeed, as the NLRA does not "work" for all employees, it is a less reliable mechanism for improving employees' terms and conditions: only employees positioned to exercise leverage through strikes have secured significantly improved terms attributable to the NLRA.)

84. Poughkeepsie Buying Serv., Inc. v. Poughkeepsie Newspapers, Inc., 131 N.Y.S.2d 515 (N.Y. App. Div. 1954); Hurley v. Eddingfield, 59 N.E. 1058 (Ind. 1901).

85. Restatement (Second) of Contracts, § 176(2) illus. 15-16. Of course, an employee's quitting a job because dissatisfied with the terms would not constitute duress, and if an employer responded by proffering better terms to induce the employee to return the resultant contract would be fully enforceable. But a concerted withholding of work, coupled with picketing and appeals for boycotts, would be considered an antitrust violation ("price" fixing) and render the ensuing contract voidable were it not for the special treatment accorded in the labor (but not the commercial) context. Clayton Act §§ 6, 20, 15 U.S.C. §§ 17, 52 (1988); Local 189, Amalgamated Meat Cutters & Butcher Workmen v. Jewel Tea Co., 381 U.S. 676 (1965) (there is a "nonstatutory exemption from antitrust sanctions" beyond the exemption furnished by the Clayton Act).

86. Congress declared, in § 1 of the NLRA, that the "inequality of bargaining power between employees . . . and employers" was one of the evils to which the Act was addressed. 29 U.S.C. § 151 (1982).

Another possible explanation is that Congress truly believed, as it said on the face of the statute, that the *process* of bargaining would lead to agreements where strikes might otherwise occur, thus averting disruptions of commerce.[87] If that is the true explanation for these features of the NLRA, there seems little reason to extend them to the individual employee context, where disruptions of commerce are not a concern.

Perhaps the best explanation for the retention of the NLRA's departures from traditional contract law is that they represent yet another kind of statutory minimum. Congress has determined that "voice" is a job condition that all employees deserve, just as they deserve a minimum wage, family leave, and a safe and healthful environment.[88] Especially as employees are obliged to assume a subservient role in virtually every aspect of the employment relationship,[89] and lack realistic opportunities to exit,[90] they ought to have a means to participate in the formulation of their terms and conditions of employment. To that end, they are entitled to a dialogue with the employer, and to resort to means that are unacceptable in other settings (economic duress) to induce agreement in order that the dialogue will be meaningful.

If this last point explains our continuing allegiance to the NLRA's scheme, it expresses values that are equally applicable to the unorganized workplace. There is an interest in vindicating employee voice there as well. Thus, I am philosophically disposed toward Matthew Finkin's proposal, in this Symposium, that employers be required to bargain with employees in nonmajority configurations.[91] But my heart is at war with my head: transporting that value to unorganized workplaces entails much higher costs, and threatens complications that do not exist when there is an exclusive representative, as I shall discuss shortly.[92]

87. 29 U.S.C. § 151 (1988) (legislative finding that unequal bargaining power has adverse effect on commerce).

88. *See* Sunstein, *supra* note 40, at 1058 ("What is accomplished by the [NLRA] that is not accomplished by a scheme of minimal terms? The answer lies in the Act's effort to create a process in which workers can use 'voice' as well as 'exit' as a means of expressing their views on how the workplace should be run.").

89. *See supra* text accompanying note 45.

90. *See supra* text accompanying note 47.

91. *See* Finkin, *supra* note 12.

92. The criticisms offered in this section are not applicable to the suggestion, made earlier, that the NLRA permit exclusive recognition for a limited menu of subjects. *See supra* text accompanying note 71. As a majority of the employees would have selected the union for those subjects, and the union would have power to bind all members of the bargaining unit, there is no

In this section, I examine two possible approaches to providing voice for unorganized employees. In the next, I examine the mechanisms for conferring bargaining leverage on unorganized employees.

1. Relaxing the Constraints of Section 8(a)(2)

As presently constituted, the NLRA imposes no requirements on employers to consult with employees who have not selected an exclusive representative, but instead places constraints upon the employer who *does* wish to initiate such a dialogue.[93] The exact scope of the prohibition in section 8(a)(2) of the NLRA is unclear,[94] but it plainly forecloses employers from initiating some dialogues with employees that employers see as desirable for improving productivity, morale, etc. These employer initiatives, no matter how self-serving, at least provide *some* voice to *some* unorganized employees, and can be the springboard for more expansive interchanges down the road. I share the impulse of many observers that section 8(a)(2) should be severely limited.[95]

Many who acknowledge that need would nonetheless constrain the employer out of the concern that originally animated the inclusion of section 8(a)(2) in the statute: that the employer may use these dialogic structures as a means to quell or discourage true unionism. Clyde Summers, in his article in this Symposium, would condition relaxing section 8(a)(2) upon the employer's acquiescence in a series of minimum requirements that, quite likely, would discourage most employers from initiating a dialogue with their employees.[96]

I appreciate the concern that animates Professor Summers's proposal, and I agree that a revised section 8(a)(2) should continue to stifle employer initiatives that are likely to squelch contemporaneous union-organizing efforts. But beyond that, I think the restrictions he proposes surrender too much for too little in return.

Initiatives that would provide *some* dialogue in the vast majority of workplaces that are unorganized and likely to remain so for a long time will be suppressed under the Summers proposal, out of concern

reason why the traditional consequences of union certifications should not apply, limited, of course, to the subjects for which the union has been certified.

93. Under 29 U.S.C. § 158(a)(2) (1988), employers engage in an unfair labor practice when they attempt to "dominate or interfere with the formation or administration of any labor organization or contribute financial or other support to it . . . ."

94. Electromation, Inc., 309 N.L.R.B. 990 (1992).

95. *See* Summers, *supra* note 46; Estreicher, *supra* note 34, at 20-21; Craver, *National Labor Relations Act*, *supra* note 7, at 429-31.

96. Summers, *supra* note 46, at 142-48.

that at the margins those initiatives might discourage unionization in the minority of workplaces where unionization is a viable possibility. This is the tail wagging the dog. Our attitude toward such employer initiatives should be driven by our views about the unlikely-soon-to-be-organized workplaces (for they employ the vast majority of America's workers) and not about the tangential effects on the potentially-organizable workplaces (which employ but a small minority).[97]

A revised section 8(a)(2) that constrained employers only where the margin was in view (i.e., where the prospect of organization was real) would best accommodate these divergent interests. For example, Professor Summers's regime of constraints might be applicable to workplaces where there was a current organizing campaign, or where there had been one within the two years prior. In these situations, the employer would have to dismantle its unilaterally-created committees or else bring them into conformity with Summers's constraints.

To be sure, limiting the application of section 8(a)(2) in this fashion would allow far-sighted employers to adopt union-avoidance dialogic structures before the reality of a unionizing effort ever materialized, and thus deter the initiation of organizing drives. There is no perfect solution. As I have suggested, this unfortunate side-effect is outweighed by the value of such structures in workplaces that have no short-term prospect of being unionized. Moreover, there is always the potential that employee-participation structures, no matter what motivated the employer to create them, will expand beyond the employer's control and in time turn into real collective-bargaining engines. That is the lesson that the NEA taught America's public school districts.[98]

2. A Statutory Duty to Bargain?

It is a tempting analogue to the NLRA to command employers of unorganized workplaces to negotiate with individual employees and/or groups that do not constitute majorities, just as they are required to do when an exclusive bargaining representative has been chosen. Such a command would fit neatly with my vision of service providers who would be competent to represent their clients in such bargaining. And there is real prospect that at least in some cases this could lead

97. It is no answer that employers who do not face realistic organizing prospects are not likely to be the subject of charges for adopting programs violative of § 8(a)(2). As any individual may file a charge, it would take only one disaffected employee (or even a union with no realistic prospects of organizing the employer) to bring down such a program.

98. *See supra* text accompanying note 35.

down the road to employee adoption of an exclusive bargaining representative.

Still, the obstacles to proposals for compelled minority bargaining are prodigious, and Professor Finkin has solved only some of them in his article.[99] Imagine an employer with 5,000 employees who wish to bargain in groups of two. Is the employer required to engage in 2,500 separate rounds of negotiation? How much time is the employer required to devote to each? The costs of individual or minority group bargaining would be prohibitive, and the costs of legally policing the employer's performance therein even more so. It is doubtful that the benefits of face-to-face dialogue would warrant the potential economic burden.

Acknowledging that difficulty, Professor Finkin suggests that perhaps the statutory obligation upon the employer to bargain should be triggered only in the case of entities that represent some substantial percentage of the employer's workforce[100] (one could imagine, e.g., a law compelling the employer to bargain with an organization designated by one-third, or forty percent, of the relevant group of employees). But notice that this qualification surrenders at the outset any obligation upon employers to bargain with what will likely remain the vast majority of America's employees, those who will *not* form themselves into groups large enough to meet the threshold trigger.

Moreover, compelling bargaining with those who *do* form such groups may be more complicated than Professor Finkin envisions. Once we create a threshold we invite litigation over the appropriate bargaining unit (forty percent of what?) and ongoing disputes about whether the threshold *continues* to be met as the dialogue goes on. There would be the difficulty of ever-shifting populations: how will the employer know, from day to day, who is within the group represented and who is not? If an agreement is reached, will the group members all be bound? Will *J.I. Case*[101] require nullification of the agreement if an exclusive representative is later chosen? (If so, the employer will be vulnerable indeed: imagine two forty percent contracts and the potential of the two groups at any time to join forces, secure joint NLRA-certification, and thus escape the contracts; the

99. Finkin, *supra* note 12, at 200-11.

100. *Id.* at 204-05.

101. J.I. Case Co. v. NLRB, 321 U.S. 332 (1944) (holding that, once a union achieves exclusive status, the employer is proscribed from dealing directly with individual employees or groups of employees, and that a collective agreement overrides inconsistent agreements negotiated prior to unionization).

employees will at all times have a one-way option to rescind the agreements reached through this process.)

What would Professor Finkin's bargaining obligation entail? Could employers make unilateral changes short of impasse? (If not, and if different minorities weigh in at different times, the employer might never be able to make changes.) Will government monitor the quality of the employer's good faith in these negotiations?

Finally, the problem of accommodating conflicting bargaining demands from rival minorities within the workforce (possibly balkanized along racial, ethnic, gender or other disquieting lines) would be an additional complication that does not accompany NLRA-mandated bargaining; indeed, perhaps the greatest value of exclusive-representation-bargaining to the employer is that the union is required to mediate the conflicting demands of the employees. What will the law require of an employer presented with mutually inconsistent demands respecting a collective good? Professor Finkin has proposals to deal with the conflicting-demands concern, but I'm not sure that they would truly solve the problem.[102]

Ultimately, the viability of the Finkin proposal depends upon a showing that the benefits (in voice) are worth the considerable cost that would be inflicted on employers. I fear that mandating a bargaining obligation of the NLRA's scope would impose costs of considerable magnitude. It bears recalling that American employers are competing in a global economy, and every cost loaded onto them makes that competition all the more difficult. Moreover, as employers are not infinitely wealthy, Finkin must prove not only that the cost of his proposal is feasible, but also that the benefit (in voice) is more valuable than other benefits that might be achieved by taxing employers in that amount (e.g., the provision of better health care, or other substantive benefits for employees). In making that assessment, we need to ask what value to assign voice if the employees lack any leverage to induce the employer to respond favorably (as the strike weapon is likely to be of little value to a minority group).

For the moment, I deem the case for compelled nonmajority bargaining to be unproved. I would be happy if my fears could be erased.

Still, it would be dangerous to create rights in employees without *any* reciprocal duty on the part of employers. If employers could simply ignore service providers, employees would be discouraged from opting for them. A compromise solution would be to impose an obli-

102. Finkin, *supra* note 12, at 203-09.

gation on employers to meet at a minimum once a month for a specified time (perhaps an hour) with each service provider who represents a specified minimum number and/or percentage of the employer's employees, the obligation to be scaled upward so that as providers represent larger numbers of employees and/or percentages the frequency (or length) of the employer's obligation to meet would grow correspondingly. This obligation-to-meet would not be accompanied by the complexities imposed by the NLRA with respect to majority representatives.[103]

I do not suggest for a moment that this is a satisfactory end point to the government's quest to confer voice on unorganized employees. I hope that Professor Finkin, or others, can perfect vehicles that would do better.

F. Bargaining Leverage: Reformulating Corporate Decision-Making

The NLRA decrees not only that employees have voice (compelling the employer to bargain) but that that voice be made meaningful through the ability to resort to economic force. As the Supreme Court has explained:

> It must be realized that collective bargaining, under a system where the Government does not attempt to control the results of negotiations, cannot be equated with an academic collective search for truth—or even with what might be thought to be the ideal of one. The parties—even granting the modification of views that may come from a realization of economic interdependence—still proceed from contrary and to an extent antagonistic viewpoints and concepts of self-interest. The system has not reached the ideal of the philosophic notion that perfect understanding among people would lead to perfect agreement among them on values. The presence of economic weapons in reserve, and their actual exercise on occasion by the parties, is part and parcel of the system that the Wagner and Taft-Hartley Acts have recognized.[104]

That choice—to license the use of "economic weapons"—is a departure from the common law of contracts, which makes voidable a contract achieved through infliction of economic duress. However meaningful this departure for organized employees (and there is reason to doubt that the strike weapon is any longer of much use to workers in most unionized workplaces), it is plain that the right to strike provides no meaningful leverage to the unorganized employee seeking to negotiate with her employer. If we accept the NLRA's

103. *See supra* notes 64-65, 99-102.
104. NLRB v. Insurance Agents' Int'l Union, 361 U.S. 477, 488-89 (1960).

premise that unionized employees are entitled to statutorily conferred bargaining leverage, it should follow that unorganized employees are as well. But how is such leverage to be delivered to the unorganized employee, who cannot possibly achieve anything by striking while others work?

There are, in truth, two questions to be answered. First, is there any longer a justification for legislative conferral of special leverage upon employees to drive a better deal with their employers? Second, if so, what form might that leverage take in a nonunion workplace?

1. Is Special Leverage for Employees Justified?

If legislatures can decree statutory minima where they think them apt, why should they be allowing employees a leg-up in negotiating for benefits above those minima? This is not meant as a rhetorical question; the answer is not self-evident, and champions of legislative empowerment of employees had better be prepared to answer it. Now that Congress has shown itself ready to decree statutory minima (as it was not in 1935), the investiture of enhanced bargaining power cannot be justified as a means to redistribute income. If not that, what?

The strongest justification for legislative leverage is that the legal deck has been stacked unfairly *against* employees, thus weakening the leverage they might have enjoyed in a world without law and making a compensatory infusion of leverage a kind of righting of the balance. Capital and labor are both needed to make a firm successful. In a world without law it is not predetermined how control of the firm might be divided between the two. But nineteenth-century law defined a corporation as "owned" by those who supplied capital, and remitted those who supplied labor to the status of third-party contractors.[105] In consequence, the law imposed a fiduciary duty on corporate officers and boards of directors to administer the affairs of the

105. The perception of the inevitably separate functions of management and labor has persisted since the Industrial Revolution. Prior to the Industrial Revolution, labor was the central factor of production. Thorstein Veblen provides an apt description of the origin of this dichotomy, indicating that labor evolved from "handicrafts" and "petty industry" toward organized, mechanistic production. *See* THORSTEIN VEBLEN, THE THEORY OF BUSINESS ENTERPRISE 270 (1932).

The advent of modern machine industry transformed the workplace. Previously, the location, pace, means and hours of work had been at the sole discretion of the workers, but now: "All these unskilled men, unused to collective work, had to be taught, trained, and above all disciplined by the manufacturer." PAUL MANTOUX, THE INDUSTRIAL REVOLUTION IN THE EIGHTEENTH CENTURY 375 (1983). *See also* Katherine Van Wezel Stone, *Labor and the Corporate Structure: Changing Conceptions and Emerging Possibilities*, 55 U. CHI. L. REV. 73, 138-47 (1988).

corporation single-mindedly for the benefit of the shareholders. The law thus compelled corporate agents to treat labor adversarily (i.e., to seek those outcomes that maximized the interests of shareholders at the expense of the employees).[106]

There was nothing "natural" about this choice of legal regime. It was adopted by legal institutions that were more responsive to corporate barons than to working people. Perhaps it reflected the relative degrees of attachment to the enterprise that predominated in that era: investors were likely to be closely affiliated with the corporations they owned, while workers tended to be itinerants with little loyalty or longevity with particular firms.

The nineteenth-century ordering of legal relations between shareholders and employees is ripe for reconsideration. Nowadays, it is the employees who devote a lifetime of investment to the business, while shareholders are often absentees who move their money from one firm to another through stock-market exchanges.[107] Indeed, precisely because shareholders are now an absentee class, many believe that in practice control of many corporations has migrated to corporate managers who run affairs largely for their own benefit.[108] Once the reality diverges from the theoretical model, it is fair to ask why managers, any more than nonmanagerial employees, should be the legally preferred beneficiaries.

Oliver Williamson has argued that the law is right in treating the shareholders as the "owners" of the corporation entitled to determine its fate, as they are the group least able to protect their interests through arms-length contracting with the corporation.[109] Williamson's confidence in employees' ability to contract is predicated upon an optimistic view of the efficacy of collective bargaining. Williamson assumes that the employees are covered by a collective bargaining agreement with a grievance-arbitration clause; he assumes, in other

Thus, the capitalist enterprise became the nexus of a social relationship between the owners of the means of production and labor, where labor was subordinate. *See* KARL MARX, CAPITAL I (Vintage ed., 1976).

106. Stone, *supra* note 105, at 145-47.

107. *See* Martin Lipton, *Corporate Governance in the Age of Financial Corporatism,* 136 U. PA. L. REV. 1, 35-36 (1987) (pointing to shareholders' capacity to "exit" by liquidating their investment on short notice). Conversely, employees are described by some theorists as investors in the firm, at least co-equal with shareholders. Workers' stake in the firm is characterized as a long-term investment of human capital. *See, e.g.,* O'Connor, *supra* note 60; Katherine Van Wezel Stone, *Employees as Stakeholders Under State Nonshareholder Constituency Statutes*, 21 STETSON L. REV. 45, 48-53 (1991).

108. Mark J. Rowe, *Some Differences in Corporate Structure in Germany, Japan and the United States,* 102 YALE L.J. 1927 (1993).

109. Oliver Williamson, *Corporate Governance*, 93 YALE L.J. 1197, 1209-12, 1227-30 (1984).

words, that employees are able to bargain effectively and collectively to a contract, and able to include in that contract a mechanism for resolving problems that arise during the life of that contract.[110] Williamson's thesis is inapplicable to the eighty-eight percent of America's employees who are not covered by collective agreements. This point has been demonstrated elegantly by Katherine Van Wezel Stone.[111]

2. Giving Employees Leverage *within* the Corporate Governing Structure

If employees cannot contract effectively to protect their interests, and "economic warfare" is antithetical to the national interest, the wiser path to empowerment may be to consider ways to enhance employee influence *within* the corporate governing structure, rather than from without via third-party contracting with the corporation. To this end, there are a number of possible approaches. The subject is too complex for extended discussion in this paper. Recently, some scholars have turned their attention to it, albeit their voices are unrepresented in this Symposium,[112] and I simply note the options here with brief observations about them.[113]

a. Employee Voice in Selecting Corporate Directors

The law could allocate to employees a voice in selecting the corporation's directors. Under German law, employees are accorded such a voice.[114] Indeed, nominally employees have equal vote with shareholders in voting for directors. The reality, however, is that employee voice is limited: in case of a tie, the shareholders decide.[115] What is more, the "employee" half of the electorate includes the managers, whose interests often will be antithetical to those of the workers covered by the NLRA.

It seems quite unrealistic to think that American law could be transformed to provide employees a large voice in selecting corporate directors—even a voice as ultimately ineffectual as that in Germany—if they are not also to bear a share of the risks associated with those

110. *Id.* at 1207-09, 1227-30.
111. Stone, *supra* note 105, at 152-59.
112. *See, e.g., id.*; Stone, *supra* note 107; O'Connor, *supra* note 60.
113. I am presently working on a paper that will explore these options more extensively.
114. Alfred F. Conrad, *Corporate Constituencies in Western Europe*, 21 STETSON L. REV. 73, 89-92 (1991).
115. *Id.* at 91.

directors' decisions (i.e., the risks to the corporation, as distinguished from the risks to their own job tenure).[116] Thus, voice in governance is more likely to emerge from the last of the proposals I tender below: conferring a share of the *ownership* of corporations upon employees.

b. Employee Representative Membership on Board of Directors

A second approach might be to mandate that the board of directors contain one or more members chosen separately by the employees.[117] Ultimately, however, this is likely to be of limited value—certainly too little to justify declaring victory and stopping the search for meaningful mechanisms for empowering employees. An employee representative on the board can assure that the other directors are aware of employee concerns (and the information pertinent to evaluating those concerns) and would have access to some information that would not otherwise be available to employees.[118] There is real value in this, and it is worth doing, but the reality will remain that the directors and managers will reach decisions that are in the interests of shareholders and managers (perhaps better decisions, because better informed).

c. Fiduciary Duties Toward Corporate Employees

A third approach might be to impose fiduciary obligations upon corporate directors toward corporate employees. A number of states have enacted "constituency" statutes which *allow*, but do not require, corporate officers and boards to consider the interests of constituencies that are tied to the corporation (including employees) in reaching corporate decisions. In other words, these statutes release corporate officials from the fiduciary obligation to prefer the shareholders over the employees.[119] These statutes are important symbolically in their recognition that employees are not strangers to the corporations for whom they work.[120] But these statutes, which are merely permissive,

116. *See generally* LEWIS D. SOLOMON ET AL., CORPORATIONS: LAW AND POLICY MATERIALS AND PROBLEMS ch. 2 (3d ed. forthcoming June 1994) (describing the economics of corporate relations as essentially involving a trade-off between risk and control).

117. *See, e.g.*, Stone, *supra* note 105, at 168-73.

118. Williamson, while arguing for preservation of shareholder control over corporations, recognized the value of allowing minority representation for other groups, simply to cure informational market defects. Williamson, *supra* note 109, at 1205, 1207-09.

119. *See, e.g.*, IND. CODE ANN. § 23-1-35-1(d), (f), (g) (West Supp. 1993); OHIO REV. CODE ANN. § 1701.59(E) (Anderson 1990).

120. The recognition may be more cynical than real: these statutes are widely understood to have been adopted to permit corporate managers to resist takeover efforts and thus prevent the acquisition of the corporation by persons disinterested in maintaining the corporation's presence

leave the decision making in the hands of officers and boards chosen exclusively by the shareholders. Thus, the choice to forego an undeviating preference for shareholders is an act of charity, not compulsion.

One could imagine statutes literally mandating that directors owe fiduciary duties to employees equal in power to those owed shareholders.[121] But given the permissiveness of the "business judgment" rule,[122] these statutes would likely be ineffective so long as directors are chosen by, resemble, and are responsive to, the shareholders. Directors' decisions that favored shareholder (or manager) interests could easily be justified under the business judgment rule.

d. Mandatory Interest Arbitration

Another approach would be to retain the existing contractual relationship, but substitute mandatory interest arbitration as the terminal point for negotiations. This idea has been much written about,[123] and I have no insights to add about its theoretical merits. I share Paul Weiler's assessment that it is outside the domain of political acceptability in this country, because it commits entrepreneurial decision making (at least as to some range of questions) to "neutrals" who are governmentally appointed.[124]

The corporate antipathy to surrendering decision-making control is exemplified by experience under the Steel Industry ENA. During the life of the ENA, negotiations never ended in interest arbitration: the parties settled. At the same time, however, steel industry labor costs rose at a higher rate than auto industry labor costs—and this was so, although auto companies were far more profitable than steel com-

in the local community. *See* ABA Committee on Corporate Law, *Other Constituencies Statutes: Potential for Confusion,* 45 Bus. Law. 2253, 2268 (1990); *cf.* Steven M.H. Wallman, *The Proper Interpretation of Corporate Constituency Statutes and Formulation of Director Duties*, 21 Stetson L. Rev. 163, 183-87 (West 1991).

121. Only Connecticut's statute purports to *oblige* corporate directors to take the interests of other constituencies into account in corporate decision making. Conn. Gen. Stat. Ann. § 33-313(e) (1991). There are no decisions interpreting this statute, and much skepticism that the courts would give it real teeth. *See* ABA Committee on Corporate Law, *supra* note 120, at 2263-68; James J. Hanks, Jr., *Playing With Fire: Nonshareholder Constituency Statutes in the 1990s*, 21 Stetson L. Rev. 97, 109-17 (voicing difficulties in formulating and enforcing new director duties).

122. Kahn v. Sullivan, 594 A.2d 48 (Del. 1991) (Chancery upholding board decision approving a charitable donation of over $50 million to construct an art museum); Dodge v. Ford Motor Co., 170 N.W. 668 (Mich. 1919) (court refusing to enjoin construction of new plant, acknowledging that "judges are not business experts").

123. *See, e.g.,* Morris, *supra* note 3; Weiler, *New Balance, supra* note 16; Robert Ackerman, *Arbitration Forums Revisited,* 43 Nat'l Acad. of Arb. 179 (1990); R.W. Fleming, *Interest Arbitration Revisited*, 26 Nat'l Acad. of Arb 1 (1973); Kleiman, *supra* note 3; Larry, *supra* note 3.

124. Weiler, *New Balance, supra* note 16, at 371-80.

panies.[125] Steel industry negotiators were paying a premium to avoid interest arbitration—a premium higher than auto industry negotiators were prepared to pay to avoid a strike.

If the corporate mentality resists so strongly the surrender of control to a neutral *selected voluntarily by the parties* (recall that the steel industry voluntarily agreed to enter into the ENA, and did so with knowledge of who the interest arbitrators would be—arbitrators that they jointly chose with the union), imagine the vigor with which they would resist legislation to *impose* interest arbitration as the terminal point of negotiation. So long as that corporate mentality can influence legislative decisions, we will not see a conversion to mandatory interest arbitration in the U.S.

e. Optional Alternatives

Another alternative would be to give corporations a choice. Interest arbitration would be the default rule, but corporations could escape it by giving employees sufficient voice in corporate governance. That voice might consist of one of the other versions discussed herein, perhaps made stronger because it is but an alternative.

f. Employees Stock Ownership

The final alternative—and the one that I think has the greatest hope of being both meaningful and politically viable—is to give employees a share of corporate ownership that provides both meaningful voice and meaningful responsibility. Employee stock ownership affords both voting power and an interest in the profitability of the corporation *qua* corporation. A mechanism that assured that employees held significant (not necessarily controlling) ownership of corporate stock would mean that employee interests would be taken into account in corporate decision making, but that employees (both in their wage demands and their stock voting) would have an interest in enlarging the corporate pie rather than simply taking the largest available slice from the existing pie.

Skeptics will note that there is a slight transitional problem with this proposal: who pays to put this stock into the employees' hands? My answer is succinct: "I'm working on it."[126]

125. See figures for steel and auto *supra* note 5, reflecting that in 1970 steel employees' earnings were slightly less than autoworkers', while by the end of the decade steel employees' earnings were substantially higher.

126. *See supra* text accompanying note 113.

3. REFORMING U.S. LABOR RELATIONS

JOEL ROGERS*

I. INTRODUCTION: A FAILED SYSTEM

Labor, management, and neutrals all recognize that the New Deal system of labor relations, codified in the Wagner (1935) and Taft-Hartley (1947) Acts, no longer works for the good of the U.S. economy. While it may have been well-suited to the industrial society of the 1930s-1950s, when it helped deliver enormous growth in real income and productivity, the New Deal system has not adjusted to the "new economic realities" of the 1990s. It currently serves neither unions nor workers nor management effectively.

The New Deal system was designed to allow worker selection of exclusive union bargaining representatives[1] through secret ballot elec-

* Professor of Law, Political Science, and Sociology, University of Wisconsin-Madison. Prepared for the AFL-CIO/Cornell University "Labor Law Reform Conference," Masters, Mates & Pilots Training Center, Linthicum Heights, Maryland, October 24-26, 1993.

In thinking about the subject matter of this essay, I benefit from ongoing collaborations with Joshua Cohen, Daniel Luria, Wade Rathke, Charles Sabel, Wolfgang Streeck, and especially Richard Freeman. *See* JOSHUA COHEN & JOEL ROGERS, BEYOND FACTION: ASSOCIATIONS AND DEMOCRATIC GOVERNANCE (forthcoming 1994) [hereinafter COHEN & ROGERS, BEYOND FACTION]; Joshua Cohen & Joel Rogers, *Associations and Democracy*, 10 SOC. PHIL. & POL'Y 282 (1993) [hereinafter Cohen & Rogers, *Associations and Democracy*]; Joshua Cohen & Joel Rogers, *Secondary Associations and Democratic Governance*, 20 POL. & SOC'Y 393 (1992) [hereinafter Cohen & Rogers, *Secondary Associations*]; Daniel Luria & Joel Rogers, Get Up and Dance! Strategies for High-Wage Metropolitan Economic Development (1993) (unpublished manuscript, on file with author); Wade Rathke & Joel Rogers, Labor Strategies (1993) (unpublished manuscript, on file with author); Joel Rogers & Charles Sabel, *Imagining Unions*, BOSTON REV. Oct.-Nov. 1993, at 10; Joel Rogers & Wolfgang Streeck, *Workplace Representation Overseas: The Works Councils Story, in* WORKING UNDER DIFFERENT RULES (Richard B. Freeman ed., forthcoming 1994); Joel Rogers & Wolfgang Streeck, *Producing Solidarity, in* REINVENTING THE LEFT (David Miliband ed., forthcoming 1994); Richard B. Freeman & Joel Rogers, *Who Speaks for Us? Employee Representation in a Nonunion Labor Market, in* EMPLOYEE REPRESENTATION: ALTERNATIVES AND FUTURE DIRECTIONS 13 (Bruce E. Kaufman & Morris M. Kleiner eds., 1993) [hereinafter Freeman & Rogers, *Who Speaks for Us?*]; Richard B. Freeman & Joel Rogers, Labor Relations: Let's Move Into the 21st Century (1993) (unpublished manuscript, on file with author); Richard B. Freeman & Joel Rogers, What Workplace Representation and Participations Do American Workers Want? (1993) (unpublished manuscript, on file with author) [hereinafter Freeman & Rogers, Workplace Representation]. The following draws freely from this joint work, while holding all co-authors blameless for errors that have survived their care.

1. The entire structure of the Labor Management Relations Act, 29 U.S.C. §§ 141-187 (1947) (Wagner Act and Taft-Hartley Act, as amended), is directed to specifying the rights, obligations, and conditions of emergence and stability of such exclusive representatives. The importance of exclusivity in turn derived from assumptions about the appropriate ambit of negotiated wage and benefit settlements. The LMRA contemplates collective bargaining on a firm rather than industry basis. It also generally does not contemplate use of "extension laws," common in Europe, extending the terms of collective agreements to firms not party to negotiation. Without

tions free of management interference, and to buttress collective bargaining between such representatives and management as a way of dividing the economic pie between labor and capital.[2] At the core of the Wagner Act was the conviction that union representation within firms was not only a moral imperative but an economic and political good. The basic economic idea was that workers, acting collectively, would be able to drive up wages. In a closed economy with unemployed resources, the resulting increase in demand would stimulate private investment and job growth. The basic political idea was that, inside the firm and out, worker organization would help American democracy by providing a "countervailing power" to otherwise overwhelming business domination.

The core ideas of this system—that workers should enjoy associational rights within and without the firm and that collective worker organizations can contribute to the vitality of the American economy—remain perfectly sound today. The problem is that the particular ways in which these ideas were institutionalized in the New Deal system are increasingly inapposite to present circumstance.

The New Deal system effectively premised: a sharp distinction between production workers, who were assumed to be solely concerned with wages and working conditions, and management, who were assumed to have full competence in running the enterprise;[3] an essentially closed economy with little international wage competition; the organization of production along "Fordist" and "Taylorist" lines, in which the dominant model of efficient production was a large firm featuring assembly-line mass production of standardized goods by un-

extension, worker gains from collective bargaining depend on worker strength within particular firms. Exclusivity is the gravamen of such power, and thus the key to stability in collective bargaining. See the discussion below.

2. Such division, of course, is not the only function of collective bargaining, much of which is concerned with nonmaterial benefits (for example, rules on notice and fair treatment); with transfers among workers (for example, "solidarity" bargaining); and with the appropriate form material gains should take (for example, wages versus benefits). Still, determining the worker share of the production surplus is the key function of collective bargaining, and the one which conditions performance of most others.

3. Reflected in the "adversarialism" that has always defined U.S. industrial relations, acceptance of this distinction was a cardinal principle on both sides of the labor-management relation. Consider the heavily circumscribed vision of George Meany, as expressed shortly after he assumed the presidency of the new AFL-CIO:

> Those matters that do not touch a worker directly, a union cannot and will not challenge. These may include investment policy, a decision to make a new product, a desire to erect a new plant so as to be closer to expanding markets, etc. . . . But where management decisions affect a worker directly, a union will intervene.

Charles C. Heckscher, The New Unionism: Employee Involvement in the Changing Corporation 59 (1988).

skilled and semi-skilled labor; and the feasibility of providing a family wage and benefit package through lifetime jobs held by single male breadwinners. Put simply, the world described by these premises no longer exists—workers have other interests, management needs more worker involvement, the economy is more open, production is more flexible and quality-driven, jobs are less stable, the workforce is more diverse—and the system based on them works poorly in the world that does exist.

The costs of this institutional mismatch are visited on everyone.[4] Unions—the only form of independent collective worker organization contemplated in the system—are effectively denied their right to organize, and escalating employer opposition[5] is rapidly "disappearing" them as a presence in national public life.[6] Individual managements, while generally welcoming the decline of unions, are denied the ability to support advanced forms of worker participation in the nonunion sector.[7] Workers are denied voice, choice among representative

4. Of course, they are not visited equally. As indicated in a moment in the text, unions are, for example, threatened with extinction, while employers are only constrained in their strategies of nonunion worker "empowerment."

5. Increased employer resistance is reflected in the sharp increase in employer unfair labor practice charges issued by the NLRB since the early 1970s. The reasons for increased resistance are many, but two bear special note. First, internationalization and the union decline itself put wages and benefits once "taken out of competition" forcefully back in. This provides clear economic incentives for firms to resist unionization. Second, increased product market instability has put a premium on flexibility in workplaces and corporate structure. While the experience of other countries (and selective cooperative programs in the United States) indicates that such flexibility can be achieved under unionization, most managers strongly prefer unilaterally imposed to negotiated flexibility.

6. The United States now approximates the "union free" environment favored by professional anti-unionists. Private sector union density now stands just above 11 percent, and on a continuation of current trends should fall to about 5 percent by the end of the decade. Of course, history has not always been kind to predictions of continued union decline. In 1932, the president of the American Economic Association spoke confidently of the "lessening importance of trade unionism in American economic organization" as one of the "fundamental alterations" of American society. George E. Barnett, *American Trade Unionism and Social Insurance*, 23 Am. Econ. Rev. 1 (1933). Without some radical changes in the conditions and strategies of union organizing, however, it seems most unlikely that the coming years will see anything like the burst in union power that made these remarks ridiculous.

7. Section 8(a)(2) of the Labor Management Relations Act makes it unlawful for an employer to "dominate or interfere with the formation or administration of any labor organization or contribute financial or other support to it." 29 U.S.C. § 158(a)(2) (1947). Deliberately, "labor organization" is elsewhere defined broadly to include not only labor unions but "any organization of any kind or any agency or employee representation committee or plan" that features (a) employee participation, (b) the representation of some employees by others, in (c) dealings with the employer regarding (d) one or more of six traditional subjects of collective bargaining: grievances, labor disputes, wages, rates of pay, hours of employment, or conditions of work. 29 U.S.C. § 152(5) (1947). For at least some nonunion employers, this imposes a restraint on desired innovations in worker participation and "empowerment" in workplace governance. For example, an employer that set out the purposes and powers of a committee making decisions about the terms and conditions of employment (for example, on health and safety, or the use of

forms, and protection from economic insecurity. The nation as a whole suffers the "denials" of lost productivity growth, rising inequality, a failure to block the "low road" response to rising international competition, ineffective enforcement of labor standards, and, less tangible but no less real, the erosion of democratic norms.[8]

For all the good reasons so many people have to be unhappy with the present system, however, the path of reform is less than clear. At present, there is no consensus on the elements of reform, nor even a sense of how consensus might be organized. Organized business and organized labor remain bitterly divided over their vision of the role of worker organization in the new economy.[9] However unfairly, both

a new technology) and subsidized that committee, or appointed some its managers to it—even if it permitted workers free choice in selecting their representatives to it—would likely be in violation of 8(a)(2).

8. While few would blame our obsolete labor relations framework and the denial of collective voice to workers for all the country's economic ills, there is growing consensus that they contribute to a host of problems and at this point pose a real barrier to economic renewal. Union decline accounts for about a fifth of the recent rise in American earnings inequality, RICHARD FREEMAN, ON THE DIVERGENCE IN UNIONISM AMONG DEVELOPED COUNTRIES (National Bureau Economic Research Working Paper No. 2817, 1989); DAVID CARD, THE EFFECT OF UNIONS ON THE DISTRIBUTION OF WAGES: REDISTRIBUTION OR RELABELLING? (National Bureau of Economic Research Working Paper No. 4195, 1992), an extreme outlier in comparative terms. Richard B. Freeman & Lawrence S. Katz, *Rising Wage Inequality: The United States vs. Other Advanced Countries, in* WORKING UNDER DIFFERENT RULES (Richard B. Freeman ed., forthcoming 1994). Union decline contributes to declining company provision of private social welfare benefits, such as pensions and health care, Joel Rogers, *Divide and Conquer: Further 'Reflections on the Distinctive Character of American Labor Laws,'* 1990 WIS. L. REV. 1; David Bloom & Richard Freeman, *The Fall in Private Pension Coverage in the United States*, 82 AM. ECON. REV. 539 (1992), and it encourages federal regulations or court rulings to resolve labor problems and protect workers that are not as flexible or effective as labor-management negotiation at specific workplaces. ROBERT J. FLANAGAN, LABOR RELATIONS AND THE LITIGATION EXPLOSION (1987); PAUL C. WEILER, GOVERNING THE WORKPLACE: THE FUTURE OF LABOR AND EMPLOYMENT LAW (1990). The more general lack of voice representation mechanisms in the present system depresses the productivity gains that would come of substantive worker involvement in enterprise management and job design, PAYING FOR PRODUCTIVITY: A LOOK AT THE EVIDENCE (Alan S. Blinder ed., 1990); UNIONS AND ECONOMIC COMPETITIVENESS (Lawrence Mishel & Paula B. Voos eds., 1992), and contributes to a "hire and fire" culture that discourages investments in human capital. MASAHIKO AOKI, INFORMATION, INCENTIVES, AND BARGAINING IN THE JAPANESE ECONOMY (1988); ROBERT E. COLE, STRATEGIES FOR LEARNING: SMALL GROUP ACTIVITIES IN AMERICAN, JAPANESE, AND SWEDISH INDUSTRY (1989); THOMAS A. KOCHAN & PAUL OSTERMAN, HUMAN RESOURCE DEVELOPMENT AND UTILIZATION: IS THERE TOO LITTLE IN THE U.S.? (Sloan School of Management, MIT Working Paper, Feb. 1991); OFF. TECH. ASSESSMENT, U.S. CONGRESS, OTA ITE-457, WORKER TRAINING: COMPETING IN THE INTERNATIONAL ECONOMY (Washington, D.C., Gov't Printing Off., 1990). On the relation between democratic performance and the level of independent collective worker organization, see Cohen & Rogers, *Secondary Associations, supra* note *; Cohen & Rogers, *Associations and Democracy supra*, note *; Freeman & Rogers, *Who Speaks for Us?, supra* note *; Rogers & Sable, *supra* note *; ROBERT D. PUTNAM, MAKING DEMOCRACY WORK: CIVIC TRADITION IN MODERN ITALY (1993).

9. Just how bitterly divided is not, I think, sufficiently appreciated. To take one recent instance: the National Association of Manufacturers and Chamber of Commerce announced opposition to the confirmation of William Gould as chair of the National Labor Relations Board, apparently for no more reason than Gould's view that unions are, on balance, a good thing to

are also generally regarded as self-serving in their proposals for reform. At the same time, each retains the power to block the other's favored agenda, and neither favors wholesale transformation of the present system of the sort that now seems needed.[10] Not surprising, given this background, the present administration is deeply ambivalent on the topic. And among the general public, whose views on the subject are barely known,[11] labor law reform is simply not an issue of great salience. In brief, labor law reform lacks a public constituency and an articulate and credible agent.

Still, the ascent of a Democratic administration, and its appointment of a Commission on the Future of Worker/Management Relations (the "Dunlop Commission")[12] has at least formally put labor law reform on the national agenda. And diffuse but accumulating dissatisfaction with the consequences of the present system create a potential general constituency for such an effort. The questions arise: "Given changed circumstances, what appear to be the general requirements of reform?" and, critically, "How might their satisfaction be organized—or, amounting to the same thing, how might reform come to be seen as in the *general* interest of American society?"

Neither question can be answered without a closer appreciation of the structure and effective collapse of the New Deal system itself. This is so not only because the institutional legacy of the New Deal system provides the natural starting point for current reform efforts. More importantly, it is because the New Deal system was not only a random experiment in democracy, but a particular social answer, offered under specific conditions, to the more general question of how improvements in democracy could be reconciled to the requirements of a productive capitalism. If "labor law reform" is to become something more than an endgame between a declining labor movement and a business community united only in its opposition to unions—if it

have around. Gould is an utterly mainstream, accomplished, "establishment" labor law professor, and an African American. Twenty years ago this appointment would have been greeted with a happy yawn—as a completely reasonable decision also evidencing progress in civil rights. Discussion today is far more exacting, and nasty, than then.

10. Albeit their reasons differ. Labor resists because its position is already so tenuous that it fears substantial change. Business resists because it can already get much of what it wants outside existing legal constraints.

11. Determining such is the major goal of the effort outlined in Freeman & Rogers, Workplace Representation, *supra* note *.

12. The Commission was so named because of its chair, former Secretary of Labor John Dunlop. The Commission is charged with investigating the current state of labor-management relations and law in the United States and recommending any changes it sees fit to improve productivity through increased worker-management cooperation and employee participation in the workplace.

is to be something of truly general interest—it is *that* reconciliation that must again be found. Seeing how it was found in the past and why the terms of its achievement were undone provides clues to the present requirements of reform.

In what follows, then, I first offer an analysis of the New Deal system and its decline. Based on that analysis, and certain "first principles" of what is sought from a labor relations system, I then address the question of present reform requirements. Finally, and more speculatively, I offer some remarks on how a constituency for reform might be organized. For concreteness, these remarks focus on what is needed from one of reform's natural beneficiaries and most likely leaders—organized labor itself.

II. The New Deal System and Its Decline

A problem arises immediately. Taking the universe of rich capitalist democracies as our field of comparison,[13] current problems in U.S. labor relations are distinctive—in many ways, indeed, increasingly so. But they are not unique.

On the one hand, the United States now has the lowest effective rate of unionization in the developed world. And now, as ever, it lacks those other institutions—worker-based political parties, mandated "works councils" or other forms of worker representation inside the firm, or general wage regulation—that elsewhere supplement or substitute for union power. By almost any measure, we are more "union free" and "worker unfriendly" than any other rich nation. And by almost any measure, it shows—in the lowest level of general social protections and highest level of wage inequality, after-tax poverty, and working class electoral abstention in the developed world.[14]

In comparative terms, U.S. labor relations have long offered an extreme instance of "low-density, decentralized unionism" (LDDU) and the union and employer strategies characteristically associated with it. For unions, this means strategies of gain not centered on society-wide political regulation of the labor market or the establishment of a high "social wage,"[15] but instead on decentralized bargaining over

13. As a practical matter, this is equivalent to taking member nations of the Organization for Economic Cooperation and Development.

14. The term "working class" is not fashionable these days, for good reasons and bad. By "working class," I mean simply, and only, the 80% of the workforce characterized as "production and nonsupervisory" workers. These are people who have to work for a living and do so under the direction of somebody else.

15. A "social wage" is a baseline packet of benefits and income guarantees provided irrespective of current job position or, in the most adventurous form, employment status.

individual firm surpluses and "job control" adversarialism in the internal labor market. Among employers, it means strategies to roll back or contain unionism at all cost. The basic reason for employer hostility is not union strength, but weakness. Given their failure to impose society-wide constraints on wages, benefits, or other terms and conditions of employment, unions in LDDU systems appear to individual employers as irritatingly distinctive burdens on their profit-taking and flexibility in organizing production inside the firm.

Traditionally, and in some measure still today, the dynamics of such LDDU systems could be contrasted with systems of "high-density, centralized unionism" (HDCU). The latter traditionally featured more "peak level" sectoral or national collective bargains and more extensive generic political regulation of the labor market. Within HDCU systems, given success in imposing society-wide terms on employers, organized labor appeared to individual employers less as a distinctive burden than a standard cost of doing business. And, secure in their social position, unions were more willing to make sure that business was done. With more power they could afford to be less adversarial. With greater protection on the external labor market, for example, they could afford to be less concerned with internal labor market rigidity. In such systems, labor and management appeared, in stark contrast to the United States, as genuine "social partners"—intent on improving economic performance within certain social bounds on the terms of economic governance and appropriate division of the social pie.

On the other hand, this contrast is less robust today. The reason is obviously not that organized labor in the United States has gotten stronger or more coordinated, but that labor elsewhere has gotten less. Virtually all rich nations show a decline in union density since 1980. Within more traditionally centralized systems, fissures have appeared within unions and union federations as employers (joined by many workers) insist on more decentralized decisions about firm organization and compensation. In consequence, once robust structures of peak bargaining have widely collapsed. And while "social wage" and other generic labor regulation remain infinitely more exacting than in the United States, many of these labor-friendly "external rigidities" are also being qualified. Labor's stature within social democratic parties has also been curtailed, and the fortunes of those parties have themselves declined.

In taking measure of the decline of the New Deal system in the United States, our distinctive experience needs to be located within this comparative frame. Things have clearly come unstuck here, but to some degree they have come unstuck elsewhere as well. To be confident in what they are about, labor law reformers in the United States need to be attentive to these deeper and more pervasive sources of derangement. And so, with due notice to be given to the peculiarities of the U.S. case, we ask: "Why is the New Deal order not working as well as it once did, *everywhere*?"

With equivalent clarity and results, the answer can be provided from different perspectives. Here, given the focus of later remarks on labor's possible role in organizing a constituency for reform, I answer from the perspective of unions.

A. *Core Elements of the Old System*[16]

In the old deal of the New Deal and the postwar era, unions functioned as the redistributive agent of the working class. They operated in essentially closed national economies where the state relied on fiscal and monetary policy to regulate the macro-economy. They demanded and got wage and benefit increases for their members—partially extracted from firms directly, partly extracted through the state. And, through the alchemy of Keynesian economics, they brought benefits to the broader society. By delivering solid and rising wage floors to their members, they boosted aggregate demand. This gave firms markets for sales, and reasons to renew investment. And that, in turn, increased productivity and lowered the costs of mass consumption goods, which was good for everyone.

Notice what happened here. Labor did something for its members or potential members of obvious usefulness—increased compensation. It solved a problem for capital that capital could not solve for itself. It created effective mass demand, which assured the existence of mass markets for goods, which increased firm productivity via the increased investment and production scale that followed. And by doing both things—by solving a problem for workers that also enhanced the productivity of capital in ways beyond those that capital itself could achieve—labor appeared as an agent of the general interest. It gained the organizational resources and social cachet that gave it political clout on other matters. The achievement was not ready-made, however. It was a fight, success in which required that unions organize both labor and capital.

16. This section draws from Rogers & Sabel, *supra* note *.

But the organization of labor was facilitated by the fact that "the working class" was a more or less determinate social group whose shared interests were spotlighted by the institutions of mass production. In a vast assembly-line factory churning out cars or refrigerators, with each worker doing a numbingly simple task, and with superordinate layers of oppressive management, it wasn't too hard to figure out which side you were on.

And the organization of capital was facilitated by the same production system. This was the age of "monopoly capitalism" in a more or less literal sense. In many of the most important industries, a few producers with vast identifiable production complexes were the key to market power. Organize them—you could organize them—and you had most of the industry. Deals struck with lead firms could be extended through most of the industry, and the deals could be good. Large firms could "afford" wage increases in a way that low-cost rivals could not. And as industry leaders, they had every incentive to cooperate with unions in removing such rivals by making sure that all firms paid the same costs.

Inside the firm, finally, unions struck a deal with management. In return for labor peace they would get pay increases proportionate to productivity advance and shared control over the movement of workers within the internal labor market of firm employees. In return for this, management kept the "right to manage"—to make essential decisions about firm structure, product strategy, production design, and the level of employment.

B. Peculiarities of the U.S. Case

Of course, as already noted in the contrast of LDDU and HDCU systems, there was enormous variation across union movements in the precise structure of this deal. In most countries, particularly continental European ones, generalization of the wage and benefit deal struck between labor and management was facilitated by the legalized "extension" of collective agreement to nonunionized firms and a generous social wage. In the United States, by contrast, generalization was achieved, if at all, only by brute economic strength—unionization or its threat. Accordingly, much importance was assigned the precise terms under which collective bargaining rights would attach within individual firms and what the conditions of maintaining the fruits of organizing success within firms required. The arcana of American law regarding the formal certification of bargaining representatives and the requirement that those representatives be exclusive were solutions to the problem of contested, decentralized unionization and wage bargaining. Without a general presumption of unionization, or its equivalent in wage and benefit guarantees, employer assumption of these costs was justified only upon a showing of majority support. Without generalizing support from the state, the welfare of individual workers depended unusually on their bargaining power vis-à-vis specific individual employers. In relation to those employers, exclusivity in representation—a guarantee of a single collective voice—was the gravamen of worker power.

In addition to thus establishing effective minima on material benefits in their nonunion sectors, most countries also established minima on employee "voice" and consultation in firm decision making through mandated works councils.[17] Generalization of this "second channel" of industrial relations was facilitated by the "first channel" of encompassing collective bargaining, itself led on the side of workers by supra-firm union organizations. In effect, the latter created a deficit of effective intra-firm worker organization and the political wherewithal to insist on some general measure of "economic democracy." In the U.S. case, by contrast, the "first channel" was never developed. Lacking a social mandate, moreover, worker representation in the nonunion sector depended by definition on the will of employers. Given the disastrous experience with employer-dominated "company unions" in the 1920s, however, the expression of this will in the form of material support or assistance to representative nonunion labor organizations was itself barred.[18]

As a consequence of both these distinctive features, collective worker representation in the U.S. private sector came to center more and more narrowly on an "all or nothing" choice between exclusive majority unions and, indeed, nothing. The employer's duty to bargain

17. The variety of forms of these works councils and their evolution across different European systems is explored in WORKS COUNCILS: CONSULTATION, REPRESENTATION, COOPERATION (Joel Rogers & Wolfgang Streeck eds., forthcoming 1994).

18. For the rationale for such a bar—employer interference with autonomous employee choices about representation—we do no better than to consider the first case decided by the National Labor Relations Board, Pennsylvania Greyhound Lines, 1 N.L.R.B. 1 (1935), *enforced in part and denied in part*, 91 F.2d 178 (3d Cir. 1937), *rev'd*, 303 U.S. 261 (1938), *cited in* Electromation, Inc., 309 N.L.R.B. 990, 994 (1992). As the Greyhound manager in charge of the company union challenged there summarized management's goals:

> [I]t is to our interest to pick our employees to serve on the committee who will work for the interest of the company and will not be radical. This plan of representation should work out very well providing the proper men are selected, and considerable thought should be given to the men placed on this responsible Committee.

Electromation, Inc., 309 N.L.R.B. at 994.

with collective organizations of workers came gradually to be understood as an obligation attaching only to majority unions; union organizing came even more quickly to accept majority status per se as its goal, rather than simply increasing the membership and effectiveness of worker organizations inside firms; failure to achieve such usually resulted in abandonment of the field. Employers rested content with resisting unions and, in the context of that resistance, invoked the "company union" ban as a bar to effective nonunion forms of collective representation.

Within the unionized firm, moreover, the scope and function of collective worker power in the United States was even more sharply circumscribed than elsewhere. The scope of "mandatory" topics of collective bargaining was drawn narrowly to exclude worker involvement in firm management. Information and consultation rights, nonexistent in the expanding nonunion sector, were limited to the terms of negotiated contracts within this circumscribed frame. Lacking statutory supplements on intra-firm power, lacking guarantees even of information about what the firm was doing, and barred from using economic force to invade the "core of entrepreneurial control," unions in the United States, more than elsewhere, concentrated on the division of the firm surplus much more than its production.

C. Core Elements of Decline[19]

These peculiarities of the U.S. case aside, most rich capitalist countries featured the three essential elements of the New Deal system—a Keynesian, "demand-based" national policy framework, "ready made" blocks of workers able to cut and enforce deals, and large, dominant, stable firms through which the deals could be cut. What explains the general decline of unions, however, is that over the past twenty years each part of this system has fallen apart.

Keynesianism is qualified. A combination of market saturation and the entrance of new competitors into the saturated markets undercut the autonomy of national economies, uprooting the foundations of Keynesian policy. By the early 1970s most people in the advanced economies who could afford cars, radios, or washing machines had them, so the growth rates of national manufacturers in those industries slowed. At the same time firms in newly industrializing countries like South Korea or Mexico got better at producing the less sophisticated goods demanded in the advanced countries, while

19. This section also draws from Rogers & Sabel, *supra note* *.

Japan got better at producing the more sophisticated ones. With new producers crowding into already overcrowded markets in the United States and Western Europe, domestic firms were driven to look for new export outlets. But once firms began looking for export markets, it became difficult to regulate the growth of any economy by stimulating consumer demand. If the French government, for example, tried to accelerate growth in France by putting more money in consumers' pockets, nothing prevented German or Italian firms from beating the French firms to the market. Even the fear of such cross-border raids was enough to dampen the stimulative effect of Keynesian stimulation. Firms were unlikely to expand capacity to meet the new demand if they had to worry that a foreign competitor could capture the market before their new facilities were ready.

Firms reacted to these pressures in two sharply contrasting ways, both of which had the long-term effect of undermining their self-sufficiency and thereby killing the stable firms that comprised another core element of the old system. One response—especially common in the United States—was to meet the competition by cutting costs, primarily wage costs. To achieve these cuts, large firms were broken up into separate profit and cost centers, thus achieving the "transparency" needed for strategic planning. Labor-intensive, low-skill operations were then transferred abroad to low-wage countries in the developing world, while the remaining domestic workers were told that their jobs would be next if they (and their unions, where they had them) did not make concessions on wages and benefits. This "sweating strategy" obviously drains work from rich countries to poor, depresses living standards at home, and wrecks lots of communities along the way. U.S. firms were naturally drawn to such a strategy in the 1980s because union weakness kept it available, and because the semi-skilled workforce relied on for generations of "assembly line" mass production provided a weak basis for more advanced and versatile production strategies.

Another response—more common in Western Europe—was to compete on quality and product differentiation rather than price. The basic idea was to allow skilled workers operating sophisticated, flexible machines to customize products to customers' needs. Although goods made this way cost more than mass-produced items, buyers will pay a premium to get what they want that more than covers the difference. This "high-wage, high-skill" strategy is obviously better for domestic workers and community stability. Western European firms were naturally drawn to it in the 1980s because stronger unions blocked "sweating," and ample reserves of skilled workers made upgrading possible.

Today, however, the lineup between countries and strategies is much less clear. Both U.S. and European firms discovered hidden costs to their strategies. Now they borrow from the other's model.

The news from the United States is that many firms have figured out that sweating is a losing strategy. There is always a lower-wage competitor ready to pounce on the low-wage subsidiary just established, and the divisions in firm operations occasioned by the search for cheap labor—between planning and production, between conception and execution—make it harder to avoid and learn from manufacturing mistakes. At least some firms (still a distinct minority) are seeking radical quality improvement and product customization and differentiation, and are placing a corresponding emphasis on the skill and shopfloor responsibility needed to get better integration of product design and execution. While others (still a distinct majority) continue with their sweating strategy, what they once did with conviction they now do with hesitation.

The news from Europe is that skill is not enough to stay abreast of the market. Firms get stuck in specialty niches. The craft hierarchies established inside firms—in which those with more skill are supposed to solve the problems that the less skilled cannot—thwart the needed flow of authority to the shopfloor. And long-term relations between the component-making and assembly divisions of the same firm degenerate into cronyism as the company's traditions of technical flare become a pretext for not worrying about costs. Inspired in part by U.S.-style administrative decentralization, the response all across Europe has been to break large concerns into autonomous profit or cost centers with the power to restructure their own operations and then sink or swim. Typical is Volkswagen's hire of the Spanish head of General Motor's purchasing operations, with the aims of reorganizing its relations to its external suppliers and building effective shopfloor teams in its own plants.

In both the United States and Western Europe, the upshot of all this firm-level reorganization is to undercut the integrity of workers as a group with distinct and compact interests—killing off the third element of the old system. There are fewer places for unskilled or semiskilled workers in manufacturing, and even where such places exist there are fewer career ladders connecting them to skilled work in the same plants. Thus, just as unions' core constituency is squeezed out of the well-paying manufacturing jobs, it becomes more difficult to advance the interests of their (less skilled) remaining members. Moreover, managers are increasingly vulnerable to job loss. Middle managers in large corporations disappear when the profit centers they once supervised are given the authority to make their own way; senior managers get the ax if their profit centers do not make it. Often it seems as though these groups have more in common with the skilled workers than the latter do with their less-skilled colleagues.

With their role in national macro-economic management limited by the decline of Keynesianism, with their role as the administrator of labor markets in large firms and well-defined industries limited by the massive decentralization of corporations, and with their core constituencies divided and disoriented, it is hardly surprising that even the strongest unions are on the defensive, and the weakest ones, as in the United States, are facing a rout.

III. The Requirements of Reform

Given this general experience, and the place of the United States within it, what lessons are to be drawn about labor law reform?

One lesson commonly drawn is that, especially as the more worker-friendly labor relations systems of other countries come under pressure, the United States itself should not engage in substantial amendment of its own. On this reading of the evidence, forces are abroad in the world that effectively moot the original purposes of New Deal system—in particular, again, its commitment to reconciling associative rights for workers and resulting limits on inequality with productive capitalism. This mooting may be welcomed—by those who believe that a core value of "liberty" requires that all collective organization be minimized, or that inequality is a necessary spur to the effort on which all social wealth depends. Or it might be regretted—as a tragically "realistic" response to a world in which effective social control over the economy and its organization is no longer possible. Those who argue that the internationalization of capital and product markets is effectively complete, or who slide from that proposition to the claim that the combination of essentially mobile factors of production are all that wealth-generation is about, may fall into either camp.

Again, however, I take the problem to be one of institutional mismatch, not weakness in the core ideas. Other things equal, the free exercise of associative rights is a good thing, for workers as well as others.[20] Gross inequalities are a bad thing, and not helpful to economic performance.[21] Moreover, current economic integration does not preclude some political management of the terms of economic cooperation.[22] So consideration of more suitable institutional means of achieving the good and avoiding the bad, in ways again consistent with a productive capitalism, is not idle. Institutional arrangements that no longer facilitate the achievement of core purposes simply need to be changed in ways that do—in light of the changes in the organization of production just described.

What this means, in very broad terms, is that the forms of worker organization need to be amended in ways responsive to the greater diversity of employee interest and potentially more autonomous role of workers in governing the productive enterprises. The mechanisms of wage and benefit regulation need to be changed in ways responsive to decentralization and casualization in labor markets to permit restructuring without diminution in the quality of life and to get some lower bound on income and welfare. And, throughout, labor relations needs to be seen through a productivist supply-side optic as much as a demand-side one. For democracy again to appear in the general interest, under capitalism, the alchemy of particular-to-general interest will this time likely arise more from labor's contribution to "effective supply"—of skilled labor, technology diffusion, comparability across establishments in ways that promote flexibility, linkages of firms in ways

20. The basic criterion of the moral judgment expressed here is respect for the moral equality of persons. For elaboration, see COHEN & ROGERS, *supra* note *.

21. Among others, see TORSTEN PERSSON & GUIDO TABELLIN, IS INEQUALITY HARMFUL TO GROWTH? (National Bureau of Economic Research Working Paper No. 3599, 1991), and the review and findings in Lane Kenworthy, Equality and Efficiency: The Illusory Tradeoff (1993) (unpublished manuscript, on file with author).

22. This issue deserves more attention than can be given it here. Briefly, however, those who argue that capital and product markets are now completely integrated mistake stylized facts for reality. National savings and investment rates still correlate closely—belying the first claim; for the vast majority of U.S. firms, including manufacturers, buying and selling is still overwhelmingly domestic—belying, at least in the U.S. case, the second. The fact that economic activity is more and more taken up with untraded services qualifies it further. Even if they were completely integrated, however, the picture of production as consisting only in the rearrangement of the classic factors of land, labor, capital, and technology is incomplete. In the real world, transactions costs and externalities, bearing on the costs of factors and the efficiency of their combination, are heavily mediated by the institutional infrastructure of the economy. Even if factors themselves slop across borders, these institutional arrangements do not. This describes the possibility that politics may in fact shape the direction of the economy. In the U.S. case—given the enormous size of our domestic economy (at nearly $6 trillion, nearly twice the size of the annual $3.5 trillion volume of world trade); relatively low rates of import penetration and export reliance (their additive share has been stable, at about 23%, for years), and the dimensions of publicly controlled investment (aggregate government spending, at all levels, is approximately $2 trillion)—it is very hard to believe the public has no capacity to set the terms under which economic production and exchange will occur or to influence directly that which does.

that promote general economic upgrading, private multipliers, and supplements to state regulatory efforts—as much if not more than its contribution to effective demand.

Many, perhaps most, of the ways this might be done have already been suggested in present reform debates. In this section, I consolidate some of these suggestions along the lines of the core values and concerns that are presently at stake—free association, equality, democratic productivism—while noting that the specific form reform takes should be influenced by a party not yet heard from with any clarity—the general population. The discussion is deliberately general. I argue from basic principles with some notice of the context in which they now need to be enacted. In the next section, with greater explicitness, I use the example of the labor movement to suggest how the suggestions might be knit together, and advanced, through a labor-led strategy of reform.

A. *Free Association*

Assuming, again, that *ceteris paribus* free association is a good thing for diverse workers as well as others, and recognizing various imperfections in the "market" of associational choice bearing on representation of worker interests, efforts here should be directed to perfecting that market. This means widening the range of employees permitted collective representation, reducing the direct cost of their choosing such, and widening the range of choice itself.

Widening the range of protected employees would mean abolishing most, if not all, restrictions on the free choice of farm workers, individual contractors, and supervisors, as well as those public employees in that half of the United States that have still not recognized even minimal rights to self-organization.

Reducing the direct costs to employees in choosing representation would mean institutionalizing respect for individual freedom in choice and collective worker deliberation about how it might best be made. At present, as regards the only available form of collective representation—unions—this condition is clearly not satisfied. Whatever one's opinion of unions, current levels and kinds of employer resistance to them clearly impose direct costs on employees and corrupt the process of deliberation.[23] Getting closer to free deliberation would

23. Apart from repeated documentation of employer violations of the spirit and letter of the LMRA and the close correlation between such resistance and union failure in representation elections, perhaps the best evidence for the importance of management resistance on current

thus appear to require more effective sanctions on such employer behavior, quickly applied.[24] Moreover, while informed consideration of the merits of alternatives is desirable and takes time, some significant expediting and simplification of the current election process in ways respectful of free employee choice—in the form of a return to "card check" certification or very rapid elections—seems desirable. In labor relations, as in democracy generally, the law is simplified and strengthened by a presumption that those in whose name power is exercised have the capacity to exercise that power themselves. Choosing collective representation is a choice for workers, not managers, to make. Finally, choices for collective representation in bargaining are meaningless if immediately frustrated by effective refusals to bargain. At present in the United States, only about one half of the units won by unions in representation elections before the NLRB ever make it to first contract. If employees want a union to negotiate for them, they should be assured the fruits of genuine negotiation. If the union and employer reach impasse, a neutral third party arbitrator should be empowered to force agreement.

Application of the same principle of free employee choice, however, would mandate expansion of the range of representative forms—a move that seems recommended in any case by the diversity of the employee population. There is no good reason to reify majority unionism as the only possible form of independent worker association. If a group of individual workers short of a majority in a relevant unit wish to concert, to join a union, to present grievances to employers, or otherwise to act to advance their interests in the employment relation, there is no compelling reason why they should not be permitted to do so—absent the prior and continuing existence of a majority union.[25] Neither—assuming conditions of employee free choice are institution-

employee choices is provided by the public sector. Controlling for age, income, race, sex, occupation, and all other conceivable individual and group variables, unionization in the public sector—essentially free of management resistance—runs better than three times as high as in the private sector.

24. Sanctions might include such things as outright fines and treble compensatory damages for actual violations of the law, or disqualification from government contract eligibility for repeat offenders. Speed might be achieved by a requirement of hearings and determination of the merit of employer unfair labor practices within 30 days of filing.

25. On their face, §§ 9(a) and 8(a)(5) provide no suggestion that employers are *not* obligated to bargain with such "minority unions." Contrary NLRB and court interpretations have stood so long, however, that statutory amendment would now probably be required to establish this obligation. Apart from administrative difficulties in handling the claims of multiple such unions (themselves navigable through threshold representation requirements and rules on their interaction), there seems no reason why it should not be—again, in the absence of an elected majority representative. *See* Clyde Summers, *Unions Without Majority: A Black Hole?*, 66 Chi.-Kent L. Rev. 531 (1990).

ally respected—is there compelling reason why representative committees or "employee caucuses" enjoying the support of management should not also be permitted.[26]

B. Equality

American labor markets, where the wages of most workers have been falling for years, are now marked by punishingly high degrees of inequality in wages and benefit compensation. For those at the bottom of our increasingly dispersed wage structure, the results are clearly horrible, and in comparative terms, increasingly anomalous. (In real purchasing power parity terms, for example, the wages of the bottom decile of American workers are now only one half those of their counterparts in Europe.)[27] Within the union sector and without, moreover, inequality is exacerbated by the fact that compensation is heavily determined by firm or industry specific rents. Even as they share in the division of such rents, however, conflicts between particular labor organizations and particular managements over benefits—even basic benefits of generally recognized social importance, such as health care—often preclude their constructive cooperation. Finally, in an age of increasingly casualized employment, the firm-based character of the American benefit system—with health care, vacation time, pensions, and more determined on a firm-specific basis, and receipt of

26. What such "institutional" respect for free choice might look like is suggested by Alan Hyde's proposal for an "employee free choice" defense to a § 8(a)(2) complaint. Leaving the section intact, and assuming a return to the early breadth of that denoted by "labor organization":

> An employer who would otherwise violate that section by establishing or supporting a system of employee representation or communication may defend against unfair labor practice charges by showing: (a) that the system was authorized by a majority of employees in a secret ballot; (b) that before the ballot, employees were specifically advised of their right to oppose the creation of such a plan without reprisal; (c) that such authorization expires in some uniform period of time, perhaps three years, unless reauthorized.

Alan Hyde, *Employee Caucus: A Key Institution in the Emerging System of Employment Law*, 69 CHI.-KENT L. REV. 149, 188 (1993). To these provisions we might add:

> (d) that the system may be abolished by a majority of employees in a secret ballot at any time; and (e) that the system cannot at any time be unilaterally abolished by the employer.

Were such conditions satisfied, employer "domination" in the current sense of the law—that which § 8(a)(2) *quite rightly* seeks to prevent, would be effectively extinguished. It would thus be possible to define current controversy over nonunion forms of worker representation not in terms of a choice between "unions or nothing" but between "independent (not employer-dominated) forms or nothing." How many employers would, under such clarification, actually seek nonunion independent worker representation is, of course, an open question. How many workers, assuming enactment of the other reforms suggested here, would choose this over rival representative forms is as well. The real values at stake, however, would be clarified in a way that they are not in the present debate.

27. This fact comes from Richard Freeman.

those benefits conditioned on continuance in that firm—further threatens equality in provision.

These familiar facts suggest that the basic structure of employment compensation in the United States—long defined by highly decentralized wage and benefit determination and a very low "social wage" of generic minima—is in need of reform. Equality concerns and, increasingly, efficiency concerns recommend a move toward more encompassing wage setting and higher guaranteed social minima.[28]

Raising social minima is in principle simple enough. Whether administered through firms or not, certain basic benefits would be guaranteed on a society-wide basis, much as is currently being promised for health care. The efficiency benefits of doing this are many. As against other means, minima are an efficient way to redistribute income, especially when receipt is conditioned on employment.[29] By raising the base price of labor, minima can also be an important spur to more productive labor use, setting dynamic efficiencies in motion. And, by generalizing certain standards of behavior and performance, minima facilitate flexibility in the deployment of productive resources. As emphasized in recent discussions of health care benefits, socializing benefits promotes greater allocative efficiency in the labor market. A Firm A employee economically (given skills, taste, whatever) best suited to Firm B is more likely to find her way to Firm B if B does not suffer from a crippling shortfall in benefits provided by A. The most obvious benefit, however, is to the level of equality itself. By removing a chunk of individual welfare from wage competition, minima make it more likely that those less fortunate in that competition will still live a decent life.

For all the same reasons, greater uniformity and generalization of wage bargaining is also desirable. While the United States seems unlikely ever to contemplate truly peak bargaining between unified union federations and a unified business community, nor even anytime soon to contemplate the full use of extension laws in the unor-

28. Is this an appropriate topic of labor law reform? It is if that reform is seen as it should be—as an effort aimed not only at addressing issues of worker representation or management prerogative inside the firm, but of the appropriate design of a society-wide system of production and reward.

29. For a recent argument to this effect and a more general review of the evidence on minima, see Richard B. Freeman, Minimum Wages—Again!, Paper Delivered at the Conference on Economic Analysis of Base Salaries and Effects of Minimum Wages, Arles, France (Sept. 30-Oct. 1, 1993).

ganized sector,[30] more modest efforts to facilitate wage generalization on a regional or sectoral basis might be considered. The law on multi-employer bargaining might be amended, shifting the presumption away from the voluntariness (and, inevitably, instability) of such arrangements and toward their requirement.[31] And more ambitious schemes of "sectoral bargaining," of the sort now being discussed in Canada, might be usefully considered.[32] In a given area or industry grouping or both, sectors of employees, defined by common occupational positions across different employers, could be defined (e.g., "restaurant workers in New York City"). Unions demonstrating support among members of the sector at different sites would be permitted to bargain jointly with all the employers corresponding to those sites. In subsequent organizing during the term of the resulting contract, union certification at additional sites would automatically accrete their employers to the population covered by the contract, with that employer joining in the multi-employer bargaining in the next round.[33] To make the scheme more palatable to employers and the general public, its application might be limited to traditionally low-wage, under-represented sectors, characterized by highly uniform conditions of work.

Such efforts would facilitate greater wage coordination among stable employees of large firms. Their larger and more important effect, however, would be to extend the benefits of wage generalization to employees in smaller locations—too small, under present circumstances, to support the costs of the negotiation and enforcement of separate contracts—or operating in more casualized or "independent" employment relations. There is no good reason why shifts in the structure of employment—in recent years, toward smaller firms, independent contracting, and less stable employment—should be associated *per se* with diminution in the quality of employment. By effectively reducing the costs of establishing a "commonality of inter-

30. The only extension laws in the United States are "prevailing wage" statutes. The reach of these is limited and, at present, shrinking.

31. We are speaking of presumptions here. It would be important in any scheme to permit employers a chance to show why the conditions of their enterprise were sufficiently distinct from those with whom they were asked to join to defeat the presumption.

32. *See* John Baigent et al., Recommendations for Labour Law Reform, A Report to the Honourable Moe Sihota, Minister of Labour, British Columbia, Canada (Sept. 1992); Judy Fudge, *Labour Needs Sectoral Bargaining Now*, Canadian Dimension, Mar.-Apr. 1993, at 33.

33. Again, it would be important to leave room for some variation due to local circumstance. Authority to make such allowances might be assigned regional offices of the Department of Labor, or the NLRB, or a more formal and new system of regional labor market boards.

est" with others, this sort of reform would permit adjustment to changed structures without a sacrifice in quality.[34]

C. Democratic Productivism

If the "equality" reforms of the sort just described were implemented, many of the most enduring sources of labor-management conflict would be shifted, at least slightly, to a resolution basis above or beyond that of the individual firm. If the "free association" reforms were implemented, the forms of collective worker organization inside the firm would become more finely attuned to the variety of employee interests and identities, unions would be more self-confident, and management would be freer in the nonunion sector to experiment with its own ideas of how best to organize employee voice. In combination, this should enlarge the role of the employee in productivity enhancement, both within and without the firm.

Within the firm, as determinations about shares of the "pie" came to be determined more externally, the concentration of all parties could turn more squarely to increasing the size of the pie itself.[35] As the market for representation cleared and its results were granted legitimacy, another source of haggling would be removed, and talk could again turn more easily to cooperation. Outside the firm, the increased reach of worker organizations—and their increased definition as organizations supporting social minima and comparability across sites of employment—will yield a potentially powerful multiplier on government and firm efforts to diffuse productivity-enhancing changes in the organization of production and to secure effective monitoring and enforcement of such efforts. Effective systems of training and technology diffusion, for example, are easier to achieve when there are linkages across firms. Regional labor market programs are easier to administer when worker organizations are more spatially defined. Such improvements would be made more likely by the reforms already discussed.

But the enhancement of firm and state efficiency through use of workers and worker organizations might also be aimed at explicitly.

34. I leave unattended the need for specific reforms in the law governing successorship. If something like the scheme suggested in the text were adopted, most of those would disappear.

35. Standard principles of rational behavior imply that when the share of the pie is exogenous, self-interested parties will cooperate to make a bigger pie, as this is the only way they can benefit themselves. When the share of the pie is "up for grabs," by contrast, there is danger of noncooperative, low-output solutions to prisoners' dilemma problems, including strikes, withholding information that might raise output, and the like.

The American economy currently suffers from the fact that the "low road" sweating response to new competition is not sufficiently foreclosed by public policy, while the "high road" of advanced, high-involvement, high-wage, quality competition is not sufficiently supported. While the reforms already suggested would go some distance toward the first goal, the second also needs attention. This is where explicit aiming may be recommended, in several areas.

We know that vast efficiency gains can be achieved within firms and in labor markets if information flows more freely to workers. General reporting requirements of firms to workers—on current performance, future plans, upcoming choices about products, technology, workforce restructuring, and the like—of the sort most advanced firms do already, ought to be considered.[36]

We know that genuine involvement of workers in solving firm problems requires not only that they see some reward from that involvement, but that they have genuine power to affect choices made. In light of this, where workers are organized, the ancient mandatory/permissive distinction in bargaining seems overdue for overhaul.

We know that in most areas of workplace regulation, the sheer number, heterogeneity, and dispersion of workplaces forbids their effective monitoring by any plausibly sized state inspectorate, and that "private attorneys general" pursuing civil claims also cannot be relied on to achieve desired results. In such areas, increased explicit reliance on worker, or worker-manager, committees for monitoring and enforcement might usefully be explored. Occupational health and safety is one familiar area of such experimentation, but "worker based" models of regulation might also be extended to other areas of pressing national concern—training and technology among them.[37]

36. As one instance of a more general effect, most of the empirical literature on advance notice of plant closing supports the notion that workers gain from early notice, *see, e.g.*, RONALD G. EHRENBERG & GEORGE H. JAKUBSON, ADVANCE NOTICE PROVISIONS IN PLANT CLOSING LEGISLATION (National Bureau of Economic Research Working Paper No. 2611, 1988), with the most negative studies claiming only that notices are neutral. John T. Addison & Pedro Portugal, *Advance Notice and Unemployment: New Evidence from the 1988 Displaced Worker Survey*, 45 INDUS. & LAB. REL. REV. 645 (1992); John T. Addison & Pedro Portugal, *The Effect of Advance Notification of Plant Closings on Unemployment*, 41 INDUS. & LAB. REL. REV. 3 (1987).

37. LINDA J. MORRA, U.S. GEN. ACCT. OFF., OCCUPATIONAL SAFETY AND HEALTH: WORKSITE SAFETY AND HEALTH PROGRAMS SHOW PROMISE, GAO/T-HRD-92-15 (1992), reviews some of the U.S. experience with occupational safety and health committees. See as well the review of Canadian experience in Elaine Bernard, *Canada: Joint Committees on Occupational Health and Safety, in* WORKS COUNCILS: CONSULTATION, REPRESENTATION, COOPERATION (Joel Rogers & Wolfgang Streeck eds., forthcoming 1994). Among others, Kochan & Osterman, *supra* note 8, suggest that worker committees be used in the administration of national training policy. And with training integrated with technology diffusion on a multi-firm regional basis (see below), the thought might naturally be extended. More general "productivity

We know that in regional labor markets and (commonly metropolitan) industry agglomerations the provision of skill and diffusion of technology is seldom "to standard," in part because no credible institutions exist to define standards and diffuse practice based on them. Explicit efforts to promote regional skills and technology consortia, consisting of labor organizations, area employers, and relevant public authorities, and to devolve to such consortia responsibility for executing regional policies in these areas, according to national standards on performance, might also be usefully encouraged.[38]

In brief, we know that modernization and industrial upgrading efforts, as well as workplace regulation, require institutional supports within and across firms—to facilitate communication, organize key players, reward cooperation, punish free-riders, monitor performance, diffuse best practice, use "local knowledge" to devise efficient compliance strategies with social mandates, and more. The sorts of institutional supports extend well beyond those supplied within the markets versus states ("live free or die") governance dichotomy on which conventional policy discussion remains transfixed. Specifically, they extend to the encouragement of a variety of *associative* forms of governance, across as well as within firms. Labor law reform should in part be about building this institutional infrastructure of high-wage productivism. Among other things, this means explicitly encouraging our existing "social partners" to assume a socially needed task of economic governance—"incentivizing" the voluntary establishment of appropriate association forms—with special benefits and protections they receive from public authority conditioned on their willingness to assume this burden.[39]

committees" with responsibility for intrafirm administration of broader training and technology diffusion agreements to which that firm was party might be natural spokes on the wheel of regional upgrading efforts.

38. The desirability of such in the United States is emphasized in the recent recommendations of the Modernization Forum Skills Commission. MODERNIZATION FORUM SKILLS COMM'N, SKILLS FOR INDUSTRIAL MODERNIZATION (1993). For treatment of the general point of which this is one instance, see Cohen & Rogers, *Secondary Associations, supra* note *; Cohen & Rogers, *Associations and Democracy, supra* note *; COHEN & ROGERS, BEYOND FACTION, *supra* note *. For a concrete example of what this might look like in the U.S. context with unions and management both involved, see ERIC PARKER & JOEL ROGERS, THE WISCONSIN REGIONAL TRAINING PARTNERSHIP: A MODEL FOR REGIONAL SKILLS CONSORTIA? (forthcoming 1993).

39. The thought here is simple, if perhaps remote from conventional policy discussion in this most liberal of liberal politics. Assuming it makes sense, for all the reasons given, for the state to provide explicit support to associative partners in governance, it is appropriate to condition such support on those partners' antecedent agreement to, and ongoing satisfaction of, what the public regards as appropriate behaviors. For general discussion and advice on design, again see Cohen & Rogers, *Secondary Associations, supra* note*; Cohen & Rogers, *Associations and Democracy, supra* note *; COHEN & ROGERS, BEYOND FACTION, *supra* note *.

D. *What We Don't Know*[40]

While these broad directions for appropriate reform can be signalled with some confidence, one large gap in our knowledge about what is desirable commands caution, and some work. The gap is public opinion on all these matters. The work is finding out what the structure of worker demand for representation and participation actually is. Without some better sense of public concerns in this area than we have now, many of the details of reform, and perhaps much more than detail, cannot be resolved.

The limits of our knowledge are these. Over the last decade, scattered national polls have explored the attitudes of workers toward workplace representation.[41] Most of these focus on whether people are favorable or unfavorable toward unions. They show that about two-thirds of the public have "favorable" attitudes, but in a vague way,[42] and that about one-third of nonunion workers would vote union in an NLRB representation election if given the opportunity.[43] The polls also indicate considerable public awareness of management opposition to unions, recognition that trying to organize a union is risky and confrontational, and concern over noncooperative labor relations.

Few polls explore anything beyond attitudes toward unionism. A 1988 Gallup poll asked about worker attitudes toward collective representation other than that provided by unions. A 1988 Harris poll asked office workers about their desire to have a say in workplace

40. This section draws on Freeman & Rogers, Workplace Representation, *supra* note *.

41. See the review in Freeman & Rogers, *Who Speaks for Us?*, *supra* note *. Cited polls include those reported in Gallup Org., Public Knowledge and Opinion Concerning the Labor Movement (1988); Fingerhut/Powers, National Labor Poll (1991); Robert P. Quinn & Graham L. Staines, The 1977 Quality of Employment Survey: Descriptive Statistics with Comparison Data from the 1969-70 and 1972-73 Surveys (1979); Louis Harris & Associates, A Study on the Outlook for Trade Union Organizing (1984); James A. Davis & Tom W. Smith, *General Social Surveys, 1972-1991, available in electronic database,* NATIONAL OPINION RESEARCH CENTER (1991); Henry Farber & Alan B. Krueger, *Union Membership in the United States: The Decline Continues in Employee Representation: Alternatives and Future Directions in* EMPLOYEE REPRESENTATION: ALTERNATIVES AND FUTURE DIRECTIONS 105 (Bruce E. Kaufman & Morris M. Kleiner eds., 1993).

42. As evidence of the vagueness of perceptions of unions: the public vastly overestimates the extent of unionization; few people (even in unions) recognize Lane Kirkland as head of the AFL-CIO; few know the names of any other union leader; and there is considerable confusion on the current state of the law regarding union organizing or administration.

43. A recent Penn & Schoen poll, Penn & Schoen, # 2200—National—5/93 (1993), commissioned by the Employment Policy Foundation and circulated to all Dunlop Commission members in advance of their first meeting in support of the proposition that pro-union reform is *not* needed or desired at this time, found that 39% of workers would vote to form a union "if there were an election by secret ballot among you and your co-workers." This is better than twice the actual level of unionization in the United States.

decisions. But no general survey has explored attitudes toward possible new forms of labor-management arrangements or systematically linked the issue of workplace representation directly to productivity, cooperation, and competitiveness.

The 1988 Gallup Survey found that ninety percent of all workers wanted a workplace association of some (vague and unspecified in the survey) form. Most important, it showed that eighty percent of persons unfavorable to unions desired such an association at their workplace. But it did not determine the type of association people wanted, what they wanted it to do for them, how it might affect their work behavior, or how willing they would be to pay dues or other charges for its services.

In addition to national polls, companies often survey their workers to determine employee attitudes toward existing human resource or pay and benefit practices, firm organization, supervision, and other aspects of the workplace. Similarly, unions routinely survey their members or prospective members to determine the same things, as well as the demand for unionization, attitudes toward current organizing drives or initiatives, and the like. These surveys, however, are usually undertaken only by large "best-practice" firms and unions; and as proprietary surveys, their results are not widely disseminated. The extent to which their findings could be generalized to the nation is questionable, and the picture they give of worker desires is not well-known or well-probed.

In sum, no extant poll or survey tells us much about possible worker desires and responses to potential labor reforms. They do not probe attitudes toward existing representative structures in any depth, ask about the desired predicates of alternatives, or ask what workers would be willing to pay for those alternatives. They do not probe the reasons for the structure of preferences—the degree, for example, to which attitudes toward unions are shaped by aversion to the labor-management conflict with which unions are commonly associated, or the degree to which willingness to join a union is shaped by fear of employer reprisal. Nor do they ask for specifics of what workers see as useful ways to increase participation in workplace activities, how hard they might work to make a system of representation or participation succeed for them and their companies, or their views on how alternative modes of workplace organization might affect work performance and company competitiveness.

Thus, entering the labor law reform discussion, the nation has little good information on what workers want, and why they want it, in the area of workplace representation and participation. If employee representation or participation in firm decisionmaking is thought of as a product, we do not know what the "customer" employees want that product to look like, why they want that, or what they are willing to pay for it. This gap in knowledge, rather obviously, needs to be substantially filled.[44]

IV. Who Might Do It, and How

However desirable reform might be, and however well-refined reform suggestions are by further research on public wants, reform will inevitably face opposition. It needs a committed agent to succeed.

This is not likely to be the American business community, which is sharply divided on the desirable future path of economic development in the United States, although it could very easily include some segments of the business community. Nor it is likely to be the present administration—which is deeply ambivalent about "traditional" labor organization, accepting of budget constraints so harsh that they will limit the side payments likely needed, and in general loathe to enter conflicts with the business community of the sort that will inevitably be required.[45] Nor will it come from the disorganized public, as yet far from up-in-arms about the topic.

This leaves labor. For reasons already reviewed, reform is also unlikely to come, even given intense labor mobilization, if it is seen as piecemeal, let alone narrowly self-serving. To put across something like the package talked about here, even to get needed discussion of that package going, reform must come to be seen as something in the

44. This is the aim of the project outlined in Freeman & Rogers, *Who Speaks for Us?*, *supra* note *.

45. What role for the Dunlop Commission does this assessment imply? I think the best thing this Commission could do is document the pathologies of the present system and thus help establish the arena as one demanding public attention. It could as well, of course, inventory the range of reform suggestions, and suggest ways in which they might be knitted together into a more coherent and satisfying system, but I take its political power to be very limited, and the possibilities of "cutting a deal" amongst labor, business, and government to be nearly hopelessly constrained in the absence of organized public concern of the sort that does not yet exist. Creating a constituency for reform is the first, most important, and perhaps only role for the Commission. As bears on the narrower question of worker representation, two specific tasks seem most urgent. The first, already mentioned, is to provide a credible documentation of the real structure of employee demand for representation and participation. The second is to consider just why that demand is not now being met. For the only form of independent representation and participation that now exists—unions—the latter effort would usefully include documentation of the range and effects of employer resistance.

general interest of the society. Its agent must be seen as a paladin of the general will.

How might labor cast itself as such a paladin? Some speculations follow.

A. General Strategy[46]

In very broad terms, "unions"—in our revised system, here meant only to mean "independent collective worker organizations"—need more self-consciously to create and occupy a place analogous to their old one. What that means, again, is that they need to find a way to serve their members' interests in a way that also serves the interests of capital and (precisely because it serves both) enables labor to claim to advance a general will that stands above the special pleading of any particular group.

Take first the problem of serving members' interests. In the old system the unions provided job security though a combination of Keynesian demand management and internal labor market administration. As we have seen, difficulties in controlling macro-economic demand and the internal structures of the firm make that much more difficult today. Accepting this, the alternative is to aim more for career security rather than job security, and to develop mechanisms of insurance rooted more in "effective supply" than effective demand. Instead of trying to define a worker's place in a fixed structure, a new unionism would seek to ensure workers power in fluid ones. The way to do that is to provide all workers with the advanced technical (and, increasingly, "business") training and counseling needed to assert power in the design of the work teams in which they are increasingly employed, and to move freely in external labor markets as their current employer goes under.

Notice that while workers desperately want such training and counseling services, there is little likelihood that firms themselves will provide them. After all, the firms are busy forming cost and profit centers precisely because they have no idea what is working well enough to justify additional investment. Notice too that such services cannot be easily provided through (though they might be funded by) the state, which is certainly no more able than firms to ascertain the sorts of services needed. They will need to be provided by institutions that are actually rooted in the economy, extend across the population

46. Again, this section draws from Rogers & Sabel, *supra* note *.

of firms, and have workers' interests chiefly in mind. They will need to be supplied by unions.

Unions cannot equip members for careers independent of particular firms, however, if compensation and work rules in the corporate way stations of a likely career are so diverse that no one with an acceptable job will dare to move. As discussed, this problem, familiar from the way people today cling to jobs to preserve firm-based pension or health benefits, can only be solved by generalizing compensation and organizational practices. Barriers to mobility arising from the cross-firm differences—in performance review or dispute-resolution procedures, stock option plans or opportunities for skill acquisition, and compensation itself—that have in part arisen from decentralization now stand as a barrier to worker mobility. Just as unions can serve their members' interests by making their skills more versatile, they should serve them by pressing both firms and the state to establish greater uniformity in the conditions of compensation (itself increasingly tied to skill) and employment.

Here again, notice that unions have unique capacities to perform this role. If they are in touch with their members, they will have a much better idea than government or managers of just what underlying standards of equity need to be respected in establishing "comparable" work settings. As institutions spread across firms, they will have wider-ranging experience of the different kinds of jobs that cluster into careers than even the most decentralized, joint-venturing corporation. Firms and groups of employees trying to reconcile differences sufficiently to establish a workable workplace could thus well look to the unions when conflicts arise over the definition and application of rules. Moreover, as institutions of workers in the economy itself, unions are indispensable vehicles for enforcing standards—with the local knowledge and capacity for disruption needed to play that role.

Next consider how the interests of firms are advanced by this two-fold strategy of new-model unions. On the first,—training and counseling—while members want a combination of technical and managerial skills to protect themselves against the risks of the labor market, firms would like to wave a magic wand over their current work force and have employees with precisely these skills costlessly appear. If the unions can help firms figure out how to make effective use of the vast public funds available for training, they can be the magic wand.

On the second,—achieving comparability across firms in conditions of work and compensation—employers, too, have an interest in this goal. As firms decentralize and cooperate more and more closely with outsiders, there is less connection between who employs a person and where and with whom that person works. If an automobile firm and an airbag manufacturer codevelop a new product, a project group from one might easily spend six months on the other's site. Or if a manufacturing firm subcontracts its information-system work to a data-processing firm, technicians employed by the data processor might work fulltime at the manufacturing site. In such cases, cooperating firms are in trouble if they tell their respective employees to treat their new co-workers as partners, and then themselves treat the partners very differently. Without some generalization in work conditions, rules, and compensation, advanced forms of cooperation are far more difficult to enter into, manage, and fold when the task is done.

Just as in the old system, then, unions can play an economic role that both advances their members' interests and solves economy-wide problems beyond the capacity of any firm. Organizationally, their doing so will inevitably require them to be attentive to a wider variety of worker interests than they are identified with at present and—to get deals cut across diverse firms—to be more defined by geographic region and less by economic sector. (Here, recent signs of revival among U.S. metropolitan central labor councils are suggestive.) At the same time, since people still work in particular settings (and the places are still largely described by firm ownership) it is vital that unions extend the reach of worker power in such settings throughout the economy—including sites where unions themselves have relatively few members. This will require getting state supports for generic baselines of worker representation. All three changes will give unions more of a "political" flavor than they have at present. Moreover, the reemergence of unions as innovative, moral, and rational social agents of general benefit will award them a fair degree of political capital with the general public. People will see the "point" of unions more clearly than they do now.

In combination, these changes suggest a basis for a new political role for unions, at both the local and national levels, as advocates for the legislated social protections and supports needed to ensure equity as well as innovation. As already discussed, the welfare state needs to be moved from a jobs-based system to one of more generic social entitlement. Public programs—as in unemployment insurance and training—need to take full measure of increases in job mobility and risk.

And, especially in the United States, the state needs to help spur industrial upgrading of the desired sort not only by rationalizing its services to firms, but by using its residual powers of direction (purchasing power, direct regulation of wage and production standards) to encourage movement in the right direction. New-model unions, as agents of the general interest, could play an important role in making sure that all this happens.

B. *Internal Reform*

The labor movement that did these things would have very broad appeal. It would also, however, be a labor movement that looked rather different from the one that now exists. While many unions in particular locales already engage in just such practices, a commitment to this sort of egalitarian productivism is not, in general, the way unions would characterize their role. Taking that commitment seriously would imply, among other things: (1) sustained efforts within the labor movement to develop the technical capacities for guiding human capital systems, technology diffusion programs, and firm management itself; (2) a massive increase in organizing, coupled with a willingness, even eagerness, to accept "nontraditional" collectivities of workers as allies; (3) a much more active, and independent, political role, at all levels of government; (4) an overhaul of internal rules on jurisdiction to get new institutional boundaries carved along genuinely functional lines and to permit the direction of inter-union cooperation on issues of cross-cutting concern; (5) generalization of an "organizing" model of unionism with much heavier reliance put on membership involvement and democratic direction; (6) consolidation of directive powers, under democratic guidance, at the core of the labor movement—a two-step process perhaps best accomplished by greater direct membership election of national officers; (7) and more. In brief, the labor movement would need, in ways manifest to the general public, to "reinvent" itself as a lively, democratic, intellectually self-assured, popular force for egalitarian productivism. This will involve breaking some eggs inside the labor movement.

C. *Putting It Together*

Suppose however, through means best known to it, the labor movement made such moves and signalled their making to the general public. Suppose it announced, in public fashion, what it now saw as its vision, given a changed economy, along the lines suggested. Suppose it offered something like the general reform package suggested, noticing with the reader that all of its elements are perfectly consistent with, even supportive of, such a transformed social role. And suppose then that it said to business, government, and the general public:

> What we intend to do is manifestly good for the country. To do it, however, we need labor law reform. The reform we seek is not self-interested. In part, indeed, it will pose a challenge to our past practices, even as it permits us the space for internal transformation on which we are now bent. It respects free association, equality, and the requirements of a productive capitalism. It expands choice for all, while limiting inequality and providing the basic security needed for flexibile adaptation to today's economy. All evidence suggests that it will promise a vast improvement in human happiness and welfare, not to mention competitiveness. Have you got something that does all those things better?

Suppose, that is, that labor sought to make "labor law reform" congruent with "labor's transformation" and offered "labor's transformation" as something manifestly guided by declared interest in meeting very general concerns—about economic well-being, insecurity, competitiveness, some residuum of democratic feeling—alive and well in the general population. Would there be takers? Would a number of people see their stake in labor law reform, so described and understood? Would they be more prepared to join the fight that will inevitably be needed to make it happen? I think so. And I see no realistic alternative equally as hopeful.

4. EMPLOYEE VOICE AND EMPLOYER CHOICE: A STRUCTURED EXCEPTION TO SECTION 8(a)(2)

Clyde W. Summers*

Introduction

There is no need here to restate the reasons employees should have a voice in the decisions which affect their working lives. Nor is there need to revisit the voluminous literature detailing how employee participation increases productive efficiency and quality, and how it enhances democratic values and personal dignity. I leave that to my fellow contributors and their industrious footnoting.

There are few in politics, personnel management or academia who would openly argue that employees should have no voice in the terms and conditions of their work. The debate is largely over how much voice they should have, and in what decisions; though the underlying dispute is often whether the employees' right to voice is matched by management's duty to listen.

Participation is often limited to the one-way channel of the "suggestion box" through which employees may speak but seldom receive answers. Or participation may be through a two-way "communications" system in which messages are shuttled up and down the hierarchical chain with no dialogue or shared decisions. "Quality of work life" programs with "quality circles," "production teams," and "employee involvement programs" may provide some voice in performance of tasks, daily work assignments, production goals and minor shop floor problems. But these devices provide no voice in larger matters of job training and promotion rights, health and safety, wage payments and benefits, employment policies and job security.

The search for new forms of employee representation is driven by an assumption that these forms of participation which have such limited substance are not adequate; that workers should have a collective voice in all decisions, both small and large, which significantly affect their working lives. At present, the only channel for participation is through a majority union acting as exclusive representative in collective bargaining. But less than thirteen percent of all employees in the

* Jefferson B. Fordham Professor of Law, University of Pennsylvania.

private sector are now represented by unions; eighty-seven percent have no voice in substantial matters affecting their working lives.

The search is primarily for some meaningful form of employee representation other than traditional collective bargaining which goes beyond what the NLRB described in *Electromation, Inc.* as a "'communication device' to promote generally the interests of quality or efficiency."[1] The purpose here is to suggest one direction the search might take.[2]

I. The Usefulness of Foreign Experience

Not surprisingly, some of those searching for new forms or representation have looked to the labor relations systems of other countries, particularly our chief international competitors, Germany and Japan. Professor Weiler, whose book *Governing The Workplace* has energized the current discussion, has proposed establishing, by statutory mandate, "Employee Participation Committees," (EPC) built on the model of the German works council. He has sketched out the elements of such a committee's structure, responsibilities, resources and finances following generally the outlines of the German Works Constitution Act,[3] but with modifications to fit the American situation.[4] Professors Freeman and Rogers would move in the same direction, but without a statutory mandate. They would encourage employers to create Employee Participation Committees by tax breaks and other government incentives, and allow less than a majority of employees to trigger their formation.[5]

Comparable efforts have not been made to build on the model of the Japanese enterprise unions which, in practice, bear many similari-

1. Electromation, Inc., 309 N.L.R.B. 990, 997 n.28 (1992).

2. This is merely an elaboration of a suggestion floated in Clyde W. Summers, *Industrial Democracy: America's Unfulfilled Promise,* 28 Clev. St. L. Rev. 29 (1979).

3. Betreibsverfassungsgesetz, Vom 15. Januar 1972 (officially translated by The Federal Minister of Labour and Social Affairs in *Co-determination in the Federal Republic of Germany*).

4. Paul C. Weiler, Governing The Workplace: The Future of labor and Employment Law 282-95 (1990).

5. Richard B. Freeman & Joel Rogers, *Who Speaks For Us? Employee Representation in a Nonunion Labor Market, in* Employee Representation: Alternatives and Future Directions 13 (Bruce E. Kaufman & Morris M. Kleiner eds., 1993). Similar suggestions have been made earlier. *See* R.J. Adams, *The Unorganized: A Rising Force?, in* Jobs and Labour Peace—An Agenda for Action 40 (Lisa R. Cohen ed., McGill University Industrial Relations Centre 31st Annual Conference 1983); Roy J. Adams, *Should Works Councils Be Used as Industrial Relations Policy?* Monthly Lab. Rev. July, 1985 at 25; David M. Beatty, Putting The Charter To Work: Designing A Constitutional Labour Code 144-55 (1987); Clyde Summers, *Past Premises, Present Failures, and Future Needs in Labor Legislation,* 31 Buff. L. Rev. 9, 28-30 (1982).

ties to the German works council, but which are built on a statutory base modeled on the Wagner Act.[6] American employers, however, have borrowed heavily from the Japanese in creating quality circles and other work group structures. If not barred by section 8(a)(2),[7] employers would likely copy the Japanese consultation committees and encourage the organization of enterprise unions to fend off or supplant traditional American unions.

No responsible person seriously suggests that German works councils or Japanese enterprise unions can be transplanted unchanged to American soil. Modifications, some major, would need to be made. Professor Weiler has flagged some of those necessary changes. Without detailing how it might be done, it is enough for my purposes here to state that I believe that a works council system modeled on the German system could be structurally superimposed on our collective bargaining system. It could be done in a way which would provide a form of representation to those not now represented by unions without undermining or weakening our present collective bargaining system, and perhaps substantially strengthening it. The obstacle is not structural, but political. It could work *if* employers and unions were willing to let it work. That, however, in my view, is a forbidding, if not preclusive *if.*

Although we can not, or will not, mandate works councils, we can learn from German and Japanese experience. The most important and illuminating question to ask is why they seem to work so well. That may give us some better understanding of what is required if we are to develop new forms of effective representation for ourselves and the difficulties we face if that is to be achieved.

German works councils and Japanese enterprise unions have several factors in common which underlie their effectiveness. First, they are rooted in the workplace, focused exclusively on problems of the enterprise.[8] Membership in German works councils is, by law, limited to the establishment;[9] council members are employees in the workplace, elected by other employees in the workplace and accountable only to those employees.[10] Where an enterprise has several establishments, separate works councils may form a central works council, but

6. Taishiro Shirai, *A Theory of Enterprise Unionism, in* CONTEMPORARY INDUSTRIAL RELATIONS IN JAPAN 117, 120 (Taishiro Shirai ed., 1983).

7. Labor Management Relations Act, 29 U.S.C. § 158(a)(2) (1988).

8. *See generally* Clyde W. Summers, *Worker Participation in the U.S. and West Germany: A Comparative Study from an American Perspective,* 28 AM. J. COMP. L. 367 (1980).

9. Works Constitution Act 1972, §§ 1, 5. (F.R.G.).

10. *Id.* § 8.

the structure is confined to the enterprise.[11] This focuses the works council on the welfare of the enterprise and focuses the employer on the welfare of its employees. This minimizes external influences; outsiders and outside influences do not intrude.

It is true that three-fourths of the works council members are union members, often elected on a union slate. But once elected they consider themselves responsible to their fellow employees and not to the union. Frequently they refuse to follow union policy, even to the extent of being disowned by the union and denied a place on the union slate in the next election. They may then win reelection on an independent slate.[12] Even though the works council asserts its independence, the union provides it technical assistance and advice when asked, for the union, not the works council, is the suitor.

Japanese enterprise unions are similarly rooted in the workplace or enterprise, for there is no parent national union as we know it.[13] The enterprise unions may be affiliated with a national confederation which provides some coordination, particularly in bargaining for general annual increases in the *shinto* or "spring offensive."[14] But the enterprise union is essentially independent, and its officers and members consider it a part of the enterprise. Its purpose, in their view, is to serve the enterprise as well as its members.

Second, employers in Germany and Japan generally accept, indeed support, the system of plant level representation. German employers accept that employees are entitled to collective representation and a voice in decisions of the enterprise. They recognize that the works council can help solve problems and find mutually acceptable solutions. When such solutions are agreed upon, employers rely on the works council to persuade employees to accept them and carry them through. As a German employer said to me, "I could not run the plant without the help of the works council." But employers also recognize that works councils cannot serve these functions unless there is genuine sharing of information and decision making.

It is worth noting that although German employers accept collective bargaining with unions at the national or sectional level, they refuse to recognize or deal with unions at the plant level and have

11. *Id.* § 47.

12. Summers, *supra* note 8, at 373.

13. *See generally* Shirai, *supra* note 6, at 117-44.

14. THE JAPAN INSTITUTE OF LABOUR, JAPANESE INDUSTRIAL RELATIONS SERIES NO. 2, LABOR UNIONS AND LABOR-MANAGEMENT RELATIONS 18-20 (1986).

resisted establishment of union steward systems in the workplace.[15] They accept the works council because, "they are our people."

Japanese employers similarly accept enterprise unions and find them useful, although they predominate only in the large enterprises, and less than one-third of all workers are in enterprise unions.[16] Where they exist, they are not viewed as adversaries of management, but as integral parts of the enterprise. This results, in part, from the fact that the practice of internal promotion results in many of those in management having once been officers of the unions in Japan.[17] Japanese employers, unlike German employers, are not confronted with potential intrusion from "outside" unions, for there are no substantial "outside" unions in Japan. But there is reason to believe that they would be equally resistant to such unions at the plant level.

Underneath this acceptance of plant level representation is a third and more subtle factor—a recognition that employees are not just another factor in production, their labor to be purchased like supplies or energy. Instead, they are considered members of the enterprise and entitled to a voice in its decisions, with a share in the enterprise because of their contribution to its production and profitability. This is the articulate premise of the German Works Constitution Act[18] and the Codetermination Acts[19] providing for employee representation on corporate boards, but it is reflected in other legal rules and practices.

For example, German dismissal law proceeds from the premise that an employee has a right in his or her job and can not be dismissed without "social justification."[20] Although employers are not required to retain unnecessary workers, an employee cannot be dismissed if there is another job available in the enterprise which the employee can perform; and the employer may be required to provide the employee training for that job.[21] If a going enterprise is transferred, the

15. Summers, *supra* note 8, at 384.

16. The Japan Institute of Labour, *supra* note 14, at 11-14.

17. Shirai, *supra* note 6, at 139.

18. *Supra* note 3.

19. Montan-Mitbestimmungsgesetz, Vom 21. Mai 1951 (Codetermination in the Coal and Steel Industry) (officially translated by The Federal Minister of Labour and Social Affairs in *Codetermination in the Federal Republic of Germany*); Mitbestimmungsgesetz, Vom 4. Mai 1976 (Co-determination Act) (officially translated by The Federal Minister of Social Affairs in *Codetermination in the Federal Republic of Germany*).

20. Annegret Dose-Digenopoulos & Armin Holand, *Dismissal of Employees in the Federal Republic of Germany*, 48 Mod. L. Rev. 539, 542-44 (1985).

21. Manfred Weiss, Labour Law And Industrial Relations In The Federal Republic of Germany 85-86 (1987).

employee's job rights are transferred with the enterprise and the successor assumes the obligation for continued employment with existing seniority rights.[22] In cases of mass dismissal or plant closure, the employer has an obligation to work out with the works council a comprehensive plan for helping employees make the change. This may include staged timing of lay offs, transfers to other parts of the enterprise, job retraining, moving allowances, and severance pay. If full agreement is not reached, the dispute is submitted to arbitration, which may assess substantial severance pay.[23]

Japanese recognition that employees, especially permanent as contrasted with so-called "temporary employees," are members of the enterprise is even more pronounced. The common expression is that permanent employees are "members of the family," and the employment relation takes on many family attitudes. "Lifetime employment" expresses the principle that employees are members of the enterprise and all measures possible should be taken to preserve that relationship. If cutbacks in employment become necessary, lifetime employees may be "dispatched" or "farmed out" to work for other employers at their existing salaries until they are again needed and returned to their regular jobs.[24] The plant may be completely closed for a number of weeks, with the employees receiving eighty percent or more of their regular pay, half of which is reimbursed by the government to employers of more than 300 employees, and two-thirds to smaller employees.[25]

Lifetime employment is limited almost entirely to large employers; small employers are unable to provide such assurance. However, the recognition that regular employees are members of the enterprise with a claim to continued employment is widely shared. For example, the practice of closing operations for a limited period and paying employees eighty percentage of their pay is more prevalent among small employers than large employers.

Although lifetime employment is an employment practice, not a legal concept, the Japanese courts have recognized the underlying principle and developed rules protecting employees from dismissal.[26]

22. *Id.* at 92-93.

23. Works Constitution Act 1972, §§ 111, 112; Weiss, *supra* note 21, at 167-68.

24. Kazuo Sugeno, Japanese Labor Law 375-82 (1992).

25. Nishikawa Shunsaku & Shimado Haruo, *Employment and Unemployment 1970 to 1975*, *in* The Labor Market in Japan 124, 137-38 (Shunsaku Nishikawa ed., Ross Mouer trans., 1980).

26. The courts have used the "abuse of rights" theory to void dismissals not based on "objectively reasonable grounds [which can] receive general social approval." Sugeno, *supra* note

They will review dismissals based on lack of work and inquire into whether the dismissals were compelled by economic necessity or whether the employer could have borne the burden of retaining the employees.[27] These inquiries will be made even though the employees are not lifetime employees.[28]

It is true that lifetime employment does not fully protect so-called temporary or part-time employees. They are used to provide much of the flexibility needed to protect the lifetime employees. They are not "members of the family." This, however, only reinforces the relation between the employer and the enterprise union, for the enterprise union does not include the temporary and part-time employees.[29] The relation remains entirely within the "family."

When employees are treated as members of the enterprise, not hired hands providing labor, they come to think of themselves as belonging to and having a stake in the enterprise. They develop a loyalty to the enterprise and a concern for its welfare. When they are given full information about the financial condition of the enterprise and a voice in its decisions, they are more ready to promote its productivity and profitability. It is this shared view of the employees' place in the enterprise which reduces the adversarial character of plant relations in Germany and Japan and fosters a process of mutual problem solving and accommodation.

The fourth factor which makes the German work councils and Japanese enterprise unions work is that when disagreements arise between management and the employees' representative, devices are available to bring pressure on management. In Germany, a wide range of issues are subject to "codetermination." That means that if the works council and management are unable to agree, the dispute is submitted to arbitration—in effect, binding interest arbitration. This includes issues such as work schedules, overtime and short time, methods of wage payment, technical devices to monitor employees, prevention of accidents and occupational diseases,[30] guidelines for hiring,

24, at 402. If a dismissal is not for "just" cause, it is an "abuse of right," and "just" cause is strictly applied with the courts voiding dismissals for misconduct, inefficiency, laziness, or even theft. *See* T.A. HANAMI, LABOUR LAW AND INDUSTRIAL RELATIONS IN JAPAN 89 (2d ed. 1985).

27. SUGENO, *supra* note 24, at 407-10; Fumito Komiya, *Dismissal Procedures and Termination Benefits in Japan*, 12 COMP. LAB. L.J. 151, 156, 158-60 (1991).

28. The doctrine of "abusive dismissal," requiring that there be reasonable and objective grounds for dismissal, has been applied to employees with contracts of indefinite duration, including "temporary workers" whose term contracts have been repeatedly renewed. SUGENO, *supra* note 24, at 155-56. It also has been applied to part-time employees. *Id.* at 162.

29. THE JAPAN INSTITUTE OF LABOUR, *supra* note 14, at 13-14.

30. Works Constitution Act 1972, § 87.

transfers and dismissal,[31] implementation of vocational training programs,[32] and severance pay in cases of mass dismissals and plant closures.[33] Although these may not reach the "core of entrepreneurial control,"[34] the threat to carry a codetermination issue to the slow, expensive and uncertain process of arbitration provides leverage to obtain agreement on issues not subject to codetermination. Indeed, works councils regularly negotiate for wages above the minimum prescribed by collective agreements. Although works councils are by law prohibited from striking, the danger of unauthorized strikes cannot be totally discounted.

Japanese enterprise unions have a variety of devices to use in disputes, designed more to embarrass than injure the employer.[35] The strike is legally available but strikes are customarily very short[36] or may often take the form of a protest demonstration of wearing badges or arm bands or posting hand bills to show their dissatisfaction.[37] Such methods are often sufficient because employers take seriously such publicity of unhappiness within the family and give weight to the union's demands.

What conclusions might we draw from these characteristics of the German and Japanese systems that are relevant to our search for new forms of employee representation? The initial reaction is that the search is a futile quest; at least, these models provide no guide. We lack the fundamental attitudes which make these models work. American employers generally do not accept that employees are entitled, as a matter of right, to collective representation; quite the opposite, as our experience distressingly demonstrates. Many employers favor employee involvement programs, but these are largely limited to communications systems or quality circle type programs which give employees no voice in larger decisions that vitally affect their working lives. More substantial forms of nonunion participation have been barred by section 8(a)(2), but there is little reason to believe that its

31. *Id.* § 95.
32. *Id.* § 98.
33. *Id.* § 112.
34. Fibreboard Paper Prod. Corp. v. NLRB, 379 U.S. 203, 223 (1964) (Stewart, J., concurring).
35. HANAMI, *supra* 26, at 133.
36. THE JAPAN INSTITUTE OF LABOUR, *supra* note 14, at 43-44. More than two-thirds of the strikes are less than four hours long. Yasuhiko Matsuda, *Conflict Resolution in Japanese Industrial Relations*, *in* CONTEMPORARY INDUSTRIAL RELATIONS IN JAPAN 179, 194 (Taishiro Shirai ed., 1983).
37. SUGENO, *supra* note 24, at 563-68; HANAMI, *supra* note 26, at 137.

repeal would lead employers generally to accept much broader shared decision making.

Mandating works councils or employee representation committees, even if politically possible, would be accomplished over the determined opposition of employers. When defeated politically, many employers would wage guerilla warfare in the workplace or engage in sabotage. At the very least, they would bring to the process an adversarial attitude which would shrivel the possibilities for cooperation and mutual problem solving. All of this points toward a voluntary solution which would allow those employers who recognized the values of worker participation to construct a system implementing it where there was no union. The hope would be that other employers, seeing its values demonstrated, would come to accept it as a better way to conduct labor relations.

Acceptance of employee participation through works councils, however, would not of itself provide the undergirding recognition by employers that employees are members of the enterprise, the most important factor in leading both parties to focus on their mutual interest in the productivity and profitability of the enterprise. Employment at will and its radiations deny that workers share any rights in their jobs and make them subservient to the whims of the employer. And claims of management prerogatives deny that workers shall have a voice in decisions in the workplace. Work councils can have only limited effectiveness unless employers repudiate employment at will, disclaim areas of management prerogatives and take other steps to recognize employees as members of the enterprise.

Works councils are rooted in the workplace, but our unions are also rooted in the workplace. No one seriously suggests that a new form of representation should supplant or preclude unions; the two forms of participation must, therefore, be coordinated. This is a more difficult problem than in Germany where the union bargains at the national or sectional level but has no authority in the plant. The problem here is complicated by the fact that unions seldom represent all of the employees at the workplace, and often only a fraction in the enterprise. However, coordination, or at least coexistence, of the two systems of participation is, I believe, possible.

II. Toward a New Form of Representation

Creation by the employer of any form of employee representation, except perhaps narrowly confined "communication devices to promote generally the interests of quality and efficiency,"[38] run headlong into section 8(a)(2) of the National Labor Relations Act which makes it an unfair labor practice for an employer "to dominate or interfere with the formation or administration of any labor organization or contribute financial or other support."[39]

Section 8(a)(2) effectively forecloses employee representation through any structure which is not wholly independent of employer support. For practical purposes, the alternatives are representation through a union or no representation at all, and this leads to collective bargaining through a majority union as the only available form of employee participation.

A common argument is that section 8(a)(2) limits employees freedom of choice as to how they shall be represented. Many employees, it is said, want to have a voice in decisions in their workplace, but they do not want to be represented by a union and through collective bargaining. They perceive unions and collective bargaining as creating an adversarial relation leading to strikes. These employees, it is argued, should be free to choose other forms of representation; and employers who want employee participation should not be barred from providing it where employees do not want a union.

I pass over, for the present, certain misgivings about this argument, except to say that in my view rejection of unions and collective bargaining is less a result of employee choice than of employer choice. Although hard data is not at hand, I doubt that many representation elections would result in a "no-union" vote if the employer remained neutral in the election campaign. Those doubts are reinforced by experience in the public sector where employers seldom wage vigorous anti-union campaigns and the majority seldom votes "no-union." Certainly, employees will rarely refuse to organize where the employer openly prefers collective bargaining.

Undoubtedly, there are many cases in which the majority of the employees have rejected unions and collective bargaining, at least in part, because of the employer's open opposition. This opposition may take the form of a simple declaration, massive campaigning which goes to the brink of illegality, or coercive unfair labor practices. In any event, the end result is that both the employees and the employer have rejected representation through a union, but both want some form of employee representation for purposes of participation. It is to

38. *Supra* note 1.
39. 29 U.S.C. § 158 (a)(2).

this situation which the present search for new forms of representations is addressed.

One path, which is commonly suggested, is to repeal section 8(a)(2) and allow employee free choice.[40] The result, however, would not be employee free choice, but employer free choice, for the only choice would be between the employer's proposed plan or no representation at all. Half a loaf might be better than no loaf at all, but experience warns that many employers' plans would be little more than crumbs.

Many, if not most, employers, are not prepared to give their employees a voice in substantial decisions of the enterprise, to give them adequate information enabling them to make useful judgments, and to discuss with them the potential alternatives. They may provide forms of participation, but only so long as the employee representatives' views do not depart from those of management and do not impede or cast doubt on management's decisions. Whether intended or not, the availability of such devices makes it easier for the employer to induce employees to reject unions and collective bargaining.

Repeal of section 8(a)(2) would reopen the doors to all of the evils it was intended to prevent. History warns that employee representation plans would be created for the very purpose of forestalling union organization, but they would provide only the shell of representation. Their structure and functions would be determined by the employer, they would be dependent on the employer for finances and administrative facilities, the representatives would be vulnerable to employer pressure, and the committee could be disbanded by the employer at any time. The employees' voice would be little more than an echo of management's.

It may be argued that employees will recognize a sham for what it is and reject it. History does not support this argument. Formal structures of representation can disguise the lack of substance, visible procedure can create an illusion of action. Representatives who are subservient to management, but who prize their prestige and other benefits, will help thicken that disguise and promote the illusion. If the employee representatives and management together control the

40. For an early, well-developed argument for this result, see Charles C. Jackson, *An Alternative to Unionization and The Wholly Unorganized Shop: A Legal Basis for Sanctioning Joint Employer-Employee Committees and Increasing Employee Free Choice*, 28 SYRACUSE L. REV. 809 (1977). The author would not, in form, repeal § 8(a)(2), but would limit the inquiry to employee free choice in such a way that, by his own admission, almost any violation of § 8(a)(2) would violate some other subsection of § 8. *See id.* at 838 n.119, 839 n.127.

channels of communication, the disguise becomes nearly impenetrable by ordinary employees. Moreover, if some employees penetrate the disguise or become dissatisfied with the employer's plan, their only alternative is unionization. But any movement in that direction will risk retaliation and be met by a massive anti-union campaign orchestrated by both the employer and those who purport to represent the employees. The choice presented will be between the union and the employer dominated plan. Many of the employees will not see through the disguise, and others will be persuaded that they will fare better under a representation system which the employer strongly supports than one which the employer bitterly opposes. The presence of the sham plan will thereby substantially reduce union support and employees will continue to have but the shell of representation.

The fact that some employers, out of anti-union motives, would create sham representation plans subservient to the employer, however, should not bar those employers who want to provide employees a meaningful voice. Employers should be able to create a representation system which has the independence, resources, information and scope of functions needed to speak for employees on matters of substantial concern to the employees. Our search should be for a way to permit the good while continuing to bar the bad.

In *Electromation*, Board Member Raudabaugh suggested that section 8(a)(2) be reinterpreted in the light of the present legal context and industrial condition to allow some forms of employee participation plans (EPP). He would look to four factors on a case by case basis:

> (1) The extent of the employer's involvement in the structure and operation of the committee;
> (2) whether the employees, from an objective standpoint, reasonably perceive the EPP as a substitute for full collective bargaining through a traditional union;
> (3) whether employees have been assured of their Section 7 right to choose to be represented by a traditional union under a system of full collective bargaining; and
> (4) the employer's motives in establishing the EPP.[41]

The four factors, on their face, are seedbeds of uncertainty; Member Raudabaugh's elaborations provide added fertility. When the four factors are intermixed on a case by case basis they are as likely to produce weeds as flowers, for they do not deal with the real evils of sham representation systems.

41. Electromation, Inc., 309 N.L.R.B. 990, 1013 (1992) (Raudabaugh, concurring).

If employer-initiated representation plans are to be separated into those which are permitted and those which are barred, then the line between the two should be reasonably clear. Employers who seek to create the form of participation without the substance should be clearly warned that empty shells will not do. Employers who want to give employees a meaningful voice and create a structure for effective employee participation should know what is required to keep within the letter and purpose of the law.

Section 8(a)(2) was enacted to reach a real evil—sham employee representation plans which obstructed representation through unions and collective bargaining but provided no meaningful representation in its place.[42] That evil is as potential today as it was real when the statute was enacted. Repeal of section 8(a)(2) or wholesale reinterpretation would open the door to the return of that evil.

The genesis of our present discussion is that section 8(a)(2) reaches beyond the evil to prohibit all forms of non-union representation. The solution should better take the form of carving out an exception to section 8(a)(2) which would allow employers and employees who have rejected collective bargaining to construct a system which will serve the employees' right to a voice and the employer's need for employee participation. The purpose of carving out an exception is to make available a system of participation where employees have rejected unionization. The exception, therefore, must be so defined as to be used only by those employers who are genuinely ready to share decision making with their employees.

III. The Outline of a Proposal

The core of my proposal, in simple terms, is to permit employers to establish employee representation plans free from the strictures of section 8(a)(2), if the plan met certain specified requirements. Those requirements would guarantee, so far as possible, that the employees' representatives had the independence necessary to speak freely on behalf of the employees,' that they were the voice of the employees, not the echo of the employer. The suggested requirements, drawn largely from the German works councils, should be cast in general terms so as to provide flexibility. The central principles would be guaranteed independence from the employer and the guarantee of a meaningful voice.

42. *See generally* Mark Barenberg, *The Political Economy of the Wagner Act: Power, Symbol, and Workplace Cooperation*, 106 Harv. L. Rev. 1379 (1993).

This alternative should not be available to an employer which has interfered with its employee's free choice; its purpose is to provide a form of employee representation only where employees have freely chosen not to have a union. Therefore, an employer should not be allowed to establish such a plan when there was an active organizing campaign under way or a representation preceeding was pending. Nor should an employer be allowed to establish such a plan where an unfair labor practice proceeding against the employer was pending or there had been a final determination of an unfair labor practice against the employer in the preceding three years. The availability of an alternative should not provide the employer an incentive to interfere with an employee's freedom of choice.

The requirements which an employee representation plan should meet to be exempt from section 8(a)(2), I would suggest, include the following:

First, although the structure would be framed at the outset by the employer, the employees should be free to modify the structure by majority vote after consultation with the employer, so long as the structure is kept within the specified requirements. Once established, the plan could be abolished or disbanded only by the employees.

Second, supervisory and administrative employees should be represented separately from non-supervisory employees in order to insulate employee representatives from management influence or control. This should not preclude inclusion of first line foremen in the non-supervisory employee group where both agree, but the representatives of the non-supervisory groups must, themselves, be non-supervisory employees. The plan should call for joint meetings of representatives of all employee groups with representatives of management. But to assure continued independence, the representatives of the non-supervisory employees must retain the right to meet alone with representatives of management to deal with matters of their concern.

Third, the employee representatives should be elected by those they represent, free from outside influences. The elections should be at reasonable intervals and the nomination and election process should be subject to basic safeguards similar to those provided in Title IV of the Landrum-Griffin Act[43] for election of union officers.

Most important, the choice must be that of the employees, uninfluenced by the employer. The employer should be barred from giving any support of any kind to any employee candidate, just as section

43. Labor Management and Disclosure Act of 1959, 29 U.S.C. § 401.

401(g) of Landrum-Griffin prohibits employers from promoting any candidate for union office.

Fourth, the employee representatives must be provided the resources needed for performing their functions. This would include paid time off for meetings with management, meetings with employees, handling of grievances, and internal discussions. The minimum amount could be fixed, as in Germany, by the number of employees covered. Employee representatives must also be provided office space and secretarial support, and have the right to hold employee meetings on company premises.

Most important, an employee representative plan must have guaranteed financial support for various organizational and educational purposes, and for hiring professional services and experts. This would include such costs as arbitration of grievances, enforcement of employees' legal rights, use of experts in health and safety matters and job evaluation programs. Again, the amount could be determined by some prescribed formula, to be paid by the employer. The employees should be free to supplement the amount with a check-off by majority vote.

Fifth, employee representatives should be protected from fear of retaliation for their activities. They should not be subject to dismissal or discipline, except upon employer proof of just cause, and they should not be subject to lay off so long as there was work available which they were qualified to perform. Prohibiting discrimination does not provide adequate protection because proving motive is too difficult. The representative should be able to enforce this right either by suit for dismissal contrary to public policy or by arbitration for dismissal without just cause, as well as by an unfair labor practice proceeding.

Sixth, the employer should have a duty to confer with the employee representatives on all matters which substantially affect the employees' working lives. Because the underlying principle of employee participation is to treat employees as members of the enterprise and give them a voice, there is no reason for drawing the troublesome and divisive line between bargainable subjects and management prerogatives. The only duty on management will be to confer; management will still retain the ultimate right to decide. The right of employees to strike would not be enlarged or reduced, for the only change in the National Labor Relations Act would be to provide an exemption from section 8(a)(2).

Employers would no doubt prefer to prescribe the subjects with which employee representatives could deal. This, however, would enable employers to limit the subjects and create a structure of elected representatives with no voice, a shell with no content. This is the kind of sham which section 8(a)(2) was designed to prevent. Any attempt to allow an employer to limit the subject matters to be discussed, but at the same time guarantee a substantial measure of participation would require line drawing which would generate uncertainty and controversy. The best test of whether a matter is of substantial interest to employees is their insistence on discussing it, and if it is of substantial interest to employees, the employer will undermine the purpose of participation if it insists that the subject is none of the employees' business.

The employer's duty should be to "confer" or "consult," not to "bargain," if for no other reason than to avoid the image of an adversarial process. But there would be a more fundamental difference; conferring or consulting would be a continuing process. Problems would be discussed and resolved as they arose, not bargained as a package and frozen for two or three year intervals. The duty on both sides would include, of course, the duty to meet, exchange views, and consider proposals and counter proposals for dealing with the problems in an effort to find a mutually acceptable solution. This solution would become the governing rule or principle to be followed by the parties until it was changed through the process of consultation.

Perhaps the most important aspect of the duty to confer would be the duty of the employer to provide the employee representatives all relevant information; they can not speak to a problem without all the relevant facts. This must include information which will enable them to make responsible judgments of the ability of the enterprise to bear the costs or burdens of potential solutions. The employees have as much concern as management with the continued viability of the enterprise. The scope of information required may be borrowed from the German Works Constitution Act. This includes giving information "in full and good time" of any plans concerning the construction, alteration or extension of the plant, works processes or jobs; matters relating to manpower planning such as manpower needs, staff movements and vocational training; and financial matters such as the economic and financial situation of the company, the production and investment programs, rationalization plans, introduction of new work methods, reduction of operations, and plan transfers or closures, or any "other circumstances and projects that may materially effect the interests of employees of the company."[44]

Finally, the employee representatives should have the authority and ability to aid employees in enforcing any statutory or other legal rights, including those arising under individual contracts of employment. Where the employer and the employee representatives have agreed upon any rules or benefits, whether stated in the form of employer policies or written agreements, these should be enforceable by any employee for whose benefit they are made as a part of their contract of employment, and also by the employee representatives. The plan should include a provision that disputes over rights under individual contracts of employment and under agreements between the employer and the employee representatives should be submitted to binding neutral arbitration.

These are the broadly stated standards which I believe an employer-created representation plan should meet to be entitled to exemption from section 8(a)(2). There remains the question of how such a proposal would be administered and enforced. If an employer-created plan, on its face, did not fully meet these standards, its creation would be an unfair labor practice and the order should be for the employer either to disestablish the plan or, if it met most of the standards, to amend it to meet the standards. If the plan, on its face, met the standards, but the employer in practice violated any of them, those violations would be unfair labor practices, leading to the usual order to cease and desist. If those violations were extensive or persistent, evidencing an unwillingness of the employer to observe the standards, then the plan should be disestablished.

The existence of such employee representation plans would not structurally change unionization or collective bargaining. Where the union represented some, but not all, of the employees in the establishment, the employee representation plan would include only those not covered by the union. The two forms of employee participation would coexist. This might well create some tension because their scope and functions would be different, but each could operate independently. Unions would retain all of their rights under the statute to organize, petition for elections, and to become an exclusive bargaining representative. If the majority in an appropriate unit voted for the union, this would demonstrate those employees' choice to be represented by

44. Works Constitution Act 1972, § 106. *See also*, *id.* §§ 90, 92, 99, 100, 110, 111 (stating other requirements of information).

the union rather than the employer-created plan and the union would become the statutory representative. The employer would then be barred from dealing with the plan's representatives on issues involving employees in the bargaining unit and would be required to bargain with the union. This might require a new election of representatives by those outside the bargaining unit, but the plan could continue for those not represented by the union.

All employees would retain all of their rights under the National Labor Relations Act, including their section 7 right to engage in concerted activity for mutual aid and protection. Any two or more employees who were dissatisfied with any of their terms and conditions of employment could, like the employees in *Washington Aluminum*,[45] refuse to work until their demands were met. Certainly, the employee representatives should not be able limit or surrender that right of employees to strike as a union may do in agreeing to a no-strike clause.

A substantial question is whether employee representatives could be barred by agreement or otherwise from calling a strike. German works councils are, by law, prohibited from engaging in "acts of industrial warfare," but they have the leverage of being able to demand arbitration on a number of issues. Employee representatives would have no such leverage. Their practical ability to call a strike would be very limited because they would have little or no resources to support a strike. Moreover, the very nature of their establishment and operation would not look toward use of economic force as a method of resolving differences. It seems to me that they should have available at least this limited instrument to encourage the employer to make serious efforts to reach mutually agreeable solutions.

An employee representation plan under this proposal has obvious weaknesses; it is not the equivalent of representation by a majority union. At the outset, it may not be the fully free choice of the employees. In an NLRB election campaign the employer may bring its full weight to bear to defeat the union so long as it avoids being found guilty of an unfair labor practice. The employer's touting the availability of an alternative plan which it prefers will add to its anti-union arguments. The election outcome will reflect the employer's choice even more than it does now.

Policing the requirements would present substantial burdens. Every plan could raise questions as to whether it conformed in all respects to the requirements. These problems could be eased by rule-

45. NLRB v. Washington Aluminum Co., 370 U.S. 9 (1962).

making and advisory opinions if the Board forced itself from the self-imposed blinders of case by case adjudication. In any case, it would, for at least a time, add substantially to the work load of the Board.

Most important, it would be difficult to legally prevent employers from making the process of consultation an empty shell. The danger is that the employer would establish the formal structures, provide the required information, meet with the employee representative, pretend to listen, but give the employees' representative's view no weight. Proving refusal to consult in good faith would be an even more ephemeral pursuit than proving refusal to bargain in good faith. There could, in reality, be no employee participation; the employee voice would be hollow. Even with the requirements, there is a danger that the plan would carry the seeds of company unionism.

The employees would have three potential responses to induce the employer to listen. *First*, the employer would largely lose the values of increased employee cooperation and efficiency. The plan would serve no purpose other than potentially forestalling unionization. *Second*, the employees could engage in concerted action. A traditional strike would have limited potential, but short term strikes, slow downs or even sabotage could exact a price. The employers failure to live up to the promises held out in establishing the plan could provide an incentive for such activities. *Third*, the employees, on finding that the plan was a shell, could readily convert it into a union and become the legal bargaining representative.

All of these responses provide only limited leverage to induce the employer to listen and consult in good faith. But the threat of these responses would exert some pressure on employers. The creation of a representation plan which met the stated requirements would create a level of employee expectations and provide an organizational structure which would substantially increase the likelihood and ability of the employees to make these responses effective. This would decrease the incentive of employers to create plans for sham purposes, but not discourage employers who had a genuine desire to provide for employee participation.

There may be relatively few employers who, when confronted with the possibility, will be willing to give their employees the voice which this proposal would provide. Most employers may prefer to limit employee involvement to suggestion boxes, communications systems or quality circles now allowed under section 8(a)(2). The proposal is designed only to meet the needs of those who want to give their employees a meaningful voice, however few or many they may be.

Conclusion

This proposal is not presented as an ideal solution for providing employees meaningful participation in the decisions which affect their working life. In my view, collective bargaining between unions and management could potentially provide a much better instrument. If we had sixty or seventy percent unionization and employers fully accepted unions and collective bargaining, then Sweden, with its Codetermination Act of 1976,[46] might provide a model. But we do not have a comprehensive system of collective bargaining; most American employers do not accept unions; and collective bargaining in this country has a predominate adversarial character. Providing participation through collective bargaining is at present impossible for the great majority of employees.

Mandated works councils built on the German model, with any three employers able to call for the election of a works council, would in my view, be the next best solution. Such a system could be structurally adapted to our present situation by the relatively simple device of providing for works councils where no majority union held representation rights. This would create less problems and tensions than now often exist when two or more unions have bargaining rights in the same enterprise.

The proposal here to provide a structured exception to section 8(a)(2) has only two claims to serious consideration. It will provide an alternative to the two present polar choices—representation by a majority union or no representation at all. The other virtue is that it appears to be within the range of present possibilities. It will provide an alternative for employers who recognize the values of employee participation, but whose employees reject unionization, without opening wide the doors to the evils barred by section 8(a)(2).[47]

46. Lag om Medbestammande i arbetslivet.

47. I doubt many employers will opt for this alternative. Their reaction may be, in Professor Finkin's words, "With a works council like this, why not have a union and be done with it?" That reaction, however, will betray many wanting to talk of employee participation but not provide it. We might then ask just how much employee participation do employers generally want, and how much decision making are they willing to share? If employers do not want real participation, then § 8(a)(2) should remain with full vigor.

5. EMPLOYEE CAUCUS: A KEY INSTITUTION IN THE EMERGING SYSTEM OF EMPLOYMENT LAW

ALAN HYDE*

If union density does shrink to five percent of the American workforce, how will employees express and act on their grievances with their employers? The not-very-radical initial thesis of this Article is that, in thinking about this admittedly speculative question, one should look to how American employees in nonunion settings actually pursue their interests. The conclusions that will be developed are that (1) the voluntary, informal caucus of employees will emerge as a crucial institution of employee representation, particularly in the vast majority of workplaces that have no unions; (2) such caucuses will often emerge along ethnic, racial, gender, or sexual identity lines; (3) such caucuses, though surely not envisaged as part of the Wagner Act system,[1] are already significantly protected by federal labor law; and (4) if one concentrates on the emerging caucus, one can see certain aspects of labor law that frustrate or impede their development that will come under scrutiny over the next decade and might profitably be altered.

Employee representation through caucuses is most developed among higher-educated employees in high technology workplaces who communicate through computer networks. As such, it is of interest even if it never spreads much beyond those workplaces. However, I believe, and will argue—most speculatively—that the high technology workplace will play roughly the role in the American imagination that the automobile factory did in the first half of the century, and that the institutions of employee voice that develop in that industry will be

* Professor of Law and Sidney Reitman Scholar, Rutgers, the State University of New Jersey, School of Law—Newark. Visiting Professor, Yale Law School. This Article benefited from conversation with Karl Klare, James Pope, and Joel Rogers and the research assistance of Stephen C. Payne at Yale.

1. The Wagner or National Labor Relations Act is codified at 29 U.S.C. §§ 151-169 (1982). The "Wagner Act system" includes the practices that were encouraged by and reinforced that legislation, of which the archetype was always collective bargaining in the automobile industry: exclusive representation by a majority, industrial union; formal, written collective agreements; industrial action limited to interest disputes at the termination of the agreement; grievance processing, conceived as distinct from interest disputes, through formal channels ending in arbitration. The best analysis of the relationship among American law, the economy, and institutions of industrial relations is CHARLES C. HECKSCHER, THE NEW UNIONISM: EMPLOYEE INVOLVEMENT IN THE CHANGING CORPORATION 15-33 (1988).

a major symbolic reference point far beyond their site of origin.[2] Employee caucuses thus have the potential to become, if they are not already, the dominant institution of employee voice in the United States.[3]

I. Competing Institutions of Employee Voice

Most of what is written about American labor law these days responds to the dramatic decline in union representation; it is not necessary to repeat the facts here. This Article shares the common assumption that, for most employees, work will continue to be less than perfect; complaints, grievances, and disputes will arise; and institutions will continue to be necessary for their resolution.

Scholars of industrial relations and labor law have not exactly covered themselves with glory as forecasters. Few predicted the dramatic decline in union density (just as few at the turn of the 1930's predicted the increases of that decade). I do not claim any great skill as a forecaster and admit that informal caucuses may never play any great role in employee relations. This might be the case if employees

2. I am in the very early stages of preparing a book on the emerging system of employment law and relations in high-technology professional employment as a basis for reshaping American employment law generally. The key elements of the new system of employment law, as I see them, are: pluralistic representation, in which employees are represented at different times by a variety of formal and informal caucuses, none of which purports to speak as an "exclusive" representative; flexible compensation arrangements, including heavy use of profit sharing and employee ownership; representation designed to monitor and enforce these flexible compensation arrangements and including direct participation in corporate management, such as through employee directors, employee share ownership, and joint action committees or teams; all the arrangements of flexible compensation, and other products of pluralistic representation, understood as implicit contracts; appreciation of employees as intellectual laborers, including articulate norms on the ownership of employee ideas and knowledge; and a more developed sense of employee autonomy and privacy.

The larger work will develop these themes with many examples from American workplaces that are prototypes of these approaches. The present Article, however, was designed to be brief and punchy; I will use only two major examples and spare the reader extensive documentation of many broad assertions I hope to establish in the larger work.

3. "Caucus" is not a term of art and was selected because it presently has no technical meaning whatever in labor or employment law. I mean to emphasize the loose and informal organization of such groups. For purposes of this Article, the most significant forms of "caucuses" will be (1) unorganized networking and griping; (2) internal pressure groups that form in protest of *ad hoc* decisions; and (3) "identity" groups like women's, Black, Latino, Asian, or gay and lesbian caucuses.

"Employee voice," which has become almost a cliche, is a concept developed and made popular in Richard B. Freeman & James L. Medoff, What Do Unions Do? (1984), applying to employee relations the conceptual scheme of Albert O. Hirschman, Exit, Voice, and Loyalty: Responses to Decline in Firms, Organizations, and States (1970). It does not have a precise operational meaning and is meant to refer loosely to union activities that affect management through mechanisms other than the creation of a cartel or monopoly over the price of labor stressed by neoclassical economists. In practice it amounts to the revival of what used to be known as "institutional" labor economics.

come instead to be routinely represented either by labor unions as we have known them, or by some alternative institutions, such as statutorily-required works councils or employee participation committees. I favor statutory changes to facilitate union organizing[4] and to require experimentation with different forms of required employee councils. However, I do not expect either to emerge as a typical or modal way of representing employees.

It is possible that unions will find the way to reach the growing ranks of white collar, professional, managerial, and technical workers that has eluded them so far, and the same may be true for poorer-paid service workers.[5] Success in organizing either group would plainly require some changed union attitudes, and perhaps legal change as well. Unions historically negotiate wage and employment stability chiefly in the context of large enterprises, preferably oligopolistic sellers that can adapt to lengthy and inflexible contracts, formal job descriptions, and seniority ladders. There are simply fewer and fewer such enterprises in the American economy, and will be fewer yet if mass production industry is encouraged to relocate to Mexico under the North American Free Trade Agreement. Unions in the Wagner Act framework have not been able effectively to address issues of individual career development and enterprise planning and culture that obsess professional workers.[6]

4. The best thought-out proposal is PAUL C. WEILER, GOVERNING THE WORKPLACE: THE FUTURE OF LABOR AND EMPLOYMENT LAW 225-81 (1990).

5. For a detailed analysis of how American union structure, organization and practices represent adaptations to an economy of mass production industry, see HECKSCHER, *supra* note 1, at 15-33.

6. From the unscientific sample of people I happen to talk to, including my own students, no complaint about unions of teachers, professors, or other professional workers is more common than the charge that the union seems interested only in wages, benefits, and parking fees and uninterested in issues of the scope, direction, and quality of the enterprise (e.g., education or children). These attitudes are deeply ingrained in American union practice and would be unlikely to be affected by the modification of National Labor Relations Act § 8(a)(2), 29 U.S.C. § 158(a)(2) (1988), to accommodate collegial organization, as advocated by David M. Rabban, *Can American Labor Law Accommodate Collective Bargaining by Professional Employees?*, 99 YALE L.J. 689, 754-56 (1990). The issues that my students and I would like to see unions of professional employees address—I speak here as one represented by the American Association of University Professors—are not the issues that a defender of collective bargaining for professional employees shows their unions addressing. That list includes such issues as work load and job descriptions that are much closer to a traditional industrial union agenda, though Rabban also shows some bargaining over professional standards, organizational policy, and commitment of organizational resources. David M. Rabban, *Is Unionization Compatible with Professionalism?*, 45 INDUS. & LAB. REL. REV. 97, 99-110 (1991). It is possible that fairly major changes in § 8(a)(5), increasing union access to company information and bargaining over areas now defined as managerial prerogatives, might help spark union bargaining in these areas, though in my opinion the deficiencies have more to do with union tradition and culture than the legal framework.

Recently, scholars have begun investigating mandatory elected statutory works councils such as are required by law in Germany, the Netherlands, France, and Italy.[7] I agree with scholars who have observed that such councils perform many valuable public functions, such as lowering information costs for employers and employees, and enforcing statutory labor standards with less governmental bureaucracy.[8] Some governmental subsidy or regulatory programs have begun to require organized employee representation as part of the program, which in nonunion workplaces means some kind of elected council. One can predict further experiments, which I favor, in mandated employee representation.[9] Perhaps after some years of experimentation with elected councils in nonunion workplaces, consensus will form on an appropriate format that might be required in all work-

On the vast areas of enterprise planning and culture that are effectively unreachable by employees under American collective bargaining, see Karl E. Klare, *The Labor-Management Cooperation Debate: A Workplace Democracy Perspective*, 23 HARV. C.R.-C.L. L. REV. 39, 40-56 (1988) (needs of working people unmet through collective barganing unless supplemented by democratic, participatory institutions); Katherine Van Wezel Stone, *Labor and the Corporate Structure: Changing Conceptions and Emerging Possibilities*, 55 U. CHI. L. REV. 73, 86-147 (1988) (legal exclusion of workers from enterprise participation). Employers are, of course, absolutely privileged to refuse to recognize representatives of the large, undefined set of "managerial employees." NLRB v. Yeshiva Univ., 444 U.S. 672 (1980) (ordinary university professors are "managerial employees" excluded from NLRA). *See* David M. Rabban, *Distinguishing Excluded Managers from Covered Professionals under the NLRA*, 89 COLUM. L. REV. 1775 (1989) [hereinafter Rabban, *Distinguishing Excluded Managers*] (supporting exclusion); Karl E. Klare, *The Bitter and the Sweet: Reflections on the Supreme Court's Yeshiva Decision,* 13 SOCIALIST REV, Sept.-Oct. 1983, at 99 (criticizing exclusion).

7. Richard B. Freeman & Joel Rogers, *Who Speaks for Us? Employee Representation in a Nonunion Labor Market*, *in* EMPLOYEE REPRESENTATION: ALTERNATIVES AND FUTURE DIRECTIONS 13-79 (Bruce E. Kaufman & Morris M. Kleiner eds., 1993) [hereinafter EMPLOYEE REPRESENTATION]; WORKS COUNCILS (Joel Rogers & Wolfgang Streeck eds.) (forthcoming); WEILER, *supra* note 4, at 282-95; Clyde W. Summers, *Worker Participation in the U.S. and West Germany: A Comparative Study from an American Perspective*, 28 AM. J. COMP. L. 367 (1980).

8. Clyde W. Summers, *Effective Remedies for Employment Rights: Preliminary Guidelines and Proposals*, 141 U. PA. L. REV. 457, 540-45 (1992) (advocating statutory safety committees as a supplement to the comparative failure of bureaucratic and common law remedies).

9. The proposed new program for national health insurance may have provisions for formal representation of employees in the health industry.

For another example, I would favor mandatory statutory elected councils of employees who work at home. The difficulties in enforcing labor standards for workers working at home, on which see Gemsco, Inc. v. Walling, 324 U.S. 244 (1945) (upholding Department of Labor ban on homework in seven industries because of difficulty in enforcing labor standards); Fair Labor Standards Act § 11(d), 29 U.S.C. § 211(d) (1988) (authorizing Department to ban homework); International Ladies' Garment Workers' Union v. Donovan, 722 F.2d 795 (D.C. Cir. 1983), *cert. denied,* 469 U.S. 820 (1984) (Secretary must consider alternatives to deregulation before lifting ban on homework in knitted outerwear); International Ladies' Garment Workers' Union v. Dole, 729 F. Supp. 877 (D.D.C. 1989) (permitting Secretary to replace ban on homework with certification system in five small handiwork industries, relying in part on infrequency of departmental investigations of homework); HOUSE COMM. ON GOV'T OPERATIONS, HOME-BASED CLERICAL WORKERS: ARE THEY VICTIMS OF EXPLOITATION?, H.R. DOC. NO. 99-677, 99th Cong., 2d Sess. (1986); could be reduced by requiring employers employing home workers to divulge records of hours worked and compensation to an elected home workers' council.

places above a certain size, as in the European statutes. I do not believe, however, that there is any such understanding now that would permit imposition of a uniform format on all American workplaces. I also do not believe that representational structures having no organic relationship to existing worklife have much chance of being successfully imposed by statute.[10]

In any case, the typical American employee in 1993—as in any other year in American history[11]—is represented neither by a labor union nor an elected works council. If this fact does not change, and if this employee has a complaint, grievance, or dispute on the job, what is she or he likely to do?

The worker might quit her job. In the blessed world of law and economics, this happens costlessly and painlessly; if the worker quits, a new worker is hired at the same rate, and the worker who quits immediately finds a new job that pays her the value of her marginal product. Alas, there are no professional labor economists who believe that this is the way things work. On this descriptive issue, neo-classicists like Edward Lazear of the University of Chicago have done outstanding, pioneering work on the implicit labor contracts that tie workers to firms over the long term, of which the most significant feature is the wage that increases over time, irrespective of changes in productivity.[12] Of course, many of these implicit employment contracts lie in ruins after the last decade.[13] For present purposes, however, it is enough to note that we are nowhere near the happy land of

10. A sobering recent failure are the Auroux laws of President Mitterand's administration in France, which were supposed to institutionalize direct, unrepresented expression by workers at the workplace and turned into a vehicle for employers to introduce quality circles or management-dominated organization. W. RAND SMITH, CRISIS IN THE FRENCH LABOUR MOVEMENT: A GRASSROOTS' PERSPECTIVE 215-19 (1987); Francois Eyraud & Robert Tchobanian, *The Auroux Reforms and Company Level Industrial Relations in France*, 23 BRIT. J. INDUS. REL. 241 (1985).

11. *See generally* Sanford M. Jacoby, *Norms and Cycles: The Dynamics of Nonunion Industrial Relations in the United States, 1897-1987*, *in* NEW DEVELOPMENTS IN THE LABOR MARKET: TOWARD A NEW INSTITUTIONAL PARADIGM 22-25 (Katherine C. Abraham & Robert B. McKersie eds., 1990).

12. Edward P. Lazear, *Why Is There Mandatory Retirement?*, 87 J. POL. ECON. 1261 (1979). For further economic analysis of implicit employment contracts, the best starting points are the anthology EFFICIENCY WAGE MODELS OF THE LABOR MARKET (George A. Akerlof & Janet L. Yellen eds., 1986), and the survey, Sherwin Rosen, *Implicit Contracts: A Survey*, 23 J. ECON. LIT. 1144 (1985). For legal implications, see WEILER, *supra* note 4, at 63-71, 134-52 (wrongful termination law as enforcement of expectations justified under implicit employment contracts); Alan Hyde, *In Defense of Employee Ownership*, 67 CHI.-KENT L. REV. 159, 176-79, 199-203 (1991) (employee ownership as solution to social externalities and inefficient incentive structure associated with implicit employment contracts); Marleen A. O'Connor, *Restructuring the Corporation's Nexus of Contracts: Recognizing a Fiduciary Duty to Protect Displaced Workers*, 69 N.C. L. REV. 1189, 1203-18 (1991) (summarizing economic literature on implicit employment contracts).

13. *See, e.g.*, Louis Uchitelle, *Strong Companies are Joining Trend to Eliminate Jobs*, N.Y. TIMES, July 26, 1993, at A1.

law and economics in which there are no workplace disputes because unhappy employees just go elsewhere. Rather, employer abrogation of implicit employment contracts is a fertile source of reported employment litigation.[14]

So, for practical purposes, the contemporary American worker with a gripe has no union, no works council, and may not feel like quitting. Of course, she or he may "lump it"—the world's most common and time-honored method of dispute resolution[15]—and internalize the dispute. While some such "lumping it" is socially useful—people cannot be encouraged to fight every grievance—one may well question whether the levels of internalization common in American employment are socially optimum.[16] She may retaliate quietly against the employer; it is impossible to form any judgment of the frequency of this or the social costs imposed.[17]

She may find a lawyer and litigate. Increasingly, this is what employees do, at least, comfortable upper-level employees who can afford lawyers,[18] and the field of individual employee litigation is now a law school course all by itself. It would be hard, however, to find anyone who believes that the nation has enough judges and courthouses to make common law litigation the modal institution of employee grievance processing.

So, while legal and practical alternatives for employees do exist and may even flourish over the next decade, the fate of spontaneous and informal employee responses to their grievances is worth some examination as a fundamental institution of employee representation in the nonunion workplace.

14. Employment contracts "implied in fact" from consistent employer practice: Gilbert v. Durand Glass Mfg. Co., 609 A.2d 517 (N.J. Super. Ct. App. Div. 1992); Sanders v. Parker Drilling Co., 911 F.2d 191 (9th Cir. 1990), *cert. denied*, 111 S. Ct. 2014 (1991) (Alaska law); Foley v. Interactive Data Corp., 765 P.2d 373 (Cal. 1988) (contract created by course of employer conduct); Wilkerson v. Wells Fargo Bank, 261 Cal. Rptr. 185 (Cal. Ct. App. 1989). Obligations of "good faith" implied in the employment contract: Tymshare, Inc. v. Covell, 727 F.2d 1145 (D.C. Cir. 1984) (Scalia, J.); Fortune v. National Cash Register Co., 364 N.E.2d 1251 (Mass. 1977).

15. William L.F. Felstiner, *Influences of Social Organization on Dispute Processing*, 9 L. & Soc. Rev. 63, 81 (1974); William L.F. Felstiner, *Avoidance as Dispute Processing: An Elaboration*, 9 L. & Soc. Rev. 695 (1975).

16. Marc Lendler, Just the Working Life: Opposition and Accommodation in Daily Industrial Life (1990).

17. Sabotage in the American Workplace: Anecdotes of Dissatisfaction, Mischief and Revenge (Martin Sprouse ed., 1992); Ben Hamper, Rivethead: Tales from the Assembly Line 206-09 (1991).

18. *See* Summers, *supra* note 8, at 467 ("Because of litigation costs, all but middle and upper income employees are largely foreclosed from any access to a remedy for wrongful dismissal.").

II. Case Study of an Employee Caucus I: Networking at TekCo

The literature on informal employee groups in nonunion settings is surprisingly sparse.[19] Professors Elizabeth L. Bishop and David I. Levine have graciously shared the following account from their unpublished research on the large, high technology company they call TekCo.[20]

TekCo is a major high technology company with over eight thousand employees, most highly trained. Almost every employee has a work station at his or her desk, capable of accessing electronic mail, including an internal electronic bulletin board. TekCo encourages employee use of the internal bulletin board; its training materials note that "the TekCo Recycles program, . . . got started when someone suggested it in a [network] discussion. TekCo's policies on hiring minorities, allowing smoking in TekCo buildings, naming conventions for shared computers, and many other issues have been hashed out thoroughly in these discussions."[21] Fifty top executives receive periodic two-page summaries of the main issues discussed on the network, under the title "What employees want."[22]

In January 1990, TekCo management announced revisions in the profit sharing plan that would have eliminated any payments to employees in quarters with slow sales growth. "Literally hundreds of postings were entered on [the electronic bulletin board] in the busiest days. All told, on the order of one thousand messages were received. This issue elicited a greater volume of response than had any event in the history of the company. The system was literally swamped."[23] Most responses attacked the reductions, often bitterly, while a minority defended them. A common early theme was that "employees wanted a complete explanation for why the change in profit-sharing

19. One of my favorite books about work disputes resonates with many of the themes of this study and is surely overdue for a revival. Deena Weinstein, Bureaucratic Opposition: Challenging Abuses at the Workplace 57-106 (1979), studied how workers in bureaucratic organizations—disproportionately female, white-collar, nonunion—changed their work. It includes rare academic discussions of basic techniques of "labor struggle" known to all such workers but ignored by scholars fixated on male industrial workers. These include leaking; informing higher-ups, including going to the Board; making your supervisor look incompetent; working to rule, and the like.

20. Elizabeth L. Bishop & David I. Levine, Computer-Mediated Communication as Employee Voice: A Case Study (Jan. 16, 1993) (unpublished paper presented at IFIP WG 9.1, Working Conference on NetWORKing, on file with author).

21. *Id.* at 12 (quoting TekCo's training materials entitled TekCo, An Introduction to The Network).

22. *Id.* at 14.

23. *Id.* at 17.

was necessary, and how it would encourage growth as management claimed."[24] TekCo's CEO did write such explanations to the bulletin board, but many employees remained unconvinced:

> The electronic uproar had a dramatic effect. As reported in a Harvard Business School case on TekCo: "Ultimately, the collective resistance that came through [the electronic bulletin board] caused management to change the formula." The causal role of the electronic resistance was supported by all of our respondents, both employees and human resource managers.[25]

Meanwhile, one employee looked through bulletin board transcripts and recorded all of the contributors to the profit sharing debate who had used their actual names. He wrote to them, suggesting a meeting. A small group formed and met quietly several times that winter. Independently, a second employee sent a bulletin board message calling for the formation of a concerned employees' league. The groups later merged under the name Employees for One TekCo. Fifty employees attended the first meeting of the merged group, announced on the bulletin board, in May 1990.

The group sought the restoration of the "corporate culture they recalled (perhaps in a somewhat idealized form) from a few years previous."[26] They sought greater communication with top management, fewer management "perks" and other divisions among staff, and an institutionalized voice for employees:

> Members of One TekCo repeatedly pointed out that they loved TekCo. Conversely, most members and leaders we interviewed went out of their way to note that they were opposed to a union at TekCo . . . they did not want outsiders involved and they did not want a union bureaucracy to intervene between employees and managers.[27]

Management, however, has resisted formal employee representation and to date the only real effect of this agitation has been the formation of an Employee-Executive Forum in which fifteen employees, randomly selected from among volunteers, discuss their concerns with top managers. The Forum has no rights to infomation or consultation and no decision making authority; it was supposed to meet quarterly but in fact meets even less often.[28]

24. *Id.*

25. *Id.* at 18 (quoting Michael Gibbs, Strategic Human Resource Management at TekCo: Managing Morale and Corporate Culture, Harvard Business School Case N-1-491-041 (1991)).

26. *Id.* at 20.

27. *Id.*

28. *Id.* at 24.

Both the spontaneous complaints to the network, and the later formation and activity of Employees for One TekCo, are examples of the broad category of employee action that I have been calling "caucuses": (1) They arise in nonunion workforces; (2) They are not experienced by the participants as "unions," not even nonmajority unions.[29] In fact, they may appeal to particular employees precisely because they are not "unions."[30] (3) They raise both demands that unions might raise in unionized workplaces, and demands that unions rarely raise. The demand for restoration of the old profit-sharing formula, the accompanying demand for information backing management's position, and the demand for specific institutions of employee voice are demands that unions might and do raise in collective negotiations.[31] The demand for a more egalitarian and participatory corporate culture could theoretically be the subject of negotiations, but does not look much like what unions typically negotiate about or are institutionally equipped to implement. The demand for reductions in management compensation is strictly a permissive subject of bargaining to which management need not even respond, even if raised by a union, and as to which unions are forbidden recourse to economic ac-

29. On nonmajority unions, see Richard R. Carlson, *The Origin and Future of Exclusive Representation in American Labor Law*, 30 Duq. L. Rev. 779, 849-865 (1992); Matthew W. Finkin, *The Road Not Taken: Some Thoughts on Nonmajority Employee Representation*, 69 Chi.-Kent L. Rev. 195 (1993); Alan Hyde et al., *After Smyrna: Rights and Powers of Unions that Represent Less than a Majority*, 45 Rutgers L. Rev. 637 (1993); Robert J. Rabin, *The Role of Unions in the Rights-Based Workplace*, 25 U.S.F. L. Rev. 169, 205-63 (1991); Clyde W. Summers, *Unions Without Majority—A Black Hole?*, 66 Chi.-Kent L. Rev. 531 (1990).

30. In determining caucuses' legal powers, rights, and obligations, it is unnecessary to determine whether they are "unions," a term which lacks legal significance. The relevant issues, discussed *infra* pp. 163-90, are whether the networking and formation of Employees for One TekCo are "concerted activities for . . . mutual aid or protection" under National Labor Relations Act § 7, 29 U.S.C. § 157 (1988) (to which the answer is, yes), and whether either is a statutory "labor organization" under National Labor Relations Act § 2(5), 29 U.S.C. § 152(5) (1988), which is a much more difficult question.

31. The demand for information would have to be a demand raised in bargaining, since the National Labor Relations Act's duty to bargain in "good faith" does not entail any duty on the employer to share financial information with unions, absent specific claims of poverty not made by TekCo (and rarely made by employers advised by counsel). Nielsen Lithographing Co., 305 N.L.R.B. 697 (1991), *review denied sub nom.* Graphic Communications Int'l Union, Local 508 O-K-I v. NLRB, 977 F.2d 1168 (7th Cir. 1992). *See* Leslie K. Shedlin, *Regulation of Disclosure of Economic and Financial Data and the Impact on the American System of Labor-Management Relations*, 41 Ohio St. L. J. 441 (1980).

While the creation of institutions of employee voice is generally a mandatory subject of negotiations with a union, certain kinds of committees are "employer assisted labor organizations" within the meaning of §§ 2(5) (defining "labor organization") and 8(a)(2) (prohibiting employer assistance to labor organizations). *E.g.,* E.I. DuPont de Nemours & Co., 311 N.L.R.B. No. 88, 143 L.R.R.M. (BNA) 1121 (May 28, 1993) (joint safety committees); Electromation, Inc., 309 N.L.R.B. 990 (1992) (joint "action committees"). The relevance of this body of law to employee caucuses will be considered *infra* notes 70-123.

tion.[32] (4) They limit themselves to employees of a particular employer. This has obvious strengths and weaknesses, the strengths being greater spontaneity, loyalty to the group, and ease of mobilization without professional union staff or bureaucracy, and the weaknesses being difficulty in linking up with potential support outside, a scale too small to permit retention of professionals, and a difficulty in long term planning, as illustrated by the reactive mode of the TekCo groups. (5) Just like unions, they have successes and failures. However, in this particular case, the success and failure are not necessarily what one might predict. When I discuss informal employee caucuses with people experienced in labor relations, a common, indeed near-universal reaction is that, while such groups might succeed in establishing employee "voice," they could never engage in successful economic bargaining. One anecdote may or may not tell us much, except perhaps not to cling too tightly to our prejudices. However, at TekCo, the agitation over profit sharing was by all accounts stunningly successful, while the efforts to establish organized employee voice have accomplished little.[33]

32. For examples of management compensation as a permissive subject of bargaining *compare* Allied Chemical & Alkali Workers, Local 1 v. Pittsburgh Plate Glass Co., 404 U.S. 157 (1971) (changes in benefits paid to already-retired workers are a permissive subject of bargaining) *with* Keystone Consolidated Industries, Inc., 309 N.L.R.B. 294 (1992) (changes in management pension plan are mandatory subjects of bargaining where some employees participate both in management and unit plan and changes in former have impact on latter). The TekCo employees alleged that changes in management compensation had an "impact" on their work culture and relations at work every bit as concrete as the "impact" on employees of the changes in management compensation in *Keystone.* One doubts, however, that the Board would find management compensation a mandatory subject of bargaining, were there a union at TekCo that sought bargaining on management "perks."

A union's recourse to economic action over a permissive subject of bargaining violates § 8(b)(3). Summers, *supra* note 7, at 382; *See* Theodore J. St. Antoine, *Legal Barriers to Worker Participation in Management Decision Making*, 58 Tul. L. Rev. 1301 (1984).

33. This may of course reflect differences, not in the underlying demands, but in the tactics and organization deployed by employees. Employees were successful when, lacking any organization, they complained on the electronic network. After forming an organization and trying to establish channels of communication, they accomplished little. This may not be a coincidence but a generalizable theory of political action. *See generally* Frances F. Piven & Richard A. Cloward, Poor People's Movements: Why They Succeed, How They Fail (1977) (case studies of successful popular protest or insurgency transformed by organizers into ineffectual mass permanent organization). It is ironic that the Employees For One TekCo should be putting energy into as silly a mechanism of employee voice as meetings with management, when their electronic network already gives them a mechanism of employee voice as efficient and powerful as any in the world.

By contrast, TekCo employees do lack mechanisms of exerting power on management. Meetings with management will, however, not give them this. Of course, unions may not either.

III. How Typical Is TekCo?

At this point, it would be helpful for my argument to point to studies showing the typicality of the TekCo story: how many American employees participated in spontaneous protest last year, or work at a workplace with a women's or Black or Latino or Asian or gay and lesbian caucus (as opposed to a recognized union). I am unaware of any such data, so at this point the reader and I are left with our intuitions. I do spend a lot of time talking to people about their work, and am just beginning a longer-term study of employment relations in nonunion high technology (to speak pleonastically) workplaces. I can report anecdotally on the frequency of the three basic types of employee caucus we have now identified. (1) Networking and griping, without formal organization that abides over time, are of course practically universal. (2) Internal pressure groups like Employees for One TekCo seem fairly rare. (3) "Identity" groups like women's, Black, Latino, Asian, or gay and lesbian caucuses appear to be quite common in nonunion professional employment.

So, for our present purposes, let us leave the issue there, and each reader will decide for her or himself whether we are talking about thirty, sixty, or ninety percent of American workplaces. Under any of these assumptions, we have more American workplaces with informal caucuses than are unionized or likely to become so. It is worth our while to assess, insofar as we can, the strengths and weaknesses of informal employee caucuses and the existing legal framework of their rights and organization.

IV. Potential and Extant Limitations of Informal Employee Organization

Recent discussions of institutions of employee representation have contrasted collective bargaining through more or less traditional labor unions; newer "associational" unions limited to single employers; and mandatory statutory employee councils. Whatever the merits of each of these plans, each would function better in a world with employee caucuses than in a world without caucuses.

A. Unions

The main problem with collective bargaining as the dominant institution of employee representation is that there is not very much of it, partly because employers resist it strenuously, partly because labor law makes it difficult to organize workplaces, and partly because many employees, like employees of TekCo, want no part of it.[34] Caucuses, as we have seen, bring an institution of employee voice to workplaces that lack any. Caucuses also permit a targeted organizational appeal that might not be open to unions. A women's caucus need not choose between organizing around "women's issues" or "class issues."[35] Caucuses might function as way stations on the road to unionism.[36] Or, failing that, unions might find ways of representing subgroups of employees even in workplaces in which the union does not represent a majority.[37]

Caucuses would be at war with collective bargaining under only two scenarios. First, it is possible that a workplace with a functioning caucus system might for that reason be more difficult for unions to organize. I know of no evidence suggesting this, and, for reasons discussed in the preceding paragraph, the contrary hypothesis strikes me as more plausible. Personally, I have no difficulty with employees choosing to be represented by caucuses instead of unions, so long as the choice is truly theirs. However, if a defender of collective bargaining demanded a guarantee from me that public policies to encourage informal employee caucuses would not impede union organization, I regret that I cannot give such assurance.

Second, if caucuses would not impede collective organization, could they coexist with it? Again we have little real knowledge here; not, I repeat, because caucuses have not been coexisting with unions, but because scholars have not really studied the relationship.[38]

34. Those three facts are obviously related to each other. For present purposes it is unnecessary to settle on any particular explanation for the decline of collective bargaining. *Compare* Henry S. Farber & Alan B. Krueger, *Union Membership in the United States: The Decline Continues*, *in* EMPLOYEE REPRESENTATION, *supra* note 7, at 105-34 (declining employee demand for unions) *with* Joel Rogers, *In the Shadow of the Law: Institutional Aspects of Postwar U.S. Union Decline*, *in* LABOR LAW IN AMERICA: HISTORICAL AND CRITICAL ESSAYS 283 (Christopher L. Tomlins & Andrew J. King eds., 1992) (emphasizing shifts in underlying employment and legal environment).

35. *Cf.* ROBERTA GOLDBERG, ORGANIZING WOMEN OFFICE WORKERS (1983) (making contrast); KAREN BRODKIN SACKS, CARING BY THE HOUR: WOMEN, WORK AND ORGANIZING AT DUKE MEDICAL CENTER (1988).

36. This was the strategy of some groups of women office workers such as 9 to 5, which organized around women's issues and later became a division of the Service Employees' International Union. There is a book waiting to be written about this experience.

37. This is the theme of the articles cited *supra* note 29.

38. This Article focuses on the legal status of employee caucuses in the nonunion workplace. Consequently, the issue of the coexistence of employee caucuses and exclusive majority representatives is left for another day. The main issue here is the continuing force of Emporium Capwell Co. v. Western Addition Community Org., 420 U.S. 50 (1975) (employees represented by a union are not protected by § 7 when they seek separate bargaining to address alleged race discrimination). This case, which has not often been followed, looks increasingly anachronistic, the last gasp of a pure system, of exclusive representation by the majority union, that fell apart in the following decade.

I see the continued existence of caucuses within labor unions as a potential antidote to some of the problems of unions: their bureaucracy, weak internal democracy, and low rates of participation. An

Today, employees represented by a majority union may neverthless be covered by additional, explicit and implicit individual or group contracts governing workplace rights, that they may enforce in suits under the common law of contracts. The Supreme Court has held that employees may enforce such "individual" agreements if they were entered into at a time the employees were not represented by a union. Belknap, Inc. v. Hale, 463 U.S. 491, 498-512 (1983) (replacement workers may enforce contracts of permanent employment in state court despite contrary provisions of strike settlement agreement); Caterpillar Inc. v. Williams, 482 U.S. 386, 396 (1987) (laid off employees may enforce promises of job security made to them at times they held supervisory positions; a "plaintiff covered by a collective-bargaining agreement is permitted to assert legal rights *independent* of that agreement, including state-law contract rights, so long as the contract relied upon is *not* a collective-bargaining agreement"); *see also* Berda v. CBS, Inc., 881 F.2d 20, 24-28 (3d Cir. 1989) (employee may enforce promise of job security made orally to him in employment interview despite contrary provisions in collective agreement applicable to him once he took the job), *cert. denied*, 493 U.S. 1062 (1990).

Employees may also, however, enforce promises made to them even at the time they were represented by a union, so long as the promises were not part of a collective agreement, according to four courts of appeals. Milne Employees Ass'n v. Sun Carriers, Inc., 960 F.2d 1401, 1407-10 (9th Cir. 1991) (unionized employees may sue in state court alleging employer's fraudulent promises of job security since such promises were not made in a collective agreement but in speeches made directly to employees), *cert. denied*, 113 S. Ct. 2927 (1993); White v. National Steel Corp., 938 F.2d 474, 484 (4th Cir.) (oral promises to induce acceptance of supervisory positions, promising right to bump back into unit, enforceable in damages despite collective agreement prohibiting such bumping), *cert. denied*, 112 S. Ct. 454 (1991); Wells v. General Motors Corp., 881 F.2d 166 (5th Cir. 1989) (employees may sue in state court to enforce employer's oral promise made during ratification of severance pay plan that employees who accepted severance could reapply as vacancies opened up), *cert. denied*, 495 U.S. 923 (1990); Anderson v. Ford Motor Co., 803 F.2d 953, 958 (8th Cir. 1986) (probationary employees allegedly promised permanent positions but bumped by laid-off employees on national preferential hiring list created by collective agreement), *cert. denied*, 483 U.S. 1011 (1987).

Finally, employees may enforce promises made to them even when the promises themselves may be unfair labor practices. For example, in Kinoshita v. Canadian Pacific Airlines, Ltd., 724 P.2d 110, 113 (Haw. 1986), the employer greeted the union drive with a proposed new set of employee rules, including inter alia the right to appeal from discipline. Certainly an employer covered by the NLRA would violate § 8(a)(1) in making such a promise. *See* NLRB v. Exchange Parts Co., 375 U.S. 405, 409 (1964) (§ 8(a)(1) prohibits "conduct immediately favorable to employees which is undertaken with the express purpose of impinging on their freedom of choice for or against union organization and is reasonably calculated to have that effect"). The employees voted down the union. Kinoshita was later summarily disciplined and denied a right to appeal. *Kinoshita*, 724 P.2d at 114, 15. The state court held that Kinoshita was entitled to enforce in contract the employer's promise. The fact that the employees voted down the union was said to be evidence of their reliance on the promise. *Id.* at 117-18.

If the above cases are correct, the employees in *Emporium Capwell* could have negotiated binding individual or group promises on job discrimination, had the employer been willing, and could have enforced those promises in suit in state court. It is thus difficult to explain why they could be fired for asking for such negotiations, unless we have one rule for scabs negotiating replacement jobs and another for African-American employees negotiating to end discrimination. Nor were the employees in *Emporium Capwell* unprotected because of the manner in which they sought separate negotiations (that is, picketing the store); the Board had not found that conduct "disloyal"; the Court of Appeals had remanded for just such findings; but the Supreme Court held that § 7 did not protect minority bargaining no matter how that demand was advanced. For a critique of *Emporium Capwell* from a different perspective, see Elizabeth M. Iglesias, *Structures of Subordination: Women of Color at the Intersection of Title VII and the NLRA. Not!*, 28 HARV. C.R.-C.L. L. REV. 395, 415-31 (1993).

active caucus system could encourage participation, provide loyal opposition to union leadership, and create a richer internal union political life without weakening the union in its relations with employers. At least, that was the conclusion of the classic study of the classic deviant case.[39] However, it is possible that some workforces would be put into the position of choosing between caucuses and unions. Still, where unions have been rejected, I see no possible objection to choosing caucuses over nothing.

B. Associational Unions

Charles Heckscher has written an interesting and important book advocating the evolution of union structure toward what he calls "associational unionism"—unions that are linked to specific employers and develop, monitor, and enforce flexible arrangements of job assignment and compensation.[40] Space does not permit a fuller summary of his views, which are definitely required reading for anyone concerned about employee representation. Employee networking and caucusing at TekCo might be seen as a rough start to Heckscher's associational unions. Certainly they combine receptiveness to cooperation with the employer with organizational forms designed to accommodate flexible compensation arrangements such as profit sharing. That is, they do not negotiate job descriptions or uniform pay scales. They do monitor employee compensation, demand that management back up changes with information, and force management to share information with them.

The biggest weakness, however, that I see in Heckscher's call for associational unionism is the isolation of these loyalist associations—their inability to link up with workers at other employers.[41] While employee networks and groups like Employees for One TekCo share this problem, "identity" caucuses do not. Civil rights and community

39. SEYMOUR M. LIPSET ET AL., UNION DEMOCRACY: THE INTERNAL POLITICS OF THE INTERNATIONAL TYPOGRAPHICAL UNION (1956) (study of a union with a functional system of internal political parties).

40. HECKSCHER, *supra* note 1, at 177-231.

41. Antitrust law reinforces this conundrum. For example, if associational unions became common it should not be difficult to create a practice in which the employees' association would nominate or even in practice select a member of the corporate Board of Directors. However, the Department of Justice has taken the position that it is a violation of § 8 of the Clayton Antitrust Act for a labor union representing employees at competing employers (there, Chrysler and American Motors) to have "representatives" (even if not formal "agents") on the board of each. Letter from Sanford M. Litvack, Assistant Attorney General, Antitrust Division, to United Automobile Workers, 7 Trade Reg. Rep. (CCH) Current Comment, ¶ 50,425 (1981). So if board representation is important, employees may be forced to select associational (rather than national) unions.

orgnizations can link (say) Latino caucuses to each other, as well as help them undertake activities that apparently are constitutionally protected when undertaken by civil rights organizations but said to be forbidden to labor organizations.[42]

C. *Statutory Works Councils*

Finally, as mentioned above, while mandatory works councils offer intriguing possibilities for efficient administration of labor statutes and employee voice,[43] as imposed organizations they would create potential problems of unresponsiveness, bureaucracy, low participation, and the need to impose legal duties of fair representation. While such problems could be solved in many ways, a functioning system of employee issue and identity caucuses would help counter trends toward bureaucratic representation.

V. THE EXISTING LEGAL FRAMEWORK FOR EMPLOYEE CAUCUSES IN NONUNION WORKPLACES

Five recent articles discuss different aspects of the role of the labor union that represents some, but less than a majority, of a workforce.[44] Since "labor union" is not a legal term of art, most of what is said there applies as well to a caucus of employees that does not describe itself as a union, and so need only be summarized here. Perhaps the most important point is that this recent flurry of interest in nonmajority unions may in practice be realized not by "unions" at all, but by identity caucuses or other informal employee groups.

The most important point of labor law necessary to grasp, in order to understand the rights and powers of caucuses, is that three crucial concepts of labor law are legally independent of each other: (1) the right of "employees" to engage in "concerted activities for . . . mutual aid or protection"[45]; (2) a "labor organization";[46] and (3) the status of "exclusive representative for purposes of collective bargain-

42. *Compare* NAACP v. Claiborne Hardware Co., 458 U.S. 886 (1982) (boycott of white merchants protected by First Amendment from application of state tort law) *with* FTC v. Superior Court Trial Lawyers Ass'n, 493 U.S. 411 (1990) (group refusal of lawyers to accept court appointments until fees raised violates Federal Trade Commission Act). *See* Gary Minda, *Rediscovering Progressive Labor Politics: The Labor Law Implications of* Federal Trade Commission v. Superior Court Trial Lawyers Association, 16 VT. L. REV. 71 (1991); James G. Pope, *Labor-Community Coalitions and Boycotts: The Old Labor Law, the New Unionism, and the Living Constitution*, 69 TEX. L. REV. 889 (1991).

43. *See supra* notes 7-10 and accompanying text.

44. *See supra* note 29.

45. National Labor Relations Act § 7, 29 U.S.C. § 157 (1988).

46. National Labor Relations Act § 2(5), 29 U.S.C. § 152(5) (1988).

ing" given to "representatives designated or selected for the purposes of collective bargaining by the majority of the employees in a unit appropriate for such purposes."[47]

As we shall see, a half century of labor law has been built on the distinctness of these three concepts. This point is rarely stressed in labor law classes, because under the "law in action" "Wagner Act system," the three concepts ideally approach identity.[48] The preferred mode of employee activity, as of labor organization, was the labor union. Normal union practice was not to attempt to organize a unit, unless the union would represent a majority and thus be the "exclusive representative."[49] Thus, under these ordinary assumptions, the three concepts were intimately linked, as they described temporally an idealized evolution. "Concerted activities" were normally simply an inchoate organizational form leading up to action by a "labor organization," which would in time either become the "exclusive representative" or simply fail to operate at a given workplace altogether.[50]

It is long past time for scholars of labor law to appreciate the legal disaggregation of these three concepts, as they have broken apart in practice in American workplaces, of which TekCo is but one example. Here is a primer of the definitions and uses of the two concepts crucial to caucuses, "protected concerted activities" and "labor organization." It may be old hat to labor law scholars, but this material is so rarely applied, and on occasion so misunderstood by courts, that a primer-like exposition may have value. It will emerge that

47. National Labor Relations Act § 9(a), 29 U.S.C. § 159(a) (1988).

48. One of the greatest strengths of American labor law scholarship of the Wagner Act period was precisely to treat the contents of negotiated collective agreements and the decisions of private labor arbitrators as part of "labor law," as may be seen in any introductory casebook. This approach helped inspire some of the most powerful European scholarship, e.g. GINO GIUGNI, DIRITTO SINDACALE 11 (8th ed. 1988) (the opening sentence of which defines union law as including norms propounded by the state and by worker organizations), often operating against positivistic traditions under which only the product of state actors could possibly be seen as "law." I am trying to continue, not criticize, this tradition. This accounts for the concededly cumbersome formulations in text. There is a sense in which the formal "labor law" of the United States has always kept the three concepts distinct, but there is also a very real sense in which lived "labor law" for half a century tended to elide the distinctions.

49. Herbert Schreiber, *The Origin of the Majority Rule and the Simultaneous Development of Institutions to Protect the Minority: A Chapter in Early American Labor Law*, 25 RUTGERS L. REV. 237 (1971); Ruth Weyand, *Majority Rule in Collective Bargaining*, 45 COLUM. L. REV. 556, 563-64 (1945).

50. For an example of this assumption in an otherwise most valuable article, see Charles J. Morris, *NLRB Protection in the Nonunion Workplace: A Glimpse at a General Theory of Section 7 Conduct*, 137 U. PA. L. REV. 1673, 1677 & n.17 (1989) ("This Article . . . cover[s] only employee *pre-organizational* activity . . . . Pre-organization activity includes any mutual activity covered by NLRA § 7 when no union is present. It does not necessarily contemplate a union organizational drive.") (emphasis added).

nearly everything that employee caucuses do is "protected concerted activity"—protected against employer retaliation. Whether caucuses are "labor organizations" is relevant mainly where employers contribute support to them. Answering that question is unnecessarily difficult and illustrates the need for reforms to that body of law.

A. *Protected Concerted Activities*

"Concerted activities for . . . mutual aid or protection" (hereinafter abbreviated, as labor lawyers do, "protected concerted activities") set the boundaries for *employer retaliation.* It is an unfair labor practice "for an employer to interfere with, restrain, or coerce employees in the exercise of the right[ ]" to engage in such concerted activities.[51] "Protected concerted activities" are also part of drawing the line between areas of federal and state regulation.[52]

Since the language of section 7 itself protects *both* the right to "form, join, or assist labor organizations, to bargain collectively . . . , and to engage in other concerted activities for the purpose of collective bargaining" *and* such activities "for the purpose of . . . other mutual aid or protection" it has been easy to hold, as a consistent feature of labor law, that employers may not retaliate against employees who engage in concerted activities even when there is no union and no prospect of one.[53] When TekCo employees complained on the electronic bulletin board about profit-sharing reductions, or contacted other employees to form a group, or held a meeting, or formed Employees for One TekCo, they were in each case engaging in "concerted activities for . . . mutual aid or protection" and, as such, were pro-

51. National Labor Relations Act § 8(a)(1), 29 U.S.C. § 158(a)(1) (1988). While an employer may not discharge or discipline employees for engaging in protected concerted activities, the employer may, under a well-known historical anomaly, replace them. NLRB v. Mackay Radio & Tel. Co., 304 U.S. 333, 345-46 (1938) (dictum). The complexities of permissible and impermissible retaliation against protected activities are beyond the scope of this Article.

52. States are forbidden to regulate activity "arguably protected" by § 7 or "arguably prohibited" by § 8. San Diego Bldg. Trades Council v. Garmon, 359 U.S. 236, 245 (1959). There are numerous exceptions, of unclear scope. Baker v. General Motors Corp., 478 U.S. 621 (1986) (state may deny unemployment compensation to workers who "finance" a protected strike with special dues); Sears, Roebuck & Co. v. San Diego County Dist. Council Carpenters, 436 U.S. 180 (1978) (state may enforce trespass laws against picketing "arguably protected" by § 7 where employer had no way of obtaining NLRB ruling on whether picketing was protected).

53. The leading case is NLRB v. Washington Aluminum Co., 370 U.S. 9, 14-16 (1962), in which seven unorganized machinists were discharged when they went home rather than work in an unheated and bitterly cold shop; the discharges violated § 8(a)(1). *See also* Mike Yurosek & Son, Inc., 306 N.L.R.B. 1037 (1992) (refusing to work overtime as protected activity where a protest either against inconsistent management demands or against pay reduction); Quality C.A.T.V., Inc., 278 N.L.R.B. 1282 (1986) (two linemen refusing to climb wet poles, protected against discharge).

tected against discipline or discharge. TekCo employees may not think they have much use for unions, but it is the NLRA, and the NLRA alone, that protects them from getting fired for the above activities.[54]

This Article argues that labor law should commit itself to protecting employee caucuses as a fundamental institution of employee voice, not merely as a "pre-organizational" state. Should the nation follow that advice, the fact that the law under section 7 protects nonunion employee organization would provide a good start. Nevertheless, there are flaws in section 7 as protection for employee caucuses, mostly quite well-known, that show up clearly in the glaring light of the nonunion workforce, particularly one unfamiliar with unions and collective bargaining.

First, by longstanding administrative interpretation, "managerial" employees, a category wholly unknown to and undefined by statute, are not "employees" protected by section 7. Moreover, the Board and Supreme Court have differed on the definition of "managerial employees"; there is no agreed-on definition; and the Supreme Court's most recent attempt, to the extent it is comprehensible at all, is wildly overinclusive.[55] Labor law committed to voice for professional employees should consider abandoning the nonstatutory exemption for

54. It is possible that their discharge might in some jurisdictions be a tortious violation of public policy. In California, however, that tort is apparently limited to public policy with "a basis in either the constitution or statutory provisions," Gantt v. Sentry Ins., 824 P.2d 680, 687-88 (Cal. 1992) (dictum).

55. NLRB v. Yeshiva Univ., 444 U.S. 672 (1980) (university professors are "managerial employees," reversing contrary determination of NLRB). Managerial employees "represent management interests by taking or recommending discretionary actions that effectively control or implement employer policy." *Id.* at 683. This nondefinition is on a collision course with much commented trends in work organization that encourage all employees to supervise each other. For example, in Jhirmack Enters., 283 N.L.R.B. 609 (1987), an employee was engaged in "protected concerted activity" when she warned a co-worker that employees had been complaining about his slow performance. "The employee complaints were prompted by their concern that Ramsey's performance adversely affected their chances of winning the weekly production award and increased the possibility of overtime work. Allison's purposes in relaying the complaints to Ramsey was to encourage him to take corrective action to protect his job." *Id.* at 609 n.2. The Board held that Allison was engaged in protected concerted activity. *Id.* at 609. It seems to me that she could as easily have been held to be a "managerial" employee under *Yeshiva*, particularly if the company's team organization gave employees formal responsibility to monitor each other. The line between "employee" and "manager" is blurrier yet in professional employment, blurrier still where employees work at electronic work stations with access to the same data base, monitoring each other. *See generally* Shoshanna Zuboff, In the Age of the Smart Machine: The Future of Work and Power 255-63 (1988).

Rabban, *Distinguishing Excluded Managers*, *supra* note 6, at 1824-32, documents the post-Yeshiva morass and struggles to develop a better distinction, deriving from the sociological literature on the professions a distinction between "managerial" and "practicing" professionals, that regrettably just restates the problem. *Id.* at 1832-56. Rabban does not deal with team organization, mutual employee monitoring, and the like.

"managerial" employees, as the Board once attempted to do (only to be told that Congressional action would be required).[56]

Second, as a very able line of recent scholarship shows, while section 7 protects group action in the nonunion workplace, the hypertechnical nature of its boundaries provides shaky protection for employees who take spontaneous action in pressured situations without assistance from any formal organization.[57] This comes about because of the lingering assumption that all of this is just "preorganizational" activity. When we recognize that, for most American employees, the only voice is the inchoate voice of the network, the bulletin board, or at most the caucus, much of labor law that assertedly protects employees becomes either of limited value or a trap for the unwary.

For an example different from those discussed in the recent scholarship, consider the Supreme Court's ruling in *Eastex, Inc. v. NLRB*.[58] The president of a union local sought permission to pass out to employees his own four paragraph newsletter urging members to register to vote and to write state legislators to oppose adding a prohibition on union security to the state constitution. The Supreme Court, affirming the Board, held that the newsletter was "protected concerted activity" under section 7. In context, this meant that the newsletter could be handed out by employees in nonworking areas of the plant during nonworking time. By implication, discharge or discipline of employees for handing out the newsletter would similarly have been an unfair labor practice.

In finding the newsletter protected, however, the Supreme Court applied no simple, bright line test—for example, that employees be protected in any nonviolent communication, irrespective of content.[59] Nor did the Court simply defer to the Board's finding that the newsletter was protected. Rather, the Court read the entire text of the

56. NLRB v. Bell Aerospace Co., 416 U.S. 267 (1974). Eliminating the exemption for "managerial employees" might leave intact the 1947 statutory exemption for "supervisors" with personnel authority. National Labor Relations Act § 2(11), 29 U.S.C. § 152(11) (1988), although this too does not sit well with the more interesting developments in autonomous work teams, on which see HECKSCHER, *supra* note 1, at 138-52.

57. Matthew Finkin, *Labor Law by Boz—A Theory of* Meyers Industries, Inc., Sears, Roebuck & Co., *and* Bird Engineering, 71 IOWA L. REV. 155 (1985); Richard M. Fischl, *Self, Others, and Section 7: Mutualism and Protected Protest Activities Under the National Labor Relations Act*, 89 COLUM. L. REV. 789 (1989); Robert Gorman & Matthew Finkin, *The Individual and the Requirement of "Concert" Under the National Labor Relations Act*, 130 U. PA. L. REV. 286 (1981); Morris, *supra* note 50.

58. 437 U.S. 556 (1978).

59. A test I suggested some years ago. Alan Hyde, *Economic Labor Law v. Political Labor Relations: Dilemmas for Liberal Legalism*, 60 TEX. L. REV. 1 (1981).

newsletter itself, noted the newsletter's "relationship to employees' interests as employees," and "assume[d] that at some point the relationship becomes so attenuated that an activity cannot fairly be deemed to come within the 'mutual aid or protection' clause."[60] The Board and lower courts have since identified "political advocacy" that, despite being addressed by employees to other employees on matters of employee concern, is not protected by section 7.[61]

In this state of the law, and particularly given the Fifth Circuit's recent refusal to defer to the Board,[62] distribution of political litera-

60. 437 U.S. at 567-68.

61. NLRB v. Motorola, Inc., 991 F.2d 278, 283-85 (5th Cir. 1993) (reversing Board; literature prepared by community group but distributed by employees, urging passage of city ordinance banning mandatory workplace drug testing, not protected; "distinguishing" *Eastex*: "[W]hat is political is not necessarily the content of the literature, but the purpose for which it was to be distributed—to advance CAPP's political agenda."); Local 174, UAW v. NLRB, 645 F.2d 1151 (D.C. Cir. 1981) (R.B. Ginsburg, J.) (affirming Board; urging votes for specific candidates, on the basis of their record on labor issues, not protected).

62. *Motorola*, 991 F.2d at 278. This is an unbelievably stupid opinion. As the excerpt in note 61 shows, the court reverses the Board on just the sort of line-drawing judgment normally committed to the Board. Far worse, however, the court ignores the approach of the Supreme Court precedent, *Eastex*, 437 U.S. at 567-68 (§ 7 protection depends on content of literature) and substitutes a "test" never before employed by any Board or court—§ 7 protection for literature depends on the "purpose" for which literature is distributed; a "political" purpose is bad. The court fails to define the terms "purpose" of distribution, or "political" purpose. Nor does the court attempt to reconcile the result with existing law under § 7, which involves a great many cases classifying literature, or explaining how the conclusion that "political" purposes are impermissible can be squared with the *Eastex* decision itself.

I have been critical of the law that makes § 7 protection turn on the content of the literature, for reasons familiar from First Amendment law, and have urged, unsuccessfully, that § 7 protection turn only on "time, place, and manner" restrictions, not on the content of peaceful employee communication. Hyde, *supra* note 59. But whatever its faults, the "content" approach, consistently applied for a generation or more, must be preferable to a new approach pulled from the sky, with no regard whatever for its constitutional or labor law problems. It is *exactly* as if protection of speech or literature for First Amendment purposes depended not on the content of the speech, or any harm caused by it, but rather on the speaker's "purpose"—and "political" purposes, entirely lawful and previously held protected, could now serve to deny the speech protection.

The *Motorola* court gives the game away with the opening line of its opinion: "In this case, we are faced with determining 'how much is too much' on-the-job activism by employees." 991 F.2d at 279. With all respect, the court is faced with no such issue. The court is faced with review of an NLRB rule that found literature, distributed by employees to other employees, urging political action on workplace drug testing, to be protected by § 7. Courts of appeals have no general or specific warrant to decide when job activism by employees is "too much," and neither does the NLRB, as the Supreme Court has pointed out. American Ship Building Co. v. NLRB, 380 U.S. 300, 316 (1965) (§ 8(a)(3) and (1): "[W]e think that the Board construes its functions too expansively when it claims general authority to define national labor policy by balancing the competing interests of labor and management."); NLRB v. Insurance Agents' Int'l Union, 361 U.S. 477, 489-98 (1960). Under § 8(a)(5):

> The presence of economic weapons in reserve, and their actual exercise on occasion by the parties, is part and parcel of the system that the Wagner and Taft-Hartley Acts have recognized . . . . Our labor policy . . . [does not] contain a charter for the National Labor Relations Board to act at large in equalizing disparities of bargaining power between employer and union . . . . [The Board] has sought to introduce some standard of properly "balanced" bargaining power, or some new distinction of justifiable and

ture carries considerable risk, for the line between what may and may not be distributed is exactly the same as the line between what may and may not get you fired. In the context of late 1970's America, when the *Eastex* case was decided, responsible advice to unions and employee caucuses was to make sure that a lawyer reviewed all political, or otherwise questionable, literature going out to employees. In that context, *Eastex* was a blow for bureaucratic control and against spontaneous employee communication.

In 1990's America, focusing on this problem through the lens of the informal caucus of unorganized employees, doctrines that expose employees to discharge for a good faith attempt to invoke protected group action that fails to anticipate subtle and shifting legal doctrine are truly traps for the unwary. The problem is not unique to the definition of "political" literature; it applies equally to the intricacies of "concerted" activity,[63] "impermissible" partial strikes,[64] "disparage-

> unjustifiable, proper and "abusive" economic weapons . . . this amounts to the Board's entrance into the substantive aspects of the bargaining process to an extent Congress has not countenanced.

If the Board cannot determine what economic weapons are "too much," neither it nor a reviewing court can determine generally how much "activism" is "too much."

This case would be a good candidate for oblivion.

63. *See supra* note 57 and accompanying text.

64. "Normal" Wagner Act assumptions are reinforced by cases that deny protection to various forms of labor protest that can be successfully deployed by nonmajority caucuses or informal groups, and thus restrict protection only to orthodox total cessation of work. *See, e.g.*, International Union, UAW-AFL, Local 232 v. Wisconsin Emp. Rel. Bd., 336 U.S. 245 (1949) (calling union meetings at irregular times during working hours); Ford Motor Co., 246 N.L.R.B. 671 (1979) (demonstration in plant aisles); Elk Lumber Co., 91 N.L.R.B. 333 (1950) (refusal to work at previous capacity, as a protest against reduced wages). *See* JAMES B. ATLESON, VALUES AND ASSUMPTIONS IN AMERICAN LABOR LAW 44 (1983); Craig Becker, *"Better Than a Strike": Protecting New Forms of Collective Work Stoppages Under the National Labor Relations Act*, 61 U. CHI. L. REV. (forthcoming Spring 1994).

These cases are full of fine distinctions that often trip up the unrepresented employees who act spontaneously. For a heartbreaking example, see Charge Card Ass'n v. NLRB, 653 F.2d 272, 275 (6th Cir. 1981). Unorganized keypunch operators, dissatisfied after a day of meetings with the company vice-president, called in sick on the following day. The court, denying enforcement to the Board's order, held that they were properly discharged. The court noted that a walkout would have been protected under the *Washington Aluminum* case, discussed *supra* note 53. However, the court held:

> [T]here is not substantial evidence to support the conclusion that the reason for disciplining the employees was to punish them for engaging in a protected walk-out . . . . This Court cannot excuse lying even if in the context of protected activity . . . . Just as employees cannot express dissatisfaction with work conditions by physically abusing their supervisors, employees cannot express their dissatisfaction with work conditions by lying.

Id. at 275.

The court did not discuss any reasons why the keypunch operators might have called in sick rather than struck. Is it possible they were emulating the well-publicized actions of public employees, who, forbidden striking, sometimes call in sick with what in the case of policemen is sometimes called "blue flu"? Didn't they probably think they were somehow *more* protected by

ment" of the employer's product,[65] and "offensive" belittling of supervisors.[66] All these subtle and treacherous limitations on section 7

calling in sick? Is it conceivable that they understood that a strike or walkout would have been protected while calling in sick was not?

If, as this Article urges, labor law treats employee action through informal and spontaneous groups as a fundamental element of labor policy, these cases will have to be rethought. Section 7 should protect any employee protest that does not violate criminal law. The Board cannot continue the callous indifference to unrepresented employees represented by the following:

> [A]lthough employees who are unrepresented and are working without an established grievance procedure have a right to engage in spontaneous concerted protests concerning their working conditions, the precise contours within which such activity is protected cannot be defined by hard-and-fast rules. Instead, each case requires that many relevant factors be weighed.

Waco, Inc., 273 N.L.R.B. 746, 746 (1984) (holding unprotected nine employees discharged for gathering in the lunchroom and demanding that the manager meet with them as a group). The Board went on to state that "In our view, by the time these employees were discharged, late in the morning, they had overstepped the boundary of a protected, spontaneous work stoppage, and were occupying the facility in a manner which was unprotected." *Id.* When the Board refuses "hard-and-fast rules" and reserves to itself the power to "weigh many relevant factors," it subjects employees who attempt to advance their interests, particularly unrepresented employees, to serious risk of job loss.

65. The Supreme Court held in NLRB v. Local 1229, I.B.E.W., 346 U.S. 464 (1953), that certain disparagement of the employer's product is "disloyal" and unprotected. This has launched a dispiriting forty years of cases that have not succeeded in defining this doctrine and cannot be reconciled with each other. *See* Sierra Publishing Co. v. NLRB, 889 F.2d 210 (9th Cir. 1989), reviewing (but not reconciling) the line of cases.

66. Employees, like all subordinate groups, frequently challenge authority and demonstrate group solidarity through Rabelaisian, carnivalesque satire or lampooning of supervisors. *See generally* MIKHAIL BAKHTIN, RABELAIS AND HIS WORLD (Helene Iswolsky trans., 1968). Employees without union representation are particularly likely to resort to struggle through satire. WEINSTEIN, *supra* note 19, at 90. The Board generally protects this material, but the courts of appeals often have a hard time with it. Two courts of appeals recently split on whether to protect sarcastic letters in which employees lampooned the style and orders of supervisors. *Compare* New River Indus. v. NLRB, 945 F.2d 1290 (4th Cir. 1991) (unprotected) *with* Reef Indus., Inc. v. NLRB, 952 F.2d 830 (5th Cir. 1991) (protected).

On rehearing, the Fifth Circuit in the latter case was challenged to reconcile the two holdings, and held that the distinction was the presence of a labor union:

> In *New River Industries*, "the record shows that there had been no union activity at the plant for about eight years . . . ." As Judge Niemeyer noted in writing for the Fourth Circuit, "the decision to discipline [the employees] for the letter was not even in the context of union activity." Furthermore, the sole purpose for the employees' action in *New River Industries* was to belittle the company's gesture—not to call attention to offending conduct by management or other conditions of employement. In stark contrast, the tee shirt incident in the instant case was intimately connected, both substantively and temporally, with union activity . . . .

Reef, 952 F.2d at 840.

This is surely wrong. In fact, it is the precise mistake referred to *supra* notes 45-54 and accompanying text: confusing the protection given by § 7 with status as a "labor organization" or perhaps even "exclusive representative." Section 7 protects employee group action that is not and never will be union action. NLRB v. Washington Aluminum Co., 370 U.S. 9 (1962) (unorganized employees who go home rather than work in an unheated shop). *See also* NLRB v. Magnavox Co., 415 U.S. 322 (1974) (§ 7 right to distribute literature belongs to employees, not to their union; union may not waive employees' right to distribute literature). The right of employees to distribute literature and t-shirts satirizing their bosses cannot depend on the presence or absence of a union.

Obviously if labor policy comes to protect employee caucuses as a basic unit of employee voice, *New River* is wrongly decided and *Reef* is correct. Without unions, employee voice is

have historically performed the function of reinforcing bureaucratic unionism, by eliminating the kinds of quick, spontaneous action that groups at low levels of organization (such as industrial unions in 1930's America) may undertake.

If labor law does undertake seriously to protect the informal network or caucus as a basic institution of labor law, many of these interpretations of section 7 will have to be loosened up to give breathing space to unorganized employees. In all cases, the search should be for tests for protection that correspond to actual patterns of employee culture without the necessity of careful lawyers' advice. Any legal standard in which the Board purports to pursue a "case-by-case" approach provides no practical protection for employees.[67]

B. Labor Organization

Some caucuses receive financial or material support from employers, or permit supervisors or managers to participate.[68] This raises potential issues under section 8(a)(2) if the caucus in question is a statutory "labor organization."[69]

simply going to be more spontaneous, more raw, and probably more witty as well in coming decades. The statute protects employee self-organization, however, and prohibits employers from interfering with it.

In truth, it is not necessary to adopt any special fondness for employee caucuses to see that *New River* is incorrect. In its insensitive hostility to employee self-organization, it gets my vote for the worst judicial failure in recent years to understand the most basic principles of the National Labor Relations Act.

Personally, I continue to adhere to my belief that, by analogy to the First Amendment, § 7 protects all employee attempts to communicate with each other that are not violent, obscene, or incitements to illegal action. Hyde, *supra* note 59.

67. *Cf. Waco, Inc.*, 273 N.L.R.B. at 746. The theory is familiar by analogy to First Amendment overbreadth doctrine: the idea that expressive, communicative, and organizational activities are easily chilled by vague legal standards that sweep broadly into protected areas and can only be applied retrospectively. *See generally* Richard H. Fallon, Jr., *Making Sense of Overbreadth*, 100 YALE L. J. 853, 867-75 (1991).

68. *See, e.g.*, Caitlin Deinard & Raymond A. Friedman, Black Caucus Groups at Xerox Corporation, Harvard Business School Cases 9-491-047 (Mar. 22, 1991) and 9-491-048 (Feb. 10, 1991) (describing Xerox's 1974 decision to pay expenses for up to twenty national leaders to attend all regional black caucuses in order to help coordinate regional caucuses).

69. National Labor Relations Act § 8(a)(2): "It shall be an unfair labor practice for an employer to dominate or interfere with the formation or administration of any *labor organization* or contribute financial or other support to it . . . ." (emphasis added).

The only other relevance to status as a "labor organization" is that under § 8(b), only a "labor organization or its agents" may commit an unfair labor practice. The literature so far on informal employee caucuses does not show these groups doing anything that might constitute an unfair labor practice.

For one thing, several of the most significant unfair labor practices in § 8(b) can, either de jure or de facto, be committed only by organizations that function as exclusive majority representatives or seek to do so. Section 8(b)(3) imposes a duty to bargain, limited to majority representatives. Section 8(b)(2) prohibits labor organizations from causing employer discrimination that encourages union membership. In theory, a nonmajority caucus could induce such discrimi-

This is not the place for yet another comprehensive review of section 8(a)(2). My aim is rather to shed a cross-light on the interpretation of that section through the lens of employee caucuses. Employer assistance to employee caucuses might well be legal, as these groups might fit into one of a number of "exceptions" to the statutory definition of "labor organization" that have been opened recently by the courts of appeals and the Board. I do not favor most of these exceptions. Instead, I will offer a possible reform of section 8(a)(2) that will preserve the traditional reading of that statute, but permit employer-assisted representation when it is knowingly and freely chosen by affected employees.

1. Case Study of Employee Caucuses II: Black Caucuses at Xerox[70]

The first black caucus group at Xerox was started by black sales representatives in the San Francisco Bay area in 1969 and was called BABE (Bay Area Black Employees). Those employees in turn helped organize a similar group in Los Angeles. Their main goal at first was to increase the number and quality of black employees at Xerox. BABE met with regional management and convinced them to assign one black interviewer to each black candidate; together with personal recruiting by BABE members, this helped increase black employment.

Soon the group became concerned about the assignment of inferior sales territories to black sales representatives and filed suit against Xerox. This suit was settled when top Xerox management flew to San Francisco, reversed local management, announced new territory assignments and some management promotions on the spot, and an-

nation, but in the vast majority of cases under § 8(b)(2) the discrimination comes about under union shop contracts that nonmajority groups may not lawfully negotiate. § 8(a)(3)(i). Section 8(b)(7) prohibits certain picketing for the purpose of obtaining recognition. Under the predecessor of this statute, it was held that picketing to achieve recognition as the representative solely of one's members is not picketing for recognition proscribed by § 8(b)(4)(C), the language of which was later copied into § 8(b)(7). Douds v. Local 1250, Retail Wholesale Dep't Store Union, 173 F.2d 764, 770 (2d Cir. 1949) (L. Hand, J.).

Caucuses might conceivably violate § 8(b) by inducing individuals at another employer to refuse to work (§ 8(b)(4)(i)(B)); picketing a "neutral" entity to get it to boycott another (§ 8(b)(4)(ii)(B); NLRB v. Retail Store Employees, Local 1001, 447 U.S. 607 (1980) (picketing insurance agencies urging consumer cancellation of policies of targeted insurance company)); or generally coercing employees under the catchall § 8(b)(1)(A). Should any of these occur, it would be relevant whether a given caucus was a statutory "labor organization."

70. This account is drawn from Caitlin Deinard & Raymond Friedman, *supra* note 68. "Black" is not capitalized in their account and I have followed that usage, which is apparently current at Xerox, here.

nounced that checks to equalize past earnings would be written and paid that afternoon.

In 1973, a similar group in Washington, D.C. called a weekend conference for black Xerox employees that was attended by 75 or 100 employees. Most of the conference consisted of information sessions and self-help workshops. Employees paid their own expenses. Organizers told Xerox that they would be holding the conference; some hostility from management was expressed.

By 1974, caucuses were functioning in six regions. Their leaders stayed in touch and attended each others' conferences, and there was some interest in forming a national caucus. Xerox managers demanded to meet with the leaders to clarify their groups' status. As the senior corporate Human Resource manager recalled:

> There was a lot of concern that they would go from making suggestions to demands. If we recognized the blacks, then women and Hispanics and native Americans, every other group would [demand similar recognition] . . . and the managers would spend full time meeting with caucus groups. Things would get out of hand. People said if blacks and other protected classes had problems, they should talk to the affirmative action managers; that's what they're there for. We don't need another vehicle to address this.[71]

Leaders of regional caucuses did meet with some top managers at Xerox. The result of the meeting was that "there would be no national caucus meeting and no attempt to form a national group. Instead, Xerox would pay travel and hotel expenses for up to 20 people so that the leadership could all regularly attend each regional caucus conference." This leadership group took on formal responsibilities in conveying complaints that emerged at the caucuses about particular managers or other problems. In the 1980's, caucuses for Hispanics, Asians, and women did form at Xerox; and the Xerox groups have been models for groups at other large companies.

2. The Statutory Definition

The statutory definition of "labor organization" is unchanged since the original Wagner Act.[72] It was designed to be broad, and was

71. *See supra* note 68.

72. National Labor Relations Act § 2(5):

> The term "labor organization" means any organization of any kind, or any agency or employee representation committee or plan, in which employees participate and which exists for the purpose, in whole or in part, of dealing with employers concerning grievances, labor disputes, wages, rates of pay, hours of employment or conditions of work.

The intellectual background and legislative history of this definition and the companion proscription of employer assistance in § 8(a)(2), are discussed in Mark Barenberg, *The Political*

further broadened in the drafting process[73] in order to outlaw employer-sponsored representation plans that had become popular in the 1920's. It was frequently applied in the early years of the Act,[74] and its only significant ambiguity was definitively resolved by the Supreme Court in 1959 in holding that even organizations that did not bargain collectively might still be "labor organizations" if they handled grievances or made "proposals and requests" of management.[75]

Under the law as it was in 1959 and for a generation thereafter, it would appear clear that the black caucuses at Xerox are statutory "labor organizations." They are organizations in which employees participate; they raise grievances with management; and they make "proposals and requests." They are not illegal, but they are "labor organizations," and management's financial support to them, in the form of the subsidies to the national leadership, and the participation of some managerial employees, would violate section 8(a)(2).

Some supporters of collective bargaining feel that perforce they must be opponents of any alternative form of employee representation. They make just the sort of formalist argument made in the last paragraph—a sort of section 8(a)(2) fundamentalism: Congress meant to outlaw it, so outlaw it we must. This is certainly a valid legal argument, but the modern legal mind generally craves something more: a sense of *why* Congress outlawed the employer-sponsored representation plan. This question turns out to be surprisingly difficult to answer. By far the best treatment of the 1930's sources, in fact a major contribution to the intellectual historiography of the New Deal, is the recent article by Professor Mark Barenberg.[76] Barenberg concludes

Economy of the Wagner Act: Power, Symbol, and Workplace Cooperation, 106 HARV. L. REV. 1381, 1442-61 (1993); Thomas C. Kohler, *Models of Worker Participation: The Uncertain Significance of Section 8(a)(2)*, 27 B.C. L. REV. 499, 518-535 (1986).

73. The phrase "or any agency or employee representation committee or plan" replaced Wagner's original "labor union, association, corporation or society" in order to capture employer groups that consisted only of plans for electing representatives, without any more formal organization. *See* Electromation, Inc., 309 N.L.R.B. 990, 999 (1992) (reviewing legislative history).

74. *See, e.g.*, Servel, Inc., 11 N.L.R.B. 1295, 1299-1319 (1939) (good review of early principles).

75. NLRB v. Cabot Carbon Co., 360 U.S. 203, 210-14 (1959) (statutory term "dealing with employers" is broader than collective bargaining and includes at least presentation of grievances and making requests and proposals).

76. Barenberg, *supra* note 72. Professor Barenberg shows how crude and ahistorical are the categories often deployed in this debate. For example, Senator Wagner did not favor an "adversarial" system over a "cooperative" system, a distinction frequently drawn by those seeking to weaken the force of § 8(a)(2). *See, e.g, Electromation*, 309 N.L.R.B. at 1011 (Raudabaugh, Member, concurring) ("The Wagner Act signified a choice of the adversarial over the cooperative model."); Hertzka & Knowles v. NLRB, 503 F.2d 625 (9th Cir. 1974), *cert. denied*, 423 U.S. 875 (1975) (distinction between "purely adversial" and "cooperative" arrangements). Rather,

that the precise vice of the employer-sponsored representation plan (as compared with the nonunion workplace not outlawed by the Act), is the power of institutions of "representation" to shape, not merely "represent," the preferences of those supposedly being represented. He argues that proponents of section 8(a)(2) "viewed the cadre of company union representatives under managerial control as a political machine that penetrated the social infrastructure of the workforce. That penetration illegitimately distorted group deliberation and coerced worker choice more systematically than did the nonunion workplace."[77]

This sounds right as an historic explanation of section 8(a)(2). However, it seems to me to make that section make sense only if one has some kind of baseline of "normal," dare I say "objective," worker interests, next to which the output of company unions might be described as "distorted."[78] While the framers of the Wagner Act had such a baseline,[79] I agree with Professor Barenberg that we can no longer identify unions with objective worker interests.[80] A further problem with Professor Barenberg's work is that it does not leave us with a very workable test for defining "labor organization" or "domination, interference, or support" (although it is not clear that this is Professor Barenberg's goal, at least in this article). In our current state of empirical uncertainty about the institutional determinants of worker preferences, it does not seem plausible to define statutory "labor organizations" as, say, organizations that *ex ante* or *ex post* "distort" worker preferences.

Senator Wagner strongly supported labor-management cooperation, Barenberg, *supra* note 72, at 1412-30, but "anticipate[d] that effective, collaborative relations would grow only within the protective shell of collective bargaining." *Id.* at 1461.

77. *Id.* at 1459.

78. If worker preferences were and are *wholly* endogenous to institutions of workplace representation and labor law, then company unions would indeed produce one or more sets, as would nonunion workplaces, craft unions, industrial unions, and so forth. But on what possible ground could public policy prefer one set over another? If worker preferences were wholly endogenous to institutions, what possible meaning could it have to say, as Barenberg does, that company unions were tainted because of their "systematic coercive and distorting effect on workers' choice over modes of workplace governance . . . ." ? *Id.* at 1458; *see also infra* note 80. By what standard of "normality" do the company unions "distort"?

79. Mark Barenberg, *Democracy and Domination in the Law of Workplace Cooperation: From Mass Production to Flexible Organization*, 94 COLUM. L. REV. (forthcoming Apr. 1994).

80. He describes a belief in determinate objective worker interests as "untenable" and "essentialist." Barenberg, *supra* note 72, at 1460. So we believe, we who have passed through Marxist objective class interests by way of the New Left and into postmodern social theory. So I believe, which is why, among other reasons, I believe that exclusive representation by majority unions is dying and will be replaced by the genuine pluralism of caucus organization.

A possible defense of section 8(a)(2) different from Professor Barenberg's is that company unions and representation plans are forbidden for the same reason that discriminatory discharge of union adherents, surveillance of union meetings, and threats to retaliate are forbidden: they are particularly effective disincentives to employee votes for unions. This is an empirical claim that has not been well researched. Quality circles or quality of work life groups may well make union organizing more difficult, although these groups are never found to violate section 8(a)(2).[81] By contrast, the groups that are scrutinized under that section—company unions in the 1930's, joint employer-employee committees—rarely seem to impede union organizing in the short run. The CIO achieved much of its success in the 1930's by taking over company unions.[82] More recent examples show the same technique.[83]

If section 8(a)(2) exists in part to limit a particularly effective anti-organizing technique, its reach is far broader than necessary for this purpose. Returning again to the black caucuses at Xerox, it is hard to see how they impede union organizing in the short run: if any union sought to organize sales representatives, the black caucuses would not seem to offer much of a problem. Of course, there is a more long-term sense in which employees in a workplace where employers have encouraged numerous identity caucuses may be less interested in unions.

81. For an account of an employer's use of its quality circle program as the vehicle for an effective and manipulative anti-union campaign, see GUILLERMO J. GRENIER, INHUMAN RELATIONS: QUALITY CIRCLES AND ANTI-UNIONISM IN AMERICAN INDUSTRY (1988).

Professor Joel Rogers has graciously shared with me unpublished internal AFL-CIO memoranda surveying organizing campaigns in the early 1980's and reporting that, "[t]hose few companies that had quality of worklife plans were virtually impossible to organize"—success rates of 8% in manufacturing and 33% in health care, as opposed to overall success rates of 36% and 54% respectively. This was a fairly informal survey and one may question whether there was adequate control for endogenous variables. Organizations with employer-sponsored representation plans are probably disproportionately employers that unions do not organize well anyway.

In any case, this study dealt only with "quality of work life plans," which, despite a great deal of agitation, have never been found by the Board to violate § 8(a)(2). The recent application of that section, as discussed *infra* notes 84-122, has been mainly against committees with employer and employee representation. Such committees are rarely as potent psychologically as quality circles or quality of work life groups. I am unaware of any literature discussing their impact, if any, on subsequent union organization campaigns.

82. Barenberg, *supra* note 79, carefully reviews the "company unions" of the 1930's for their effects on employee consciousness and later union organizing, finding them generally less powerful than the early reformers had feared.

83. One recent account of a union organizing campaign at a hospital sees the triggering event as management's abolition of a joint management-employee policy commitee. RICK FANTASIA, CULTURES OF SOLIDARITY: CONSCIOUSNESS, ACTION, AND CONTEMPORARY AMERICAN WORKERS 126-27 (1988).

3. Recent Judicial and Administrative "Exceptions" to the Definition of "Labor Organization"

The Board, and to a greater extent some courts of appeals, have shared this disquiet with the underlying purpose behind the application of section 8(a)(2) to joint committees and elected representation plans. Rather than state clearly an underlying philosophy for the section, they have either carved out or intimated a laundry list of possible exceptions to the statutory definition of "labor organization."[84] Some of these exceptions might well be applied to declare that the black caucuses at Xerox are not "labor organizations." This is partly because the exceptions are mostly vague, lack theoretical appeal, and seem designed mostly to give the Board and courts a free hand to approve employer plans that they like. The structure of broad definitions modified by vague exceptions creates uncertainty in the law. Moreover, many of the exceptions can survive only as *ad hoc* exceptions; if carried out consistently, they would cause serious harm to more important values in labor law.

a. Communication Device

Some decisions have suggested that a body representing employees that is merely a "communicative device" is not "dealing with" employers and is therefore not a "labor organization."[85] The Board has not adopted this theory, though it expressly reserved judgment on it in *Electromation, Inc.*,[86] and one member, writing individually, has suggested a variant of it.[87]

The Supreme Court has already considered and rejected just this argument. In *NLRB v. Cabot Carbon Co.*,[88] elected employee committees met monthly with management. The purpose of the commit-

84. The first of these cases was NLRB v. Streamway Div. of Scott & Fetzer Co., 691 F.2d 288 (6th Cir. 1982). Before that case, courts of appeals that denied enforcement to Board § 8(a)(2) findings held that the employer's actions did not amount to "domination," "interference," or "support." *See, e.g.,* Hertzka & Knowles v. NLRB, 503 F.2d 625 (9th Cir. 1974), *cert. denied*, 423 U.S. 875 (1975); Coppus Eng'g Corp. v. NLRB, 240 F.2d 564 (1st Cir. 1957); Chicago Rawhide Mfg. Co. v. NLRB, 221 F.2d 165 (7th Cir. 1955); S. Mark Tuller, Note, *New Standards for Domination and Support Under Section 8(a)(2)*, 82 YALE L.J. 510 (1973). None of these cases doubted that the assisted organizations were statutory "labor organizations."

85. *Streamway*, 691 F.2d at 295 ("The Board offers no evidence that anyone viewed the committee as anything more than a communicative device.").

86. 309 N.L.R.B. 990, 997 n.28 (1992).

87. *Id.* at 1002 (Devaney, Member, concurring) stated that a "communications committee" that is a "management tool" is not a statutory "labor organization." (citing Sears, Roebuck & Co., 274 N.L.R.B. 230 (1985), discussed *infra* note 103). This combines two exceptions that I am analyzing separately.

88. 360 U.S. 203 (1959).

tees was described in their bylaws, as paraphrased by the Court, to provide "a procedure for considering employees' ideas and problems of mutual interest to employees and management."[89] The court of appeals held that since such groups did not bargain collectively, they were not "dealing with" the employer. The Supreme Court reversed, holding that "dealing with" was broader than collective bargaining, and was satisfied here when the committees made "proposals and requests."[90] The Sixth Circuit, in *NLRB v. Streamway Div.*,[91] sought to distinguish *Cabot Carbon* as "a more active, ongoing association between management and employees, which the term dealing connotes, than is present here."[92] The distinction is specious. Both sets of committees met monthly, and in any case the frequency of meetings was not important to the Supreme Court.

It is not clear what the difference is between a "communicative" group and a group that "deals," particularly since "dealing" consists only of the making of "requests and proposals"; what is left for a "communicative" group to "communicate" that is not a "request or proposal"?[93] Nor is it clear why such a distinction should be drawn, except to seize anything that comes to mind to weaken section 8(a)(2). If this exception endures, it is big enough to save the black caucuses at Xerox from being "labor organizations," as it is easy enough to describe the black caucuses as merely "communicative." However, I do not understand this exception or expect it to endure.

89. *Id.* at 205. The Court continued: "Examples of the problems of mutual interest to employees and management to be considered at the Committee-Management meetings were stated in the bylaws to be, but were not limited to, safety; increased efficiency and production; conservation of supplies, materials, and equipment; encouragment of ingenuity and initiative; and grievances at nonunion plants or departments." *Id.* at 205 n.2.

90. *Id.* at 214.

91. 691 F.2d 288 (1982).

92. *Id.* at 294.

93. The *Streamway* court did not attempt to distinguish its "communicative" committees on the basis of their subjects of interest, which did not appear to be restricted and had covered at least such subjects as vacation policy. 691 F.2d at 295 n.11.

A later case in the Sixth Circuit relied on *Streamway* to hold that a President's Advisory Council, through which elected employee representatives complained about attendance and leave policy and job bidding, was merely a "means of communication." Airstream, Inc. v. NLRB, 877 F.2d 1291, 1296 (6th Cir. 1989). *Cabot Carbon* was distinguished as a case in which elected representatives "made specific proposals about all manner of work conditions . . . . The *Cabot Carbon* scenario is a far cry from the circumstances of this case." *Id.* at 1296. Obviously, all the facts of *Cabot Carbon* mentioned by the *Airstream* court are present in its own case, that is, elected employee representatives making specific proposals about all manner of work conditions, except that the committees in *Airstream* did not adjust grievances, an independent ground of decision in *Cabot*, 360 U.S. at 213.

b. Group "Proposals" v. Collected Individual Suggestions

The *Streamway* court, in listing the "several factors" that convinced it that the In-Plant Representation Committee was no labor organization, noted that its elected representatives were limited to three-month terms and could not serve more than three months in a calendar year.[94] The court described this as "continuous rotation of Committee members" that made "the Committee resemble more closely the employee groups speaking directly to management on an individual, rather than a representative, basis . . . ."[95]

The Board has now apparently applied this distinction. In a recent case "to provide guidance for those seeking to implement lawful cooperative programs between employees and management," the Board, in a lengthy section unadorned by case citation and irrelevant to the facts before it, stated that it would not apply the label "labor organization" to "a 'brainstorming' group" the purpose of which was "simply to develop a whole host of ideas," or a committee for "sharing information with the employer."[96] The Board went on to hold that quarterly all-day safety conferences in which participants made safety suggestions were not employers "dealing" with employees.[97]

This loose language is at the very least overinclusive, stretching substantially into the activities of unions engaged in collective bargaining, never before doubted to be "labor organizations." Collective bargaining may well involve both "brainstorming" and "sharing information." What the Board must have meant is that a group that does *no more than* generate and transmit "individual" proposals is not a "labor organization." Although the Board does not say this, a more coherent account of these remarks might be that every "labor organi-

94. 691 F.2d at 290.

95. *Id.* at 294-95. Of course, the committee was elected, and called the In-Plant *Representation* Committee, but these facts were omitted by the court from its discussion here.

96. E.I. DuPont de Nemours & Co., 311 N.L.R.B. No. 88, 143 L.R.R.M. (BNA) 1121, (May 28, 1993).

97. *Id.* at 1125-26. The relevance of this observation is unclear, as the conferences were not alleged to violate § 8(a)(2). They were alleged to violate § 8(a)(5), the bad faith involved in bypassing a union and dealing directly with employees. The Board found that the safety conferences did not violate § 8(a)(5). Such a violation would not normally turn on whether the vehicle through which the employer communicated with employees was or was not a statutory "labor organization." In the best-known cases of employers violating § 8(a)(5) by bypassing the union, the employers simply communicated with individual employees. *E.g.*, Medo Photo Supply Corp. v. NLRB, 321 U.S. 678 (1944); Order of R.R. Telegraphers v. Railway Express Agency, Inc., 321 U.S. 342 (1944). There was no attempt to set up any kind of structure; there were just individual negotiations with employees. If the Board is now suggesting that an employer may violate § 8(a)(5) by bypassing the exclusive representative only if the bypassing fits the Board's new restrictive definition of "dealing" with employees in a "bilateral" mechanism, it has carelessly overturned a half century of law on exclusive representation.

zation" must at some point make a "proposal" in the name of the group.

If this "exception" to the statutory definition "exists" and makes sense, it was surely misapplied in *Streamway*, the only court case even arguably applying such an exception.[98] The court provided little detail about the operation of the "In-Plant Representation Committee," but no support whatever for the idea that its members spoke only as individuals. What would be the point of having a "representative" from each department, of electing the "representatives," of calling the group a "Representation Committee"?[99]

However, even if no case law supports this exception, is there a case for letting employers set up and dominate groups of employees that collect "individual" suggestions but never make a group "proposal"? This exception gets no support in the statutory language, which does not contain the word "proposal." Indeed, the word "proposal" is not a term of art in labor law and has no meaning at all that I can see. I suspect that the emphasis on "proposals" is just a way of distinguishing *Cabot Carbon*, which, as explained above, did note that the committees there made "proposals and requests." It takes more than a word, however, to distinguish *Cabot Carbon*. The thrust of that case was that, both in 1935 and 1947, Congress had adopted a deliberately broad, nontechnical term ("dealing") to describe the kinds of employee activities (not simply "representation") that could not be undertaken through employer-dominated entities. The recent attempt to give "dealing" a restricted and technical meaning flies directly in the face of *Cabot Carbon*.[100]

98. The *Streamway* court cited General Foods, 231 N.L.R.B. 1232 (1977). As discussed *infra* note 108, the autonomous employee teams there were a unit of organizing work assignments and in no way may honestly be described as groups that collected "individual" thoughts for management action.

99. 691 F.2d at 289-90 & n.2.

100.
> [T]he concept of "dealing" does not require that the two sides seek to compromise their differences. It involves only a bilateral mechanism between two parties. That "bilateral mechanism" ordinarily entails a pattern or practice in which a group of employees, over time, makes proposals to management, management responds to these proposals by acceptance or rejection by word or deed, and compromise is not required.

E.I. DuPont de Nemours & Co., 311 N.L.R.B. No. 88, 143 L.R.R.M. (BNA) 1121, 1123 (May 28, 1993). The Board's prototype of "dealing" reflects the continued primacy of the collective bargaining paradigm. The Board completely fails to explain how its attempt to give "dealing" some technical, extrastatutory meaning can be squared with the Supreme Court's refusal to do so in *Cabot Carbon*, all the more so since that case held expressly, as the Board acknowledges in word if not deed, that "dealing" was broader than "bargaining." The Board's recent nondefinition ("ordinarily entails," i.e., except if we hold otherwise) of "dealing" seems to equate it with "bargaining," despite the Supreme Court's admonition in *Cabot Carbon*.

Finally, a rule that permits employers to dominate groups that make "individual" suggestions but never "representative" "proposals" is almost impossible to police and tantamount to licensing employer evasion of section 8(a)(2) so long as "communication" uses the right labels. The black caucuses at Xerox show the difficulty of applying this exception. The apparent quid pro quo for Xerox's limited financial support of the leadership group is the leadership group's transmittal of the concerns and complaints of the regional caucuses. When this occurs, are the leaders making a "group proposal" or "communicating" an "individual" idea? For what policy purpose should this distinction be drawn?

c. *No Anti-Union Animus*

Another of the "several factors" relied on by the *Streamway* court to find that the committee there was not a labor organization was the absence of employer anti-union animus.[101] The Board has expressly rejected this idea.[102] It does not appear to promote clarity in the definition of "labor organization" to make employer motive a factor. It would be idiotic, however welcome to a beleaguered union movement, to have the question of whether a group is liable at all under section 8(b) (unfair labor practices committed by "labor organizations") turn on employer motivation respecting that group, so that only the creatures and darlings of hostile employers could be guilty of unfair labor practices.

d. *Management Tool*

An administrative law judge, affirmed without opinion (on this point) by the Board, held that a "communications committee" with rotating membership, one representative from each department, was not a "labor organization" but rather a "management tool that was intended to increase company efficiency."[103] Company officials testified that the committee was "a vehicle to discuss such matters as uniforms, tools and equipment," "designed to help employees understand each other's jobs so that there would be more understanding when a problem arose." In practice, the committee discussed such employee complaints as technicians' inability to get parts, equipment left so as to create safety hazards, and employee needs for training.

101. 691 F.2d at 294-95.

102. Electromation, Inc., 309 N.L.R.B. 990, 995 n.24 (1992).

103. Sears, Roebuck & Co., 274 N.L.R.B. 230, (1985). Member Devaney cited this case with approval in his separate concurrence in *Electromation*, 309 N.L.R.B. at 1002.

The Administrative Law Judge admitted that the committee thus discussed "work performance and working conditions" but was nevertheless not a "labor organization." "The Communications Committee was not an employee representative or advocate. The Commitee did not deal with the Company on behalf of the employees."[104]

As formulated, this exception to the statutory definition seems spectacularly underdefined. Presumably any management group that sets up a representation plan, even one specifically and expressly expected by the 1935 Congress to be outlawed by section 8(a)(2), does so as a "management tool" "created by the Company for company purposes." If this becomes a functioning part of Board law, some narrower explanation will be necessary.[105]

e. *Delegated Management Function*

Three Board cases, all from 1977, were cited with approval in *Electromation* and generalized as cases where groups, in which employees participated, were nevertheless not statutory "labor organizations" because their "purpose [was] limited to performing essentially a managerial or adjudicative function . . . ."[106] This is the most coherent and workable "exception" to the statutory definition yet put forward. It is also, in my opinion, the most pernicious. In trying to divide employer-assisted groups from collective bargaining by restricting each's agenda, the Board risks paralyzing *both* institutions.

The three Board cases dealt with teams or committees on which management personnel and employees sat together. Two involved joint committees with the effective power to resolve grievances. Each involved a pool of employees, elected by their fellows, who heard grievances in panels on which one management representative sat.[107]

104. 274 N.L.R.B. at 66.

105. *Sears* does not appear to have been cited by the full Board for its § 8(a)(2) holding.

It is possible that *Sears* and *Streamway* will come to stand for the narrow proposition that a group, the members of which rotate, is not a "labor organization." This is coherent and workable, but I cannot see what policy goal it advances. When one employee is there from each department, it is clear that the employee is expected to act as a representative in passing along complaints and grievances; the employees in both those cases so understood their roles.

106. *Electromation*, 309 N.L.R.B. at 995.

107. There were a few minor distinctions between the two grievance committees that did not appear to affect the analysis. In Sparks Nugget, Inc., 230 N.L.R.B. 275 (1977) (2-1 decision), the Sparks Nugget Employees' Council was unilaterally implemented by management—a violation of § 8(a)(5), as the employees were represented by a union. Panels consisted of the elected employee from the grievant's department, the director of employee relations, and an employee selected by the first two. Decisions of the panel were binding on all parties. The panels were strictly adjudicatory and made no proposals to management.

In Mercy-Memorial Hosp. Corp., 231 N.L.R.B. 1108 (1977) (3-2 decision), the Grievance Committee evolved from open discussions but was then unilaterally imposed by management.

The third case involved the most far-reaching work innovation to come before the Board—self-governing teams of employees who made their own job assignments and schedules.[108]

The Board held that none of the three groups violated section 8(a)(2), for none was a "labor organization." The Board thus did not construe "domination, interference, or support."[109] None was a labor organization, for all had power, either the power to decide grievances or to assign work. The Board seemed to say that, under the NLRA, "labor organizations" may not have power, and therefore anything that *has* power is no labor organization.

The fact that the grievance committees actually had power is thus what, in the wonderful world of Board logic, permits employers to dominate them. If either grievance committee had only the power to remonstrate, either would plainly have been a "labor organization" under the very words of the statute.[110] Employer representatives may not sit on "grievance committees" that plead or remonstrate. Give the committee real power, however, and the Board washes its hands of the matter.[111]

(These employees too were represented by a union, but General Counsel did not issue a § 8(a)(5) complaint.) Panels consisted of four employees selected by the grievant from the 10 elected employees, and a department head, from a department other than the grievant's or a committee member's, selected by the grievant. Decisions of the panel were effectively binding, although the rules provided for appeal to the personnel committee of the Board of Directors. The Grievance Committee had authority under its rules to recommend changes in rules to management, but had exercised this authority only once in a minor manner. The Board dissenters seized on this last fact in an attempt to distinguish *Sparks Nugget.*

108. General Foods Corp., 231 N.L.R.B. 1232 (1977). Similar teams at another plant of this employer were the subject of considerable academic and journalistic interest at the time. *See* Richard E. Walton, *Work Innovations at Topeka: After Six Years*, 13 J. APPL. BEHAV. SCI. 422 (1977); Robert Schrank, *On Ending Worker Alienation: The Gaines Pet Food Plant, in* HUMANIZING THE WORKPLACE 119 (Roy Fairfield ed., 1974); *Stonewalling Plant Democracy*, BUS. WK., Mar. 28, 1977, at 78-82. For continued academic interest in autonomous or self-governing teams, see HECKSCHER, *supra* note 1, at 138-52.

109. The Board might have held in each case that the presence of one management representative capable of being outvoted did not equal employer "domination, interference, or support." However, the Board continues to adhere to the view that the mere presence of a supervisor or manager constitutes potential "domination" or "interference," and implicitly maintained that view in these three cases. The Board's rigidity in the standards under § 8(a)(2) contrasts with its flexibility under § 2(5), and has been criticized judicially. *E.g.*, NLRB v. Northeastern Univ., 601 F.2d 1208, 1213-14 (1st Cir. 1979) (calling for standard of "actual" not "potential" "domination").

110. National Labor Relations Act § 2(5): "any organization of any kind, or any agency or employee representation committee of plan, in which employees participate and which exists for the purpose, in whole or in part, of dealing with employers concerning *grievances* . . . ." (emphasis added).

111. The "Grievance Committee" at the hospital did not "exist for the purpose . . . of dealing with" the Hospital "concerning grievances," as Alice might have been told by one of Wonderland's stranger denizens, since it did not "present" or "discuss" or "negotiate" with management. It decided grievances for itself. Mercy-Memorial Hosp. Corp., 231 N.L.R.B. 1108 (1977).

The mildest criticism that might be made of these decisions is that this is at least a restriction on the statutory definition not found in its text. "[O]rganization *of any kind*" that "exists for the purpose, in whole *or in part*, of dealing with employers" does not easily admit of a reading that says: "unless that organization is performing a managerial function." "Managerial function" is not a statutory term of art, and thus this malleable exception may easily swallow the rule. Absolutely everything that genuine, labor union-type "labor organizations" do was once a "managerial function" and still is in nonunion workplaces: articulating employee preferences, forming collective action, administering benefits.

So as a statutory term, "managerial function" has no meaning and does not distinguish among the activities of employee organizations. What gives the "managerial function" exception its apparent content however is the analogous use of similar language in the law of mandatory subjects of bargaining under section 8(a)(5). That section merely creates a duty to bargain collectively. As late as 1958, counsel representing an employer in the Supreme Court came close to arguing that the duty applied to any lawful demand made by one party on another.[112] However, in that year the Supreme Court accepted the view of the Eisenhower Board that some bargaining topics were "permissive" in the Pickwickian sense that the party served with the demand need not discuss it, and the party making the demand would violate its "duty to bargain" in "insisting" on such a "permissive" subject.[113]

The "permissive" demands in that case were petty issues over which the Board did not want to see negotiations snarled: the union's internal ratification procedures and the substitution of the local for the international union as bargaining representative. Quickly, however, "permissive" subjects became not subjects too trivial, but subjects too important—to management. In an influential concurring opinion, Justice Stewart denied that management had to bargain about "*managerial* decisions which lie at the core of entrepreneurial

The grievance committee at Sparks Nugget did not "deal with" management. "Rather, it appear[ed] to perform a function for management." Sparks Nugget, Inc., 230 N.L.R.B. 275 (1977). One does not have to be a Hegelian to see the flaw here. What is a delegation except a partial invitation to negotiate the terms of that delegation, in deed and word?

112. Theodore J. St. Antoine, *Legal Barriers to Worker Participation in Management Decision Making*, 58 Tul. L. Rev. 1301, 1305 n.25 (1984).

113. NLRB v. Wooster Div. of Borg-Warner Corp., 356 U.S. 342 (1958). For a critique, see Note, *Major Operational Decisions and Free Collective Bargaining: Eliminating the Mandatory/Permissive Distinction*, 102 Harv. L. Rev. 1971, 1977 n.30 (1989).

control."[114] This category has expanded, not contracted, in recent years as cases stake out increasing "managerial prerogatives" as to which management need not bargain, and unions may not insist on their positions or employ economic force.[115]

It is presumably this body of law that the Board purports to import into section 2(5). Together with section 8(a)(5), they would create a sort of workplace kashrut. All "company" decisions are either "managerial" or "bargainable." "Managerial" decisions need not be taken up with the union and may instead be submitted to any body of management's choice, even one it chairs or dominates. "Bargainable" decisions require a different path to management unilateralism. If management creates a body with power over "bargainable" decisions (such as grievances), that body is therefore "managerial" and may be dominated by management. Under this scheme, "labor organizations" definitionally exercise no power and at most receive information and make requests as to a constricted list of issues. This bifurcation, lacking any statutory basis, has long debilitated collective bargaining.[116] Over the next generation, it has the potential to debilitate alternatives to collective bargaining as well.

114. Fibreboard Paper Prods. Corp. v. NLRB, 379 U.S. 203, 223 (1964) (Stewart, J., concurring) (emphasis added). His examples included decisions to invest in labor-saving machinery or to liquidate assets and cease operations.

115. First Nat'l Maintenance Corp. v. NLRB, 452 U.S. 666 (1981) (decision to drop a customer, eliminating jobs); Newspaper Guild Local 10 v. NLRB, 636 F.2d. 550, 560-61 (D.C. Cir. 1980) (codes of ethics):

> [P]rotection of the editorial integrity of a newspaper lies at the core of publishing control .... [A] news publication must be free to establish without *interference*, reasonable rules designed to prevent its employees from engaging in activities which may directly compromise their standing as responsible journalists and that of the publication for which they work as a medium of integrity.

Id. at 560-61 (citations omited) (emphasis added); Wells v. General Motors Corp., 881 F.2d 166, 170 (5th Cir. 1989), *cert. denied*, 495 U.S. 923 (1990) (dictum) (eligibility standards for rehiring employees is nonbargainable managerial decision). For a sustained critique of the category of "managerial prerogatives," see ATLESON, *supra* note 64, at 111-135; Karl E. Klare, *Workplace Democracy and Market Reconstruction: An Agenda for Legal Reform*, 38 CATH. U. L. REV. 1, 49-52 (1988); Katherine Van Wezel Stone, *Labor and the Corporate Structure: Changing Conceptions and Emerging Possibilities*, 55 U. CHI. L. REV. 73, 86-96 (1988).

116. Connoisseurs of hypocrisy particularly enjoyed the crocodile tears of Justice Blackmun's footnote in Fall River Dyeing & Finishing Corp. v. NLRB, 482 U.S. 27, 39 n.6 (1987) ("The Union was confronted with the layoff .... Moreover, despite the Union's desire to participate in the transition between employers, it was left entirely in the dark about petitioner's acquisition."). Justice Blackmun unaccountably failed to note that for two decades or so before 1981, the Board normally imposed a duty to bargain over decisions that resulted in job loss for employees. However, in that year, the Supreme Court held that "the harm likely to be done to an employer's need to operate freely in deciding whether to shut down part of its business purely for economic reasons outweighs the incremental benefit that might be gained through the union's participation in making the decision ...." *First Nat'l Maintenance*, 452 U.S. at 686 (Blackmun, J.).

Enthusiasts for joint teams and committees normally emphasize their flexibility, adaptability, and ability to reach into problem areas that might elude collective bargaining or unilateral managerialism.[117] While this upside potential is far from clearly established in the literature, there is no doubt that a problem-solving group or team will be ineffectual and disintegrate quickly if it is excluded as an initial matter from areas important to the participants.[118] While I am agnostic about the long term potential of autonomous work teams and joint groups, I am confident that they will achieve little if their agendas are limited from the beginning to lists of controlled topics.

Unfortunately, if the Board continues to adhere to this approach in defining "labor organizations," it will also draw the line between caucuses that employers may support and caucuses they may not. To return to black caucuses at Xerox, their functions have changed over time, as befits a group that is employee-created and substantially employee-controlled. Yet for the Board, the question of whether Xerox may pay travel and other expenses for group leaders is just the question of the group's "purpose" at any moment in time, and the boundary lines are vague and shifting. If black caucuses "present" grievances, they are labor organizations and may not receive any employer support. If they merely "communicate" grievances on a "non-representative" basis, then under some court of appeals decisions

It is true that a footnote immediately following this sentence "intimate[d] no view as to other types of management decisions, such as . . . sales." *Id.* at 686 n.22. However, a chief impact of the decision in *First National Maintenance* has been to remove any obligation to share information with the union over decisions leading to job loss, so that the union is unable to evaluate whether the decision is bargainable or not. One might say that the union is "left entirely in the dark." *See, e.g.*, Knappton Maritime Corp., 292 N.L.R.B. 236 (1988) (partial sale of business; sales agreement not "presumptively relevant"; union must establish relevancy; established here when union showed "reasonable basis" for assuming sale not bona fide and purchaser merely alter ego of seller).

117. *See, e.g.*, Heckscher, *supra* note 1, at 138-52. Enthusiasts do not have much else to emphasize. Despite all the hoopla about employee participation and productivity, there is no evidence that joint committees enhance productivity and some evidence that they do not. A rare, and fascinating, set of data on joint committees is provided by Maryellen R. Kelley & Bennett Harrison, *Unions, Technology, and Labor-Management Cooperation*, *in* Unions and Economic Competitiveness 247 (Lawrence Mishel & Paula B. Voos eds., 1992). Manufacturing plants accounting for nearly all machining activity in American industry were studied for productivity and willingness to adopt new technology. Plants with joint labor-management problem-solving committees, found in more than 47% of plants, were on the whole less efficient, less invested in new technology, and more likely to outsource, than the 13% of plants with unions.

118. Most observers believe this impeded development of Quality of Work Life or Employee Involvement groups in the automobile industry in the early 1980's. "You run out of diddlysquat things to do . . . you get tired of trying to figure out what you can do and what you can't." Robert J. Thomas, Participation and Control: New Trends in Labor Relations in the Auto Industry 4 (U. Mich. Ctr. for Res. on Soc. Org., Working Paper #315, n.d.) (quoting worker who had recently quit his "problem-solving group"); *see also* Harry Katz, Shifting Gears: Changing Labor Relations in the U.S. Automobile Industry 83 (1985).

Xerox may pay the travel expenses. At the other end, should they actually be given power to decide something, they might be "delegated management authority," in which case management might fund them however it likes, perhaps even if its avowed intent is to discourage unionization.

We have then one of those depressing corners of Board law that will only grow worse over the next decades unless its first principles are radically rethought. Unfortunately, all the reform proposals of section 8(a)(2) that I have seen create more or other vague "exceptions" relating to the *purpose* or *agenda* of the plan. These respond to no principled generalization but merely multiply the possibilities for unions that lose representation elections to litigate.

4. A Proposed Solution: An Employee Free Choice Defense to a Section 8(a)(2) Complaint

I propose doing away with all attempts to define "labor organization" (or to limit that definition) that turn on groups' agendas. Such definitions make planning innovative employee representation impossible, and destroy the very flexibility that is the only argument in favor of joint committees and teams. I oppose generally this dominant conception of section 8(a)(2). However, it is particularly inappropriate when we focus specifically on the problems of employee caucuses, as the growing, lively, vital mode of employee representation. It would probably be livable and might even be desirable to forbid such a group from receiving any support from employers. To me, however, the story of the black caucuses at Xerox suggests a more flexible approach. At crucial moments in the growth of spontanenous employee organizations, employer support may assist the group in better employee representation without posing any danger to national policy or to employees themselves—if employees know of the support and freely choose that form of representation.

To implement this strategy, the Board should return to the broad statutory definition of "labor organization," as drafted by Congress in section 2(5) and construed by the Supreme Court in *Cabot Carbon*: if employees participate in it and it "deals with" employers concerning any conditions of work, it is a labor organization. The "exceptions" for "managerial tools," "communicative groups," or "delegated" arms of management should be eliminated. "Deals with" should not have a technical meaning but should include, as argued above, "communication" and "delegated managerial authority."

If management wishes to support, assist, organize, chair, or participate in any employee group under this definition, it should be able to do so only if employees have consented. To accomplish this, the Board—after reestablishing the breadth of statutory "labor organizations" and eliminating the poorly-thought-out exceptions—should establish, through case law or rule-making, an "employee free choice" defense to section 8(a)(2) complaints. An employer who would otherwise violate that section by establishing or supporting a system of employee representation or communication may defend against unfair labor practice charges by showing (1) that the system was authorized by a majority of employees in a secret ballot; (2) that before the ballot, employees were specifically advised of their right to oppose the creation of such a plan without reprisal; and (3) that such authorization expires in some uniform period of time, perhaps one year initially and three years thereafter, unless reauthorized in a new election.

I would encourage recourse to these three steps by making them a genuine safe haven for employers who follow them: if employees genuinely authorize it, they may lawfully be represented by *anything* they choose. The Board does not often establish genuine safe havens, preferring to reserve total freedom to itself through vague standards that, as we have seen, turn on "all the circumstances."[119] As I have said, if there is any value at all in joint or employer-assisted representation as an alternative to collective bargaining, or a successor to it, or just something that some firms and employees find helpful that does not harm the economy, employers who set these things up must know what they may do.[120]

I would let the employer conduct the authorization ballot and simply retain the documentation of the assurances given to employ-

119. For example, in E.I. DuPont de Nemours & Co., 311 N.L.R.B. No. 88, 143 L.R.R.M. (BNA) 1268, 1270 (May 28, 1993), the Board comically described as "safe havens" its "exceptions" to the statutory definition of "labor organization" for (1) "isolated instances in which the group makes ad hoc proposals to management followed by a management response of acceptance or rejection by word or deed"; (2) groups that "brainstorm" but "make no proposals"; and (3) groups that "share information with the employer" but "make no proposals." These are not "safe havens" in the sense that an employer may consciously create such a group and be confident that the Board will not find it in violation of § 8(a)(2). The idea of an employer creating an "isolated instance" group is pretty amusing. Rather, they are vague and manipulable labels that reserve to the Board the freedom to apply that section essentially however it likes. Management counsel routinely assist clients in the creation of such groups, but one doubts that counsel consider them "safe havens." I assume that professionally responsible advice is that any such group potentially buys Board litigation.

120. If there is no value to employer-assisted joint committees, we should return to § 8(a)(2) fundamentalism. I think in a world in which most employees have no union and never will that we owe them some experimentation in alternative representation.

ees. The Board has no authorization to conduct such ballots now, unless the joint team or committee sought certification as an exclusive bargaining representative, which seems unnecessary and undesirable to me (for one thing, it would bar unions' organizational efforts).

This proposal attempts to respond to some courts of appeals that have been groping for the employee free choice idea.[121] While I applaud this interest in employee free choice, if sincere, the problem is the absence of mechanisms for reliably determining employee desires in a nonunion workplace.[122] The Board would perform a valuable service if it provided incentives for employers establishing joint committees or support for caucuses to discover what employees really want. The current regulatory regime cares about employee concerns only as an afterthought; its thrust is to encourage employers to design whatever plan they want and hope the Board or court of appeals will see things their way.

The precise details of the employee free choice defense could be altered, of course. I think it is important that it not be too onerous for

121. For example, the *Streamway* court noted that:

> Two certification elections have occurred in the span of time covered by this litigation. No unfair labor charges were filed. [Other than the charges that were the subject of the enforcement proceeding before the court!] Those elections provided the employees with an uncoerced opportunity to make an intelligent choice between the status quo and the alternative benefits of . . . collective bargaining . . . . This was their choice. We see no reason under the Act to disturb that choice or to tip the scales against it and in favor of that which the employees themselves have twice rejected.

NLRB v. Streamway Div. of Scott & Fetzer Co., 691 F.2d 288, 295 (6th Cir. 1982).

In holding a system of joint committees not employer dominated, another court laid almost exclusive emphasis on what it saw as employee free choice:

> The sum of this is that a § 8(a)(2) finding must rest on a showing that the employees' free choice, either in type of organization or in the assertion of demands, is stifled by the degree of employer involvement at issue . . . . [Here] the idea was still that of an employee, and it was approved by the employees . . . . The question essentially comes down to the significance of having management partners on the committees . . . . Yet this feature too was chosen by the employees, and it is one with which, for all the record shows, they are not dissatisfied.

Hertzka & Knowles v. NLRB, 503 F.2d 625, 630-63 (9th Cir. 1974), *cert. denied*, 423 U.S. 875 (1975).

122. In *Streamway*, the committees were set up and implemented by management. 691 F.2d at 289-90. The sole support for the court's assertion that the employees favored the system was the employees' contemporaneous rejection of union organization.

In *Hertzka & Knowles*, management called a meeting after a union had been defeated in a decertification election (later set aside by the Board which found that the employer had threatened reprisals if the firm stayed union). Management "asked for suggestions . . . on how to accomplish a management-employee dialogue," to which request, amazingly enough, an employee suggested a system of joint committees. 503 F.2d at 629. Those assembled at the meeting adopted the proposal. The court, reversing the Board, characterized this as "employee free choice," although it was required to resort to a litotes in order to establish this characterization. *Id.* at 630-31 (quoted *supra* note 121). I am less willing to equate the results of an open employee show of hands, under the eyes of a management that has just threatened employees with reprisals unless they decertify their union, with "employee free choice."

employers to establish. Requiring elections conducted by neutrals, for example, would offer little real benefit to employees but encourage employers not to avail themselves of the "free choice" defense. On the other hand, it might be desirable to restrict availability of the "employee free choice" defense to employers with no unfair labor practices in the preceding three years. To my mind, the important points of this defense are a firm statement that employees may select their own form of employee voice and that they are free to reject or alter the employer's plan.

I am well aware that describing such a defense as "free choice" is at best a metaphor. It is impossible to ignore the ways in which the daily exercise of employer power in any form shapes worker consciousness and sense of alternatives. I do not mean to suggest that voting for a joint committee plan that the employer clearly wants is "free choice" under any strong political theory of self-realization. I am making only the weaker, but still significant, claim that under present law there is neither the requirement that nonunion representation plans be acceptable to employees nor any real incentive to obtain such acceptance. The right to say no to the employer may not exactly be "employee free choice," but it is more than employees have now.

Employers would have incentives to design plans with which their employees would be supportive (and not merely "not dissatisfied"). Employers who wanted "communication" groups, brainstorming sessions, joint committees, autonomous teams, or joint grievance committees could have them—so long as employees voted them up in a simple yes-or-no ballot. How could any employer genuinely interested in "communication" and "dialogue" resist this proposal in good faith?

Conclusion: Labor Law for Yuppies?

The depressing quality about most labor law scholarship these days, that adopts a perspective in favor of employee voice, is that nobody seems to believe publicly or privately that labor unions will ever represent more than twenty percent of the workforce; few think that legal reforms could bring even that about; yet nobody wants to begin to talk publicly about forms of employee representation that will succeed unions, except for mandatory works councils. While there is much in this Article that is speculative and much that will be disagreed with, I hope I have started a discussion about forms of representing employees that are actually found in American workplaces and could become the basis for new labor law policies.

I have also tried to show that this choice is not trivial. Of course it would be possible to protect employee caucuses as we have for fifty years—by sporadic invocation of section 7 of the NLRA. Nevertheless, I have argued, a real commitment to spontaneous employee self-organization requires attention to the actual forms of contemporary self-organization, of which the most significant include networks, informal caucuses, and "identity" caucuses. It also requires a willingness to reexamine doctrine, under disparate areas of labor law, that presupposes a world of collective bargaining and must be rethought if we become committed to spontaneous employee organization. This Article has identified two such areas: the protection of concerted activities and the law of employer assistance to labor organizations. This Article, however, merely begins that rethinking process.

I have tried to draw here briefly on some observable accounts of how employees in high tech industry pursue their interests. I am therefore confident that I will be accused of pushing a sort of "labor law for yuppies" that is irrelevant to the needs of the sweaty working class.[123] Since nothing could be farther from my intention, I want to close with a few brief speculative thoughts on the importance of the high technology workplace as a paradigm.

Scholars of labor law and industrial relations are comfortable with something they think they understand, called the system of "collective bargaining." It is rarely appreciated that this is in large part an intellectual construct. Out of the thousands of American workplaces, intellectuals generalize the images we carry of "workplace," "worker," "employer," "grievance," "contract," and "strike." Nobody can carry around thousands of images of these things. These are thoughts that the mind organizes around prototypes.[124] Like all generalizations, they are to some extent normative.

123. *Cf.* Michael H. Gottesman, *Wither Goest Labor Law: Law and Economics in the Workplace*, 100 YALE L.J. 2767, 2776 (1991) (reviewing PAUL C. WEILER, GOVERNING THE WORKPLACE: THE FUTURE OF LABOR AND EMPLOYMENT LAW (1990)) ("yuppie justice"); Matthew Finkin, *Back to the Future of Labor Law*, 32 WM. & MARY L. REV. 1005, 1022-23 (1991) (reviewing PAUL C. WEILER, GOVERNING THE WORKPLACE: THE FUTURE OF LABOR AND EMPLOYMENT LAW (1990)).

124. *See generally* GEORGE LAKOFF, WOMEN, FIRE, AND DANGEROUS THINGS: WHAT CATEGORIES TELL US ABOUT THE MIND (1987) (discussion of the research in cognitive science backing up the importance of prototypes). Lakoff's work has become popular among some legal scholars in recent years to prove a number of points with which I am not comfortable, including a somewhat positivistic identification of some cognitive categories as derived from universal body experiences and thereafter limiting what is thinkable (except by the researcher criticizing

For most of us, when we talk about "collective bargaining" or "labor relations," the prototypes come from the automobile industry. For half a century, the "worker" has been a male automobile worker, "work" an automobile factory, "contracts" automobile contracts. This is a complex psychological phenomenon that reflects generic American fascination with the automobile,[125] the high levels of achievement of the automobile workers in militant action and in their collective agreements, and the high quality of many individuals associated with labor relations in the automobile industry.[126] I do not, in other words, think there is any conspiracy here. I do think it is time to reexamine whether adherence to this prototype may disable us from understanding today's workplaces.[127]

The system of collective bargaining as an intellectual construct lies in disarray, a victim of the decline in American manufacturing, including automobiles, and the decline of unions. It is unlikely that "nothing" will take its place. Out there now, a new generation of intellectuals, scholars, and publicists are constructing a new "system" of work relations that will function for the next generation as the primacy of automobile labor relations functioned for fifty years. Even a regime of common law employment contracts may be described as a "system."

others' limited thoughts and who has miraculously escaped the constraining force of these metaphors). I cite Lakoff only as an introduction to the literature on the cognitive significance of prototypes.

125. *See, e.g.*, Christopher Finch, Highways to Heaven: the AUTO Biography of America (1992); James J. Flink, The Automobile Age (1988).

126. Among the most important for lawyers is Dean Harry Shulman, permanent umpire under the Ford-UAW contract, whose influence on his friend and former Yale colleague William Douglas is apparent in such cases establishing labor disputes as a separate sphere, largely impervious to legal regulation, as United Steelworkers v. Warrior & Gulf Mfg. Co., 363 U.S. 574 (1960). *See* Katherine Van Wezel Stone, *Re-envisioning Labor Law: A Response to Professor Finkin*, 45 Md. L. Rev. 978, 1004-12 (1986).

127. A recent line of scholarship has attacked the primacy of the concept of the male industrial worker: working full-time, functioning well in jobs defined tightly by contractual job descriptions, projecting power in customary male fashion, through tough-talking narratives of violence. Marion Crain, *Feminism, Labor, and Power*, 65 S. Cal. L. Rev. 1819 (1992); Joanne Conaghan, *The Invisibility of Women in Labour Law: Gender-neutrality in Model-building*, 14 Int'l J. Soc. L. 377 (1986); Gillian Lester, *Toward the Feminization of Collective Bargaining Law*, 36 McGill L.J. 1181 (1991). These articles are often alarmingly vague when they turn to the "female" alternative—vague calls for cooperative organization that those comfortable with collective bargaining will dismiss as simple accommodation or timidity. Crain, *supra*, at 1874-75 (quoting papal encyclicals); Lester, *supra*, at 1213 (vague call for cooperative structures). That kind of dismissal was my first response to these articles too—until I realized that my kind of "tough talk" is itself part of the narrative of threatened male violence which is an essential element both of the general power of men over women and the specific styles of unions as we have known them.

While we do not know the content or all the elements of the emerging system of employment law, I am confident that there is or will be such a system, for the simple fact that nobody could even think about "workplace dispute" without some kind of an intellectual picture of workplaces and disputes. Moreover, that system will function through prototypes. It will provide us with a stereotyped set of prototype "workers," "employers," and "disputes" that will fit some cases quite well, and into which others will be stretched and pulled, in order to fit—for that is how prototypes work.[128]

Computers, cybernetics, and high technology are somewhat ill-defined terms that seem to exert a great deal of fascination on people, particularly young people, today. Is it not possible that the images of work relations in those industries—networks; caucuses, along with team-based work; flexible compensation including stock options and ownership shares; and employees conceptualized as intellectual laborers with valuable ideas in their heads—may come to be the prototypes for employment law in the way that the United Automobile Workers, their grievances and strikes, were for an earlier generation?

128. Legislation, particularly legislation accompanied by devices to enhance its public salience, often symbolizes such a cognitive reorientation to new imagery of "worker" or "workplace" or "dispute," for example the symbolized importance of shop-level representation in Italian labor relations of the late 1960's, crystallized in the Statuto dei Lavoratori of 1970. *See generally* Alan Hyde, *A Theory of Labor Legislation*, 38 BUFF. L. REV. 383, 456-63 (1990).

6. THE ROAD NOT TAKEN: SOME THOUGHTS ON NONMAJORITY EMPLOYEE REPRESENTATION

MATTHEW W. FINKIN*

In 1919, Woodrow Wilson called for legislation "based upon a full recognition of the right of those who work . . . to participate in some organic way in every decision which directly affects their welfare or the part they are to play in industry."[1] The call was made in the wake of decades of labor unrest, was grounded in the experience of federal labor policy during the Great War, and drew upon Progressive efforts at labor reform—for the realization of an "industrial democracy." But it came to naught. The Republic was to experience another decade and a half of labor unrest, employer resistance, judicial hostility, and reform efforts before Congress embarked upon the legislative experiment of the National Labor Relations Act (NLRA).[2]

The "tap-root and trunk"[3] of the Act is found in section 7, which guarantees employees the right to "self-organization" and "to bargain collectively through representatives of their own choosing."[4] The elemental notion embraced by the Act was that the individual employee acting alone and without assistance could have little influence upon the employer, and that only through collective representation could some rough equality be achieved. This statutory proposition, however, was neither novel nor especially controversial: It was taken verbatim from section 7(a) of the National Industrial Recovery Act (NIRA),[5] which borrowed from the declaration of policy of the Norris-LaGuardia Act,[6] and which, in turn, was prefigured in the principles adopted by the War Labor Conference Board of 1918. What was novel—and heavily contested at the time—were the means of realizing that policy, especially on two issues: Congress prohibited em-

* Albert J. Harno Professor of Law and Professor in the Institute of Labor and Industrial Relations, University of Illinois.

1. 58 CONG. REC. 40, 41 (1919).
2. National Labor Relations (Wagner) Act, 29 U.S.C. §§ 151-169 (1988) [hereinafter Labor Act].
3. Clyde Summers, *Unions Without Majority—A Black Hole?*, 66 CHI.-KENT L. REV. 531, 531 (1990).
4. National Labor Relations Act, § 7, 29 U.S.C. § 157 (1988).
5. National Industrial Recovery Act, Act of June 16, 1933, ch. 90, 48 Stat. 195 (1933) (declared unconstitutional in Schecter Poultry v. United States, 295 U.S. 495 (1935)).
6. Norris-LaGuardia Act, ch. 90, 47 Stat. 70 (1932) (current version at 29 U.S.C. §§ 101-115 (1988)).

ployer interference in or support of a labor organization, as defined expressly to include "any kind" of employee representation committee or plan; and it established the principle of exclusive representation by majority rule.

Over the next three decades, and despite the blunting effects of the Taft-Hartley amendments, that experiment was a modest success: The bulk of the production workers in major, nationally based manufacturing industries were organized under the Act, and the standards set in bargaining for these employees—especially the creation of internal labor markets—were widely emulated by nonunion firms.[7] But over the course of the past two decades union density has drastically declined, to about the same percentage of the private sector non-agricultural work force as at the time the Labor Act was passed. Although this development has been explained by a variety of factors, in which the law may or may not play an especially prominent part, the result has caused a number of observers to return to President Wilson's plea; to find, as Paul Weiler put it, some alternative means for "direct indigenous representation."[8]

Two broad ideas for legislative reform have been proposed. The one more discussed calls for the creation of employee works councils, either by voluntary employer action or as mandated by law such as in Germany.[9] The one less talked about calls for provision of "members only" representation.[10] Each, in other words, would unmake one of the more contested legislative choices made in 1935: The former considerably to modify or repeal the "company union" prohibition;[11] the latter to modify or abandon exclusive representation by majority rule.

The former draws not only from European developments but upon the American experience as well. The stimulation of works

7. *See generally* SANFORD M. JACOBY, EMPLOYING BUREAUCRACY: MANAGERS, UNIONS, AND THE TRANSFORMATION OF WORK IN AMERICAN INDUSTRY, 1900-1945 (1985).

8. PAUL C. WEILER, GOVERNING THE WORKPLACE: THE FUTURE OF LABOR AND EMPLOYMENT LAW 295 (1990).

9. *Id.* at 282-95. *See also* Jamin B. Raskin, *Reviving the Democratic Vision of Labor Law*, 42 HASTINGS L.J. 1067, 1098-99 (1991) (reviewing Weiler's book); JANICE R. BELLACE, MANDATING EMPLOYEE INFORMATION AND CONSULTATION RIGHTS, PROCEEDINGS OF THE FORTY-THIRD ANNUAL MEETING, INDUSTRIAL RELATIONS RESEARCH ASSOCIATION 137 (John F. Burton ed., 1991) and the papers presented by Roy J. Adams, Richard B. Freeman, and Otto Jacobi and commented on by Joel Rogers in the same proceedings under the heading of "Statutory Works Councils," *id.* at 319-48.

10. *See* Summers, *supra* note 3. *See also* Charles McDonald, *U.S. Union Membership in Future Decades: A Trade Unionist's Perspective*, 31 INDUS. REL. 13 (1992).

11. Paul C. Weiler & Guy Mundlak, *New Directions for the Law of the Workplace*, 102 YALE L.J. 1907, 1922 (1993). *See also* Raymond L. Hogler, *Worker Participation, Employer Anti-Unionism, and Labor Law: The Case of the Steel Industry, 1918-1937*, 7 HOFSTRA LAB. L.J. 1, 68-69 (1989).

councils for otherwise unrepresented employees was federal policy during World War I. Following that, a number of employers established employee representation plans and committees in the 20s, at the height of which efforts about ten percent of workers in large manufacturing enterprises were so represented.[12] Employee representation plans were more widely adopted in the 30s as part of management's response to section 7(a) of the NIRA—resulting in the Labor Act's "company union" prohibition. Consequently, many of the same arguments made against that prohibition at the time are heard again today, especially the need to foster "cooperative" as opposed to "adversarial" labor relations.

But the idea of "members only" representation also draws from the historical wellspring in practice and, to a limited extent, in law as well.[13] On the former, the tradition of American "trades unions" throughout the nineteenth and the early twentieth century was to bargain only for their members; but this was coupled to the demand that employers hire union members exclusively—hence the sometimes violent struggle over employer demands for the "open shop." On the latter, under the Principles of the War Labor Conference Board, giving employees the right "to bargain collectively, through chosen representatives," the War Labor Board recognized the right of employees "through the agency of any union to which they may belong" to select a committee "to represent the union men" in the company's employ.[14] Following that principle, the idea that the law should authorize unions to represent those—and only those—who have voluntarily chosen them was embedded in the text of the Labor Act. Section 7 gives employees the right to representatives "of their own choosing"—not of someone else's choosing, whether that someone else is the employer or a group of co-workers. Such was a tenable reading of section 7(a) of the NIRA, until the then National Labor Relations Board (old) adopted the requirement of majority rule giving the "their" of "their own choosing" a collective rather than individual reference.[15] In consequence of the prior reading, however, the Automobile Settlement of March 25, 1934, provided for representation by any organization freely chosen by individual employees, although the Automobile

12. H.M. Gitelman, Legacy of the Ludlow Massacre 333-34 (1988).

13. *See generally* Richard R. Carlson, *The Origin and Future of Exclusive Representation in American Labor Law*, 30 Duq. L. Rev. 779 (1992).

14. Bureau of Labor Statistics, U.S. Dep't of Labor, Bull. No. 287, National War Labor Board 213 (1992).

15. *See* Minier Sargent, *Majority Rule in Collective Bargaining Under Section 7(a)*, 29 Ill. L. Rev. 275 (1934).

Labor Board promptly converted that provision into a kind of super works council, by a system of proportional representation.[16] But whatever potential the law might have had to effect a system of "members only" representation was eliminated by the Labor Act's embracing the principle of majority rule shortly thereafter. As the President of the American Federation of Labor's Office Employees International Union explained:

> Prior to the Act, unions were free to organize in whatever manner they found to be most effective. Frequently, a union would build its membership in a shop by first organizing a small group of workers who had the fortitude to stand strong for the union. Upon the organization of such group, certain job improvements would be obtained for them from management. And this working example of the gains to be achieved through organization frequently formed the most potent organizational appeal to other workers in the shop, and they too would join to improve their conditions. Now, trade unions must conform their organization activities to the appropriate bargaining unit patterns laid down by the Board. *They cannot organize and bargain for those workers in a plant who are interested in collective bargaining, they must organize and bargain for all workers within "an appropriate bargaining unit."*[17]

In sum, Congress took a provision, borrowing from prior law, that at the threshold granted to each individual employee the right to his or her chosen representative, and attached to it a provision requiring the employer to bargain only with a majority representative. However, the threshold grant of individual rights was not altered by the provision for majority rule. In the absence of an exclusive representative, concerted activity by work groups for better working conditions is statutorily protected, and nothing prohibits an employer from contracting with a union for terms applicable only to its members. The law simply makes no provision requiring employers to deal on that basis.[18] As a result, the ability of a nonmajority group to require the employer to deal with it is entirely a function of the group's strategic

16. *See* AUTOMOBILE LABOR BOARD, FINAL REPORT (Aug. 6, 1935). *See generally* SIDNEY FINE, THE AUTOMOBILE UNDER THE BLUE EAGLE (1963).

17. Paul R. Hutchings, *Effect on the Trade Union*, *in* THE WAGNER ACT: AFTER TEN YEARS 72, 73 (Louis G. Silverberg ed., 1945) (emphasis added).

18. Clyde Summers has argued that, "The plain words of section 7, section 8(a)(1) and section 8(a)(5) would seem to require an employer, in the absence of a majority union to bargain collectively with a non-majority union for its own members." Summers, *supra* note 3, at 539. It is a provocative argument; but it would require an unusually bold Labor Board (and judiciary) so to hold, against the weight of a contrary conventional wisdom. Accordingly this essay proceeds upon the assumption that legislative action would be required.

situation in the workplace.[19] But an unstrategically situated "bargaining unit" majority would be equally unable to compel the employer to deal with it, save for the Act's imposition of a duty to bargain. What follows will examine whether the road not taken in 1935 is worth exploring in the search for an alternative to the current system: Whether it would make sense today, with the hindsight of the Labor Act's experience, to think about extending bargaining rights on a "members only" basis.

The benefits of such an extension were dealt with in a comprehensive (and prescient) study by George Schatzki in 1975 and need only be briefly rehearsed.[20] All the regulation and delay attendant to unit determinations, election campaigns, and elections themselves would be eliminated (as well as the whole body of law surrounding successorship). Inasmuch as the employer would be required to bargain with any organization on behalf of its members, all the organization need supply to establish a bargaining relationship is a membership list. (Such, in fact, was part of the 1934 Automobile Settlement.)[21] To be sure, the submission of such a list to the employer could facilitate anti-union retaliation. But even now, a retaliatory discharge—for example, during the course of union organizing—requires proof of the employer's knowledge of the employee's union sentiment, membership, or activity; and the potential exacerbation of the prospect of unlawful employer retaliation only emphasizes the current need to strengthen legal safeguards against it.

Moreover, in consequence of "members only" representation an employee would not be forced to be represented either in bargaining or in the handling of grievances by a representative not of his or her "own choosing," whether a union elected by a majority under the current law,[22] or an elected works council either mandated by law or es-

19. For an assessment of how a nonexclusive representative might function under the current state of the law see Alan Hyde et al., *After Smyrna: Rights and Powers of Unions that Represent Less than a Majority*, 45 RUTGERS L. REV. 637 (1993).

20. George Schatzki, *Majority Rule, Exclusive Representation, and the Interests of Individual Workers: Should Exclusivity Be Abolished?*, 123 U. PA. L. REV. 897 (1975).

21. The lists, however, were submitted not to the employer but to the Automobile Labor Board, and the several difficulties with their use were obviated by the electoral machinery for proportional representation adopted by the Board. FINE, *supra* note 16, at 260-61. One difficulty was the fact that some employees joined more than one organization; but that could be dealt with by requiring the employee to make an election of membership for representation purposes in one organization only, failing which he or she would be considered unrepresented.

22. The fact that under majority rule a union selected by the slimmest of margins was required to represent employees unsympathetic or hostile to it—and to preclude their separate representation—continued to vex critics well after the Act's passage, to the point of an argument for a partial accommodation by requiring the Board to exclude from any bargaining unit em-

tablished unilaterally by the employer. Professor Schatzki dwells at some length on the implications of a true voluntarism, but to oversimplify, the prospect is likely to be one of greater individual participation and organizational responsiveness.

The arguable disadvantages of the proposal are two, both of which harken back to the debate over majority rule: The first goes to the issue of union bargaining power; the second goes to the employer's ability to bargain on a "members only" basis.[23] The first is concerned that nonmajority unions will be weaker in their dealing with employers relative to the power they can wield as exclusive representatives. The second is concerned that employers will be unable to deal efficiently with a multiplicity of different organizations representing otherwise fungible employees; it conjures up the spectre of three operatives working side-by-side performing identical tasks under common supervision and working conditions being represented by three different organizations. Each of these should be taken in turn.

The ability of a "members only" representative more sharply to focus shared concerns would be offset by a lessened ability to command a broader front in dealing with the employer. But a similar caution has been made with respect to bargaining unit determinations under the existing Act,[24] and that has not deterred the Board from finding units of relatively narrow congruent interests to be appropriate—for example, just the food service workers in a single outlet of a large retail chain like F.W. Woolworth.[25]

Moreover, it remains to be seen how effective the solidarity of coerced representation really is. The United States Supreme Court has limited a union's ability to command the financial support of the

ployees of a craft, class, department or plant division that had evidenced less than thirty percent support for the union. THEODORE R. ISERMAN, INDUSTRIAL PEACE AND THE WAGNER ACT 78-79 (1947).

23. *See* LEVERETT S. LYON ET AL., THE NATIONAL RECOVERY ADMINISTRATION 539 (1935):

> Majority rule in collective bargaining is justified by experience, which proves that collective bargaining is nullified in practice wherever the workers are divided. Majority rule is also necessitated by the fact that labor standards cannot be properly set for all the workers of a plant, craft, or industry, if different sets of representatives bargain at the same time with the same employer.

24. ROBERT A. GORMAN, BASIC TEXT ON LABOR LAW 68 (1976).

25. F.W. Woolworth Co., 144 N.L.R.B. 307 (1963). So, too, has the Board found to be appropriate a unit of only the meat department employees of a single outlet of a grocery chain, NLRB v. Joe B. Foods, Inc., 953 F.2d 287 (7th Cir. 1992), and of only the "front desk" employees of a hotel, Dinah's Hotel Corp., 295 N.L.R.B. 1100 (1989), which may, again, be part of a chain.

bargaining unit.[26] And in the strike situation, where solidarity is a necessary (if not sufficient) condition of economic power, the emphasis placed by the United States Supreme Court on the individual right to break with the strike and on the employer's privilege to induce breach of solidarity[27] weakens the argument to the bargaining strength of majority representation.

Some of the reservations about the current system can be illustrated by a relatively recent and altogether unremarkable decision, *Continental Web Press, Inc. v. NLRB*.[28] In 1980, a union petitioned to represent a unit of thirty-six pressmen in a lithographic printing plant. The Company argued that the unit should include seven preparatory employees. The Regional Director decided the unit petitioned for was appropriate and ordered an election. The union won the election 19 to 11, with 6 not voting, but the Company sought Board review. In 1982, the Board sustained the Regional Director, relying upon the different training (apprenticeship), supervision and work hours of the two groups and the lack of interchange between them.[29] The employer, however, refused to bargain on the ground that the unit was inappropriate. The union filed a charge of unfair labor practice, and in 1983 the Board ordered the employer to bargain.[30] The employer then sought review in the court of appeals. The court opined that had the case been one of first impression, a separate pressmen's unit might well have been appropriate; but the Board had held in other cases that preparatory employees and pressmen were part of a continuous lithographic process, which, by analogy, would mean that the Board in this case had placed the employees at the beginning of an assembly line in one unit and those at the end in another.[31] And so—four years after the election—the court applied that principle of administrative law requiring the Board adequately to explain a departure from established precedent, or to announce its reasons more fully were it to be adopting a new policy, and remanded for the Board's reconsideration.

One is driven to inquire whether something is not amiss in these events: Why should the 19 of 36 pressmen who desire union represen-

26. *See generally* Kenneth G. Dau-Schmidt, *Union Security Agreements Under the National Labor Relations Act: The Statute, the Constitution, and the Court's Opinion in* Beck, 27 HARV. J. ON LEGIS. 51 (1990).

27. *See, e.g.*, Matthew W. Finkin, *Labor Policy and the Enervation of the Economic Strike*, 1990 U. ILL. L. REV. 547.

28. 742 F.2d 1087 (7th Cir. 1984).

29. Continental Web Press, Inc., 262 N.L.R.B. 1395 (1982).

30. Continental Web Press, Inc., 266 N.L.R.B. 841 (1983).

31. *Continental Web Press, Inc.*, 742 F.2d at 1091.

tation be denied that representation because seven nonpressmen were not included in the unit? Even if the pressmen constituted "an" appropriate unit, as the court conceded could be the case, would a union with 19 supporters of 36 in the unit (with 11 hostile and 6 arguably indifferent) be measurably stronger as a representative of the entire unit than one that represents only its members? If the union had lost the election in a pressmen's unit—15 for, 15 against, and 6 not voting—why should those fifteen be denied a representative "of their own choosing" because an equal number of their co-workers were contrary minded (and six arguably indifferent)? And even if the union in both these cases is in a weaker bargaining position representing only its members than it would be representing all the pressmen—which is by no means obvious—neither is it obvious that employees are better off in the aggregate with the current "high stakes" game, which encourages employer resistance and litigation and in which unions secure majority support less than half the time,[32] than with a "lower stakes" game that assures representation automatically to all those who desire it even if their bargaining position may be of lessened strength.[33]

The more difficult or, at least, perplexing problem is the prospect of a proliferation of organizations each demanding to bargain for its members over the same subjects and to which the employer would owe an equal duty to bargain in good faith. The difficulty will be discussed presently. But the perplexity derives from the Act's misleading vocabulary and from the want of any statutory guidance on the question of bargaining structure.

The Act speaks in terms of exclusive representation of "an appropriate bargaining unit"—the group of jobs the union represents. But, what the Board in reality is determining is an appropriate election unit for the designation of a bargaining agent, which may or may not coincide with the group of jobs actually represented at the bargaining table. From this perspective, the function of the "community of interests" test the Board applies to decide unit questions is only partly a concern for management's ease of bargaining and more importantly one of assuring sufficient homogeneity of employee interests for the purpose of selecting an exclusive representative and minimizing the

32. In 1990 the NLRB ran 4,210 representation elections. Unions won 1,965 of them—or 46.7 percent. The total vote over the fiscal year was about 108,000 employees voting for unions and 121,000 against. 55 NLRB ANN. REP. 11 (1992).

33. *Cf.* McDonald, *supra* note 10, at 27-28.

number of conflicting interests the representative might be called upon to reconcile.[34]

In the case of the Woolworth outlet adverted to earlier, the union sought a unit of only the food service workers, and the employer insisted that only a unit of all the store's employees would be appropriate. Accordingly, the Board attended to differences in work, supervision, and working conditions as well as to similarities in wages, benefits, and personnel policies to decide whether or not the unit petitioned for represented a true community of interests. But at no point does either the Board majority or the dissenting Board members advert to how an enormous national retail chain, with over a thousand outlets, is to bargain effectively over wages, medical insurance, pension benefits, and seniority (including transfer and "bumping" rights) with either a representative of the employees of just a single store *or* of only that single store's food service workers; nor does the Board contemplate the Company's situation were it required to bargain with representatives of potentially thousands of such units.

The Board's silence is not surprising for it mirrors the statute's silence on this point. The duty to bargain under the Act requires the employer to send a representative to the bargaining table with power to make an agreement; thus, the selection of a union by the single outlet's food service workers compels the employer to bargain on company-wide policies such as wages, hours, and benefits. But the Act is silent about, is unconcerned with, how the employer is to do that. Consequently, the practical difficulty for "members only" representation flows from the Act's lack of concern with bargaining structure.

Under the current state of the law, a union may attempt to rationalize the structure of bargaining for the various units it represents. If it is selected at food service counters elsewhere in the company, it may propose to bargain for them all as a single unit; but it may not insist upon that demand for such an alteration in "the bargaining unit" is only a permissive bargaining subject. If the Company agrees, however, the union may negotiate a single company-wide contract even though it was elected counter by counter, store by store. In that case, the actual "bargaining unit" will transcend the election districts from which the union derived its bargaining rights. Further, a group of unions representing different groups of the employer's employees may form a coalition and bargain jointly with the employer; but they may

34. GORMAN, *supra* note 24, at 67-68.

not insist that the employer bargain on that basis for that too would alter "the bargaining unit" which the Board determined to be appropriate.[35] For the same reason, neither may the employer insist upon joint bargaining. In the Woolworth example, the employer could not insist upon meeting jointly with the separate representatives of the food service workers and store clerks to negotiate a common issue such as seniority in consequence of employee interchange.[36] Nor may either party condition agreement in one unit upon the satisfactory conclusion of negotiations for another unit.[37] Thus the prospect of a variety of organizations—some affiliated with national labor organizations, some entirely indigenous—each representing its own members, each desiring to bargain about employer policies that may affect them in common, each owed a duty to bargain in good faith by the employer has the potential of exacerbating the difficulties an employer would face under the current state of the law, where it might be required to bargain with a variety of unions, each the exclusive representative of one or more of a number of bargaining units.

One can be skeptical that the actual number of organizations demanding to bargain for their members would be outlandish. A recent study based on the empirical and theoretical literature has concluded that, "[C]ollective action tends to happen when a critical mass of interested and resourceful individuals can coordinate their efforts."[38] And it remains to be seen how many such critical masses there are in a given workplace, or how sustainable a number of organizations can be on a given potential membership base. (If multiplicity were considered to be a serious potential problem, the statute could require that organizational membership reach a certain practicable level as a condition of recognition, perhaps as a minimum percentage of the workforce in the establishment, division, department, class or craft.)[39]

35. *See generally* William N. Chernish, Coalition Bargaining (1969). However, each of the unions in the coalition may sit with one another's bargaining committee as a technical representative of the then bargaining union. General Elec. Co. v. NLRB, 412 F.2d 512 (2d Cir. 1969).

36. F.W. Woolworth Co., 179 N.L.R.B. 748 (1969).

37. *See* United Paperworkers Int'l Union Eriez Local 620 (International Paper Co.), 309 N.L.R.B. 44 (1992) (applying this principle to a "pooled voting ratification procedure"). For criticism of the decision (and the doctrine) in the context of the precise labor dispute in question see Julius G. Getman & F. Ray Marshall, *Industrial Relations in Transition: The Paper Industry Example*, 102 Yale L.J. 1803 (1993).

38. Gerald Marwell & Pamela Oliver, The Critical Mass in Collective Action: A Micro-Social Theory 123 (1993).

39. *See, e.g.,* Exec. Order No. 10,988, 3 C.F.R. 521 (1959-1963). It provided for recognition of an employee organization in the federal service as the exclusive representative of the employees in an appropriate bargaining unit upon designation by a majority of those employees. But it also provided for "formal recognition" short of exclusive bargaining rights of an organization "as

Nonetheless, nonmajority representation may complicate conduct of bargaining and arguably heighten the potential of whipsawing or leapfrogging by different organizations. In other words, explicit provision for "members only" representation would bring to the fore an issue currently imbedded in but ignored by the Labor Act. And although it is likely that employers and unions would work out the practical problems of bargaining structure without statutory attention, just as they do now—either by bargaining consensually on a multi-union basis or by a "pattern" bargain with a single union which is then insisted upon by the employer in bargaining with the others—the potential exacerbation of the problem argues for legislative facilitation of the bargaining process; that is, for a coalition-accommodating and, if need be, a coalition-forcing statutory provision.[40]

If one were to fashion a statute that accepted the principle of majority rule but required that units be configured to relatively narrow sets of congruent interests, an analogous problem of a potential proliferation of bargaining obligations would be presented. Such a statute was drafted to deal with a rather more rarified question in public sector collective bargaining;[41] but the approach it took would seem to be applicable to the possible proliferation of bargaining obligations under a system of "members only" representation. Assuming that section 9(a) were amended so to require, section 8(a)(5) could be amended as follows:

> It shall be an unfair labor practice for an employer—
>
> * * *
>
> (5) to refuse to bargain collectively with a representative of his employees; but it shall not be an unfair labor practice—

the representative of its members" in a unit defined by the governmental agency when *inter alia* it has "a substantial and stable membership" of at least ten percent of the employees in the unit.

Such a provision arguably could invite litigation much like the current determination of an "appropriate bargaining unit." But an "establishment" is a fairly well-defined entity for federal wage and hour law purposes. 29 C.F.R. § 779.23 (1992). Unlike the multifactored test for what is an appropriate unit, what constitutes an employer's own "department" or "division" would seem to be a much simpler determination; and only less so what constitutes a "class" or "craft." Thus challenges on the ground of insufficient membership or level of subscription would be likely to arise only on the margin; and the incentive to such challenges would be reduced by strengthening the remedies for wrongful refusal to bargain, a much needed reform irrespective of any change in majority rule.

40. Professor Schatzki observes that unions could engage in coalition bargaining and that employers could be required to deal with them on that basis. Schatzki, *supra* note 20, at 919. But he does not attend to what a coalition-forcing mechanism would be, save for suggesting on the issue of seniority that the contract made with the first union be made to serve as a pattern. *Id.* at 936.

41. David E. Feller & Matthew W. Finkin, *Legislative Issues in Faculty Collective Bargaining, in* FACULTY BARGAINING IN PUBLIC HIGHER EDUCATION 74 (Carnegie Council Series 1977).

> (a) for two or more labor organizations to demand joint bargaining with an employer with respect to matters which have customarily been provided on a uniform basis among the employees represented by such organizations; or,
>
> (b) for an employer (i) to demand joint bargaining by two or more organizations with respect to matters which have customarily been provided on a uniform basis among the employees represented by such labor organizations, or (ii) if joint bargaining is not agreed to by those organizations or no agreement is reached acceptable to all parties, to conclude an agreement as to such matter with the organization or organizations which represent the largest number of employees and to refuse to bargain further with any other organizations as to such matters unless that other organization agrees to accept the terms so negotiated.[42]

These provisions give the employee representatives and the employer the power directly to confront and to rationalize the bargaining structure. Subparagraph (a) makes joint bargaining a mandatory bargaining subject. Inasmuch as the statutory concern is for the employer's ability to bargain, the employer need not be required to bargain with a coalition; but where the employee representatives fear an effort to play one off against another, it permits the different organizations to require the employer directly to confront the issue. Subparagraph (b) is concerned with the reverse situation, where the employer sees the need to rationalize its bargaining structure and the representatives prove resistant. Accordingly, the proposed provision gives the employer the power to impose a coalition in the face of such recalcitrance. But both are limited to issues that have customarily been settled on a uniform basis, to preserve separate negotiations on matters of particular interest to the organization that raise no issue of common concern. Thus the operation of subparagraph (b) has been explained by its drafter:

> [It] makes clear that the employer cannot, after joint bargaining, take advantage of the permissible pattern bargain by settling with the weaker organizations (at least in terms of the total number of employees represented) and imposing that settlement on the stronger. For the same reason the employer cannot impose terms on an organization to which the demand for joint bargaining had not been directed or which had not been a participant in unsuccessful joint bargaining. The provision does, however, give real meaning to the joint bargaining procedure, because a settlement with a coalition representing the largest number could be binding even on the nonconsenting representative of the single largest . . . [member-

42. *Id.* at 161. This draft accordingly omits the current requirement—"subject to the provisions of section 9(a)"—in section 8(a)(5).

ship]. As a result, the bargaining agents are under considerable pressure to come together and arrive at a mutually acceptable resolution.[43]

The proposal has its most obvious application where the several organizations represent members in work groups who conceive of themselves as uniquely situated or as having special concerns—those who might be subsumed in a more heterogeneous bargaining unit determined to be appropriate by the Labor Board. But even if one were to speculate that employees doing otherwise the same work for the same pay and under the same supervision might choose different organizations to represent them, such would seem possible because these organizations successfully appeal to different workplace concerns. It would be possible, arguably, for employees to segregate themselves into organizations emphasizing divergent interests, for example, of health insurance and pensions for the older, of job training and retraining for the younger, of flextime and child care, especially for female employees with young children, and of safety in certain hazardous jobs. Even in such a speculative situation, a coalition-forcing provision would compel these groups to make compromises with one another in order to achieve an overall package on matters of common policy.

However, the availability of self-segregating organizations holds open the possibility for a variety of "civil rights" organizations to assert the interests of their members.[44] This may well give pause, for the argument runs that the opening of a channel for these groups separately to assert their members' "voice" would virtually insure that it would be utilized. And while added "voice" is often to be welcomed, too much voice—like too much exit—may become dysfunctional.[45]

Under the current state of the law, the bargaining agent is required to accommodate the unit's various interests and desires in fashioning its bargaining demands and trade-offs, subject to external accountability under a statutory duty of fair representation, in which intra-organizational accommodation the employer has nothing to say. What is different today from when the duty of fair representation was

43. *Id.* at 163-64. The statutory provision and the analysis were drafted by David Feller who is not responsible for its extension into this setting.

44. Professor Schatzki acknowledges the prospect of racial self-segregation. Schatzki, *supra* note 20, at 933-34. That such is a distinct possibility *see* Black Grievance Comm. v. NLRB, 749 F.2d 1072 (3d Cir. 1984), *cert. denied*, 472 U.S. 1008 (1985).

45. Albert O. Hirschman, Exit, Voice, and Loyalty 31 (1970) ("But voice is like exit in that it can be overdone: the discontented . . . could become so harassing that their protests would at some point hinder rather than help . . . .").

created in 1944, to deal with a racial distinction drawn by collective agreement, is a proliferation in the number of groups with statutory rights to assert in the workplace—on grounds of sex, ethnicity, religion, age, physical and mental handicap, citizenship and lawful immigration status in addition to race—and the emergence of other groups identifying themselves as needful of similar solicitude, most prominently on grounds of sexual orientation.

To see how this might complicate the contemporary workplace, contemplate the situation where a number of Spanish-speaking employees desire to converse with one another in that tongue even as other English-only speakers—perhaps African Americans—feel put off by the use of that language, possibly feeling themselves to be the object of comment (or ridicule) they do not understand. Their desire for an "English only" rule on company premises is strongly resisted by the Spanish-speakers. Now play out the possibility of such competing claims on racial, ethnic and sexual grounds to training and promotion opportunities, to claims for out-of-seniority accommodation to religious observance and physical handicap, and on down an expanding list of potential claims and claimants, and the "civil rights" scenario becomes a sobering one entirely apart from the additional regulation of some of these issues by civil rights law.

The argument derives its considerable force from the depiction of a multiplicity of competing interest groups clamoring to be heard. But if that is so, if all these conflicting claims are nascent in the workplace, the question presented is whether it makes sense to continue to call upon a single exclusive employee representative to reconcile them. There is much to be said for a model of minorities successfully negotiating their differences with one another. But if "too much" voice may harass an employer, it is at least equally possible that too much voice internal to an employee organization may place more burdens upon its political processes than it reasonably should be asked to accommodate.

It is true that under "members only" representation, employees who believe they would be better represented separately could insist on dealing with the employer (subject, if need be, to some minimum membership requirement).[46] But this may suggest in return that such groups should be heard if they desire, and that the responsibility for orchestrating their claims may rest just as well if not better with the

46. *See supra* note 39.

employer, subject to its invocation of the proposed coalition-forcing provision.

The shifting of this responsibility to the employer raises a related concern. Under the instant proposal, a collective representative would be free to set its own membership requirements so long as it does not violate any civil rights law. It could not, for example, refuse to admit African Americans, Mexican Americans, women, or the like. But it could restrict membership to those who perform certain tasks or who have certain training; and there is no reason why it could not also require a certain level of skill. The consequence may give separate "voice" to the more highly skilled and better trained—those whom the employer might be most anxious to retain (and reward) but whose voice would be submerged in larger noncraft bargaining units—and who may be better positioned to exact a wage premium (or "rent") at the expense of those less skilled or less in demand.[47] This, in turn, may contribute to the widening of the wage inequality that the Republic has experienced over the past decade or two.[48]

If this consequence was thought relevant to the fashioning of a system of employee representation, we could regulate the membership policies of employee representatives to blunt these effects; to require, for example, that an organization that admits any employee of an employer admit all employees of that employer.[49] But that approach would cut against the principle of free association that undergirds nonexclusive representation. It would also require a reintroduction of some externally imposed notion of statutory fair representation that the instant proposal eliminates.[50]

47. Professor Schatzki confronted this possibility, *see supra* note 20, at 933:

> For example, skilled workers may be prepared to work for no less than, say, eight dollars an hour. But they may hope for nine dollars, and might be able to realize that greater salary if they are able to negotiate on their own; the employer could then compensate by offering less to the unskilled workers, who are more easily replaced if they are not satisfied with the employer's pay scale. Under the present state of affairs, with skilled employees merged in collective bargaining units with less skilled or more easily replaced employees, the union may aim only for the eight dollar figure, on the thesis that the skilled employees will be minimally satisfied and more will be left over for the unskilled workers. If one has some concern for the status and rewards of the less able, skilled, or fortunate workers, the consequence I describe should be unsettling.

48. W. Norton Grubb & Robert H. Wilson, *Sources of Increasing Inequality in Wages and Salaries, 1960-80*, MONTHLY LAB. REV., April 1989, at 3; Paul Ryscavage & Peter Henle, *Earnings Inequality Accelerates in the 1980's*, MONTHLY LAB. REV., Dec. 1990, at 3.

49. This is the approach taken by Professor Schatzki, *supra* note 20, at 920.

50. This is not to suggest that unions would have no externally imposed limit on their treatment of their members. But such would derive from the general law governing the internal affairs of membership organizations and not from the Labor Act. *Cf.* Zechariah Chafee, Jr., *The Internal Affairs of Associations Not For Profit*, 43 HARV. L. REV. 993 (1930). Nor should the Landrum-Griffin Act, requiring union democracy, be affected.

Alternatively, one could require the fundamentals of the wage bargain to be centrally set at a supra-enterprise level as is done in some European countries, of which Sweden is probably the most well known.[51] But that would require a massive change in American law and practice of dubious workability; even Sweden has experienced "wage drift"—an increase in wages at the firm level beyond the centrally set contractual standard.[52]

What remains to be seen is whether the incomes inequality problem ought to be addressed through the statutory structure of employee representation. If one conceives of the collectively bargained wage as a means of distributing the total wage sum among differing groups in society, then the call to statutory concern would make a lot of sense—in fact, the call should be for mandatory unionization and a centralized bargaining structure. But at the enterprise level the wage may be a tool for the effective organization of work, even a system of reward for work that bears some relationship to productivity. The giving of "voice" to the better trained and more highly skilled might well widen the wage differential within organized firms; but it might also conduce toward greater productivity—else why would employers more readily accede to these demands than those of the unskilled—and possibly encourage the unskilled to undertake more training.

Thus the "wage gap" argument is a reprise of the conventional solution to the "civil rights" problem: In that case, to place the burden of reconciling conflicting ethnic claimants on the union, so to filter them in the process; in this case, to resolve the "wage gap" problem by the same means, in the sure and certain hope that a majoritarian body will tend to compress the wage for the better skilled relative to the larger number of un- and semi-skilled.[53] There is one difference between the two, but it only emphasizes the role the submergence of interest plays; that is, the terms of the bargain in the former case must withstand scrutiny under the civil rights laws. But no such scrutiny is afforded in the latter. In fact, the Supreme Court has explained that "[t]he workman is free, if he values his own bargaining position more than that of the group, to vote against representation . . . ."[54] What that workman is not given is the privilege to associate

51. *See* Lei Delsen & Tom van Veen, *The Swedish Model: Relevant for Other European Countries?*, 30 Brit. J. of Indus. Rel. 83 (1992).

52. Hans-Göran Myrdal, *The Hard Way from a Centralised to a Decentralised Industrial Relations System—The Case of Sweden and SAF, in* Employers' Associations in Europe: Policy and Organisation 191 (Dieter Sadowski & Otto Jacobi eds., 1991).

53. *See supra* note 47.

54. J.I. Case, Co. v. NLRB, 321 U.S. 332, 339 (1944).

only with others who value their bargaining position equally with his, in contradistinction to membership in a governmentally defined bargaining unit. The result was supported in the debate on majority rule by an analogy of industrial to political democracy: Just as a Congressman represents all the voters in the Congressional district, including those who voted for her opponent or who didn't bother to vote at all, so does the representative elected by a majority of the bargaining unit. But the analogy is flawed: Residence in an electoral district represented by a disliked politician does not preclude those voters from banding together financially and in other ways to support other members of the same deliberative body who may be sympathetic to their views. Those residents may also lobby the executive or legislative branches in opposition to "their own" representative's position. Neither channel is available under the system of exclusive representation: No other workplace representative is allowed for dissatisfied employees to influence; nor may they effectively deal with their employer to advance a position contrary to that of the exclusive representative. Collective bargaining under the Labor Act is a form of industrial democracy; but it is a one-party State.[55]

If a consequence of an authentic freedom of workplace association is to contribute to a widening of wage disparities, and if that consequence is of concern to the body politic (as it well may), the better approach would be for the body politic to confront the issue of wage inequality directly—perhaps via a national incomes policy—and not to compel workers to be represented by organizations they do not want or who may not want to represent them.

Thus far this excursion has assumed for simplicity's sake that whatever pluralism emerges in employee representation at the plant or office would occur more or less simultaneously. But the duty to bargain might arise sequentially. Return, for example, to the *Continental Web Press* case and assume that after negotiations have been concluded with organization A, binding only on its members, organization B is formed and insists upon different terms. Because B could not have been subject to an employer demand for joint bargaining, the Company could not refuse to bargain with it. But the Company could insist upon the terms agreed with organization A. Were it to agree to better terms with B, it would in effect be deciding which is to be the

55. Nor is this state of affairs mitigated by the intramural political structure of most unions. *See* Clyde W. Summers, *Democracy in a One-Party State: Perspectives from Landrum-Griffin*, 43 MD. L. REV. 93 (1984).

dominant organization. To be sure, A's "no strike" obligation would bind only its members. Consequently, in this sequential bargaining scenario B would be free to strike were the Company to insist on the pattern made with A.[56] But in simultaneous bargaining, a nondominant organization would be equally free to strike in an effort to secure better terms than those agreed upon with the dominant organization or coalition. In other words, the "sequential bargaining" scenario does not differ greatly from the situation an employer faces under the current state of the law when it bargains with a number of organizations who differ among themselves as to which will be the pattern setter.

The prospect of sequential bargaining obligations ripening as new organizations emerge raises a question: How is the employer to carry on its day-to-day operations when the duty to bargain in good faith imposes a limit upon the employer's ability to take unilateral action over bargainable subject matter pending the exhaustion of its bargaining obligation? This would be a serious concern if a statute were configured to require the exhaustion of a "meet and confer" obligation with any organization claiming to represent any members of a bargaining unit before any change could be made in terms and conditions of employment for the unit as a whole. But, the sequential ripening of nonmajority bargaining obligations would not seem to differ materially from the situation a company—say, Woolworth—would face as various bargaining units—say, each of its food counters—proceed to unionize over time. The bargain struck with one organization representing either only its members or a bargaining unit would be binding upon those it covers; and the terms agreed to might be extended unilaterally by the employer to nonrepresented employees. But whatever the existing employment terms are, they constitute the status quo to which the unilateral action rule would apply as new organizations secure bargaining rights, just as they do now.

To be sure, were a hundred or more tiny and so economically unsustainable organizations—of, say, two or three employees each—sequentially to demand to represent themselves, the unilateral action rule would significantly hobble the employer's ability to act—so significantly, in fact, that it would be a virtual certainty that the exception to the rule would be held to apply, allowing the employer to act

56. So, too, might A, in cautious anticipation of any new organization emerging, negotiate a "me too" clause that would give it the benefit of any better bargain struck with another organization.

out of business necessity.[57] But the mere theoretical possibility of such a scenario should not lend credence to it as a likely reality: Why *would* three hundred production workers feel it necessary—or useful—to form a hundred organizations? In any event, if an excess of legislative caution were thought prudent, that potential could be dealt with along the line of a mandatory minimum membership.

A final aspect of the workability of "members only" representation concerns not negotiation but contract application and administration, for it contemplates a system where organizations represent not jobs, as under the current system, but people. Return to *Continental Web Press* and assume that in addition to organization A, which represents nineteen pressmen, organization B represents the eleven pressmen who were hostile to A (for whatever reason) as well as three preparatory workers, and that each is statutorily entitled to represent its members. How is it possible for the employer to give better terms to A than to B, or to A and B but not to extend these terms to the unrepresented without violating section 8(a)(3), which forbids discrimination in terms and conditions of employment to encourage or discourage union membership? And if the grievances of A's and B's members are presumably to be dealt with through the grievance arbitration provisions of their respective representative's agreements, how are the unrepresented nonmembers to be dealt with? In other words, for these purposes must there not have to be some notion of a "bargaining unit"—a cluster of common jobs subject accordingly to common treatment?

Under the existing statutory regime, differences in terms and conditions of employment between represented employees, or between the represented and the unrepresented, that reflect the respective bargaining powers of the organizations and are not rooted in an intent to favor one union over another or to sanction the represented in favor of the unrepresented do not work a violation of section 8(a)(3).[58] It is possible for one group of employees—Woolworth's food service workers—to unionize while another, their fellow retail clerks, do not. As a result, the former may secure improvements and protections the latter do not then enjoy, even though they heretofore had the same pay scale, hours, and benefits, had some interchange of duties, and worked in the same location under the same store management. And

57. *See* George Schatzki, *The Employer's Unilateral Act—A Per Se Violation—Sometimes*, 44 TEX. L. REV. 470 (1966).

58. *See generally* Soule Glass & Glazing Co. v. NLRB, 652 F.2d 1055, 1077-78 (1st Cir. 1981).

per contra an employer may pay its nonunionized workers at a higher rate than the unionized,[59] even where it is entirely conceivable that the two groups could have comprised "an" appropriate bargaining unit,[60] where, that is, the major distinction between the two is the fact of unionization. Neither does it violate the Act for an employer to institute welfare or pension benefits that exclude unionized workers from coverage on that basis alone, so long as the employer has not instituted the benefits to defeat the union and does not preclude the union from bargaining for them.[61] In other words, as the Labor Act currently stands, a cluster of common jobs may nevertheless be disaggregated for unit purposes along the lines of more narrowly focused communities of interests.[62] This in turn may result in different terms and conditions of employment for persons who had been governed by common terms heretofore, which differences derive from the fact of such separate representation.

In a sense, a great many unions already bargain on a nonmajority basis to the extent the units they represent (albeit on an exclusive basis) comprise a minority of the employer's eligible employees or a minority even within alternative configurations of appropriate bargaining units. Consequently, bargaining on a nonmajority, "members only" basis should pose little difficulty for reconciliation with section 8(a)(3).[63]

But most important, under the proposed statutory provision the Company is given the power to assure that the similarly situated are in fact treated similarly if it desires (or where antidiscrimination law requires)—in the lithographical hypothetical, by insisting on a coalition,

59. *Cf.* Viacom Cablevision, 267 N.L.R.B. 1141 (1983) (no unfair labor practice for employer to call a meeting of its unionized workers to inform them of the better wages and benefits paid to their nonunion counterparts).

60. *Cf.* Lennox Indus., 308 N.L.R.B. 1237 (1992) (breaking up what had been a single bargaining unit not due to any change in the work but because of the employer's organizational restructuring).

61. *See* Dallas Morning News, 285 N.L.R.B. 807 (1987); Fabric Warehouse, 294 N.L.R.B. 189 (1989), *aff'd*, 901 F.2d 669 (1990).

62. But section 9(c)(5), added in 1947, provides that in determining the unit appropriate for bargaining, "the extent to which the employees have organized shall not be controlling." 29 U.S.C. § 159(c)5 (1988).

63. *See* NLRB v. Reliable Newspaper Delivery, Inc., 187 F.2d 547 (3d Cir. 1951) (refusing to sustain a section 8(a)(3) violation where a minority union, bargaining only for its members, secured a retroactive pay raise that was not extended by the employer to nonmember employees). It should follow that a collective agreement could not forbid an employer from extending its gains to nonmembers. Nor can an employer agree to prefer union members over nonmembers as such in a layoff. Radio Officers' Union v. NLRB, 347 U.S. 17 (1954); NLRB v. Erie Resistor Corp., 373 U.S. 221 (1963). But the employer could agree with a "members only" representative (or coalition) upon the configuration of the unit within which seniority would operate and to extend that definition unilaterally to the unrepresented.

failing which it could settle with organization A and effectively impose those terms on organization B, to assure that the terms accorded to the pressmen via each of their organizations are substantially the same. (However, the Company would be required to bargain separately with organization B for any special terms or conditions pertaining only to the three preparatory workers.) And, as a practical matter the employer is free, and would be expected to extend the negotiated terms—putting the grievance procedure aside—to the technically "unrepresented" nonmember pressmen and preparatory employees respectively.

Inasmuch as the unrepresented are likely to benefit from whatever is secured by the bargaining representative (or coalition), and because there could be no compulsory dues for nonmembers, a question remains of whether such a system would not encounter an insuperable "free rider" problem. But with a sufficient "critical mass" of participants,[64] the fact of free riding would not seem to disable an otherwise economically sustainable representative organization to a significantly greater extent than does the current system where the gains of an exclusive representative may be extended by the employer to its "free riding" nonunionized employees. In addition, the major difference between the represented and the unrepresented would be the grievance-arbitration procedure available only to the member as a swift, inexpensive, and effective means of enforcing contract rights. To be sure, the employer is free unilaterally to establish a grievance-arbitration procedure for the unrepresented,[65] so long as it does not violate section 7 in so doing.[66] But the one critical feature that such a procedure would lack is the institutional presence and participation of the employee's representative organization—its expertise, indepen-

64. *See* MARWELL & OLIVER, *supra* note 38, at 101:

> [S]imultaneous coordinated action is modeled as an all-or-none contract. The organizer is conceived as asking others to participate in a risk-free agreement to make contributions if enough others also agree. . . . [G]roup members will agree to contribute if the total benefit they would experience from the "contract" exceeds their own share of the cost. . . . [T]he model would . . . apply to any small group whose members have decided to pool their resources and act in concert, as if they were one complex person.

65. *See generally* Samuel Estreicher, *Arbitration of Employment Disputes Without Unions*, 66 CHI.-KENT L. REV. 753 (1990).

66. *Cf.* NLRB v. Stone, 125 F.2d 752, 756 (7th Cir.), *cert. denied*, 317 U.S. 649 (1942) (finding individual agreement to submit "all complaints and disputes" to "final" arbitration constitutes a per se violation of the Labor Act). *Compare* Matthew W. Finkin, *Commentary on "Arbitration of Employment Disputes Without Union,"* 66 CHI.-KENT L. REV. 799 (1990) *with* Samuel Estreicher, *Reply to Professor Finkin*, 66 CHI.-KENT L. REV. 817 (1990), on the role of section 8(a)(2) in regulating nonunion arbitration plans.

dence, and resources.[67] Moreover, the right to participate in the organization's decision-making, to influence the terms of the bargain, flows exclusively from membership. These lawful differences between members and nonmembers should tend to mitigate the free rider problem.

Last, but of no small significance, nonmajority representation holds open a degree of flexibility arguably better attuned to the contemporary workplace. As the Foreword to this Symposium points out, the Nation is now legislatively committed to a variety of workplace protections, and the common law has recognized employee dignity—reputation, privacy, and emotional well-being—as legally protected interests. But these legislative goals and societal values depend upon the happenstance of administrative intervention or individual litigation for their vindication. If society is serious about realizing them, there would seem to be no more effective means than well informed, adequately financed, and truly independent employee organizations active in the shop or office. Take, for example, the earlier discussion of the emergence of a critical mass of employees concerned only with a single workplace issue such as pensions. Under the Employee Retirement Income Security Act, which regulates both welfare and pension benefits, an employer is under no obligation to inform benefit plan participants of its intention to alter or even to abrogate a benefit, let alone any obligation to bargain with them about such change.[68] The United States Supreme Court has opined that "employee resistance" is a "significant check" on an employer's ability to terminate a pension plan;[69] but the Court did not explain how that resistance would be manifested or marshaled. An exclusive bargaining agent would serve to focus and channel that resistance—because pension benefits are a mandatory bargaining subject and because the duty to bargain under the Labor Act requires an employer to bargain to impasse before it may implement a change. What remains to be seen is why employees concerned about their benefits should be given the Hobson's Choice of only that one model of representation: Why should a group of employees who desire to be informed of impending

67. *See* Julius G. Getman, *Labor Arbitration and Dispute Resolution*, 88 YALE L.J. 916 (1979), and Martha S. West, *The Case Against Reinstatement in Wrongful Discharge*, 1988 U. ILL. L. REV. 1, respectively on the significance of unions in the arbitration process, and of a union presence in the workplace to the effectiveness of the arbitral remedy of reinstatement for wrongful discharge.

68. The cases are collected in 1 HOWARD A. SPECTER & MATTHEW W. FINKIN, INDIVIDUAL EMPLOYMENT LAW AND LITIGATION § 1.80, at 153 (1989).

69. Pension Benefit Guar. Corp. v. LTV Corp., 496 U.S. 633, 651 (1990).

changes in employer benefits and to negotiate over them, and who notify their employer to that effect, first be required to become the exclusive bargaining agent of an appropriate bargaining unit?

So, too, of information sharing more generally. The Labor Act requires an employer to disclose job-related information in its possession necessary for the employees' agent to deal with terms and conditions of employment as well as with employee grievances. But absent some other law requiring disclosure, an employer need not disclose that information to unrepresented employees. Some employers, for example, keep even their supervisory rules governing discipline and discharge a secret from the employees governed by them.[70] Again, it remains to be seen why a group of employees who desire to know what the rules are should be required first to become certified as an exclusive bargaining representative. Under the instant proposal, all they need do is submit a membership or subscriber list—and ask to see the rules. And if they are able to contribute funds sufficient to retain a lawyer to represent them, there is no reason why their employer should not be required to deal with her.[71]

In addition, nonmajority representation would have the potential of being more responsive than is the current system to the growing use of "contingent" (or "atypical") workers who are hired for short terms of service and who cannot expect to have a permanent or long term relationship with any single employer.[72] On the one hand, the expectation of impermanence (and, in some cases, the lack of even a central workplace for those who are employed to work at home) makes it difficult if not impossible for these employees to secure representation.[73] But on the other hand, these sequential short-term job holders may be most in need of representation. For example, with the acceleration in job mobility—with the growing reality for many entrants to the labor market that they cannot expect to have a career with a single employer for the duration of their working lives—the assumption that

70. This has emerged in litigation on whether the terms so secreted can be contractually binding on the employer. The prevailing view is that they are not. SPECTER & FINKIN, *supra* note 68, § 1.01, at 6 n.11 (1989).

71. The Labor Act speaks in terms of a "representative" designated or selected by the employees. A statutory representative need not be a labor organization. Under existing law, a majority of a bargaining unit could designate a single person, *e.g.* a lawyer, as their exclusive bargaining representative.

72. *See generally* RICHARD S. BELOUS, THE CONTINGENT ECONOMY: THE GROWTH OF THE TEMPORARY, PART-TIME AND SUBCONTRACTED WORKFORCE (1989).

73. *Cf.* Dorothy S. Cobble, *Union Strategies for Organizing and Representing the New Service Workforce, in* PROCEEDINGS OF THE FORTY-THIRD ANNUAL MEETING, INDUSTRIAL RELATIONS RESEARCH ASSOCIATION 76 (John F. Burton, Jr. ed., 1991).

employees will be assured of post-employment income via a single company's pension plan becomes increasingly unrealistic. The grant of representational rights to occupationally based organizations that automatically represent their members, hired even as contingent workers, and so able to negotiate fully vested and fully portable pension systems would fill a growing and important need.[74]

This excursion has been unconcerned with the political reality that any legislative reform is highly unlikely unless it holds some tangible benefit to management and to organized labor, however defensible from the point of view of individual employee freedom of choice. Nonmajority representation offers a trade-off to both. Labor would get the benefit of automatic representational rights, but in an arguably more weakened bargaining position vis-a-vis employers. Management would not be able to resist collective representation, at least not by dilatory litigation and election campaigns, but would be given the statutory power to rationalize its bargaining structure under terms that would seem to concede it a commanding bargaining position in most cases. This is essentially the trade-off perceived in the debate over majority rule in 1935 that was acceptable to management but unacceptable to organized labor at that time. It remains to be seen whether it is politically sufficient today. But if "direct indigenous representation" in the workplace is a social good, should nonmajority representation not merit consideration?

74. *See generally* Daniel J.B. Mitchell, *Social Insurance and Benefits, in* RESEARCH FRONTIERS IN INDUSTRIAL RELATIONS AND HUMAN RESOURCES 587 (David Lewin et. al. eds., 1992).

7. REFLECTIONS ON LABOR LAW REFORM AND THE CRISIS OF AMERICAN LABOR

SANFORD M. JACOBY*

In 1932, when the American labor movement was at its nadir, experts like George Barnett predicted the demise of collective representation in the United States. The AFL had given up on organizing the mass production industries, while the company union movement was moribund.[1] Yet five years later the situation changed dramatically, as millions of workers became members of affiliated and employer-initiated (company) unions. There were several causes of this turnaround: legal reforms emanating from Washington; the emergence of new or redesigned representational forms, including the industrial union and the federal labor union; and competition between these new forms and more traditional craft and company unions.

The CIO's industrial unions can be thought of in Darwinian terms as a successful adaptation to the economic environment of the 1930s. The environment, however, has changed over the last sixty years. Today's markets are global, so industrial unions cannot take wages out of competition; neither do high union wages guarantee Keynesian prosperity for the American economy. (Any stimulative impact from union wage premiums is lost when union members spend their incomes on imported goods.)[2] On top of this, unions face a multitude of organizing barriers, including hostile employers and a skeptical workforce.

What is needed, argue this Symposium's contributors, is a spark from Washington that would touch off a proliferation of representational forms better suited to the present environment. Precisely what these forms might look like the contributors do not agree, although most of them think that enterprise-oriented representation (works

* Professor of History and Industrial Relations, UCLA, Los Angeles, CA.

1. On Barnett and other pundits, see David Brody, *The Expansion of the American Labor Movement: Institutional Sources of Stimulus and Restraint, in* INSTITUTIONS IN MODERN AMERICA: INNOVATION IN STRUCTURE AND PROCESS 11 (Stephen E. Ambrose ed., 1967).

2. *See* THE WORKERS OF NATIONS: INDUSTRIAL RELATIONS IN A GLOBAL ECONOMY (Sanford M. Jacoby ed., 1994) [hereinafter THE WORKERS OF NATIONS]. *See also* Daniel J.B. Mitchell, *Inflation, Unemployment, and the Wagner Act: A Critical Reappraisal*, 38 STAN. L. REV. 1065 (1986).

councils, plant participation plans, nonmajority representation) would offer a better "fit" than traditional unionism.

One may question, however, whether economic reality justifies this Symposium's focus on enterprise representation. The past ten years have seen not only economic globalization but also the disintegration of the stable employment relationships which are a prerequisite to enterprise representation. Large nonunion companies like IBM and Eastman Kodak no longer guarantee quasi-lifetime jobs. A rapidly increasing share of the workforce is comprised of contingent employees (part-time, temporary, and contract workers) whose ties to the employer—and whose employers' ties to them—are weak. Of all the contributors, only Finkin, Gottesman, and Rogers mention this problem. Like the promoters of the AFL-CIO's associate member program, Gottesman envisions the emergence of an associational unionism whose cohesion does not depend on stable ties between employers and employees.[3] Similarly, Rogers envisions a labor movement that helps members with their training and counseling needs regardless of who employs them, if anyone.[4] Although I have doubts about the political feasibility of the legal reforms needed to support these ideas, I do, however, think that Gottesman and Rogers are on the right track. Enterprise-oriented representation constitutes but a portion of what is required to close the "representation gap."[5]

Nevertheless, expansion of enterprise-oriented representation remains a worthy objective of industrial relations policy. After all, the supply of relatively stable, career-type jobs may be declining, but there still are many of them around. Properly designed, enterprise representation can serve, like European works councils, as a complement to traditional multi-employer unionism; it can also stand alone. This point is made forcefully by Estreicher[6] and Summers[7] (and by

3. Michael H. Gottesman, *In Despair, Starting Over: Imagining a Labor Law for Unorganized Workers*, 69 CHI.-KENT L. REV. 59 (1993).

4. Joel Rogers, *Reforming U.S. Labor Relations*, 69 CHI.-KENT L. REV. 97 (1993). For related ideas, see CHARLES C. HECKSCHER, THE NEW UNIONISM: EMPLOYEE INVOLVEMENT IN THE CHANGING CORPORATION (1988); Dorothy Sue Cobble, *Organizing the Postindustrial Work Force: Lessons from the History of Waitress Unionism*, 44 INDUS. & LAB. REL. REV. 419 (1991).

5. The AFL-CIO's associate membership program similarly recognizes this fact. Paul Jarley & Jack Fiorito, *Associate Membership: Unionism or Consumerism?*, 43 INDUS. & LAB. REL. REV. 209 (1990).

6. Samuel Estreicher, *Labor Law Reform in a World of Competitive Product Markets*, 69 CHI.-KENT L. REV. 3 (1993).

7. Clyde W. Summers, *Employee Voice and Employer Choice: A Structured Exception to Section 8(a)(2)*, 69 CHI.-KENT L. REV. 129 (1993).

Rogers[8] in his other writings). Each outlines overlapping proposals under which employers would establish works councils to provide channels for employee voice, and for participative problem-solving in the workplace.

The proposals divide on a couple of practical issues. First, there is the matter of whether employers should be pressured, in some fashion, to set up works councils or whether their choice should be unconstrained by policy. The former is Rogers's position; he has urged that employers be given positive incentives to create works councils, perhaps by allowing the councils to supervise the enforcement of OSHA regulations or to implement federal on-the-job worker training programs.[9] Some employers would welcome this decentralized regulatory approach; works councils would devise safety and training policies tailored to idiosyncratic employer needs rather than the "plain vanilla" variety emanating from Washington. Rogers has also suggested that the government's administrative savings on decentralization be refunded to employers in the form of tax breaks.[10]

To some, using employer incentives to promote works councils may sound far-fetched. Estreicher, for one, is opposed (he calls it "a bad idea"). Rather than legislate new forms of representation, Estreicher would prefer simply to amend the company union prohibition in section 8(a)(2) of the National Labor Relations Act, and confine the section's reach to "truly coercive or deceptive practices."[11] Once section 8(a)(2) is amended, a variety of alternatives to traditional unionism will, presumably, come bubbling forth, each variant designed to meet local conditions.

Summers picks up where Estreicher leaves off, filling in the details of how, precisely, section 8(a)(2) should and should not be amended. According to Summers, works councils may be created by the employer and would "meet and confer" rather than engage in bargaining. Otherwise, however, works councils would be subject to the entire range of unfair labor practice rules presently in place. Getting rid of these section 8(a)(2) and other unfair labor practice restrictions would, Summers fears, open up a Pandora's box filled with regressive

8. Richard B. Freeman & Joel Rogers, *Who Speaks for Us?: Employee Representation in a Non-Union Labor Market*, *in* EMPLOYEE REPRESENTATION: ALTERNATIVES AND FUTURE DIRECTIONS (Morris Kleiner & Bruce Kaufman eds., 1993).

9. *Id.* at 63.

10. Id. at 64-65. *See also* Sanford M. Jacoby & Anil Verma, *Enterprise Unions in the United States*, 31 INDUS. REL. 137 (1992).

11. Estreicher, *supra* note 6, at 35.

historical phenomena; a plethora of "sham" company unions might return to haunt us.[12]

But radical reform of section 8(a)(2) is not likely to take industrial relations back to the Dark Ages. After all, we have had nearly sixty years of experience under the Wagner Act. Unions are more institutionally secure than in pre-Wagner days. And, whatever one's position on the *Law and Reality* debate, modern employees are more sophisticated than after the Second World War, when NLRB chair Paul Herzog testified to Congress, "This is 1947, not 1935; in the interim employees have learned much about protecting their own rights and making their own choices with the full facts before them."[13] Changing section 8(a)(2) is necessary and such reform should be more expansive than Summers would allow.

Merely changing section 8(a)(2) is, however, insufficient. In today's legal climate, most nonunion employers do not find section 8(a)(2) to be an impediment to establishing employee involvement (EI) plans (pace *Electromation, Inc.*[14]). Hence something more than a change in section 8(a)(2) is needed to spur employers without EI plans to adopt them and to get existing plans to deal with a broader range of topics, especially the enterprise-wide issues that most EI groups do not address. In other words, employers must be given incentives (other than the negative incentive of an organizing campaign) to experiment with collective representation. The idea of employer incentives is not as far-fetched as it might sound. It has the attention of President Clinton's new Commission on the Future of Worker Management Relations, which hopes to promote works councils as part of an overall strategy for "decentralizing and internalizing responsibility for administering or enforcing government policies."[15] If safety-and-training-oriented councils can reduce the government's administrative and enforcement costs, then it is efficient to share those savings with employers. Incentives are also a way to kick-start the process of representational innovation and diffusion.

A second point in contention is the scope of permissible bargaining issues. Rogers would prohibit works councils from bargaining

12. Summers, *supra* note 7, at 137-48.

13. Detroit Edison Co., 74 N.L.R.B. 267, 279 (1947). *See also* JULIUS G. GETMAN, ET AL., UNION REPRESENTATION ELECTIONS: LAW AND REALITY (1976).

14. 309 N.L.R.B. 990 (1992).

15. Thomas A. Kochan, *Toward a Mutual Gains Paradigm for Labor-Management Relations*, 44 LAB. L.J. 455, 458 (1993); *GAO Launches Examination of Workplace Regulations*, Daily Lab. Rep. (BNA) No. 173, at A-8 (Sept. 9, 1993).

over distributive issues such as wages, hours, and benefits;[16] Estreicher and Summers would allow them to address any and all matters that affect employees' working lives and/or the competitive position of the firm.[17] Rogers's position draws on the German and Japanese experiences, where national wage norms established through centralized bargaining or *shunto* serve to reduce economic adversarialism at the plant level. This permits German works councils and Japanese enterprise unions to focus more easily on integrative issues such as plant conditions and competitiveness. Because they focus on "win-win" topics, works councils and enterprise unions are viewed favorably by employers and employees; in the German case, this focus reassures national unions that their economic functions are not being usurped by the works councils.

Here lies the strongest argument in favor of prohibiting American works councils from pursuing wage bargains: such a ban would differentiate national unions from works councils, thus drawing support for a councils proposal from national unions and from employers. National unions would still have the unique role of representing workers wishing to bargain over pay; employers may be reassured that the integrative benefits of works councils could be obtained without the costs associated with wage bargaining.[18]

Back in the 1930s, critics faulted employee representation plans for failing to assimilate wage bargaining into their integrative approach. Senator Robert F. Wagner wrote in 1934 that the company union "has improved personal relations, group welfare activities, discipline and the other matters which may be handled on a local basis. But it has failed dismally to standardize or improve wage levels, for the wage question is a general one whose sweep embraces whole industries, or States, or even the nation."[19] Wagner's criticism had found the Achilles heel of 1920s-style employee representation. But

16. Rogers, *supra* note 4.

17. Estreicher, *supra* note 6, at 29-30; Summers, *supra* note 7, at 143.

18. The same argument can be made about strikes: prohibiting works councils from striking would facilitate enterprise cooperation and differentiate councils from national unions. The "peace obligation" of German works councils is based on this idea. Most U.S. advocates of the German approach support a ban on concerted activity for employer-initiated councils.

19. Robert F. Wagner, *Company Unions: A Vast Industrial Issue*, N.Y. TIMES, Mar. 11, 1934, § 9, at 1. Company unions that survived the Wagner Act evolved into independent labor unions (ILUs), a hybrid combining the cooperativeness of an enterprise union with the economic assertiveness of an affiliated union. Companies with ILUs were saddled with high labor costs, sometimes exceeding national union wage levels. Although companies preferred ILUs to affiliated unions, they shed the ILUs as soon as a lower-cost alternative became available, namely, the "new" nonunion model of the 1960s, which provided the same integrative benefits as ILUs but at lower cost. Jacoby & Verma, *supra* note 10.

the argument has little meaning today. Wage standardization no longer serves the economic function once envisioned by underconsumptionists like Wagner. And in contrast to the situation in 1934, national unions are today entrenched in those sectors of the economy still prone to oligopoly.

That still leaves open, however, the question of how wages would be determined in a works council system. In his article for this Symposium, Rogers suggests the possibility of regional wage standardization along lines currently being tried in Canada,[20] an interesting idea which, potentially, could facilitate either enterprise or multiemployer unionism. The proposal is not so far-fetched; analogues already exist in the form of the Davis-Bacon Act[21] and other prevailing wage laws. Another route to solving the wage problem would be to jettison the outdated notion of wage standardization and instead encourage employers to tie compensation to their firm's ability to pay. Many firms already are doing this, although in piecemeal and haphazard fashion. Employers would, undoubtedly, be less averse to the promulgation of revenue-or gain-sharing formulas than to wage bargaining or mandated standardization. Works councils could play an auditing role, ensuring employees of the reliability of the employer's financial data and revenue allocations. Of course, this kind of system would, *ceteris paribus*, raise rather than reduce pay inequality. Inequality could, however, be remedied through the fiscal system (e.g., negative income taxes, which the Clinton administration already has endorsed) instead of the labor market.[22]

One point on which this Symposium's participants agree is the continued importance of, and need for, national unions. New representational forms—be they works councils, nonmajority groups, or whatever—are seen as supplements to, not substitutes for, national unions. Just how important national unions will be in the future the authors do not say, though the implied range runs from traditionalists like Summers (very important) to skeptics like Estreicher and Gottesman (not very).

The traditionalists argue comparatively: Like the United States, other countries have experienced intensified global competition and

20. Rogers, *supra* note 4, at 115-16.

21. 40 U.S.C. §§ 276a to 276a-5.

22. MARTIN L. WEITZMAN, THE SHARE ECONOMY: CONQUERING STAGFLATION (1984). Even in Germany and Scandinavia, where the local wage issue supposedly is mooted by industry bargaining, wage problems still crop up at the plant level, leading to inequality in the form of wage drift ("black wages"). To the extent that such inequality is reduced, the process occurs outside of, rather than within, the labor market.

decartelization, yet their union sectors have not declined nearly so much as our own. Causal reasoning then leads to two key factors differentiating the U.S. experience: a flawed legal regime and a highly decentralized bargaining system. Both of these factors, say the traditionalists, encourage employer resistance to unionism; such resistance is more important than economic circumstances in causing low union density in the United States. Because no one expects wage bargaining in the United States to ever become as centralized as in northern Europe[23] (or, under *shunto*, as coordinated as in Japan), that leaves reform of the legal regime as the main device for allowing national unions to realize their potential.

The skeptics recognize the need for labor law reform.[24] But they are dubious that it will lead to large density gains, chiefly because they doubt that employer resistance has been a major cause of labor's problems. To Estreicher, what is of equal if not greater causal importance is declining demand for unions; employees feel that their needs are better met by nonunion firms, by statutes, and by the market.[25] There is merit in this view. But Estreicher underemphasizes the importance of employer resistance. After all, a declining demand for unionism is not inconsistent with employer resistance; the latter may well have a chilling effect that turns workers away from unions.

These supply-demand issues are best considered in a comparative context. Canada provides a useful illustration; its workers and managers are similar to those in the United States but its legal framework is quite different. Yet according to a recent study, demand factors account for only twenty-nine percent of the private-sector union density difference between Canada and the United States; most of the differential is due to supply factors.[26] Such findings support the claim that employer resistance (and a less favorable legal environment) have reduced the relative supply of unionism in the United States. Thus labor law reform, including a smaller role for the courts and streamlined

23. Rogers's claim that, in Europe, "once robust structures of peak bargaining have widely collapsed" is surely an exaggeration. *See* Miriam Golden, et al., *The End of Corporatism?: Wage Setting in the Nordic and Germanic Countries, in* THE WORKERS OF NATIONS, *supra* note 2.

24. One reform advocated by Estreicher concerns the contract bar rule. The rule, he believes, determines contract durations, which he thinks are too brief. However, historical analysis suggests the reverse: the rule has been keyed to existing contract durations. Moreover, the bar has never been an obstacle to parties wishing to negotiate contracts with durations exeeding the bar. *See* Sanford M. Jacoby & Daniel J.B. Mitchell, *Does Implicit Contracting Explain Explicit Contracting?, in* PROCEEDINGS OF THE 35TH ANNUAL MEETING 319 (Industrial Relations Research Association, Barbara D. Dennis ed., 1983).

25. Estreicher, *supra* note 6, at 7-8.

26. W. CRAIG RIDDELL, UNIONIZATION IN CANADA AND THE UNITED STATES: A TALE OF TWO COUNTRIES 16 (Queen's Papers in Industrial Relations Working Paper No. 1993-1, 1993).

representational procedures, has more potential for increasing union membership than the skeptics would have us believe.[27]

In arguing for labor law reform, however, I admit to being guilty of a sin shared by all contributors to this Symposium: a notable disregard of *realpolitik*. While the contributors offer proposals that are imaginative, well-reasoned, and logical (as one would expect from professors of law), they lack calibrations of political feasibility. Take the various suggestions for works councils. Are they within the realm of political reality? Frankly, none of us knows or has attempted to find out. We must consider: What are the views of major employers' groups, national unions, unorganized employees, and Congress? How might proposals be shaped to anticipate objections from the parties? Would reform of section 8(a)(2) be strongly opposed by unions? Would such reform be sufficient incentive for employers to establish works councils?

On this last point, my own opinion is that employers will want much more than a change in section 8(a)(2) before they adopt works councils or support legislation mandating them. After all, employers realize that a works council solves the collective action problem; in one stroke, it transforms an inchoate mass of employees into an organized group ripe for the picking by union organizers. The hassle of being hit with repeated organizing drives is one reason why employers gave up on independent unions in the 1950s; the "raiding rate" for independent unions in those years was roughly 10 percent per annum. Indeed, the attraction of the modern nonunion model is its emphasis on small group activities like EI. Small groups provide to employers—and to employees—many of the benefits of collective "voice" without the NLRB-election liabilities posed by larger groupings.[28]

Or take Finkin's proposal for nonmajority representation (which fits very closely Hyde's prescriptions for "caucus law").[29] Is it realistic to think that employers will support either set of proposals? Experience with craft severance provides some evidence on this issue.[30] Em-

27. "[T]he probability that a Canadian worker who desires union status will in fact be unionized is 0.84 higher than the equivalent likelihood for an American worker." *Id.* at 17.

28. Sanford M. Jacoby, *Reckoning with Company Unions: The Case of Thompson Products, 1934-1964,* 43 INDUS. & LAB. REL. REV. 19 (1989); ARTHUR B. SHOSTAK, AMERICA'S FORGOTTEN LABOR ORGANIZATION 115 (1962); ROBERT E. COLE, STRATEGIES FOR LEARNING: SMALL-GROUP ACTIVITIES IN AMERICAN, JAPANESE, AND SWEDISH INDUSTRY (1989).

29. Matthew W. Finkin, *The Road Not Taken: Some Thoughts on Nonmajority Employee Representation*, 69 CHI.-KENT L. REV. 195 (1993); Alan Hyde, *Employee Caucus: A Key Institution in the Emerging System of Employment Law,* 69 CHI-KENT L. REV. 149 (1993).

30. The Globe Mach. & Stamping Co., 3 N.L.R.B. 294 (1937); General Elec. Co., 58 N.L.R.B. 57 (1944).

ployers traditionally have opposed the severing of crafts from industrial units because of a belief that small groups hinder representational efficiency. Employers undoubtedly would feel the same way about nonmajority representation. Moreover, employers will be concerned about adverse selection: Under nonmajority representation, employees have an incentive to form small groups that concentrate, rather than disperse, particular health and other risks.

And what about unions? Here we can to turn to theory. The collective action problem suggests that the groups most likely to take advantage of nonmajority representation will be dissatisfied factions within existing units, *not* unrepresented employees. Having factions break off from existing units will not make unions happy, just as craft severance irked the CIO in the early 1940s. On the other hand, the cost of servicing small units and the labor movement's commitment to exclusive representation make it unlikely that unions will push hard to create nonmajority units comprised of currently unorganized workers. Given all this, the political prospects for nonmajority representation are, to say the least, dim.

When it comes to proposals for workplace representation, we suffer an embarrassment of riches. What is needed, frankly, is less imagination and more practicality. The important question on the policy agenda is how to craft proposals that will be supported by a Congressional majority. We have a responsibility to consider how key interest groups—chiefly, employers and unions—will weigh the costs and benefits of particular proposals. Perhaps other interest groups should be considered; we do also need to assess the views of unorganized employees, as Rogers suggests. My hunch, however, is that no reform proposal will fly unless it is supported both by employers and by unions.[31] Absent such support, we are all just shouting in the wind.

31. Indeed, much as I like the idea of labor law for unorganized workers (Gottesman) or for caucuses (Hyde), who would sponsor such a proposal? No organized constituency—what Rogers calls a "committed agent"—is immediately obvious; this is a fatal flaw.

8. THE OVERLOOKED MIDDLE

THOMAS C. KOHLER*

> If the inhabitants of democratic countries had neither the right nor the taste for uniting for political objects, their independence would run great risks, but they could keep to their wealth and their knowledge for a long time. But, if they did not learn some habits of acting together in the affairs of daily life, civilization itself would be in peril.[1]

> In democratic countries knowledge of how to combine is the mother of all other forms of knowledge; on its progress depends that of all the others . . . . If men are to remain civilized or to become civilized, the art of association must develop and improve among them.[2]

INTRODUCTION

Humans can ignore anything, G.K. Chesterton observed, as long as the thing being ignored is big enough. The contemporary discussion swirling about the issue of labor law reform well illustrates the curious truth of Chesterton's remark. Despite the intensity with which this debate has been conducted and the air of scientific objectivity and certainty that frequently permeates it, we have managed to overlook some pretty big things. For example, we completely have failed to appreciate the fact that the better than thirty-year long decline of unions is not an isolated occurrence. Instead, it is part of a much broader and deeply troubling trend that has affected every sort of mediating group in our society. Our blinkered insistence on treating the deterioration of autonomous employee associations as a solitary phenomenon has precluded us from comprehending either the complexity of its causes or the full extent of its implications. We similarly are inclined to look past the significance of collective bargaining as a social institution as well as the conditions necessary to stable and ongoing cooperation, whether in the workplace or anywhere else.

* Associate Professor of Law, Boston College Law School. This Article reflects research on a larger study in which the author is engaged. He gratefully acknowledges the aid of the Fund for Labor Relations Studies and the generous support of Lynde and Harry Bradley Foundation in pursuit of this work.

1. ALEXIS DE TOCQUEVILLE, DEMOCRACY IN AMERICA 514 (J.P. Meyer ed. & George Lawrence trans., Anchor Books 1969) (1850).

2. *Id.* at 517.

The unifying theme in all this is our pronounced tendency to overlook the importance of the middle. By middle, I mean families, religious congregations, service and fraternal groups, grassroots political clubs, unions and like institutions that mediate the relation between individuals and the large institutions of market and state that characterize so much of public life today.[3] The healthy functioning of these mediating bodies—which Edmund Burke described as the "little platoons"[4] of society—is of crucial concern. For it is through these bodies that we literally learn and practice the habits necessary for self-rule at both the individual and social level. This fact explains why Tocqueville placed such stress on the importance of associations and mediating groups and their potential to act as "schools for democracy."[5] As he so clearly understood, individuals and societies alike become self-governing only by repeatedly and regularly engaging in acts of self-government. It is the habit that sustains the condition.

Succinctly stated, we cannot learn toleration and respect for others in a vacuum. Nor can we learn or practice self-rule in isolation. As humans, we are not self-sufficient beings. We only learn who we are, and gain some sense of the fullness of our human character, through dealing with others. Hence, it is the small associations and mediating bodies, where society is realized, that act as the seedbeds for the civic virtues. For it is in them that we learn the habits necessary to sustain democratic political life. To leave these seedbeds untended is to put the entire project of self-rule at grave risk. Our tendency to overlook the middle grows out of our curious propensity to ignore the biggest thing of all: what we are as human beings and the intrinsically social character of our personhood. By so doing, we sell ourselves short and trade over our full status for a pot of message. While we—and, more importantly, those who come after us—are bound by such exchanges, we cannot help ultimately but to be both disappointed and injured by them.[6]

One of the most complicated parts of all of this arises from the fact that the well-being of these various mediating bodies is deeply interdependent. Their existence is mutually conditioning, and the

3. For a concise discussion of the functions of mediating institutions in modern society, see PETER L. BERGER & RICHARD JOHN NEUHAUS, TO EMPOWER PEOPLE: THE ROLE OF MEDIATING STRUCTURES IN PUBLIC POLICY (1977).

4. EDMUND BURKE, REFLECTIONS ON THE REVOLUTION IN FRANCE 53 (Thomas Mahoney ed. 1955).

5. *See* TOCQUEVILLE, *supra* note 1, at 63.

6. On this matter, see Thomas C. Kohler, *Individualism and Communitarianism at Work*, 1993 B.Y.U. L. REV. 727.

health of any one of them has an impact on the rest. In short, there is more involved and more at stake in labor law reform than we may think. What follows is a brief outline of a few of the things I believe are too big to ignore in considering the shape labor law reform may take.

I. Does the Employment Order Matter? Does It Matter in the Way We Typically Think It Does?

Just as we have sold the character of our personhood short, so do we tend to understate the significance of the order that shapes the employment relationship.[7] It is tempting to ascribe this restraint to modesty, but that is one characteristic for which lawyers and academics generally are not well-known. Rather, we tend to understate the function and importance of this order because we understate or misconstrue the character of our personhood. There may be a further reason as well. Perhaps none of us really want to own-up to the responsibility that comes with suggesting and promoting a framework of norms by which peoples' lives should be conducted.

As Aristotle, Montesquieu, and Tocqueville (among others) are at pains to point out, people's habits are of more significance than their law. Yet, as they also make clear, law performs a pedagogical function. It thereby plays a direct role in shaping and developing the habits that undergird the legal order. In short, the law and the culture stand in a reflexive, mutually conditioning relationship. To understand the meaning of either, or their long-term effects and direction, one must take account of both.

The big problem with taking labor and employment law as seriously as we ought is that it is basically, well, a bit scruffy. Like family law (from which it developed),[8] labor law deals with messy things like personal relationships and seemingly mundane day-to-day issues. It lacks the cool hauteur of constitutional law and the sort of cachet that attaches to model building and theory spinning. Consequently, it is relatively easy to assign the law governing employment a low status in the legal hierarchy.

7. Throughout this portion of the Article, I have used the terms order, law, labor law, and employment law interchangeably. The terms labor law and employment law frequently imply different ordering regimes. *Cf.* Hugh Collins, *Labour Law as a Vocation*, 105 Law Q. Rev. 468 (1989). But, I mean here to talk about order in its broadest sense, including formal and informal sets of rules. On the topic of the workplace order and its relation to the social order generally, see the classic work by John T. Dunlop, Industrial Relations Systems (rev. ed., 1993).

8. *See* Mary Ann Glendon, The New Family and the New Property 143-51 (1981).

Nevertheless, it is precisely its impact on the daily, the concrete, the particular, that marks the real significance of the law governing work. People are self-constituting beings. We make ourselves to be what we are through the activities in which we habitually are engaged. Consequently, it is the seemingly insignificant routines and actions of everyday life that make all the difference. For it is through them that we literally are forming ourselves as individuals and as a society.

As David Feller pointed out twenty years ago,[9] the law governing the work relationship touches employees more directly and frequently than virtually any other aspect of the public ordering regime. That statement remains true. But it is now true of far more people, and of a far greater proportion of our populace. Indeed, the overall increase in labor force participation is one of the most striking social developments of the past forty years.

A few statistics help to illustrate the point. Currently, about ninety-three percent of adult males are in the labor force—a figure that has remained roughly steady for some decades.[10] Since 1950, however, women's participation in the workforce has climbed by more than two hundred percent.[11] Presently, seventy-four percent of women aged twenty-five to fifty-four are employed,[12] the overwhelming proportion of them full-time.[13] Not surprisingly, working hours for women have been increasing steadily over the past twenty years.[14] Additionally, one recently published major study shows that after

9. David E. Feller, *A General Theory of the Collective Bargaining Agreement,* 61 CAL. L. REV. 663, 761 (1973).

10. BUREAU OF LABOR STATISTICS, U.S. DEP'T OF LABOR, BULL. NO. 2385, WORKING WOMEN: A CHARTBOOK 48 (1991) (labor force participation for persons 25-54 years of age). Actual participation rates for men have declined slowly but steadily over the past three decades. In 1962, 96.8% of adult men were in the workforce. *Id.* For one brief consideration of the decline among men in the workforce participation, see Howard V. Hayghe & Steven H. Haugen, *A Profile of Husbands in Today's Labor Market*, MONTHLY LAB. REV., Oct. 1987, at 12.

11. Dana Priest, *Major Changes Seen in Female Labor Force; in 1990, 60% of Mothers With Young Went to Work*, WASH. POST, March 25, 1992, at A21. *See also* WORKING WOMEN: A CHARTBOOK, *supra* note 10, at 48.

12. WORKING WOMEN: A CHARTBOOK, *supra* note 10, at 48. In 1990, of 9 industrialized nations (the United States, Australia, Canada, France, Italy, Japan, The Netherlands, Sweden, and the United Kingdom), only Sweden and Canada had greater female workforce participation than the United States. Since 1970, the participation gap between Sweden and the United States narrowed, while the rate for Canadian women grew rapidly and now narrowly surpasses the U.S. rate. Significant increases in workforce participation by women since 1970 also occurred in the United States, Australia, and The Netherlands. Italy's rate of 30% was the smallest portion of the nations for which data was available. *Id.* at 9-10.

13. *Id.* at 13. The Bureau of Labor Statistics (BLS) figures show that 77% of employed adult women worked 35 or more hours weekly. Among unemployed women, 80% were seeking full-time work. Also see figures in Table A-16, at 48.

14. Thus, between 1970 and 1989, the proportion of women working on a full-time, year round basis grew from 41 to 51%. BUREAU OF LABOR STATISTICS, *supra* note 10, at 13.

years of gradual decline, the normal work week for Americans has increased to the point where the average employee now works the equivalent of an additional month more than was worked in 1970.[15]

The long and short of it is this: Working for pay now occupies more of the time of more of our populace than ever. The job has become a central part of most adults' lives and being employed (by one or more employers) is the way people spend the major share of their waking hours. Consequently, anyone with serious concerns about the kind of people we are making ourselves to be over the long run, and whether we can sustain the sorts of habits necessary to the well-being of a democracy, must pay close and critical attention to employment and the way that relationship is ordered. Briefly stated, the employment order involves far more than simply wage rates, power relationships, productivity, quality, or workplace voice. It quite literally involves the constitution of human beings.

Any extended discussion of collective bargaining is out of place here. Nevertheless, since it is the system that we are considering reforming, a few remarks about its distinct character are warranted. The term collective bargaining virtually is synonymous with the Wagner Act.[16] The core goal of that statute is the protection and enhancement of individuals' status through the defense and maintenance of freely-formed employee groups. This feature defines the statute and the unique position that the Wagner Act holds in American law. It represents the only place in our otherwise highly individualistically-oriented jurisprudence where the law has encouraged the formation of mediating groups that foster individual empowerment and promote self-determination.

It may be old news to observe that collective bargaining can provide an unmatched opportunity to involve people in making and administering the law that most directly determines the details of their daily lives. It may be slightly more novel, or at least more important, to point out that in contemporary society, work has become a—and perhaps for many the—primary source of common life for adults. As Durkheim understood, work creates a moral environment, and its influence extends to nearly every sphere of life.[17] Similarly, work is the

15. Juliet B. Schor, The Overworked American: The Unexpected Decline of Leisure 17-41 (1991).

16. 29 U.S.C. §§ 151-169 (1988).

17. *See* Emile Durkheim, Suicide 378-84 (George Simpson ed., John A. Spaulding & George Simpson trans., The Free Press 1966) (1897).

chief—and again for many the only—place outside the family where people are engaged in a common undertaking.

These points highlight one of the key aspects of collective bargaining. Unions are autonomous bodies. They stand independently both of the state as well as the organizations that employ their members. They come into being as a result of employee self-organization, and their well-being depends on the ability of the members to maintain solidarity. Winner-takes-all attitudes don't produce enduring relationships or democracies. Healthy and well-functioning employee associations can provide a place where people learn to lose a point without resentment, prevail on an argument without triumphalism, and most importantly of all, practice the art of reasonable compromise.

As things now stand, the town meeting, the neighborhood ward, grassroots political organizations, and many of the other places where these sorts of skills might be learned and practiced are withering or absent altogether. Given the degree to which people now are tied to the market, employee associations would seem to be the natural thing to stand in the place of these other institutions. The fact that unions themselves virtually have disappeared turns us to consider briefly why this is so.

II. Unions and the Vanishing Middle[18]

Accounting for the decline in union membership has become something of a cottage industry for academics during the past several years. Theories abound, some of them most ably and intelligently discussed in the other articles in this Symposium. Prominent explanations that have been put forward during the past decade include structural changes in the economy; peculiar characteristics of American labor law, combined with its weak or unsympathetic enforcement; and stiff but sophisticated employer opposition to worker self-organization. Added to these is the undoubted fact that incidents of corruption, mob influence, and wrongdoing of various sorts by union officials have had a marked and lasting impact on our attitudes toward unions.

All of the reasons offered to explain union decline have some force. But none of them, either singly or in combination, adequately account for the long and steady decline in union membership that has

18. The discussion in this section draws from a portion of a forthcoming piece by the author. For a fuller account, see Thomas C. Kohler, *Civic Virtue at Work: Unions as Seedbeds of the Civic Virtues, in* Seedbeds of Virtue: Sources of Competence, Character and Citizenship in American Society (Mary Ann Glendon & David Blankenhorn eds.) (forthcoming 1994).

occurred in the United States since the late 1950s. They don't because once again, we have overlooked the significance of the middle. Scholars and commentators seem invariably to neglect the point. Yet the plain fact of the matter is that unions went into decline in the United States at roughly the same time that all other sorts of mediating institutions began to unravel,[19] and for strikingly similar reasons. As Americans, we are deeply and increasingly ambivalent toward association in almost any form. The decline of unions is but part of a much larger story.

Once again, any lengthy discussion of that story exceeds the limited bounds of a commentary. A brief comparison of union decline with the steady withering of mainline religious denominations may help to illuminate my point.[20] As has been frequently observed, Americans are among the most religious people on Earth. Over nine in ten Americans claim they believe in the existence of God,[21] and a huge proportion states that religion is "very important" (fifty-four percent) or "fairly important" (thirty-two percent) in their lives.[22] Likewise, about six in ten Americans "believe that religion can answer all or most of today's problems."[23] Despite this, George Gallup and Jim Castelli report that "while Americans attach great importance to religion, they do not equate religion with church membership or attendance."[24] Gallup and Castelli also found that a vast majority of Americans believe that one can be a good Christian or Jew without being part of a religious congregation.[25]

These figures take on great interest for our purposes when they are compared with American attitudes toward unions. As Seymour Martin Lipset points out, extensive survey data repeatedly show that "the majority of Americans believe that unions are essential and do

19. For example, the long and steady increase in divorce rates that we experienced in the United States during the past two decades began around 1958—roughly the same year that the unbroken trend of decline in U.S. union density commenced. *See* Theodore N. Greenstein, *Marital Disruption and the Employment of Married Women*, 52 J. MARRIAGE & FAM. 657, 658 (1990) (table collecting data); Robert J. LaLonde & Bernard D. Meltzer, *Hard Times for Unions: Another Look at the Significance of Employer Illegalities*, 58 U. CHI. L. REV. 953, 953 n.l (1991) (discussing data).

20. The decline experienced by these religious congregations began around 1963, just a few years after the steady fall in union membership rates commenced. On this decline, see BENTON JOHNSON ET AL., VANISHING BOUNDARIES: THE RELIGION OF MAINLINE PROTESTANT BABY BOOMERS (1994).

21. ANDREW M. GREELEY, RELIGIOUS CHANGE IN AMERICA 13-14 (1989).

22. GEORGE GALLUP, JR. & JIM CASTELLI, THE PEOPLE'S RELIGION: AMERICAN FAITH IN THE 90's, at 35 (1989).

23. *Id.* at 39.

24. *Id.* at 45.

25. *Id.* at 252.

more good than harm, [and] that without unions employers would maltreat workers."[26] Most Americans—six in ten in the most recent poll[27]—also indicate that they "approve" of unions and an overwhelming proportion of the population believes that "workers should have the right to join unions."[28] Despite all this, only about three in ten workforce participants indicated that they would join a union if given the opportunity.[29]

Briefly stated, notions of self-sovereignty and misgivings about reliance on a mediator of whatever character are pervasive. For example, ninety percent of Americans say that they pray.[30] Nevertheless, Americans also state that they rely on themselves "rather than an outside power such as God," to resolve life's problems.[31] Similarly, while a substantial majority of Americans approve of the functions unions perform in society and think unions are necessary to protect employees and to give them a voice in the workplace, nearly the same proportion believe that they don't need a union to get fair treatment.[32] In short, we think unions, churches, and the other mediating institutions that compose civil society are great—but, for somebody else.[33]

We should not be surprised that union decline has occurred at the same time that families, churches, fraternal and service groups, local political clubs, and similar mediating institutions began to deteriorate. No single mediating structure of whatever description is likely to survive in the absence of others. All require and can ingrain the same sorts of habits: decision, commitment, self-rule, and direct responsibility. No single institution alone can inculcate or restore these habits. The existence and decline of all these bodies is mutually conditioning. The collapse or deformation of any one of them threatens the rest.

Indeed, it seems likely that the correlation between the decline of unions and religious congregations is stronger than it may first appear. For example, Catholics and Jews traditionally have been thought to be

26. Seymour Martin Lipset, *Labor Unions in the Public Mind*, *in* UNIONS IN TRANSITION: ENTERING THE SECOND CENTURY 299 (Seymour Martin Lipset ed., 1986).

27. Gallup Org., August 3, 1991 (telephone poll conducted July 18-21, 1991 of 1002 respondents) (poll data on file with the author).

28. James L. Medoff, *Study for the AFL-CIO on Public's Image of Unions*, DAILY LAB. REP. (BNA), Dec. 24, 1984, at D-2.

29. *Id.*

30. GALLUP & CASTELLI, *supra* note 22, at 45.

31. *Id.* at 69-71.

32. Lipset, *supra* note 26, at 302-03.

33. Perhaps it is not surprising that Gallup and Castelli also report that "Americans are, in fact, the loneliest people in the world" and that "four in ten Americans admit to frequent or occasional feelings of intense loneliness." GALLUP & CASTELLI, *supra* note 22, at 253.

more hospitable to union organization than other portions of the populace, and persons from Catholic or Jewish backgrounds still tend to be predominant in union leadership positions. There undoubtedly are a great many reasons for this, one of the most obvious being that as members of immigrant groups, many Catholics and Jews had strong financial incentives to become active in and to support unions.

But, I think there is more involved in all this than simple economic interest alone. For instance, Southern workers have had similar financial reasons to join unions, yet they traditionally have been resistant to organization.[34] To condense a lot into a sparse description: Habits of thought related to these two religious traditions may have had rather a lot to do with the general willingness of Catholics and Jews to become involved in or to support unions. Both traditions, for instance, place an enormous emphasis on community. Similarly, neither would tend to understand community—at least in its most profound forms—simply in terms of a voluntary association of like-minded individuals.[35] Accordingly, neither tradition emphasizes the supremacy of individual conscience over the norms authoritatively transmitted through the community. As Tocqueville observes, "Catholicism may dispose the faithful to obedience, but it does not prepare them for inequality." In contrast, however, "Protestantism in general orients men much less toward equality than toward independence."[36]

One can add to this the fact that since the issuance of the first "social encyclical" in 1891,[37] the Catholic Church officially and continuously both has sanctioned and encouraged the formation of unions.[38]

34. This may also in some way be reflective of long-standing habits. For example, writing in 1835, Tocqueville observes that the habits of direct self-rule that characterize New England town-government were not so frequently found in the South. *See, e.g.*, TOCQUEVILLE, *supra* note 1, at 33-35, 80-82.

35. Such views are characteristic of the modern liberal conception of association, which also portrays all forms of association as being instrumental. *See* Thomas C. Kohler, *Setting the Conditions for Self-Rule: Unions, Associations, Our First Amendment Discourse and the Problem of* DeBartolo, 1990 WIS. L. REV. 149, 182-86. They also tend to be far more typical of the Protestant conception of religious community, which also tends to conventionalize all forms of association.

36. TOCQUEVILLE, *supra* note 1, at 288.

37. POPE LEO XIII, RERUM NOVARUM ON THE CONDITION OF LABOR (1939). Support for unions among bishops and others involved in developing the foundation of Catholic social thought was longstanding, particularly among the Germans and Americans. For a concise discussion of the development of RERUM NOVARUM see William Murphy, *In the Beginning, in* BUILDING THE FREE SOCIETY: DEMOCRACY, CAPITALISM AND CATHOLIC SOCIAL TEACHING (George Weigel & Robert Royal eds., 1993). *See also* PAUL MISNER, SOCIAL CATHOLICISM IN EUROPE (1991).

38. The most recent statement of such support is contained in the 1991 encyclical CENTESIMUS ANNUS.

In short, whether they themselves were in any sense "religious," unions and the sorts of habits they require to sustain themselves may have been particularly intelligible to persons of Jewish or Catholic backgrounds. As both groups have become more assimilated, so has the special intelligibility of unions (and other mediating bodies) faded.[39]

The accuracy of this thesis notwithstanding, it seems likely that for the foreseeable future, we can expect a continued decline in mediating groups generally. As a nation, we fast are losing the habit of participating in organizations that require more than dropping a check in the mail. Moreover, we increasingly no longer see the need for or the significance of these mediating bodies. What we characteristically do and the sorts of things we are open to understanding—indeed the very sorts of questions that are likely to occur to us—go hand-in-hand. Since we increasingly don't participate in them, mediating bodies have lost their meaning for us. We won't make a commitment to what we don't understand. And increasingly, we don't understand what things like unions, churches, Lions' Clubs, or the Lower West Side Democratic Club have to do with anything.

Of course, the problem is that we cannot sustain a healthy democracy or polity without these bodies. So, the question is how we can intelligently and effectively work toward setting the conditions for their restoration. I do not mean to suggest that if unions were somehow magically restored, everything else would follow. Moreover, whatever form they take, autonomous employee associations will have to take on different, or at least additional, forms and function in somewhat different ways than they have during the past fifty years.[40]

39. One can speculate that the labor and the civil rights movements have had rather similar experiences in this regard. Of course, the religious voice played a central role in the civil rights movement—in this case, that voice emanated from the African-American Protestant churches. But, as that voice has receded in its predominance and has been replaced almost entirely by our dominant (and largely legalistic) rights discourse, so too does it seem that the movement's urgent moral claims on the Nation's conscience has been lost in the welter of contemporary rights' claims.

40. As noted above, the great French sociologist Emile Durkheim had significant interest in the work-life sphere. *See* text accompanying note 17. He agreed with Tocqueville's emphasis on the importance of mediating bodies, but he believed that the traditional mediating structures of town, religious congregation, and family were doomed to decline in modern conditions. He saw "occupational associations" (corporate groups of persons exercizing the same trade or occupation) as their replacement. What he did not realize was how unstable both the employment relationship and life-long devotion to a trade or occupation would become. (Witness the constant recitation of the need of the workplace for perpetual "retraining.")

Of course, along with the decline of the middle has come a significant loosening in the employment bond itself. Contingent employment arrangements are on the rise, as is the tendency of people to have two or more jobs. In these conditions, employee associations may take

What is clear is that any sort of responsible labor law reform will have to take into account the centrality of employment, its function in inculcating habits, and its role in creating a moral environment. In short, responsible reform will have to take the middle into account, and the intrinsic interdependence of mediating groups upon one another. The costs of overlooking the role and contributions of autonomous employee associations to grounding the conditions for authentic self-rule are simply too high.[41]

III. Alternatives to Autonomy: New Forms of Representation

We must live in the world as it is. And as it is, unions currently constitute a fading presence on the American scene. What sort of promise do alternative forms of worker representation hold for us? What can we do for the unorganized? Once again, these are large topics to which I can devote but a few words.

Perhaps we first should consider some of the central features of the scheme we may be reforming. Contrary to others, I see little in the essence of the Wagner Act that is tied to, or a direct result of, the patterns of economic organization of the nation in the mid-1930s. It is true enough that unions historically represent a response to changes in social organization that occurred through the rise of liberal economies. And, it is also true that the patterns of union organization and bargaining reflect the shape of industrial arrangements.

Nevertheless, little about these patterns is compelled by the statute or important to the Wagner Act's central scheme. To boil a lot down to a few words: In enacting the Wagner Act, and in sharp contrast to the course taken by the rest of the industrialized world, Congress deliberately opted for a law-making system that would involve minimal state intervention in the employment relationship. The Act stands as an example of what Gunther Tuebner calls a "reflexive" legal scheme.[42] In this sort of regime, the state establishes and sanctions a voluntary ordering system, but leaves the outcomes achieved through the process to be determined by the parties themselves, free of state influence. The goal of reflexive law, Tuebner suggests is "reg-

on more of the characteristics of a "hiring hall" than have been typical of "industrial" unions, as well as undertaking other, less-directly job related activities.

41. For a further elucidation of these points, see also Kohler, *supra* note 35, at 180-86, 200-11. Of great value is Xavier Blanc-Jouvan's incisive piece *Individualisme et "communautarisme" en droit français: le cas des relations de travail*, 1993 B.Y.U. L. Rev. 693.

42. Gunther Teubner, *Substantive and Reflexive Elements in Modern Law*, 17 Law & Soc'y Rev. 239, 254-55 (1983).

ulated autonomy," or structured self-regulation.[43] As such, reflexive schemes represent a sharp departure from statist ordering regimes.

The Act also represents an attempt to apply the principle of subsidiarity.[44] Simply put, subsidiarity is an organizational norm. It recommends that institutions of all sorts be ordered so that decision making can occur at the lowest capable level. The principle rests on the idea that the state and all other forms of association exist *for* the individual. Thus, organized bodies should not take up what individuals can do, nor should larger groups assume what smaller associations can accomplish. Conversely, the state and other large institutions have the positive responsibility to undertake those activities that neither individuals nor smaller associations are capable of performing. In this perspective, associations and social relationships exist to supply help (*subsidium*) to individuals in assuming self-responsibility. Hence, the subsidiary function of associations of any sort consists not in displacing but in setting the conditions for authentic self-rule. A key feature of the subsidiarity principle rests in its emphasis on the middle, *i.e.*, the fostering of autonomous mediating groups in which civil society exists and through which individual self-realization can occur. Not incidentally, the principle's development has stressed the importance of work, beginning with the inherent dignity of the human who performs it, as well as the social function of autonomous employee associations.

In brief, the Act sought to establish a private ordering system for developing and administering the law that governs one of the most important of relationships in modern times: employment. This was a far bolder move than it may first appear to us, the inhabitants of the modern regulatory state. It must be remembered that there was relatively little employment law in the United States in 1935. In the sixty or so years preceding passage of the Act, the ordering of the relationship had been increasingly left to the market. Other industrialized states had responded to the call for the reformation of this sort of system by legal regimes that involved rather heavy state intrusion into and regulation of the employment relationship. As noted, we went in precisely the opposite direction. The Wagner Act held out the promise of a highly flexible scheme that would permit the parties directly affected to come up with an order appropriate to their circumstances. To paraphrase the late, great Harry Shulman, this was a system that

43. *Id.*

44. On subsidiarity, see Thomas C. Kohler, *Lessons from the Social Charter: State, Corporation, and the Meaning of Subsidiarity*, 43 U. Toronto L.J. 607 (1993), and sources cited therein.

was intended to keep the state out, and ("mind you") to keep the lawyers' role in it properly understood.[45] That properly apprehended role for lawyers would be as counselors and problem-solvers, not as litigators and appellate advocates. Ultimate responsibility was to rest with reasonable and responsible actors at the ground level, not with agents of the state.[46]

In sum, the Act's central scheme avoids what Max Weber called the "iron cage"[47] in which we imprison ourselves when we see bureaucracies or the market as the sole available ordering solutions. It should come as no surprise that the piecemeal and *ad hoc* regulation of the employment relationship has grown markedly in direct correlation with the decline of the practice of private ordering through collective bargaining. The past seventy-five years, and particularly the past twenty, have taught us a clear lesson concerning employment: If ordering does not occur through the organs of civil society, it will occur through the state—whose guarantees may be more formal than effective, and whose methods will be far less supple and adaptive than privately arrived at solutions.

Our experience with the development of common law wrongful termination doctrines is illustrative in this regard. A recent study conducted by the Rand Corporation shows that as a result of a jury trial of a wrongful discharge claim in California, "the majority of employees can expect a payment that, in present value dollars, is the equivalent of a half year of work."[48] The same study found that because of the high transaction costs associated with a trial, "95 percent of all cases settle for an average of about $25,000."[49]

These findings are eerily reminiscent of the common law order that obtained generally in England and in some American jurisdictions through the middle part of the Nineteenth Century. Broadly speaking, in this regime, an employer could discharge an employee only upon proper notice, save in those cases where good cause existed

45. Harry Shulman, *Reason, Contract, and Law in Labor Relations*, 68 HARV. L. REV. 999, 1024 (1955).

46. It only seems fair to point out here that the source of much of the rigidity and perceived inflexibility in the Act rests not in its own terms, but in the judicial accretions with which it has been loaded over the years.

47. MAX WEBER, THE PROTESTANT ETHIC AND THE SPIRIT OF CAPITALISM 181 (Talcott Parsons trans., 1930).

48. JAMES N. DERTOUZOS & LYNN A. KAROLY, INST. FOR CIV. JUST., LABOR-MARKET RESPONSES TO EMPLOYER LIABILITY 36 (1992).

49. *Id.* The authors also found that fear of liability on the part of employers may have led to some increased job security generally, but at the cost of aggregate levels of employment. *Id.* at 36-45.

for not giving such notice. The amount of notice required turned on the character of the plaintiff's position, *e.g.*, one month's notice for household help, up to six months for more highly compensated employees.[50] The reported cases from this period appear not to inquire into the question of cause, but instead deal with the nature of the plaintiff's job and whether the parties intended for their relationship to be on terms other than those established by the general rules. The remedy for discharge in the absence of proper notice was the income the plaintiff would have received had that person worked through the end of the notice period.

Because they turn on the question of the existence of good cause, modern trials over wrongful discharge may be more involved, more expensive, and more intrusive upon the employer-employee relationship than their Nineteenth Century predecessors. Taken as a whole, however, (and assuming that California is any guide) the modern doctrines seem to have developed a sort of *de facto* common law rule that permits plaintiffs roughly half a year's pay in cases where some question exists about whether they were discharged with just cause. Given the costs and uncertainties associated with litigation, and the results that litigation on average produces for plaintiffs, perhaps we eventually will see a statutory regime that would require that persons to be discharged receive notice of some stated period (*e.g.* six months), and in its absence, "severence pay" in the amount of a half year's salary, or some combination of the two, save in a presumably narrow band of cases (which would be statutorily defined) where "good cause" exists to give neither. I am not urging the desirability of such a scheme. But, I think it does typify the sorts of limited results one can expect from reliance upon a public ordering regime. And indeed, it is just the sort of regime that exists in jurisdictions that do not rely upon collective bargaining systems.

In sharp contrast to bureaucratically oriented regimes, the whole scheme of the Act revolves around the formation and maintenance of autonomous employee associations. Thus, the Act's section 8(a)(2) was intended to do far more than settle a long-standing squabble about how employees might achieve voice in managerial decision making.[51] It would also serve to anchor what was supposed to be a

50. *See, e.g.*, Bleeker v. Johnson, 51 How. Pr. 380 (1876); Fawcett v. Cash, 110 Eng. Rep. 1026 (1834).

51. On section 8(a)(2) see Thomas C. Kohler, *Models of Worker Participation: The Uncertain Significance of Section 8(a)(2)*, 27 B.C. L. Rev. 499 (1986).

comprehensive system for ordering all aspects of the employment relationship.

Section 8(a)(2) had some other, undoubtedly unintended but nevertheless important, benefits as well. One of the most notable and far reaching benefits is this: Given the importance of the work-life sphere in contemporary culture, the promotion of employee self-organization could serve as a buffer against the sort of fragmentation of the polity that Tocqueville understood would deform and pervert a democracy. This fragmentation results when people lose the ability to settle on and engage in undertaking a common purpose.

The rise of this sort of fragmentation is as insidious as it is pernicious. As the circles within which they act shrink, people literally lose touch with one another, and thereby the commonality of understandings, sentiments, judgments, and goals that sustain willing cooperation and a healthy polity dissipate. The idea of some common good is replaced by factional interest, and worse, a sense of individual helplessness *vis-a-vis* the state or the large institutions of the market. With the habits of self-action weak or in desuetude, and the sentiments necessary to sustain commonality lax, people drift into a state of atomistic isolation and effective dependency on the state or other large institutions. Common action comes to appear at best a romantic yearning "for a simpler era" and self-government another way of saying every man or women for him or herself. Interest groups narrowly described replace the middle, and increasingly, only the institutions of market or state are seen as credible.

Whatever else they may do, alternative forms of "worker representation" will not truly take the place of those anchored by and developed through free-standing employee associations. The alternatives will (or, do) not represent the product of self-organizational activity. They are not autonomous. As such, they do not constitute a part of the crucial middle that I have been describing.

Nor, of course, are the alternatives intended to perform the same functions as the autonomous employee association. As George Strauss and Eliezer Rosenstein pointed out nearly twenty-five years ago,[52] participative management theory springs from entirely different sources and assumptions, and is intended to serve a rather different and far more restricted set of goals, than is the so-called collective bargaining model.[53] Briefly stated, those goals are organizational ef-

52. George Strauss & Eliezer Rosenstein, *Workers Participation: A Critical View*, 9 INDUS. REL. 197 (1969).

53. On these points, see Kohler, *supra* note 51, at 513-18.

fectiveness (as bureaucratically defined), not private ordering or employee self-determination.

These differences raise many issues. One of them is this: Do participative schemes unanchored by an autonomous employee association promise more than they deliver? There is much reason to believe that this is the case. As is frequently pointed out, "participation" is a managerial ethic. The ethic rests on the creation of an atmosphere of trust between the parties that will set the grounds for the willing and intelligent cooperation[54] by employees with organizational goals, which ultimately are established and controlled by management.

A relationship of trust implies a selflessness among the parties, for the one trusted must be constantly willing to put the others' good before his or her own. In short, trust involves a sort of self-transcendence and, as Aristotle observes, it is a hallmark of the most authentic sort of friendship.[55] Succinctly stated, participative management theories make self-transcendence easy. For they rest on the idea that there are no inherent conflicts of interest among people in work organizations that demand structural accommodation. Thus, *pace* Adam Smith,[56] the interests of employer and employed are identical. Trust as selflessness thus involves no real moral or intellectual conversion in the sense suggested by traditional religious thought or classical political philosophy. People, including those with ultimate decisional authority, simply will act in a trustworthy (i.e., selfless) manner once they understand that they should. In other words, being "good" is a matter of education, because people will do the "right" thing once they know what it is. To use Étienne Gilson's description, such ideas represent a species of "angelism." But, of course, as James Madison points out,[57] men are not angels, and hence attention must be paid to structures that can accommodate conflicting interests and to limit the *libido dominandi* that is so much a part of all of us. It comes as no surprise that participative schemes like TQM (Total Quality Management) are spoken of by their proponents as a new religion. But, like the new religion proclaimed by the boy prophet in Flannery

54. For a brief description of the conditions necessary to sustain cooperation, see Kohler, *supra* note 44. On the underlying cooperationist scheme of the Wagner Act, see the thoughtful piece by Mark Barenberg, *The Political Economy of the Wagner Act: Power, Symbol, and Workplace Cooperation*, 106 HARV. L. REV. 1379 (1993).

55. ARISTOTLE, NICOMACHEAN ETHICS 207-66 (Terence Irwin trans., 1985) (Books 8, 9). He goes on to observe that people should count themselves lucky if they have two or three real friends during the course of their lifetime. *E.g.*, *id.* at 263 (Book 9, 1171a20).

56. *E.g.*, ADAM SMITH, THE WEALTH OF NATIONS chs. 6, 8 (1776).

57. THE FEDERALIST NO. 51, at 322 (James Madison) (Clinton Rossiter ed., 1961).

O'Connor's *Wise Blood*[58]—the Church of Christ without Christ—it seems to be missing something.

Participative management theories have another deeply troubling aspect as well. Corporate bodies of whatever description, whether they be business organizations, political communities, voluntary groups, etc., all face a common issue: How we can be both one and many, or to put the matter just slightly differently, how each person can be a distinct and unique individual, yet be related to and operate cooperatively with other distinct and unique individuals. Participative management techniques attempt to resolve this problem by seeking to create a state of complete identity between the individual and the group. In other words, they reify the group as the sole individual. They do this by seeking to replace individual attitude and conscience with a group conscience, which in turn is given its shape and orientation by corporate leadership. In short, this is why participative theory techniques represent a bureaucratic adjunct. They are intended to achieve a mass that will act efficiently and as one. To use Tatsuo Inoue's term, such schemes can produce a form of "companyism" that may deny individual status altogether.[59] In the theoretical perspective from which these schemes tend to proceed, individuals exist only in and through the group; they have no separate character outside it.

I do not mean to suggest that there is nothing whatever of value to participative management schemes. That is plainly not the case. As a managerial ethic, participative schemes can enhance the scope of the individual workers to make workplace decisions *vis-a-vis* other style of managing. By increasing the organization's reliance upon the good sense of the man or woman on the spot best to figure out how to accomplish a task, such schemes also are intelligent.[60] But, given the foregoing, perhaps it is no surprise that the data show that participation plans function best, and have the best chance for survival, when they are anchored by an autonomous employee association.[61] Our do-

58. FLANNERY O'CONNOR, *Wise Blood, in* FLANNERY O'CONNOR: COLLECTED WORKS (Library of America 1988).

59. Tatsuo Inoue, *The Poverty of Rights-Blind Communality: Looking Through the Window at Japan*, 1993 B.Y.U. L. REV. 517, 530. On the term "companyism," see *id.* at 528-30. *See also* Kohler, *supra* notes 6, 44.

60. Maryellen Kelley and Bennett Harrison have found that the introduction of participation schemes in "U.S. manufacturing workplaces has mainly been part of an effort by managers in large bureaucracies to overcome the rigidities associated with this organizational form." Maryellen R. Kelley & Bennett Harrison, *Unions, Technology, and Labor-Management Cooperation, in* UNIONS AND ECONOMIC COMPETITIVENESS 247, 263 (Lawrence Mishel & Paula B. Voos eds., 1992).

61. *E.g., id.* There is nothing fundamental to the scheme of collective bargaining that requires its narrow focus simply on wage rates and benefits. Indeed, the basic scheme of the Act is

mestic experience is confirmed by the experience of other nations, which shows that devices like works councils only function well, and achieve significant results for employees, when they exist in an organized context.[62]

Like the original debate over its terms, much of the current discussion over labor law reform is concentrated upon the provisions of section 8(a)(2). Certainly, a lot has changed during the nearly sixty years that have intervened since the Act's passage. The one thing that remains constant, however, is human character. In revisiting these provisions, we revisit an ideological debate that had been fully rehearsed before Congress. By striking off in an entirely different direction, we will be attempting to do something that no one else in the world has been able to achieve: make participative devices function without some form of autonomous employee body to ground them. We will be doing more as well. We will be giving public sanction to yet another turn away from one of the institutions that grounds the middle. It may be more prudent to inquire in the other direction and to ask what sorts of steps we can take to sustain and restore these crucial institutions, including autonomous employee bodies. Problems rarely are solved by furthering the types of actions that brought the problem on in the first place.

Conclusion

Wholes cohere about a middle. But, even as they described the crucial role mediating institutions play in a liberal democratic order, the farseeing amongst us continually have warned about the destructive pressures that the institutions constituting the middle would face. At first glance, these sorts of issues would seem far removed from labor law and the employment order. The more one looks into the matter, however, the more clear it becomes how deeply interrelated the problems of the middle are with the seemingly mundane world of work. Indeed, the whole question of labor law reform presently confronts us because of the general decline in mediating institutions, including unions, and the increasing laxness in our habits of association.

consistent with broad-based cooperation. The main contribution of participative schemes to organized settings may rest simply in reawakeining our imaginations as to the great flexibility inherent in the collective bargaining model.

62. *See, e.g.*, *International Colloquium on Labor Law: Models of Employee Representational Participation*, 15 Comp. Lab. L.J. 1 (1993), and particularly the papers by Marie Mercat Bruns, *Worker Representation* at 1, and Rudolf Buschmann, *Workers Participation at the Enterprise Level in France,* at 15 and Rudolf Buschmann, *Workers Participation and Collective Bargaining in Germany*, at 26.

Succinctly stated, our ability to "compete" is not a mere matter of technology, of selecting and properly employing the right management techniques. Maintaining a liberal political and economic order is truly hard work. It requires that people possess a certain sort of discipline. However inconvenient, the plain fact remains that there is no replacement for individual goodness, intelligence, reasonableness, and responsibility. But, these characteristics are virtues. A virtue is an operative habit, and habits require inculcation and practice. In short, the health and competitiveness of our polity and our economy depend on the existence of functioning schemes that can regularly and recurrently assist people in obtaining the sorts of habits on which a liberal order depends. We must never forget that we do not just trade in time, but we constantly are trading across time as well. What we have is not solely our creation, and the effects of the order we are establishing will be felt less by us than by those who come after us.

Labor law reform confronts us with some enormously difficult and complex problems. It is tempting to ignore them, but pretending they aren't there won't make them go away. Looking past our difficulties only makes them more acute. If we are to deal with these problems in an effective and responsible way, however, we must go beyond our well-worn, comfortable because familiar, but all-too-narrow analytical boundaries and habits of thought. The employment order involves much more than we typically think.

As we consider the shape labor law reform might take, one more thing must be kept in mind: Institutional orders inconsistent with our character as humans will not survive. Consequently, the most pressing question we face is whether and to what degree our notions of ourselves as human actors is accurate. Everything turns on the answers to this query. Bluntly stated, try as we might, in the final analysis, we can't get past ourselves. We're simply too big to ignore.

9. REFLECTIONS ON EMPLOYEE VOICE AND REPRESENTATION FOR THE FUTURE

PETER D. SHERER*

The New Deal legislation, the Wagner Act and its amendments,[1] institutionalized a form of employee voice and representation (EVR) that featured employers and unions as adversaries. This legislation endured despite its growing inability to deal with changing organizational realities. These new realities have resulted in a great deal of local experimentation with forms of EVR outside of the legal regime of the New Deal legislation. During this time, organized labor and national lawmakers have in effect sat back and allowed this experimentation to go on, only occasionally speaking out against these new forms of EVR or urging their wider diffusion.

There now appears to be something of a consensus that the New Deal legislation no longer works at promoting EVR,[2] particularly because it seems irrelevant if not a thorn in the side of the large nonunion sector. Coupled with the growing awareness in industry and in government that human resource management (HRM) matters for competitive advantage and that EVR is a key HRM policy and practice, discussion of EVR has moved closer to center stage. The time is propitious for considering the role of labor law in promoting EVR.

Each of the authors in this Symposium makes use of law to propose a model of what EVR should look like in the future. These authors, however, express a wide variety of views on how the law should be modified. Their diversity of views mirrors the diversity in forms of EVR that now exists, suggesting that the role of law should not be to favor any one model of EVR over another, but to promote EVR more generally through enabling variety to emerge and flourish.

* Associate Professor of Management, The Wharton School, University of Pennsylvania. Conversations with Janice Bellace, Huseyin Leblebici, and David Lewin have contributed to my reflections in this essay.

1. National Labor Relations (Wagner) Act, 29 U.S.C. §§ 151-169 (1988).

2. *See* THOMAS A. KOCHAN ET AL., THE TRANSFORMATION OF AMERICAN INDUSTRIAL RELATIONS (1986).

I. THE NEW ORGANIZATIONAL REALITIES

Since the time of the New Deal legislation, organizations and their labor primarily have had principal-agent or employment relationships in which the employer acted as a monitor and controller.[3] The employer qua principal monitored and controlled what and how his/her employees qua agents accomplished work activities. These organizations were hierarchical because of their concern with monitoring employees.

The New Deal model, with the union acting as an adversary to management, had a certain logic in these organizations. The union moderated management prerogatives over monitoring and controlling the workforce, and it redistributed profits in favor of employees and away from stockholders.

Increased product market competition both at home and abroad has lead many firms to depart from these traditional employment relationships.[4] One alternative response has been for organizations to adopt more relational employment models, dedicating employees to their firms through lifetime employment, empowerment, and the like. The aim of organizations with these models is to have employees with dedicated assets who will provide their firms with dedicated capabilities. Flexibility and innovation in these organizations arise through employee commitment and loyalty. These organizations are invariably leaner and flatter than their traditional hierarchical counterparts.

The EVR implications with such relational models are clear. Firms must give their employees a larger voice in strategy formulation and implementation. For such firms, EVR becomes embedded in the

3. For more on this, see David Lewin & Peter D. Sherer, *Does Strategic Choice Explain Senior Executives' Preferences on Employee Voice and Representation?*, *in* EMPLOYEE REPRESENTATION: ALTERNATIVES AND FUTURE DIRECTIONS 235 (Bruce E. Kaufman & Morris M. Kleiner eds., 1993); Peter D. Sherer & Kyungmook Lee, Variation from the Standard Employment Relationship: The Character and Determinants of RRTs, ATAs, and CIRs (1993) (unpublished manuscript, on file with The Wharton School, University of Pennsylvania) [hereinafter Variation from the Standard Employment Relationship]. For the classic statement in support of the hierarchical firm, see Armen A. Alchian & Harold Demsetz, *Production, Information Costs, and Economic Organization*, 62 AM. ECON. REV. 777 (1972).

4. This argument draws from Peter D. Sherer, Variety and Selection in Organization-Labor Relationships: A Macro Organizational and Strategic Framework to Human Resource Management (1993) (unpublished manuscript, on file with The Wharton School, University of Pennsylvania). For more on the topic, see RICHARD BELOUS, THE CONTINGENT ECONOMY: THE GROWTH OF THE TEMPORARY, PART-TIME AND SUBCONTRACTED WORKFORCE (National Planning Association Report No. 239, 1989); PETER B. DOERINGER ET AL., TURBULENCE IN THE AMERICAN WORKPLACE (1991); PAUL OSTERMAN, EMPLOYMENT FUTURES (1988); Jeffrey Pfeffer & James Baron, *Taking the Workers Back Out: Recent Trends in the Structuring of Employment*, *in* 10 RESEARCH IN ORGANIZATIONAL BEHAVIOR 257 (Barry M. Staw & Larry L. Cummings eds., 1988).

way the organization manages its human resources. Indeed, the common separation between working and "voicing" becomes less visible, if at all visible, in such organizations.

Another alternative response has been for organizations to have more transactional relationships with labor, deploying labor with as much fluidity as possible. Organizations have done this largely through contracting in relationships with independent contractors, free lancers, and the like.[5] The aim of organizations with these transactional models is to have fluid human assets that will allow for fluid capabilities. Flexibility and innovation arise through the flow of human capital in and out of organizations. These organizations are also lean and flat, if not hollow, as compared to their traditional hierarchical counterparts.

The EVR implications with these transactional relationships may not be immediately obvious but they are potentially very important. Just as craft unions in the 1800s once trained and aided the mobility of labor from one locale to another through traveling cards, so too can labor organizations provide training and take the friction out of mobility for contracted in workers.[6] As Joel Rogers persuasively argues in this Symposium, labor organizations, in taking such a role, not only legitimize themselves with workers, but they also make themselves attractive to the many firms who need well trained workers.[7]

Competition has also had an effect on employee attitudes about EVR. As Michael Gottesman clearly points out, many employees have become much more concerned with their firms' competitive position.[8] These employees do not want to lose good jobs because they are hard to come by. Indeed, despite the fact that many workers are working harder and have not seen significant increases in their real wages, employee dissatisfaction hardly seems to be a pressing issue today. Many employees do not want forms of EVR, particularly unions, that create sharp differences between them and their employers.

5. The legal relationships between the organization and the labor often falls between the cracks of independent contractor relationships with and without agency. They are not fully in the capacity of employees nor are they fully outsiders in these organizations. I use the term "contracting in relationships" to refer to the many situations in which there is such a partial, or quasi-agency, relationship.

6. *See* Peter D. Sherer & Huseyin Leblebici, *The Formation and Transformation of National Unions: A Generative Approach to the Evolution of Labor Organizations*, *in* 12 RESEARCH IN THE SOCIOLOGY OF ORGANIZATIONS 75 (1993). *See generally* LLOYD ULMAN, THE RISE OF THE NATIONAL TRADE UNION (2d ed. 1966).

7. *See* Joel Rogers, *Reforming U.S. Labor Relations*, 69 CHI.-KENT L. REV. 97 (1993).

8. Michael Gottesman, *In Despair, Starting Over: Imagining A Labor Law for Unorganized Workers*, 69 CHI.-KENT L. REV. 59, 65 (1993).

Those who work in services, especially the well educated, are apt to be turned off by labor organizations that challenge employers through bluff, bluster, and strikes. Such employees appear to be persuaded by organizations that have knowledge and expertise.

Competition may be having a different effect on the attitudes of other workers, particularly those who are contracted in, are operating as "free agents employees," or in some other way no longer are permanently attached to one employer. These more nomadic or mobile workers no longer have the commitment and loyalty that they once felt for their employer and they operate more on the notion of having employability as opposed to employment security.[9] For these workers, exit may be viewed as a better option than voice.

The changing composition of the labor force also has important implications for EVR. The widely cited *Workforce 2000* makes it dramatically clear that white males will no longer dominate the labor market, especially at entry points, as they once did.[10] Women, African Americans, Hispanic Americans, and a multitude of immigrants will diversify the labor market and organizations, and they have the potential to have a very real impact on EVR. Alan Hyde's discussion of black caucus groups shows how minority concerns in a firm can become actualized into a group voice that may in fact be illegal under the New Deal legislation.[11]

II. The Union Response

Despite the highly visible self-analysis by the American labor movement in the AFL-CIO report by the Committee on the Evolution of Work of 1985, national unions have changed little.[12] They remain the dominant form of labor organization, dwarfing subsidiary local unions, independent local unions, and intermediary bodies such as city centrals and regional federations of different unions.[13]

The dominance of national unions stifles experimentation with alternative forms of EVR. As Sam Estreicher points out in this Symposium, national unions as multi-employer organizations make it very

9. *See* Rosabeth Moss Kanter, *The New Managerial Work*, Harv. Bus. Rev., Nov.-Dec. 1989, at 85, 92; *see also* Steve Lohr, *Fewer Ties Are Bonding Workers to Corporations*, N.Y. Times, August 14, 1992, at A1.

10. *See* William B. Johnston & Arnold E. Packer, Workforce 2000 (1987).

11. *See* Alan Hyde, *Employee Caucus: A Key Institution in the Emerging System of Employment Law*, 69 Chi.-Kent L. Rev. 149, 172-77 (1993).

12. *See* Committee on the Evolution of Work, AFL-CIO, The Changing Situation of Workers and Their Unions (1985)[hereinafter The Changing Situation].

13. For a fuller discussion of these issues, see generally Sherer & Leblebici, *supra* note 6.

difficult for firms to share proprietary information with the union, or to get labor costs attuned to a single firm.[14] As a result, experimentation with enterprise-like unionism is stunted. Yet, as Michael Gottesman suggests, enterprise unionism would seem to be what many unionized employees would prefer, since they want their firm to win in the competition among employers.[15]

Another key component to traditional unionism is the selection rule that membership is a product of being a member of a union and being a party to a labor contract.[16] The basic premise was that a union member needed a union contract in order for the union to be able to take wages out of the competition. As Matt Finkin points out in this Symposium, this selection rule was written into the New Deal legislation as majority rule and exclusive representation.[17] Membership-by-contract provided the needed instrument of power for the national unions both with respect to their members and employers. Yet, membership-by-contract meant no union members if less than fifty percent of a bargaining unit voted for the union. Membership-by-contract became a problem when unions lost many more elections than they won and they were not able to secure first contracts.

The labor movement's highly visible alternative to membership-by-contract was associate unionism.[18] Associate unions are based on the idea that union membership does not require coverage by a collective bargaining contract. As Michael Gottesman suggests in this Symposium, associate-like unions could act as service providers to nonunion workers by providing expertise, training and counsel, and benefits for workers that would be too costly for them to purchase as individuals.[19] To date, however, associate unionism has not had a major impact on reviving the American labor movement.

14. Samuel Estreicher, *Labor Law Reform in A World of Competetive Product Markets*, 69 CHI.-KENT L. REV. 3, 11 (1993).

15. Gottesman, *supra* note 8, at 67-68.

16. *See* Sherer & Leblebici, supra note 6.

17. *See* Matthew W. Finkin, *The Road Not Taken: Some Thoughts on Nonmajority Employee Representation*, 69 CHI.-KENT L. REV. 195 (1993).

18. *See* THE CHANGING SITUATION, *supra* note 12, at 18-29. *See also* CHARLES C. HECKSCHER, THE NEW UNIONISM 177-91 (1988); Peter D. Sherer & Huseyin Leblebici, *Union Membership Rules: What Do They Tell Us About Alternative Union Form in the Past, Present, and Future?*, *in* PROCEEDINGS OF THE FORTY-SECOND ANNUAL MEETING OF THE INDUSTRIAL RELATIONS RESEARCH ASSOCIATION 74 (John F. Burton, Jr., ed. 1990); Paul Jarley & Jack Fiorito, *Associate Membership: Unionism or Consumerism*, 43 INDUS. & LAB. REL. REV. 209 (1990).

19. Gottesman, *supra* note 8, at 80-83.

III. The Role of Law: Lagging or Enabling?

The proposals for promoting EVR in this Symposium range from fairly specific and narrow changes to major changes that require us to rethink a larger set of social institutions. Where there is a great deal of unity is in proposals for relaxing or narrowing section 8(a)(2) of the Wagner Act.[20] These proposals, with Clyde Summers' being the most reasoned and detailed statement on this matter, are aimed at encouraging nonunion employers to have employee involvement or participation plans when they do not actively subvert unions.[21] The main encouragement in these proposals is to strip away legal prohibitions against employee involvement and participation plans. Such a change in law might be expected to tip the balance toward participation plans for those employers at the margin.

What is clear, though, is that many organizations in the nonunion sector already have such plans.[22] Involvement teams, participation plans, and the like are now "best practices" in many managements' eyes. Business schools all around the country teach the virtues of using these practices. Many employers in fact believe that participation plans are useful. The issue here seems to be how much the law wants to lag organizational realities.

For those who contend that such plans are simply shams, Alan Hyde's example of Tekko illustrates that employee voice without unions can make a difference.[23] His example of the black caucus groups at Xerox illustrates too that initially local and somewhat informal groups arise to pursue their common concerns outside of unions and that these group voices do make a difference.[24] Both these examples further suggest that employees may not want a union even if they have real grievances because they believe unions lead to more problems than solutions.

Several authors in this Symposium call for unions to improve firm competitiveness through their voice effects, or what Joel Rogers calls

20. National Labor Relations (Wagner) Act § 8(a)(2), 29 U.S.C. § 158(a)(2) (1988).

21. *See* Clyde Summers, *Employee Voice and Employer Choice: A Structural Exception to Section 8 (a)(2)*, 69 Chi.-Kent L. Rev. 129 (1993).

22. For works that look at the diversity of firm practices, see generally Peter D. Sherer & Kyungmook Lee, *Cores, Peripheries, and More and Less: An Examination of Mixes of Labor Relationships in Firms*, *in* Proceedings of the Forty-Fourth Annual Meeting of the Industrial Relations Research Association 317 (John F. Burton, Jr., ed., 1993); Paul Osterman, How Common Is Workplace Transformation and How Can We Explain Who Adopts It? (1993) (working paper, on file with the Sloan School of Management, MIT); Sherer & Lee, Variation from the Standard Employment Relationship, *supra* note 3.

23. *See* Hyde, *supra* note 11, at 155-58.

24. *Id.* at 172-77.

"democratic productivism."[25] The general point is that unions can play a positive role in firm competitive advantage rather than simply exact rents from firms' competitive advantage or monopoly powers. Joel Rogers' specific strategy for unions is to press both firms and the state to move to greater uniformity in practices through imposing standards at the work place. The question here is whether such uniformity contributes to firm competitiveness at the firm or micro level. If firm heterogeneity or idiosyncracies do not contribute to competitive advantage, then Rogers' proposal makes good sense. However, if firms have idiosyncratic practices that contribute to their unique capabilities and hence competitive advantage over other firms—what the resource-based approach in the business strategy literature increasingly tells us is a key basis for firm competitive advantage[26]—then firms will surely resist the pressure for uniformity and standards. Even given the latter scenario, though, there still could be a role for unions. Craft-like or professional-like unions could train workers in transportable or general skills which firms might need.

Matt Finkin takes a different approach to promoting EVR by suggesting the possibility of nonmajority union representation.[27] As noted earlier, associate unionism has been the labor movement's answer to nonmajority representation: an associate union would be the exclusive agent of a nonmajority who wanted representation. Matt Finkin's proposal goes further by allowing for plural unions in one work place.[28] Plural unionism would provide the freedom of association for workers that Joel Rogers persuasively argues for in this Symposium, and it might provide the incentives for unions to compete amongst themselves in ways that get them to innovate. The intriguing question is how would nonmajority unionism work in a plant with employee involvement and participation plans or a majority union? Matt Finkin's proposal is also important in that it makes us recognize that experimentation with EVR can occur within firms and their establishments as well as across firms and their establishments. Law has a role in allowing both types of experimentation to occur.

Other proposals suggest a multiple stakeholder model of the firm as the means to promote EVR. Such a relational model involves a

25. Rogers, *supra* note 7, at 112.

26. *See* Peter Cappelli & Harbir Singh, *Integrating Strategic Human Resources and Strategic Management*, *in* Research Frontiers in Industrial Relations and Human Resources 165, 182 (David Lewin et al. eds., 1992).

27. *See* Finkin, *supra* note 17.

28. *Id.* at 213-18.

consensus that there are many stakeholders in the firm, not just stockholders, and that employees as key stakeholders have a long-term relationship and voice in firm matters that affect them.[29] As Michael Gottesman argues, the legal "deck" in the United States is stacked toward a stockholder model and against the stakeholder model.[30] The view that dominates in the U.S. is that corporate officers and boards of directors have a fiduciary responsibility to the corporation, which is operationalized as maximizing shareholders' value. Given these points, it is not surprising that David Lewin and I found that a sample of American senior executives ranked employees as the fourth most important stakeholder, with stockholders first, customers second, and suppliers ranked third.[31]

In contrast, as Ronald Dore has so vividly described, Japanese firms view employees as key stakeholders.[32] Japanese corporate, bankruptcy, and antitrust laws support and reflect this relational model. Japanese corporate law includes employees in its definition and conception of the firm. Japanese bankruptcy law requires that employees receive debt payments ahead of other creditors. Friendly banks provide a significant portion of the equity capital that Japanese firms require; stock and stockholders play less of a role in a firm gaining access to capital as compared to the U.S. firms.

How do authors in this Symposium suggest moving away from the stockholder model to a stakeholder model? Sam Estreicher argues that law should encourage longer-term horizons.[33] Unions and management should be encouraged to have long-term contracts and to engage in information sharing rather than information hoarding. Management, he argues, should be encouraged by tax and corporate law to be less driven by the stock market and short-term share price. Gottesman's answer is deceptively simple: give employees stock ownership so that they are stockholders cum stakeholdings in firms.[34]

Whether a stakeholder model is appropriate in all cases is certainly subject to question. There may be times when firms need to respond much more quickly and dramatically than such relational

29. Ronald Dore, *Japan's Version of Managerial Capitalism*, *in* TRANSFORMING ORGANIZATIONS 17, 18 (Thomas A. Kochan & Michael Useem eds., 1992).

30. Gottesman, *supra* note 8, at 91.

31. *See* Lewin & Sherer, *supra* note 3.

32. Dore, *supra* note 29, at 24.

33. Estreicher, *supra* note 14, at 40-42.

34. *See* Gottesman, *supra* note 8, at 93-96.

models ordinarily allow. When that is the case, a more transactional or stockholder model makes more sense.[35]

Given the diversity of the suggestions for promoting EVR, it is clear that no single model of EVR has come to supplant the New Deal legislation, nor might that need to be true at a future date. Different approaches to EVR are parts of more relational, traditional, as well as more transactional relationships that organizations have with their labor. The role of law should be to enable this variety to flourish.

35. *See* Franklin Allen & Peter D. Sherer, *The Design and Redesign of Organizational Form, in* REDESIGNING THE FIRM (Bruce Kogut & Edward Bowman eds., forthcoming 1994).

AFTERWORD

LABOR LAW REFORM: WAITING FOR CONGRESS?

MARTIN H. MALIN*

INTRODUCTION

The topic of labor law reform usually focuses attention on Congressional action to amend the National Labor Relations Act or enact other legislation. Most of the articles in this symposium are similarly focused. Presumably, so too is the work of the Dunlop Commission. The last time there was a Democrat in the White House, substantial energy went into the effort to reform the NLRA, but the effort failed. Perhaps this time will be different. There seems to be a different tenor to the debate over labor law reform. Although many acknowledge the continuing need to strengthen the NLRA's protection of collective employee action, there also is a focus on alternatives to traditional collective bargaining. This reflects another way in which this time is different. Organized labor is much weaker than it was when Jimmy Carter was president. As the editors of the recent Industrial Relations Research Association research volume on workplace representation observed,

> The long term decline in union density to 10 percent of the private-sector work force, the growth and development of new forms of worker representation in both the United States and other countries, and the interest of the Clinton administration in labor law reform, all suggest that the time may be ripe for a fundamental, broad-ranging reconsideration of the role of employee representation in the workplace and the economy.[1]

When an informed and well-respected commentator such as Professor Rogers declares that there is consensus that our traditional system of collective bargaining "no longer works," and "serves neither unions nor workers nor management effectively,"[2] and when an indi-

* Professor of Law, Chicago-Kent College of Law, Illinois Institute of Technology, J.D. 1976 George Washington University, B.A. 1973, Michigan State University.

1. BRUCE E. KAUFMAN & MORRIS M. KLEINER, EMPLOYEE REPRESENTATION: ALTERNATIVES AND FUTURE DIRECTIONS 11 (1993).

2. Joel Rogers, *Reforming U.S. Labor Relations*, 69 CHI.-KENT L. REV. 97, 97 (1993). *See also* Richard B. Freeman & Joel Rogers, *Who Speaks for Us? Employee Representation in a Nonunion Labor Market, in* EMPLOYEE REPRESENTATION: ALTERNATIVES AND FUTURE DIRECTIONS 13, 16 (Bruce E. Kaufman & Morris M. Kleiner eds., 1993).

vidual such as Professor Gottesman, who has devoted most of his professional career to representing organized labor, laments that legislatively strengthening traditional collective bargaining will add at most a few percentage points to the rate of union density,[3] it is time to focus on alternative strategies for providing collective employee voice in the workplace. The thoughtful contributions to this symposium should prove to be a major contribution to this necessary expansion of our horizons. In closing this symposium, however, I feel compelled to plead that we not lose sight of the need to maintain traditional unionization and collective bargaining as a real option for those employees who may freely choose it. I do not intend to suggest that the contributors to this symposium are hammering nails into the casket of traditional labor unions. On the contrary, all recognize the importance of strengthening the NLRA.[4] With the focus on alternatives to traditional union exclusive representation, however, it is important that the need to maintain the availability of the traditional option not get lost in the shuffle.

Several contributors to this symposium call for modifying section 8(a)(2) to enable employers to develop employee representation plans as an alternative to traditional labor unions to provide a mechanism for employee collective voice.[5] All recognize the danger that such plans could become sham methods of employer control which stifle, rather than facilitate, employee voice. What will keep such plans honest? Although many employers will recognize that it is in their best interests to provide true mechanisms for employee voice, they are not the ones who we need fear will use the plans to subvert employee voice. It is the unenlightened employers who must be kept honest. The ability of the employees faced with a sham employer-promulgated representation plan to organize a traditional union will be very important in checking abuses of any section 8(a)(2) exception that might be developed.[6]

3. Michael H. Gottesman, *In Despair, Starting Over: Imagining a Labor Law for Unorganized Workers*, 69 CHI.-KENT L. REV. 59, 61 (1993).

4. Samuel Estreicher, *Labor Law Reform in a World of Competitive Product Markets*, 69 CHI.-KENT L. REV. 3 (1993); Gottesman, *supra* note 3; Rogers, *supra* note 2; Clyde W. Summers, *Employee Voice and Employer Choice: A Structured Exception to Section 8(a)(2)*, 69 CHI.-KENT L. REV. 129 (1993).

5. Estreicher, *supra* note 4; Summers, *supra* note 4.

6. The advocates of § 8(a)(2) exceptions appear to recognize this. It is the fear of employer abuse that leads Professor Summers to confine his proposed § 8(a)(2) exception quite narrowly. Summers, *supra* note 4. Professor Estreicher recognizes, "To prevent employer-based schemes from becoming mere tools to manipulate workers, the option to choose an independent union must be a realistic one." Estreicher, *supra* note 4, at 35.

Other contributors have called for protections for employees who wish to bargain with their employers in the absence of a traditional exclusive representative.[7] When such bargaining exists, however, employers may feel free to play divide and rule. What will stop an employer from rewarding a minority faction within the workforce to gain their alliance against the interests of the majority? I suggest that one deterrent is the ability of the majority to organize and gain the status of exclusive representative.

Thus, regardless of what we do to provide alternative mechanisms of collective voice in the workplace, we must strengthen the option of traditional exclusive representation by a labor union. Many look to Congress to strengthen the NLRA. Although remedies for discriminatory discharges and prohibitions on striker replacements would undoubtedly improve the legal climate for collective bargaining, there is much that can be done without changing a single word in the statute.

During the 1980s, the legal environment for collective bargaining became extremely hostile without any relevant changes in statutory language.[8] The change in the legal environment resulted from an NLRB and judiciary populated by individuals who were themselves hostile to collective bargaining. The Clinton administration promises to appoint judges and NLRB members who are more receptive to collective bargaining. This presents an opportunity to achieve a modest level of labor law reform regardless of whether Congress enacts any statutory changes. In the remainder of this afterword I address two ways in which the Board and the courts may take a fresh look at interpreting the existing statute which, in a small way, would address two underlying problems: the law's inability to provide employees with a meaningful opportunity to choose to be represented by a union and the law's inability to thwart employers who are determined whenever employees successfully organize to ensure that no collective bargaining agreement ever takes effect.

I. Equalizing Access During Representation Campaigns

In their empirical study of union representation elections, Professors Getman, Goldberg, and Herman found a significant imbalance

7. Matthew W. Finkin, *The Road Not Taken: Some Thoughts on Nonmajority Employee Representation*, 69 Chi.-Kent L. Rev. 195 (1993); Gottesman, *supra* note 3; Alan Hyde, *Employee Caucus: A Key Institution in the Emerging System of Employment Law*, 69 Chi.-Kent L. Rev. 149 (1993).

8. *See* Julius G. Getman, *The Courts and Collective Bargaining*, 59 Chi.-Kent L. Rev. 969 (1983).

between company and union opportunities for organizational communication. They recommended that the law require that an employer who campaigns against the union on company time afford the union a similar opportunity to campaign on company time.[9] Although much of the Getman study and recommendations have been controversial,[10] its treatment of the imbalance in company and union access to employees has not been. Indeed, one is tempted to say that the conclusion is intuitively obvious.

Employer anti-union campaigns often stress that unions do not have the power to compel employers to raise wages or improve working conditions. They drive home to employees the employer's power. Employer campaigning on company time further drives home the employer's control over the employees' working time. When the union is left to respond in a less effective manner, the employer's message of union impotence is further reinforced.

The Supreme Court's decision in the *Nutone* case[11] is often thought to impede a Board requirement of equal access. In *Nutone*, the employers had maintained valid no-solicitation rules but violated their own rules to campaign against the unions. The Court rejected arguments that the combination violated section 8(a)(1) of the NLRA. In so doing, it emphasized the limited nature of the record before it:

> We do not at all imply that the enforcement of a valid no-solicitation rule by an employer who is at the same time engaging in anti-union solicitation may not constitute an unfair labor practice. All we hold is that there must be some basis, in the actualities of industrial relations, for such a finding. The records in both cases . . . are barren of the ingredients for such a finding.[12]

Nutone, thus, left open to the Board the possibility of developing an equal access rule, provided it does so on a record which discloses the need for such a rule based in the "actualities of industrial relations." Moreover, *Nutone* speaks only to the unfair labor practice implications of an employer's campaigning on company time while denying the union similar access to the employees. It does not speak to what regulations the Board may impose to ensure that a represen-

9. Julius G. Getman et al., Union Representation Elections: Law and Reality 156-59 (1976).

10. *See, e.g.,* Patricia Eames, *An Analysis of the Union Voting Study from a Trade Unionist Point of View*, 28 Stan. L. Rev. 1181 (1976); Thomas A. Kochan, *Book Review*, 29 Stan. L. Rev. 1115 (1976); Paul Weiler, *Promises to Keep: Securing Workers' Rights to Self-Organization Under the NLRA*, 96 Harv. L. Rev. 1769, 1782-86 (1983).

11. NLRB v. United Steelworkers of America, 357 U.S. 357 (1958).

12. *Id.* at 364.

tation election be conducted under conditions designed to assure free, fair and informed employee choice.

Of course, for almost three decades, the Board has recognized that "an employee who has had an effective opportunity to hear the arguments concerning representation is in a better position to make a more fully informed and reasonable choice."[13] Consequently, the Board requires that the employer furnish a list of all eligible voters' names and addresses for use by all parties to the election.[14] The same day that the Board decided *Excelsior*, requiring employers to furnish the list of voters' names and addresses, the Board also refused to adopt an equal access for campaigning rule, "prefer[ring] to defer any reconsideration of current Board doctrine in the area of plant access until after the effects of *Excelsior* become known."[15] The Board has never revisited the issue. The time has come for the Board to evaluate whether imbalances in access to employees for campaigning impedes free, fair and informed representation elections. For two reasons, the Board should do so via a rulemaking proceeding.

First, the use of rulemaking will further the goal of having elections conform to the rule. Little is served by overturning an election that has already been conducted in order to announce a new rule governing pre-election conduct. It is far better to announce the rule in advance and then hold the parties to it.[16] Second, it is clear that any equal access for campaigning rule will require considerable factual support to withstand judicial scrutiny. The rulemaking process will enable the Board to gather extensive data concerning the adequacies and imbalances in access under current Board policy. As the Board's experience with hospital bargaining units demonstrates, development of an extensive factual record in support of a rule greatly enhances its credibility when subject to judicial review.[17]

13. Excelsior Underwear, Inc., 156 N.L.R.B. 1236, 1240 (1966).

14. *Id.*

15. General Electric Co., 156 N.L.R.B. 1247, 1251 (1966).

16. Indeed, in *Excelsior*, the Board announced that its rule requiring employers to furnish voter lists would be applied prospectively only. 156 N.L.R.B. at 1240 n.5. This led the Supreme Court to consider the Board's actions to be improper rulemaking. NLRB v. Wyman-Gordon, 394 U.S. 759 (1969).

17. *See* American Hosps. Ass'n v. NLRB, 499 U.S. 606 (1991).

II. VIGOROUSLY ENFORCE THE DUTY TO BARGAIN FOR FIRST CONTRACTS

In *NLRB v. Crockett-Bradley, Inc.*,[18] the court held that the employer had engaged in unfair labor practices sufficiently egregious to justify enforcing the Board's *Gissell* bargaining order. Negotiations pursuant to that order occurred from January 30, 1976 until June 3, 1976, without agreement. The Board then brought contempt proceedings against the company, contending that it was not negotiating in good faith in violation of the court's order. A special master agreed, but the court rejected the master's recommendation because he relied too heavily on his view that the company's bargaining position was inherently unreasonable. Instead, the court emphasized that the employer had attended every bargaining session called by the union, and that the parties had made progress on such issues as bereavement pay, handling of holidays falling on weekends, and union access to company bulletin boards. The court concluded that the company was bargaining in good faith.[19]

The union in *Crockett-Bradley* faced a common problem of newly recognized unions—they frequently are unable to obtain collective bargaining agreements. The collective bargaining rights obtained through representation or unfair labor practice procedures are shallow if they do not mature into collective bargaining agreements.

The NLRA envisions a regime of private regulation of the workplace accomplished through collective bargaining. The statutory expectation is that, once charged with a duty to bargain in good faith, company and union will achieve an agreement which better fits the peculiarities of the workplace to which it applies than will direct government regulation of terms and conditions of employment. The statute is not concerned with the substance of the agreement. The NLRA merely requires the employer to open its door and, in good faith, let the union in. It says nothing about what should result from the meeting.[20]

The policy favoring free collective bargaining has greatly minimized legal scrutiny of the parties' positions at the bargaining table. Unions are not held accountable for the substantive positions that

18. 523 F.2d 449 (5th Cir. 1975).

19. NLRB v. Crockett-Bradley, Inc., 598 F.2d 971 (5th Cir. 1979).

20. *See* Archibald Cox & John T. Dunlop, *Regulation of Collective Bargaining by the National Labor Relations Board*, 63 HARV. L. REV. 389, 395 (1950) (quoting relevant legislative history); Benjamin M. Shieber, *Surface Bargaining: The Problem and a Proposed Solution*, 5 U. TOL. L. REV. 656, 657-58 (1974) (same).

they take at the bargaining table as long as their motives are proper and their positions are not so beyond a broad range of reasonableness as to be irrational.[21] Similarly, employers are not held accountable for the substantive positions they take at the bargaining table. As the leading treatise on the NLRA summarizes the state of the case law, "The Board generally does not find bad-faith bargaining solely because of the content of very aggressive contract demands made by the employer."[22]

On the other hand, the duty to bargain in good faith requires that employers negotiate with an intent to reach agreement, even though no agreement need actually be reached. Surface bargaining, or merely going through the motions of negotiating without any expectation of reaching agreement, is illegal. It is rare, however, that there is direct evidence of illegal motive.[23] Therefore, subjective intent must be inferred from objective conduct.

The NLRB has been willing to infer subjective bad faith from the content of employer bargaining proposals in two circumstances. First, the Board will find bad faith where the proposals themselves are grossly outrageous.[24] Second, the Board will cite the substantive proposals and other objective conduct by the employer and base a finding of bad faith on the totality of the circumstances.[25]

Once the Board finds bad faith, the policy of free collective bargaining limits its choices of available remedies. The Board may not order an employer to agree to a specific contract provision, even though the employer's rejection of the proposed provision was properly considered to be evidence of bad faith.[26] Consequently, the Board's typical remedy is to order the employer to bargain in good faith. Similarly, where the content of employer contract proposals, coupled with other actions which by themselves would be legal, leads the Board to conclude that the employer engaged in surface bargaining, the Board also only orders the employer to bargain in good faith.

21. Air Line Pilots Ass'n v. O'Neil, 111 S. Ct. 1127, 1130 (1991).

22. THE DEVELOPING LABOR LAW 627 (Patrick Hardin ed., 3d ed. 1992).

23. Although rare, it does happen. *See, e.g.,* Virginia Holding Corp., 293 N.L.R.B. 182, 184 (1989); Brownsboro Hills Nursing Home, Inc., 244 N.L.R.B. 269, 270-71 (1979).

24. *See, e.g.,* NLRB v. A-1 King Size Sandwiches, Inc., 732 F.2d 872 (11th Cir.), *cert. denied,* 469 U.S. 1035 (1984); Prentice-Hall, Inc., 290 N.L.R.B. 646 (1988).

25. *See, e.g.,* Virginia Holding Corp., 293 N.L.R.B. 182, 184 (1989); ACL Corp., 271 N.L.R.B. 1600, 1603 (1984) (listing conduct which may indicate bad faith but finding it not present in the instant case).

26. H. K. Porter Co. v. NLRB, 397 U.S. 99 (1970).

The Board's orders fail to provide the parties with any guidance as to what objectively the employer must do to comply.[27]

This, however, is how it should be. If an employer is in good faith unyielding at the bargaining table, the union's remedy is not to seek NLRB assistance but to exert economic pressure. If the parties are acting out of a mutual good faith desire to reach agreement, the relative strength of the parties' economic weapons will determine the content of the agreement. The statute does not, and should not, compel an employer to make concessions that the union is too weak to force.[28]

The problem with illegal surface bargaining is that the employer who engages in it probably does not fear a strike, but rather welcomes one as an opportunity to rid itself of the union. Surface bargaining is a problem only where the union is weak. A union who can shut an employer down by striking because the employees cannot be easily replaced need not fear surface bargaining. When the union is weak, however, a strike enables the employer to permanently replace the strikers.[29] Because permanently replaced strikers lose their rights to vote in a decertification election after a year, surface bargaining may be calculated to force the union to strike as a necessary step toward ousting the union.[30]

Unfair labor practice strikers, however, may not be permanently replaced.[31] Consequently, a finding of bad faith premised on surface bargaining denies the employer the opportunity to exploit the union's vulnerability to permanent replacement beyond extracting a favorable contract. Indeed, because the Board may not order the employer to make any substantive concessions, the only real effect of a finding of surface bargaining is to strengthen the union's strike weapon by denying the employer the ability to permanently replace the strikers.

27. *See* James A. Gross et al., *Good Faith in Labor Negotiations: Tests and Remedies*, 53 Cornell L. Rev. 1009 (1968).

28. *See* NLRB v. Tomco Communications, Inc., 567 F.2d 871, 883 (9th Cir. 1978).

29. NLRB v. Mackay Radio & Tel. Co., 304 U.S. 333 (1938).

30. In his classic article on the duty to bargain, Professor Archibald Cox characterized the problem of surface bargaining as follows:

> The bargaining status of a union can be destroyed by going through the motions of negotiating almost as easily as by bluntly withholding recognition. The NLRB reports are filled with cases in which a union won an election but lacked the economic power to use the strike as a weapon for compelling the employer to grant it real participation in industrial government. As long as there are unions weak enough to be talked to death, there will be employers who are tempted to engage in the forms of collective bargaining without the substance.

Archibald Cox, *The Duty to Bargain in Good Faith*, 71 Harv. L. Rev. 1401, 1413 (1958).

31. *See* NLRB v. Thayer Co., 213 F.2d 748 (1st Cir.), *cert. denied*, 348 U.S. 883 (1954).

Recognizing that what is at stake is not what substantive bargain should the employer be compelled to yield to, but instead whether the employer should be able to permanently replace if the union should strike, places the surface bargaining case in its proper role. The evil behind surface bargaining is not that an economically advantaged employer will use its superior bargaining power to extract a favorable agreement from the union; it is that the economically advantaged employer will abuse its superior power to walk away from the bargaining process entirely. Stripping surface bargaining employers of the ability to permanently replace strikers denies them the fruits of their sham bargaining.

Thus, NLRB policing of good faith in the bargaining process amounts to NLRB policing of the use of the employer's most severe economic weapon. The suggestion that section 8(a)(5) may be used to limit the use of permanent replacements to safeguard the integrity of the bargaining process is not novel. It is at the heart of the Supreme Court's decision in *NLRB v. Curtin Matheson Scientific Corp.*[32]

In *Curtin Matheson*, the Court upheld the Board's refusal to presume that permanent replacements are opposed to continued representation by the union which called the strike. The Court held that the Board acted reasonably when it did not allow an employer to withdraw recognition where the sole basis of the employer's good faith doubt of the union's continued majority status arose from the fact that permanent replacements constituted a majority of the bargaining unit.

The Court offered two bases for its holding. The first was the empirically dubious proposition that permanent replacements are just as likely as not to desire continued representation by the striking union.[33] The second was the sound policy objective of confining the ability to permanently replace strikers to an economic weapon and precluding it from undermining the bargaining process by becoming a means by which the employer walks away from the union.

The Court deferred to the Board's reasoning that a presumption that permanent replacements oppose continued union representation would discourage good faith bargaining by empowering employers to use a strike as a means of eliminating union representation by hiring enough replacements. The Court concluded, "Restricting an employer's ability to use a strike as a means of terminating the bargain-

32. 494 U.S. 775 (1990).
33. *Id.* at 780.

ing relationship serves the policies of promoting industrial stability and negotiated settlements."[34]

Recognizing that surface bargaining cases are concerned with denying employers the ability to use the permanent replacement weapon as a tool for ousting the union goes a long way to explaining why the Board's remedies for surface bargaining do not specify what the employer must do to comply with the statute. The purpose of a finding of surface bargaining is not to compel the employer to make specific changes in its contract proposals. Rather, it is to take away the employer's incentive to talk the union to death and to empower the union to move the employer into a realistic bargaining frame of mind by being able to strike without fear of permanent replacement.

Unfortunately, there are two problems with the current approach to surface bargaining. First, current law makes it relatively easy for an employer to surface bargain while creating a stream of objective evidence which will negate any finding of surface bargaining. Second, remedies for illegal surface bargaining, other than a general order to bargain in good faith, are retrospective only, thereby negating much of the economic incentive for an employer to bargain in good faith.

Current interpretations of section 8(a)(5) enable employers to bargain to avoid a contract without fear of violation. A well-advised employer will take an initial position that is extremely negative and may be calculated to ensure its unacceptability.[35] It will appear at every union-called negotiating session,[36] will listen to and discuss all union proposals,[37] and will make concessions here and there.[38] In general, the employer will avoid the outer limits of grossly outrageous proposals and will avoid conduct that would otherwise lead to an inference of surface bargaining.[39] In so doing, the employer will suc-

34. *Id.* at 794-95.

35. *See, e.g.,* NLRB v. Crockett-Bradley, Inc., 598 F.2d 971 (5th Cir. 1979).

36. *See id.* at 976; Reichhold Chemicals, Inc., 288 N.L.R.B. 69 (1988); ACL Corp., 271 N.L.R.B. 1600, 1603 (1984) (company participation in 13 negotiating sessions is evidence of its good faith).

37. *See, e.g.,* Reichhold Chemicals, Inc., 288 N.L.R.B. 69 (1988).

38. *See, e.g.,* NLRB v. General Tire & Rubber Co., 326 F.2d 832, 833 (5th Cir. 1964). In ACL Corp., 271 N.L.R.B. 1600 (1984), the company responded to union contract proposals by demanding a one year extension of the existing agreement. The company expressly disclaimed any suggestion that its position was economically necessary. It steadfastly maintained this position throughout the negotiations. Five months into the negotiations, the company coupled the one year contract extension demand with an offer of a twenty cent per hour pay increase to take effect following the one year extension. The Board found that the Company did not surface bargain, relying in part on the company's wage offer.

39. ACL Corp., 271 N.L.R.B. at 1603.

ceed in surface bargaining without incurring liability.[40] Newly recognized unions seeking contracts with the employer for the first time are particularly vulnerable to such tactics.[41]

The extreme reluctance to find surface bargaining stems from fears that such findings will effectively dictate the terms of the collective bargaining agreement.[42] If a union is dissatisfied with the employer's position at the bargaining table, its remedy is not to complain to the NLRB, but to exert economic pressure. If the union is unable to pressure the employer to move off its position, the law should not intervene.

The fear that Board regulation will replace free collective bargaining in settling contract terms ignores the limitations on Board remedies. The Board lacks the power to order an employer to agree to anything, even where it infers bad faith from the employer's intransigence.[43] The effect of a finding of surface bargaining is to enable the union to strike without fear of permanent replacement.[44] Thus, regulation of surface bargaining in appropriate circumstances actually enhances the process of free collective bargaining. By denying the employer the opportunity to rid itself of the union by provoking a strike and replacing the strikers, closer scrutiny of employer conduct for surface bargaining will provide incentives for negotiated settlements and further the national policy of promoting labor peace.

Nevertheless, it may be argued that the employees' vulnerability to permanent replacement is a factor which plays a pivotal role in free collective bargaining. When vulnerability to permanent replacement impairs the union's strike weapon, the law should not be concerned if the employer takes advantage of its superior bargaining power to extract a favorable deal.

Permanent replacement, however, has two sides to it. Although the ability to replace strikers permanently strengthens the employer's position at the bargaining table and contributes to the interplay of

40. As one NLRB attorney has summarized the situation, "An employer which meets regularly with the union and agrees to minimal concessions on some key issues will likely prevail in an unfair labor practice hearing." Bruce H. Meizlish, *Surface Bargaining: A Problem in Need of a Remedy*, 1985 Det. C.L. Rev. 721, 724.

41. *See* Paul Weiler, *Striking a New Balance: Freedom of Contract and the Prospects for Union Representation*, 98 Harv. L. Rev. 351, 357-63 (1984).

42. *See, e.g.,* ACL Corp., 271 N.L.R.B. at 1603 ("The Company's firmness in insisting on a 1-year extension of the current contract does not of itself constitute bad faith. . . . To hold otherwise . . . would be tantamount to requiring an employer to offer improved benefits . . . or be guilty of bad-faith bargaining.").

43. *See supra* note 26 and accompanying text.

44. *See supra* notes 31-32 and accompanying text.

economic forces that the statute envisions will result in agreement, it also may enable an employer to set the stage for withdrawing recognition from the union. In the latter situation, the employer will negotiate with no intention of reaching agreement, hoping to provoke a strike that will lead to replacement of the workforce and the demise of the union.

Where the employer and union have shared an ongoing relationship, there is good reason to presume that an employer's aggressive position in negotiations reflects its assessment of the parties' relative bargaining power. There is no reason to presume that an employer who has successfully bargained agreements in the past is not in good faith seeking a new deal, albeit one very favorable to it.

Newly recognized unions, however, particularly those recognized following vigorous employer opposition, are particularly vulnerable to employer tactics designed not to assert bargaining power to produce a contract, but rather to avoid a contract and thereby avoid the union. Moreover, there is reason for concern with employer tendencies to bring their opposition to collective bargaining to the bargaining table. In recognition of their vulnerability the law irrebuttably presumes that a newly certified union maintains majority status for a year.[45] Recognition of such vulnerability, coupled with the realization that surface bargaining charges concern regulation of economic weapons rather than substantive bargaining positions, justifies closer NLRB scrutiny of employer conduct for surface bargaining in negotiating first contracts.

Closer scrutiny of employer conduct for surface bargaining during first contract negotiations alone may not deprive employers of the incentive to try to talk the union to death. Under the NLRB's current approach, the employer's ability to replace strikers permanently becomes an issue only if the union strikes and the employer purports to permanently replace. In essence, the Board's processes mop up after a failed bargaining process by reinstating the replaced strikers to their jobs. If the goal is to further the statutory process of free collective bargaining by depriving employers of the incentive to avoid agreement, this mop-up approach to remedies leaves much to be desired.

An employer who surface bargains to avoid a first contract in effect dares the union to strike, wielding permanent replacement as an explicit or implicit threat to the union's very existence. Employees deterred from striking by the specter of permanent replacements tak-

45. Brooks v. NLRB, 348 U.S. 96, 104 (1954).

ing their jobs are not likely to be reassured by the potential for getting their jobs back after a prolonged legal fight.

Consequently, an employer who surface bargains during first contract negotiations is more likely to be met by an unfair labor practice charge than by a strike, even if the Board more closely scrutinizes bargaining conduct. If the charge is successful, the Board will order the employer to bargain in good faith. Such an order is akin to a parent yelling at two quarreling siblings to stop fighting and play nicely, except it may be less effective. The employer may return to the bargaining table and make a few cosmetic changes in its position, realizing that all it risks is another Board proceeding.[46]

The NLRB has been blind to the problem. At times it has ordered employers who surface bargained to reimburse the union's bargaining expenses[47] or to reimburse lost wages to employee members of the bargaining team who missed work to participate in fruitless bargaining sessions.[48] Such remedies, however, provide little incentive to the employer, upon returning to the bargaining table, to negotiate in an effort to reach rather than avoid agreement.

Although the Board has not confronted the problem, the Washington Supreme Court has. Under Washington state law, public employees do not have a right to strike and most public employee unions do not have a right to take bargaining impasses to interest arbitration. In *Municipality of Metropolitan Seattle v. Public Employment Relations Commission*,[49] the court upheld a Washington Public Employment Relations Commission order that an employer who had refused to bargain in good faith return to the table and negotiate, provided that if agreement was not reached, either party could demand mediation which, if unsuccessful would enable either party to demand interest arbitration. The court reasoned that the employer's conduct had exhibited flagrant and repeated efforts to avoid its bargaining obligations. Because the union lacked the right to strike and there was no other provision for resolving impasses with finality, the remedy was

46. *See* Meizlish, *supra* note 40, at 725-26 (detailing the example of the failure of NLRB remedies in a case involving Teamsters Local 696 and K-Mart Corp.'s Lawrence, Kansas, distribution center).

47. In J.P. Stevens & Co. v. NLRB, 623 F.2d 322 (4th Cir. 1980), the court held that the Board had authority to order the employer to reimburse the union's negotiating expenses for bargaining sessions rendered fruitless by the employer's bad faith, but denied enforcement to the order because the Board had failed to explain its apparent departure from its prior decisions denying such reimbursement. *Id.* at 329-30.

48. *See, e.g.*, Modern Mfg. Co., 292 N.L.R.B. 10, 10 n.4 (1988).

49. 826 P.2d 158 (Wash. 1992).

necessary to prevent the employer from continuing to breach its duty to bargain with impunity.

Ordering a private sector employer to bargain under threat of interest arbitration would be inconsistent with the NLRA's policy of free collective bargaining. It would be akin to ordering an employer to agree to a specific union contract proposal.[50]

The premise behind the court's decision in *Metro Seattle*, however, has much to offer for the NLRA. That premise is that where a labor relations act's ground rules for collective bargaining enable an employer repeatedly to avoid its duty to bargain in good faith, the labor board has the authority to remedy the violation by altering the ground rules in such a way as to make the bargaining process work as envisioned in the statute. Under the NLRA the appropriate remedy is not to order interest arbitration but to strip the employer of the temptation to dare the union to engage in a suicidal strike. Consequently, in cases of repeat or egregious surface bargaining, the Board should consider coupling its order to negotiate in good faith with an order prohibiting the employer from permanently replacing or threatening to permanently replace strikers during the negotiations. Such an order of affirmative relief would, in the language of section 10(c), "effectuate the policies" of the NLRA by depriving the employer of the incentive to bargain to avoid agreement and leaving the terms of the agreement themselves to be fixed through the collective bargaining process.

Conclusion

The proposals I have offered in this afterword to equalize access during representation elections and to police surface bargaining more closely and effectively during negotiations for first contracts are not intended as a panacea for what ails our nation's labor laws. Rather, my point is that as we focus on reforming our system of collective representation for American workers by taking a fresh look at our labor statutes, we should not ignore the existing statute. As our eyes turn first to the Dunlop Commission and then to Congress to take a fresh look at our statutory scheme, they should not be blind to the Board and the courts who also should take a fresh look at interpretation of the existing statutory language.

50. *See* J.P. Stevens & Co. v. NLRB, 623 F.2d at 329-30; *but see* Meizlish, *supra* note 40, at 729-30 (arguing that an order of interest arbitration would be consistent with the NLRA).